VOCABULARY BUILDER

NINTH EDITION

BY SAMUEL C. BROWNSTEIN
Formerly Chairman Science Department
George W. Wingate High School, Brooklyn, N.Y.

AND MITCHEL WEINER
Formerly Member, Department of English
James Madison High School, Brooklyn, N.Y.

BARRON'S

BARRON'S EDUCATIONAL SERIES, INC.
New York • London • Toronto • Sydney

All inquiries should be addressed to:
Barron's Educational Series, Inc.
250 Wireless Boulevard
Hauppauge, New York 11788

Library of Congress Catalog Card No. 83-26631

International Standard Book No. 0-8120-2449-4

Library of Congress Cataloging in Publication Data

Brownstein, Samuel C., 1909–
    Vocabulary builder.

    1. Vocabulary. 2. English language—Examinations,
questions, etc. 3. Universities and colleges—United
States—Entrance examinations. I. Weiner, Mitchel,
1907-   . II. Title.
PE1449.B76   1984   428.1   83-26631
ISBN o-8120-2449-4

PRINTED IN THE UNITED STATES OF AMERICA

789   410   9 8 7 6

Table of Contents

PREFACE

This book was published in response to requests from different sources. Essentially, the contents of this publication are a reprint of Chapters 5, 6, and 7 of *Barron's How to Prepare for College Entrance Examinations*. Numerous teachers of English found the material on vocabulary building in our original book so valuable that they asked for the production of this booklet. Thus, within the covers of this recently revised publication, we present a systematic, organized plan for building a vocabulary, testing progress, and applying knowledge, in accordance with the most recently revised edition of our comprehensive *College Entrance* book.

High school students looking forward to the numerous tests that they must face for college entrance should begin to use this book as early as the tenth year. Competency in English cannot be acquired within a short period.

College students who plan to take entrance examinations for advanced study, either for graduate school or for professional school, will find this book extremely helpful. They can utilize it as a study guide as well as a test of progress.

Prospective teachers of elementary education usually encounter examination questions which test vocabulary. They will find this book most valuable. Teachers preparing for higher licenses or supervisory posts will discover that the vocabulary list in this book offers adequate preparation for their specific test requirements.

In addition, many individuals applying for positions with large corporations find that placement is often based on vocabulary tests for which this book offers excellent preparation.

The reader who would like more test material on vocabulary, word relationships and reading comprehension should consult *Barron's How to Prepare for College Entrance Examinations*. This comprehensive review for the SAT (Scholastic Aptitude Test), the Achievement Tests, and other standardized college entrance examinations, also contains a thorough treatment of mathematics review, from simple arithmetic to advanced mathematics. It includes effective study guides and test material for all academic high school subjects.

We are indeed grateful to the numerous readers whose correspondence has encouraged us to produce this publication.

How and What to Study

Anyone who studies the material in this book should have a plan to master as much of the material as possible in the time available. Two plans are presented for efficient study of Barron's Basic Word List.

Plan 1

(For those who have approximately one month or less to prepare for the SAT or another examination). You must recognize that in so short a period of time it is foolish to try to master all the words in the Word List. We recommend that you concentrate on the words which appear in the Tests which follow each of the 40 Word Lists. Take one or two of these tests each day (depending on how much time you have before the day of the test).

Plan 2

(For those who begin their studying for the examination at least four months before the actual test). Use the following procedure:

STEP 1: Beginning with the Junior Word List, read through the forty-two words listed there. As you read, try to suggest a synonymous word or phrase for each word in the list. If a synonym comes to your mind, even though it is inexact, you probably know the word. When a word stimulates no association in your mind, note the unknown word by underlining it.

STEP 2: On a separate sheet of paper write down the underlined words in a vertical list on the left hand side of your paper. The very process of copying these words will add to your sense of familiarity with them.

STEP 3: Look up the definitions of these words in the Word List. Jot down brief definitions or meaningful synonyms beside each of the words. Also, if an antonym of the word comes to mind, jot that down also.

STEP 4: After an interval of time—preferably the next day—repeat step 1 for the underlined words only. Recheck the definitions of any word or words which do not stir any meaningful associations in your mind.

Repeat this process until you have completed the Junior Word List. Then move ahead to the Senior Word List on p. 7.

STEP 5: (the last two or three weeks). Take each of the 40 Tests that follow the Word Lists as outlined in Plan 1 (above). Conclude your studying by taking Synonym Test A, Synonym Test B, Antonym Test A and Antonym Test B and the seven Vocabulary Tests in Chapter 2.

If you do the work suggested in the 26 Assignments and in Plan 1 or 2, you should be able to obtain a score on the Verbal Part of the test you are taking which will reflect your effort and improved ability.

Barron's Basic Word List (40 lists) is here divided into four categories:

1. Junior Words

2. Senior Words

3. Honor Senior Words

4. Additional Honor Senior Words

It is advisable that students see how many of the words in each category they know.

JUNIOR WORD LIST

From Word List 1 (page 17)

abash, abdicate, abominate, aboriginal, abrogate, abscond, abstemious, accelerate, accessory, accolade, accomplice, accord, accost, acoustics, acquittal, acrimonious, actuate, acumen, adamant, adapt, addiction, adhere, admonish, adroit, adulation, adulterate, adverse, adversity, advocate, aesthetic, affected, affiliation, affirmation, affluence, aggregate, aghast, agility, agitate, alacrity, alias, alienate, allege

From Word List 2 (page 19)

allude, allusion, aloof, altercation, altruism, ambiguous, amble, ambulatory, ameliorate, amenable, amphitheatre, ample, amputate, anaesthetic, analogous, analogy, anarchy, andirons, animated, animosity, annals, annihilate, annul, anomalous, antagonism, anticlimax, antiseptic, apathetic, aphorism, aplomb, apocryphal, apostate, apotheosis, appellation, append, apprehensive, apprise, appurtenances

From Word List 3 (page 22)

arbiter, arbitrary, arcade, archipelago, arduous, aromatic, arraign, arrant, arrogance, ascetic, ascribe, ashen, askew, aspirant, aspiration, assail, assay, astral, astringent, atheistic, athwart, attenuate, attribute, attrition, augment, augury, auspicious, austerity, authenticate, autocrat, autonomous, autopsy, averse, avid, avow, awe, babble, badger, baffle, balk

From Word List 4 (page 24)

barb, barrage, batten, bedraggle, beguile, behoove, belated, benediction, benefactor, beneficiary, benevolent, benighted, berate, bestow, bête noir, bicameral, bizarre, blandishment, blasphemous, blatant, bleak, bloated, bludgeon, bolster, bountiful, bourgeois, bravado, breach, brevity, broach, brocade, brochure, brooch, brusque, bullion, bulwark, bungle, buttress, cabal, cadaverous

From Word List 5 (page 26)

cajole, callous, calumniate, calumny, canny, cant, capitulate, caprice, caption, caricature, carping, carrion, cascade, castigate, casualty, catapult, catastrophe, cathartic, cauterize, cavalcade, cede, celestial, censor, cerebral, cerebration, cession, chafe, chagrin, chalice, chameleon, chaotic, charlatan, chary, chasm, chassis, chastise, chauvinist, checkered, chicanery, chronic

From Word List 6 (page 29)

circlet, circumscribe, circumspect, circumvent, citadel, clairvoyant, clamber, clarion, clavicle, cleave, clemency, cliché, climactic, clique, cloister, coalesce, cog, cogitate, collaborate, collateral, collusion, colossal, comely, comity, commensurate, commiserate, compact, compatible, compilation, complacent, complaisant, complement, comport, compunction, compute, concatenate, concentric, conception, concise

From Word List 7 (page 31)

concoct, concurrent, condescend, condign, condiments, condole, congeal, congruence, conjugal, connivance, connotation, consecrate, consort, constraint, consummate, context, contiguous, contingent, contortions, contumacious, contusion, convene, conveyance, convivial, convoke, coquette, corporeal, corroborate, cortege, cosmic, covenant, covert, covetous, cower, crass, credulity, creed, crevice, criterion, crone

From Word List 8 (page 33)

culinary, cull, culmination, culpable, cursory, dally, dearth, debase, debutante, decadence, deciduous, decorous, decoy, deducible, defamation, defeatist, deference, definitive, deflect, defunct, deign, delete, delineation, delirium, delusion, demean, demeanor, demise, demolition, demur, demure, depict, deplete, deprecate, deprecatory, depreciate, depredation, derelict, derision, desiccate

From Word List 9 (page 35)

despotism, desultory, detergent, detonation, detraction, detriment, deviate, devious, dexterous, diadem, diaphanous, dictum, diffusion, digressive, dilapidation, dilemma, dilettante, dint, dire, dirge, disavowal, discernible, discerning, disclaim, disconcert, discordant, discursive, disdain, disparage, dispersion, disputatious, dissemble, disseminate, dissertation, dissimulate, dissolute, dissuade, distortion, diverge, diverse

From Word List 10 (page 37)

diversity, divest, dolorous, dolt, dregs, dross, drudgery, duplicity, earthy, ebullient, eccentricity, ecstasy, eerie, effectual, effervesce, effete, efficacy, effrontery, effulgent, effusive, egoism, egotism, egregious, ejaculation, elegiacal, elicit, elucidate, elusory, emanate, emancipate, embroil, emolument, emulate, encompass, encumber, endearment, energize, engender, engross, enigma

From Word List 11 (page 40)

enormity, enrapture, enthrall, entree, entrepreneur, epicurean, epigram, epilogue, epitaph, epithet, epitome, epoch, equestrian, equinox, equity, equivocate, erode, errant, escapade, esoteric, espionage, esprit de corps, estranged, ethereal, eulogy, evanescent, evince, evoke, exemplary, exhort, exigency, exotic, expatiate, expediency, expeditiously, expiate, expunge, expurgate, extant, extirpate, extort.

From Word List 12 (page 42)

extrude, exuberant, fabricate, facetious, facile, facilitate, faction, fallacious, fallible, fallow, fanaticism, fancied, fantastic, fastidious, faux pas, fawning, feint, felicitous, fervent, fester, fetid, fetter, fictitious, filial, finale, finesse, finicky, fissure, fitful, flaccid, flagging, flagrant, flay, flick, flippancy, flotilla, flout, fluctuation, fluency, fluster

From Word List 13 (page 44)

foible, forbearance, foreboding, forte, fortitude, fractious, frantic, fraudulent, fraught, fray, frenzied, friction, frigid, frolicsome, froward, frowzy, fruition, frustrate, fulminate, fulsome, funereal, fusion, gainsay, gamut, gape, gauntlet, gazette, generality, geniality, genteel, gentry, gesticulation, ghastly, gibber, gibbet, gibe, glaze, glean, gloaming, gloat

From Word List 14 (page 46)

glut, gluttonous, gnarled, goad, gory, gossamer, granary, grandiloquent, graphic, gratis, grueling, gruesome, gruff, guffaw, guile, guileless, gustatory, gutteral, haggle, hallowed, hallucination, hamper, harangue, harass, harbinger, harping, harry, haughtiness, hazardous, hazy, hedonism, heedless, heinous, heresy, hiatus, hibernate, hierarchy, hindmost, histrionic, holocaust, homespun

From Word List 15 (page 48)

homogenous, humane, humdrum, humid, humility, hypochondriac, hypocritical, ideology, idiom, idiosyncrasy, igneous, ignoble, ignominious, illimitable, imbecility, imbibe, imminent, immobility, immune, impasse, impending, impenitent, imperious, impermeable, impertinent, imperturbability, impiety, impious, implacable, implication, implicit, imprecate, impregnable, impropriety, improvident, impugn, inanimate, inadvertence, inarticulate, incapacitate

From Word List 16 (page 50)

incessant, incipient, incisive, incite, inclusive, incommodious, incongruity, incredulity, increment, incumbent, incursion, indefatigable, indict, indigenous, indisputable, indomitable, indulgent, inept, inexorable, infamous, inference, infinitesimal, inflated, influx, infraction, infringe, inherent, inhibit, iniquitous, inkling, innate, innocuous, innovation, innuendo, inordinate, inscrutable, insomnia, instigate, insuperable, insurgent, integrity

From Word List 17 (page 53)

interment, interminable, intimate, intimidation, intrude, intuition, invective, invidious, invulnerable, iota, irascible, ironical, irreconcilable, irreparable, irrevocable, iterate, itinerant, jargon, jeopardy, jocose, jocular, jocund, jubilation, judicious, knavery, knell, labyrinth, lacerate, laconic, laggard, laity, languid, languish, lassitude, latent, latitude, lave, lavish, lesion, lethal

From Word List 18 (page 55)

libelous, licentious, linguistic, liquidate, loathe, longevity, loquacious, lout, lucent, lucid, lucrative, luminous, lunar, luscious, lustrous, luxuriant, macerate, machinations, maelstrom, magnanimous, magnate, maim, malicious, malignant, mammoth, mandatory, manipulate, marauder, maritime, masticate, maudlin, maxim, meander, meddlesome, mediate, meditation, medley, melee, mendacious, mendicant

From Word List 19 (page 57)

mercenary, mercurial, mete, metropolis, mettle, mien, migratory, militate, mincing, misadventure, misapprehension, miscreant, misgivings, mishap, missile, mite, mitigate, mobile, mode, modicum, molten, momentous, monotheism, moodiness, morbid, morose, mortician, mortify, mote, mountebank, muddle, multiform, multiplicity, murkiness, muse, musky, mutable, mutilate, mutinous, nadir

From Word List 20 (page 59)

naiveté, natal, nauseous, nemesis, nepotism, nettle, nib, nicety, nomadic, nonchalance, noncommittal, nonentity, non sequitur, nostalgia, novice, noxious, nugatory, numismatist, nutrient, oaf, obfuscate, obliterate, oblivion, obnoxious, obtrude, obtrusive, obviate, occult, odoriferous, odorous, officious, olfactory, oligarch, ominous, omniverous, onerous, onomatopoeia, onslaught, opaque, opprobrious

From Word List 21 (page 61)

ordinance, ornate, ornithologist, oscillate, ostensible, ostracize, overt, pacifist, palatable, palatial, pallid, palpable, paltry, panacea, pandemonium, panegyric, panorama, pantomime, paragon, paregoric, parley, parody, paroxysm, parricide, partiality, passive, pastoral, pathetic, pathos, patriarch, peccadillo, pedulate, pecuniary, pedagogue, pedantic, pediatrician, pell-mell, penance, pensive, penury, perdition, perfidious

From Word List 22 (page 64)

perjury, perpetrate, perusal, pervade, perverse, perversity, pessimism, pestilential, philanthropist, philology, pied, piquant, pithy, pittance, placid, plagiarism, platitude, plebeian, plethora, podiatrist, podium, poignant, politic, polygamist, polyglot, portend, portent, portentous, portly, posthumous, postulate, potentate, potential, potion, potpourri, practical, pragmatic, prate, prattle, precarious

From Word List 23 (page 66)

precipitate, precipitous, preclude, precocious, precursor, predatory, preeminent, premonition, preposterous, prevaricate, procrastinate, profligate, profusion, progenitor, progeny, prognosticate, prolific, promiscuous, prone, propagate, propensity, propitiate, propound, propriety, propulsive, prostrate, protégé, protrude, provident, provocation, proximity, proxy, pseudonym, pugnacious, pulmonary, pulsate, pungent, puny, purge, purloin

From Word List 24 (page 68)

pyromaniac, quack, qualms, quell, querulous, quibble, quip, quirk, quizzical, rabid, ramp, rancid, rancor, rant, rapacious, rationalize, ravenous, recalcitrant, recant, recapitulate, recession, recipient, reciprocal, reciprocate, recluse, reconcile, recourse, recrimination, rectitude, recumbent, recurrent, redolent, redoubtable, redress, redundant, reek, refutation, regale, regeneration, regime

From Word List 25 (page 70)

relegate, relevancy, relinquish, remedial, reminiscence, remnant, remunerative, rend, render, renegade, renounce, renovate, renunciation, reparable, replete, reprehensible, reprieve, reprimand, requisite, rescind, resonant, respite, restitution, resuscitate, retaliate, retraction, retribution, retrieve, retroactive, revelry, reverberate, revile, revulsion, ribald, rift, rigor, risible, risqué, rococo, roseate

From Word List 26 (page 72)

rote, ruminate, rummage, ruse, sacrilegious, sacrosanct, salient, saline, sallow, salutary, sangfroid, sanguinary, sapid, sapient, sardonic, sate, satiate, satiety, saturnine, saunter, savant, savoir faire, scavenger, schism, scintilla, scourge, scrupulous, scuttle, sedate, sedulous, seethe, seine, semblance sensual, serenity, serrated, severance, shackle, shimmer

From Word List 27 (page 75)

simian, simile, simulate, sinuous, skimp, skulk, solicitous, soliloquy, solstice, somnambulist, spasmodic, specious, spectral, spurious, squalid, staid, stamina, stentorian, stigmatize, stint, stipend, stoic, stolid, strident, subjugate, sub rosa, subsequent, subservient, subsistence, substantiate, subterfuge, subtlety, subversive, succinct, succulent, suffuse, sully, sultry, sumptuous, sunder

From Word List 28 (page 77)

supersede, supine, supplicate, surcease, surly, surmise, surveillance, sustenance, swelter, sylvan, synthesis, taciturn, tactile, taint, tantalize, tautological, temporize, tenet, tenuous, terrestrial, terse, testy, tether, therapeutic, thermal, throes, throttle, thwart, timidity, tirade, titanic, toady, topography, torpid, tortuous, touchy, toxic, tractable, tranquillity, transcend

From Word List 29 (page 79)

transition, translucent, transparent, tremor, tremulous, trenchant, trepidation, tribulation, trite, truculent, tumid, turbid, turbulence, turgid, turpitude, tyro, ubiquitous, ulterior, ultimate, ultimatum, unassuming, unbridled, uncanny, unconscionable, uncouth, unctuous, unearthly, unequivocal, unfaltering, unfeigned, unique, unmitigated, unwonted, upbraid, urbane, vacuous, vagary, validate, vapid, variegated

From Word List 30 (page 81)

veneer, venerable, vent, verbose, vernal, versatile, vicissitude, vie, vilify, vindicate, vindictive, virile, virtuoso, virus, viscous, vituperative, vivacious, vociferous, volatile, voluble, voracious, vulnerable, vying, waggish, waive, wan, wane, wanton, wary, wheedle, whet, wily, winsome, witless, witticism, wizened, wont, worldly, wrest, zenith·

SENIOR WORD LIST

From Word List 1 (page 17)

abase, abhor, abjure, ablution, absolve, abstinence, accrue, acetic, acknowledge, acme, acquiescent, acrid, adage, addle, adept, adipose, affinity, agape, aggrandize, agnostic, albeit, alimentary, alimony

From Word List 2 (page 19)

allocate, alloy, amalgamate, ambrosia, amiable, amicable, amnesia, amphibian, amuck, anemia, annuity, anonymous, anthropologist, antipathy, apex, apothecary, apparition, appraise, apprehend, aptitude

From Word List 3 (page 22)

aquiline, arable, ardor, artifice, ascertain, asinine, aspersion, asteroid, atrocity, attest, audacity, audit, austere, auxiliary, awry, axiom, azure, balmy, banal, bandanna, bantering

From Word List 4 (page 24)

barrister, barterer, bauble, belabor, benign, bereft, besmirch, betroth, biennial, bigotry, bilious, bland, blighted, blithe, bogus, boisterous, bouillon, brazen, buffoonery, burlesque, buxom, cadaver

From Word List 5 (page 26)

caliber, cameo, canard, candor, canter, canvass, capacious, carat, carnal, carniverous, catechism, caustic, celibate, censure, centaur, centigrade, centrifugal, charisma, chassis, chattel, chide, chiropodist, churlish

From Word List 6 (page 29)

cite, claustrophobia, cleft, coerce, cognomen, coincident, collier, combustible, commandeer, commodious, conciliate

From Word List 7 (page 31)

condone, confiscate, conformity, congenital, connoisseur, connubial, consensus, contaminate, contentious, contraband, contrite, conversant, copious, cornice, corpulent, countermand, counterpart, coy, craven, crestfallen

From Word List 8 (page 33)

eryptic, cuisine, curtail, cynic, dais, dauntless, dawdle, debonair, decrepit, default, defection, defile, deleterious, delude, depilate, deploy, depravity, deranged, deride, dermatologist, derogatory, desecrate, despicable, despise

From Word List 9 (page 35)

devoid, devout, diabolical, diffidence, dilate, diminution, disconsolate, disgruntle, disheveled, disinterested, dismember, disparate, dispirited, dissection, dissipate, distend, distraught, diva

From Word List 10 (page 37)

divulge, docile, doff, doggerel, domicile, dormant, droll, dubious, duress, efface, effeminate, effigy, elation, emaciated, embezzlement, eminent

From Word List 11 (page 40)

ennui, ephemeral, epicure, escutcheon, ethnic, eulogistic, evasive, exasperate, exhume, exodus, exonerate, exorbitant, expatriate, extant, extemporaneous, extenuate, extol, extraneous, extricate, extrovert

From Word List 12 (page 42)

facade, fanciful, fatalism, fatuous, fauna, feasible, feign, ferment, fervid, fervor, fete, fiasco, fickle, fidelity, filch, flail, flair, flamboyant, flora, fleck, florid

From Word List 13 (page 44)

flux, foist, foment, foolhardy, foppish, forensic, formidable, foster, frailty, frenetic, frugality, furor, furtive, galleon, galvanize, gamester, garbled, garish, gist, glib

From Word List 14 (page 46)

glossy, gnome, gouge, grandiose, gregarious, grisly, grotto, gruel, guise, gullible, gusty, hackneyed, haggard, haphazard, harridan, hawser, heterogeneous, hilarity, holster

From Word List 15 (page 48)

homonym, hubbub, hybrid, hypothetical, idolatry, imbue, immaculate, impair, impassive, impeach, impetuous, impetus, import, impromptu, improvise, inalienable, inane

From Word List 16 (page 50)

incentive, inclement, incognito, incorrigible, incriminate, inculcate, indigent, indolence, infallible, infirmity, ingrate, insinuate, insipid, insolent, insolvency, integrate, intellect

From Word List 17 (*page 53*)

interim, intermittent, intrepid, introvert, inverse, irrelevant, irreverent, jaundiced, kismet, klepto-maniac, lackadaisical, lagoon, languish, lateral, laudatory, lethargic, levity

From Word List 18 (*page 55*)

lewd, lexicon, libertine, libretto, litigation, livid, lucre, luster, malediction, malefactor, mall, maniacal, marital, martial, maternal, matricide, mausoleum, mediocre, memento

From Word List 19 (*page 57*)

menial, mentor, mercantile, meringue, meticulous, migrant, mirage, misdemeanor, misogynist, modish, millify, molt, motif, muggy, mulct, munificent, musty

From Word List 20 (*page 59*)

nave, nebulous, nefarious, negation, nocturnal, obelisk, obese, obituary, oblique, obsession, obsolete, obtuse, oculist, odious, ogle, omnipotent, opiate, opportune, optician, optometrist

From Word List 21 (*page 61*)

ostentatious, palette, pallet, palpitate, papyrus, parable, paradox, parallelism, paranoia, para-phernalia, parasite, parlance, parry, parvenu, patent, patricide, pendant, pendent, perennial, perfidy, perfunctory

From Word List 22 (*page 64*)

perimeter, periphery, permeate, pernicious, perpetual, pert, pertinent, perturb, petrify, pet-ulant, phial, pillage, pinnacle, pious, pique, placate, plaintive, posterity, practicable, preamble, precedent (n)

From Word List 23 (*page 66*)

precept, prefatory, prelude, presentiment, presumption, prim, probity, prodigal, profane, promontory, protract, prurient, psychiatrist, puerile, pulchritude, punitive, purgatory, purveyor

From Word List 24 (*page 68*)

putrid, quaff, quandary, quixotic, ragamuffin, raucous, ravage, raze, realm, rebate, recon-naisance, rectify, recuperate, refectory, regatta, rehabilitate, reimburse, reiterate

From Word List 25 (*page 70*)

rejuvenate, relish, remediable, remonstrate, rendezvous, reparation, repartee, repellent, repertoire, replenish, replica, requiem, retentive, reverie, rhetoric, rife, roan, robust, rostrum

From Word List 26 (*page 72*)

rotundity, rubble, ruddy, rueful, ruthless, sadistic, saga, sagacious, salvage, saturate, savor, secession, sedentary, senility, serendipity, servile, shambles, sherbert, shoddy, silt

From Word List 27 (page 75)

sinister, skittish, sleazy, slovenly, sojourn, solvent, spangle, spatial, spawn, sporadic, stagnant, stanch, statute, stein, stellar, stupor, stymie, suavity, sublime, subsidiary, summation, sundry

From Word List 28 (page 77)

superficial, superfluity, surfeit, swathe, synthetic, tacit, tantrum, tedium, tempo, tentative, tenure, tepid, tipple, toga, tome, torso, tract, transcribe

From Word List 29 (page 79)

transgression, transient, traverse, treatise, trek, tribunal, tribute, trilogy, tumbrel, turnkey, unearth, unguent, unkempt, unruly, usury, vanguard, vantage, vaunted, veer

From Word List 30 (page 81)

vegetate, venal, venial, vent, veracious, verdant, verity, vertigo, vestige, viand, vicarious, victuals, vigilance, viper, virulent, visage, visionary, vogue, whit, wizardry, zephyr

HONOR SENIOR WORD LIST

From Word List 1 (page 17)

abettor, abeyance, abortive, abrade, abstruse, acclivity, accoutre, accretion, acidulous, actuarial, adduce, adjuration, adumbration, adventitious, affray, agglomeration, alchemy, allay, allegory

From Word List 2 (page 19)

alleviate, alluvial, amass, amenities, amnesty, amorphous, amplify, amulet, anathema, ancillary, animosity, anomaly, antediluvian, anthropoid, antipodes, antithesis, aperture, apogee, apothegm, appease, apposite

From Word List 3 (page 22)

argot, artifacts, artisan, asceticism, asseverate, assiduous, assuage, astute, atrophy, atypical, automaton, avarice, aver, avouch, avuncular, baneful

From Word List 4 (page 24)

baroque, bate, beatific, bedizen, beleaguer, bellicose, berserk, bivouac, blazon, bode, bombastic, bootless, braggadocio, brazier, bucolic, bumptious, burgeon, burnish, cache, cacophony

From Word List 5 (page 26)

calorific, canker, cantata, canto, caparison, capricious, captious, carmine, carnage, carousal, carte blanche, cataclysm, catholic, cavil, censer, centurion, cessation, chaffing, champ, chimerical, choleric

From Word List 6 (page 29)

ciliated, circuitous, clandestine, coadjutor, cockade, cogent, cognate, cognizance, cohere, cohesion, cohorts, collate, collation, colloquy, comestible, compliant

From Word List 7 (page 31)

conclave, concomitant, conglomeration, conifer, consanguinity, construe, contemn, continence, contravene, controvert, contumely, corrosive, corsair, coterie, crabbed, credence, crux

From Word List 8 (page 33)

cupidity, curry, dank, dastard, daunt, debauch, debilitate, decant, declivity, decry, defalcate, delusive, demagogue, demoniac, denizen, deposition, descant, descry, despoil

From Word List 9 (page 35)

destitute, desuetude, devolve, dialectic, dichotomy, dilatory, dipsomaniac, discomfit, discretion, discrete, disingenuous, disjointed, disparity, disport, disquisition, dissonance, dissuasion, distrait, diurnal, divers

From Word List 10 (page 37)

divination, dogmatic, dorsal, dotage, doughty, dour, ecclesiastic, edify, educe, efflorescent, effusion, egress, elusive, embellish, emblazon, emend, emetic, enamored, enclave, encomiastic, encroachment, endive, endue, enervate, enhance

From Word List 11 (page 40)

ensconce, entity, environ, equable, equanimity, equipage, equivocal, erudite, eschew, euphemism, euphonious, ewer, exaction, exchequer, exculpate, execrable, exiguous, expostulation, extradition, extrinsic

From Word List 12 (page 42)

exude, facet, factitious, factious, factotum, fain, fancier, fealty, fecundity, fell, ferret, fetish, fiat, figment, flagellate, flaunt, fledgling, flotsam

From Word List 13 (page 44)

foray, fortuitous, franchise, freebooter, fresco, freshet, frieze, fructify, functionary, fustian, gadfly, gaff, gambol, garner, garrulity, genre, gentility, germane, gig

From Word List 14 (page 46)

gorge, gourmand, gourmet, gratuitous, gusto, habiliments, halcyon, hap, hapless, harrow, hauteur, heretic, hermitage, hibernal, hieroglyphic, hireling, hirsute. hoary, hogshead

From Word List 15 (*page 48*)

horticultural, hostelry, humus, hypercritical, iconoclastic, illusion, imbroglio, immolate, immutable, impale, impeccable, impecunious, impervious, impolitic, importune, imprecate, impunity, imputation, incarcerate, incarnate

From Word List 16 (*page 50*)

incendiary, inchoate, incompatible, inconsequential, incontrovertible, incorporeal, incubate, indemnify, indenture, indignity, indite, indubitably, ineffable, ingenuous, ingratiate, inimical, insatiable, insensate, insidious, insular

From Word List 17 (*page 53*)

intelligentsia, inter, intransigent, intrinsic, inundate, inured, inveigle, inveterate, inviolability, iridescent, irremediable, jaded, jettison, jingoism, junket, junto, ken, kiosk, kith, knoll, lagniappe, lambent, laminated, lampoon, lapidary, largess, lascivious, lecherous

From Word List 18 (*page 55*)

liaison, libidinous, lieu, limn, limpid, lithe, loath, lode, lope, lugubrious, macabre, Machiavellian, madrigal, magniloquent, magnitude, malevolent, malign, malingerer, malleable, manifest, manifesto, marrow, martinet, matrix, mauve, mellifluous, memorialize

From Word List 19 (*page 57*)

meretricious, mesa, metallurgical, metamorphosis, metaphysical, mews, misanthrope, miscegenation, miscellany, misnomer, modulation, moiety, monetary, moot, mordant, mores, moribund, motley, multilingual, mundane

From Word List 20 (*page 59*)

natation, necrology, necromancy, neophyte, nexus, niggardly, noisome, nosegay, nurture, obdurate, obeisance, objugate, obliquity, obloquy, obsequious, omniscient, opalescent

From Word List 21 (*page 61*)

opulence, oratorio, orifice, ossify, paean, palaver, palliate, pander, paraphrase, pariah, parsimonious, patrimony, paucity, pelf, pellucid, penchant, penitent, penumbra, penurious, percussion, peremptory, perforce.

From Word List 22 (*page 64*)

peripatetic, permeable, persiflage, perspicacious, pertinacious, perturbation, perversion, pervious, philander, philistine, pillory, pinion, piscatorial, plauditory, plenary, plenipotentiary, plumb, poltroon, pommel, poultice

From Word List 23 (*page 66*)

precedent (adj), predilection, preponderate, presage, pretentious, primordial, pristine, privy, proboscis, prodigious, prognosis, prolix, promulgate, propitious, prorogue, proscribe, prosody, proto-col, provender, proviso, psyche, puissant, punctilious, purport, purview

From Word List 24 (page 68)

pusillanimous, quail, quay, quiescent, quietude, quintessence, qui vive, ramification, rampant, rapprocchement, rarefied, ratiocination, ravening, recondite, recreant, refection, refraction, refrac-tory, refulgent, regimen

From Word List 25 (page 70)

remiss, repercussion, repository, reprisal, reprobation, repudiate, repugnance, requite, rescission, resplendent, restive, retinue, retrograde, retrospective, rheumy

From Word List 26 (page 72)

rubicund, rudimentary, rusticate, sacerdotal, saffron, salubrious, sanguine, scintillate, scion, scullion, scurillous, sebaceous, secular, sententious, sepulcher, sequester, sheaf, sheathe, shibboleth, shoal, sidereal

From Word List 27 (page 75)

sinecure, slake, sloth, slough, sluggard, sobriety, solecism, somnolent, sonorous, soupcon, splenetic, sportive, squander, stratagem, striated, stricture, stringent, subaltern, sublimate

From Word List 28 (page 77)

superannuated, supercilious, suppliant, supposititious, surreptitious, sycophantic, synchronous, tawdry, temerity, temporal, tenacious, terminus, tertiary, theocracy, thrall, threnody, tithe, titular, traduce

From Word List 29 (page 79)

transmute, transpire, travail, travesty, trident, troth, trumpery, tryst, tutelage, umbrage, unanimity, unassuaged, unction, undulate, unimpeachable, unison, unseemly, unsullied, untenable, unwitting, uxorious, vacillation, vainglorious

From Word List 30 (page 81)

vehement, vellum, venerate, ventral, verbiage, verdigris, vertex, virago, vitiate, vitriolic, volition, voluptuous, votary, vouchsafe, whimsical, wraith, wreak, zealot

ADDITIONAL HONOR SENIOR WORDS

From Word List 31 (page 84)

aberration, abnegation, abut, abysmal, accede, acclimate, acephalous, acerbity, acquiescence, adjunct, adjure, admonition, advert, adulterated, advent, aegis, aeon, affable, afferent, affidavit, afflatus, agenda, agitation, agrarian, agronomist, alliteration, amazon, amoral, amortization, anachronism, analgesic, animus, anneal, annotate, anthropomorphic, aphasia, apiary, apocalyptic, apologue, apropos, archetype, archives, arrogate, arroyo, aseptic, assimilate, astigmatism, atavism, atelier, aureole, auroral, auscultation, avatar, avocation

From Word List 32 (page 85)

bassoon, beholden, belittle, benignity, benison, bereavement, bestial, bifurcated, oillingsgate, blanch, blasé, boorish, bowdlerize, brackish, breviary, brindled, bugaboo, bureaucracy, buskin, calligraphy, callow, capillary, carafe, carillon, cartographer, caryatid, caste, casuistry, catalyst, catharsis, caucus, celerity, centripetal, chiromancy, choreography, circumlocution, codicil, colander, colloquial, comatose, compendium, complicity, compromise, conch, concordat, conduit, conjecture, convoluted, cordon, cormorant, correlation, coruscate, cozen, credo, crepuscular, crescendo, crotchety

From Word List 33 (page 87)

cruet, crypt, cubicle, cul-de-sac, culvert, curator, curmudgeon, cursive, cynosure, debacle, debenture, decimate, decolleté, decrepitude, degraded, deliquescent, demesne, demotic, denigrate, denotation, denouement, desideratum, diatribe, didactic, disabuse, dishabille, dispassionate, distaff, doddering, duenna, dulcet, durance, dynamic, eclat, eclecticism, effluvium, embryonic, emendation, emeritus, emollient, empirical, empyreal, encomium, endemic, enigmatic, enjoin, ensue, entomology, equitable, erotic, erudition, ethnology, etymology, eugenic, eviscerate, exacerbate

From Word List 34 (page 89)

excision, excoriate, execrate, exegesis, ex officio, exorcise, expletive, explicit, fanfare, febrile, fiduciary, flinch, floe, fluted, fracas, frond, fulcrum, fulgent, galaxy, gambit, gargoyle, garrulous, gasconade, gastronomy, gauche, genealogy, generic, genuflect, germinal, germinate, gerrymander, gestate, glossary, gratuity, grimace, grovel, hackles, hegira, hermetically, hew, hoax, hoodwink, hortatory, hoyden, hummock, husbandry, hustings, hyperbole, hyperborean, hypothecate, idiosyncratic, illusive, imbrue, immure, impalpable, imperturbable

From Word List 35 (page 91)

implement, imply, imponderable, importunate, impotent, imprimatur, impute, incantation, incarnadine, incarnation, incidence, incongruous, incontinent, incredulous, inductive, inebriety, ineluctable, inertia, infer, ingenue, insouciant, integument, interdict, interlocutory, internecine, interstices, intractable, intransigeance, invalidate, inveigh, irksome, irony, irrefragable, isotope, itinerary jejune, jeremiad, juncture, jurisprudence, juxtapose, kaleidoscope, kinetic, lachrymose, languor, larceny, laudable, lechery, lectern, lexicographer, libido, limbo, lissome, litany, litotes, lubricity, ludicrous, maladroit, malcontent, mammal

From Word List 36 (page 92)

mandate, manifold, manumit, marsupial, maunder, mawkish, mayhem, mélange, mesmerize, metaphor, miasma, microcosm, milieu, militant, millennium, minaret, minatory, minion, molecule, momentum, moor, moratorium, morganatic, mugwump, murrain, myopic, nascent, nautical, neap, nirvana, nonplus, nuance, nubile, objuration, oblation, obligatory, obsidian, obstetrician, obstreperous, occident, odium, offal, offertory, omnipresent, onus, opportunist, opprobrium, optimum, opus, orientation, orison, ornithology, orotund, orthography, overweening, pachyderm, paddock

From Word List 37 (page 94)

palimpsest, palliation, panoply, paramour, paranoiac, parapet, parity, parlous, parturition, passé, pastiche, pathological, patina, patois, peculation, pedant, pediment, pejorative, pendulous, pennate, peregrination, perigee, peristyle, peroration, perquisite, personable, perspicuity, perspicuous, pharisaical, phobia, physiological, picaresque, piebald, plangent, platonic, plausible, plebiscite, polemic, polity, porphyry, postprandial, potable, preciosity, preempt, prehensile, premonitory, preponderance, prerogative, prestige, primogeniture, probes, prognathous, projectile, proletarian, propellants, prophylactic

From Word List 38 (page 96)

propinquity, proscenium, proselytize, prototype, provenance, provincial, psychopathic, psychosis, pterodactyl, pundit, purblind, putative, quadruped, quagmire, quarantine, queasy, quorum, ramify, rampart, rationalization, reactionary, recherché, recidivism, recrudescence, recusant, refurbish, rendition, reprobate, reprove, residue, resilient, resurgent, reticulated, rood, rotunda, rustic, saltatory, salver, sanctimonius, sarcophagus, sartorial, satellite, satire, satrap, satyr, scarify, sciolism, screed, senescence, sensuous, septic, sequacious, seraph, serried, sibylline, similitude

From Word List 39 (page 98)

simpering, sirocco, skeptic, slander, slattern, sleight, slither, sluice, smattering, sobriquet, solace, somatic, sophist, sophistication, sophomoric, soporific, spate, spatula, spectrum, spoliation, spoonerism, spume, staccato, stalemate, stalwart, statutory, stereotyped, stertorous, stigma, stilted, stratum, stultify, suave, subjective, subliminal, subsidy, substantive, sudorific, sumptuary, superimpose, supernal, supernumerary, supple, suppurate, suture, syllogism, symmetry, talon, tantamount, tarantula, tarn, tatterdemalion, taut, tautology, teleology, temerarious, tenacity, tendentious, tenebrous, tergiversation

From Word List 40 (page 99)

termagant, terminology, terrapin, tessellated, testator, thaumaturgist, theosophy, thyme, timbre, timorous, titillate, tocsin, tonsure, tortilla, touchstone, trajectory, traumatic, treacle, trencherman, triolet, troglodyte, trope, truckle, truncate, tundra, tureen, tutelary, ukase, unilateral, untoward, ursine, usufruct, usurpation, utopia, valance, valedictory, valetudinarian, vampire, vassal, vendetta, verbatim, vermicular, vertiginous, viable, vitreous, vivisection, warranty, wastrel, welkin, welter, whorl, yeoman, yokel

Barron's Basic Word List

2

The approximately 2,800 words in this list have been compiled from various sources. They have been taken from the standard literature read by high school students throughout the country and from the many tests taken by high school and college students. Ever since this book first appeared in 1954, countless students have reported that mastering this list has been of immense value in the taking of all kinds of college entrance and scholarship tests. It has been used with profit by people preparing for civil service examinations, placement tests, and promotion examinations in many industrial fields.

For each word, the following is provided:

1. The word is printed in heavy type (words are arranged in strict alphabetical order for ease in locating).
2. Its part of speech is given.
3. Where needed, the pronunciation of a difficult syllable or sound is indicated. For this, a simplified key is used

KEY

ā — ale	ĕ — end	ō — old	th — thin
ă — add	ê — err, her	ŏ — odd	ū — use
ä — arm	ə — event, allow	ô — orb	ŭ — up
à — ask	ī — ice	o͞o — food	zh — pleasure
ē — eve	ĭ — ill	ou — out	

4. A brief definition of the word.
5. A sentence illustrating the use of the word.
6. Whenever useful, related words are provided.
7. Following each list of words will be a group of common prefixes, suffixes, and stems. Studying these can be of help to many students in reinforcing the impression the word has made. It will help the student interpret other words he encounters. However, it must be remembered that many words have lost their original meanings and have taken on more specific and limited meanings. These prefixes, suffixes, and roots should be used as a guide when in doubt about the meaning of a strange word. There is no substitute for learning the exact meaning of each word as it is used today.
8. A cumulative listing of prefixes, suffixes, and stems follows Word List 40.

Basic Word List

WORD LIST   1   **abase - allegory**

abase V. lower; humiliate. His refusal to *abase* himself in the eyes of his followers irritated the king, who wanted to humiliate the proud leader.

abash V. embarrass. He was not at all *abashed* by her open admiration.

abdicate V. renounce; give up. When Edward VIII *abdicated* the British throne, he surprised the entire world.

abettor N. encourager. He was accused of being an aider and *abettor* of the criminal. abet, V.

abeyance (-bā´-) N. suspended action. The deal was held in *abeyance* until his arrival.

abhor V. detest; hate. He *abhorred* all forms of bigotry. abhorrence, N.

abjure V. renounce upon oath. He *abjured* his allegiance to the king. abjuration N.

ablution N. washing. His daily *ablutions* were accompanied by loud noises which he humorously labeled "Opera in the Bath."

abominate V. loathe; hate. Moses scolded the idol worshippers in the tribe because he *abominated* the custom.

aboriginal ADJ., N. being the first of its kind in a region; primitive; native. His studies of the primitive art forms of the *aboriginal* Indians were widely reported in the scientific journals. aborigines, N.

abortive ADJ. unsuccessful; fruitless. We had to abandon our *abortive* attempts.

abrade V. wear away by friction; erode. The skin of his leg was *abraded* by the sharp rocks. abrasion, N.

abrogate V. abolish. He intended to *abrogate* the decree issued by his predecessor.

abscond V. depart secretly and hide. The teller *absconded* with the bonds and was not found.

absolve V. pardon (an offense). The father confessor *absolved* him of his sins. absolution, N.

abstemious (-stē´-) ADJ. temperate; sparing in drink, etc. The drunkards mocked him because of his *abstemious* habits.

abstinence N. restraint from eating or drinking. The doctor recommended total *abstinence* from salted foods. abstain, V.

abstruse ADJ. obscure; profound; difficult to understand. He read *abstruse* works in philosophy.

accelerate V. move faster. In our science class, we learn how falling bodies *accelerate*.

accessory N. additional object; useful but not essential thing. The *accessories* she bought cost more than the dress. also ADJ.

acclivity (-klĭv´-) N. sharp upslope of a hill. The car could not go up the *acclivity* in high gear.

accolade (ak´-ə-lād) N. award of merit. In Hollywood, an "Oscar" is the highest *accolade*.

accomplice N. partner in crime. Because he had provided the criminal with the lethal weapon, he was arrested as an *accomplice* in the murder.

accord N. agreement. He was in complete *accord* with the verdict.

accost V. approach and speak first to a person. When the two young men *accosted* me, I was frightened because I thought they were going to attack me.

accoutre (-kōōt´-) V. equip. The fisherman was *accoutred* with the best that the sporting goods store could supply. accoutrements, N.

accretion (-krē´-) N. growth; increase. The *accretion* of wealth marked the family's rise in power.

accrue V. come about by addition. You must pay the interest which has *accrued* on your debt as well as the principal sum. accrual, N.

acetic (-sēt´-) ADJ. vinegary. The salad had an exceedingly *acetic* flavor.

acidulous (-sĭd´-) ADJ. slightly sour; sharp, caustic. James was unpopular because of his sarcastic and *acidulous* remarks.

acknowledge V. recognize; admit. When pressed for an answer, he *acknowledged* the existence of another motive for the crime.

acme (ăk´-mē) N. top; pinnacle. His success in this role marked his *acme* as an actor.

acoustics (-kōō´-) N. science of sound; quality that makes a room easy or hard to hear in. Carnegie Hall is liked by music lovers because of its fine *acoustics*.

acquiescent (-w-ĕs´-) ADJ. accepting passively. His *acquiescent* manner did not indicate the extent of his reluctance to join the group. acquiesce, V.

acquittal N. deliverance from a charge. His *acquittal* by the jury surprised those who had thought him guilty. acquit, V.

acrid ADJ. sharp; bitterly pungent. The *acrid* odor of burnt gunpowder filled the room after the pistol had been fired.

acrimonious ADJ. stinging; caustic. His tendency to utter *acrimonious* remarks alienated his audience. acrimony, N.

actuarial ADJ. calculating; pertaining to insurance statistics. According to recent *actuarial* tables, life expectancy is greater today than it was a century ago.

actuate V. motivate. I fail to understand what *actuated* you to reply to this letter so nastily.

acumen (-kū´-) N. mental keenness. His business *acumen* helped him to succeed where others had failed.

adage (ăd´-) N. wise saying; proverb. There is much truth in the old *adage* about fools and their money.

adamant (ăd´-) ADJ. hard; inflexible. He was *adamant* in his determination to punish the wrongdoer. adamantine, ADJ.

adapt V. alter; modify. Some species of animals have become extinct because they could not *adapt* to a changing environment.

addiction N. compulsive, habitual need. His *addiction* to drugs caused his friends much grief.

addle ADJ. rotten; muddled; crazy. This *addle*-headed plan is so preposterous that it does not deserve any consideration. also V.

adduce V. present as evidence. When you *adduce* evidence of this nature, you must be sure of your sources.

adept (-dĕpt´) ADJ. expert at. He was *adept* at the fine art of irritating people. also N.

adhere V. stick fast to. I will *adhere* to this opinion until proof that I am wrong is presented. adhesion, N.

adipose (ăd´-) ADJ. fatty. Excess *adipose* tissue should be avoided by middle-aged people.

adjuration (ăj-ə-rā´-) N. solemn urging. His *adjuration* to tell the truth did not change the witnesses' testimony. **adjure,** V.

admonish V. warn; reprove. He *admonished* his listeners to change their wicked ways. admonition, N.

adroit ADJ. skillful. His *adroit* handling of the delicate situation pleased his employers.

adulation N. flattery; admiration. He thrived on the *adulation* of his henchmen.

adulterate V. make impure by mixing with baser substances. It is a crime to *adulterate* foods without informing the buyer.

adumbration (*-brā´-*) N. foreshadowing; outlining. The *adumbration* of the future in science fiction is often extremely fantastic.

adventitious (*-tĭsh´-*) ADJ. accidental; casual. He found this *adventitious* meeting with his friend extremely fortunate.

adverse (*-vêrs´*) ADJ. unfavorable; hostile. *Adverse* circumstances compelled him to close his business.

adversity N. poverty; misfortune. We must learn to meet *adversity* gracefully.

advocate V. urge; plead for. The abolitionists *advocated* freedom for the slaves. also N.

aesthetic (*ĕs-thĕt´-*) ADJ. artistic; dealing with or capable of appreciation of the beautiful. Because of his *aesthetic* nature, he was emotionally disturbed by ugly things. aesthete, N.

affected ADJ. artificial; pretended. His *affected* mannerisms irritated many of us who had known him before his promotion. affectation, N.

affiliation N. joining; associating with. His *affiliation* with the political party was of short duration for he soon disagreed with his colleagues.

affinity N. kinship. He felt an *affinity* with all who suffered; their pains were his pains.

affirmation N. solemn pledge by one who refuses to take an oath. The Constitution of this country provides for oath or *affirmation* by officeholders.

affluence (*ăf´-*) N. abundance; wealth. Foreigners are amazed by the *affluence* and luxury of the American way of life.

affray N. public brawl. He was badly mauled by the fighters in the *affray.*

agape (*ə-gāp´*) ADJ. openmouthed. He stared, *agape,* at the many strange animals in the zoo.

agglomeration N. collection; heap. It took weeks to assort the *agglomeration* of miscellaneous items he had collected on his trip.

aggrandize (*-grăn-*) V. increase or intensify. The history of the past quarter century illustrates how a President may *aggrandize* his power to act aggressively in international affairs without considering the wishes of Congress.

aggregate ADJ. sum; total. The *aggregate* wealth of this country is staggering to the imagination. also V.

aghast ADJ. horrified. He was *aghast* at the nerve of the speaker who had insulted his host.

agility N. nimbleness. The *agility* of the acrobat amazed and thrilled the audience.

agitate V. stir up; disturb. His fiery remarks *agitated* the already angry mob.

agnostic N. one who is skeptical of the existence or knowability of a god or any ultimate reality. The *agnostic* demanded proof before he would accept the statement of the minister. also ADJ.

alacrity N. cheerful promptness. He demonstrated his eagerness to serve by his *alacrity* in executing the orders of his master.

albeit (*ôl-bē´-ĭt*) CONJ. although. *Albeit* fair, she was not sought after.

alchemy N. medieval chemistry. The changing of baser metals into gold was the goal of the students of *alchemy.* alchemist, N.

alias (*ā´-lē-əs*) N. an assumed name. John Smith's *alias* was Bob Jones. also ADV.

alienate V. make hostile; separate. His attempts to *alienate* the two friends failed because they had complete faith.

alimentary ADJ. supplying nourishment. The *alimentary* canal in our bodies is so named because digestion of foods occurs there.

alimony N. payment by a husband to his divorced wife. Mrs. Jones was awarded $200 monthly *alimony* by the court when she was divorced from her husband.

allay V. calm; pacify. The crew tried to *allay* the fears of the passengers by announcing that the fire had been controlled.

allege V. state without proof. It is *alleged* that he had worked for the enemy. allegation, N.

allegory N. story in which characters are used as symbols; fable. *Pilgrim's Progress* is an *allegory* of the temptations and victories of man's soul. allegorical, ADJ.

ETYMOLOGY 1

AB, ABS (from, away from) prefix

abduct lead away, kidnap
abjure renounce (swear away from)
abscond depart secretly and hide

ABLE, IBLE (capable of) adjective suffix

portable able to be carried
legible able to be read
interminable unable to be ended

AC, IC (like, pertaining to) adjective suffix

cardiac pertaining to the heart
aquatic pertaining to water
dramatic pertaining to drama

AC, ACR (sharp)

acrimonious bitter

acerbity bitterness of temper
acidulate make somewhat acidic or sour

AD (to, forward) prefix

adjure request earnestly
admit allow entrance

Note: By assimilation, the AD prefix is changed to
AC *in accord*
AF *in affliction*
AG *in aggregation*
AN *in annexation*
AP *in apparition*
AR *in arraignment*
AS *in assumption*
AT *in attendance*

AEV (age, era)

ā—ale; ă—add; ä—arm; à—ask; ē—eve; ĕ—end; ê—err, her; ə—allow; even; ī—ice; ĭ—ill; ō—oll; ŏ—odd; ô—orb; oo—food; oo—foot, put; ou—out; th—thin; ū—use; ù—up; zh—pleasure

primeval of the first age
coeval of the same age or era
medieval (*mediaeval*) of the middle ages

AG, ACT (to do)

act deed
agent doer
retroactive having a backward or reversed action

AGOG (leader)

demagogue false leader of people

pedagogue teacher (leader of children)
synagogue house of worship (leading together of people)

AGRI, AGRARI (field)

agrarian one who works in the fields; farmer
agriculture cultivation of fields

ALI (another)

alias assumed (another) name
alienate estrange (divert from another)
inalienable unable to be diverted from another

TEST—WORD LIST 1—*Synonyms*

Each of the questions below consists of a word printed in italics, followed by five words or phrases numbered 1 to 5. Choose the numbered word or phrase which is most nearly similar in meaning to the word in italics and write the number of your choice on your answer paper.

1. *aborigines* 1 first designs 2 absolutions 3 finales 4 concepts 5 primitive inhabitants
2. *abeyance* 1 obedience 2 discussion 3 excitement 4 suspended action 5 editorial
3. *abjure* 1 discuss 2 renounce 3 run off secretly 4 perjure 5 project
4. *ablution* 1 censure 2 forgiveness 3 mutiny 4 survival 5 washing
5. *abortive* 1 unsuccessful 2 consuming 3 financing 4 familiar 5 fruitful
6. *abasement* 1 incurrence 2 taxation 3 ground floor 4 humility 5 humiliation
7. *abettor* 1 conception 2 one who wagers 3 encourager 4 evidence 5 protection
8. *abstruse* 1 profound 2 irrespective 3 suspended

4 protesting 5 not thorough
9. *acclivity* 1 index 2 report 3 upslope of a hill 4 character 5 negotiator
10. *accoutre* 1 compromise 2 equip 3 revise 4 encounter 5 visit
11. *accrue* 1 come about by addition 2 reach summit 3 create a crisis 4 process 5 educate
12. *accretion* 1 mayonnaise 2 ban 3 increase 4 protection 5 ceremony
13. *acme* 1 pinnace 2 skin disease 3 basement 4 congestion 5 pinnacle
14. *acidulous* 1 recommended 2 witty 3 realistic 4 slightly sour 5 very generous
15. *abstinence* 1 restrained eating or drinking 2 vulgar display 3 deportment 4 reluctance 5 population
16. *acrid* 1 sour 2 bitterly pungent 3 sweetish 4 slightly acid 5 very hard
17. *adipose* 1 sandy 2 round 3 fatty 4 alkali 5 soft
18. *adventitious* 1 incidental 2 happy 3 courageous 4 accidental 5 foretelling
19. *affluence* 1 wealth 2 fear 3 persuasion 4 consideration 5 neglect
20. *allegory* 1 fable 2 poem 3 essay 4 anecdote 5 novel

WORD LIST 2 **alleviate - aptitude**

alleviate (-*lē´-vē-*) V. relieve. This should *alleviate* the pain; if it does not, we shall have to use stronger drugs.

allocate V. assign. Even though the Red Cross had *allocated* a large sum for the relief of the sufferers of the disaster, many people perished.

alloy N. a mixture as of metals. *Alloys* of gold are used more frequently than the pure metal.

allude V. refer indirectly. Try not to *allude* to this matter in his presence because it annoys him to hear of it.

allusion N. indirect reference. The *allusions* to mythological characters in Milton's poems bewilder the reader who has not studied Latin.

alluvial ADJ. pertaining to soil deposits left by rivers, etc. The farmers found the *alluvial* deposits at the mouth of the river very fertile.

aloof ADJ. apart; reserved. He remained *aloof* while all the rest conversed.

altercation N. wordy quarrel. Throughout the entire *altercation*, not one sensible word was uttered.

altruism (*ăl´-trŏō-*) N. unselfish aid to others; generosity.

The philanthropist was noted for his *altruism.* altruistic, ADJ.

amalgamate (-*măl´-*) V. combine; unite in one body. The unions will attempt to *amalgamate* their groups into one national body.

amass (-*măs´*) V. collect. The miser's aim is to *amass* and hoard as much gold as possible.

ambiguous (-*bĭg´-*) ADJ. doubtful in meaning. His *ambiguous* directions misled us; we did not know which road to take. ambiguity, N.

amble N. moving at an easy pace. When she first mounted the horse, she was afraid to urge the animal to go faster than a gentle *amble.* also V.

ambrosia (-*brō´-zhə*) N. food of the gods. *Ambrosia* was supposed to give immortality to any human who ate it.

ambulatory (*ăm´-*) ADJ. able to walk. He was described as an *ambulatory* patient because he was not confined to his bed.

ameliorate (-*mēl´-*) V. improve. Many social workers have attempted to *ameliorate* the conditions of people living in

ā—ale; ă—add; ä—arm; à—ask, ē—eve; ĕ—end; ê—err, her; ə—allow; even; ī—ice; ĭ—ill; ō—oll; ŏ—odd; ô—orb; ŏō—food; ŏŏ—foot, put; ou—out; th—thin; ū—use; ŭ—up; zh—pleasure

the slums.

amenable (-mē´-) ADJ. readily managed; willing to be led. He was *amenable* to any suggestions which came from those he looked up to; he resented advice from his inferiors.

amenities (-měn´-) N. agreeable manners; courtesies. He observed the social *amenities.*

amiable (ā´-mē-) ADJ. agreeable; lovable. His *amiable* disposition pleased all who had dealings with him.

amicable (ăm´-) ADJ. friendly. The dispute was settled in an *amicable* manner with no harsh words.

amnesia N. loss of memory. Because she was suffering from *amnesia,* the police could not get the young girl to identify herself.

amnesty N. pardon. When his first child was born, the king granted *amnesty* to all in prison.

amorphous ADJ. shapeless. He was frightened by the *amorphous* mass which had floated in from the sea.

amphibian ADJ. able to live both on land and in water. Frogs are classified as *amphibian.* also N.

amphitheater N. oval building with tiers of seats. The spectators in the *amphitheater* cheered the gladiators.

ample ADJ. abundant. He had *ample* opportunity to dispose of his loot before the police caught up with him.

amplify V. enlarge. His attempts to *amplify* his remarks were drowned out by the jeers of the audience.

amputate V. cut off part of body; prune. When the doctors decided to *amputate* his leg to prevent the spread of gangrene, he cried that he preferred death to incapacity.

amuck ADV. in a state of rage. The police had to be called in to restrain him after he ran *amuck* in the department store.

amulet (ăm´-) N. charm; talisman. Around his neck he wore the *amulet* which the witch doctor had given him.

analogous (-năl´-ə-gəs) ADJ. comparable. He called our attention to the things that had been done in an *analogous* situation and recommended that we do the same.

analogy N. similarity; parallelism. Your *analogy* is not a good one because the two situations are not similar.

anarchy (ăn´-) N. absence of governing body; state of disorder. The assassination of the leaders led to a period of *anarchy.*

anathema (-năth´-) N. solemn curse. He heaped *anathema* upon his foe.

ancillary (ăn´-sə-) ADJ. serving as an aid or accessory; auxiliary. In an *ancillary* capacity he was helpful; however, he could not be entrusted with leadership. also N.

andirons N. metal supports in a fireplace for cooking utensils or logs. She spent many hours in the department stores looking for a pair of ornamental *andirons* for her fireplace.

anemia (-nē´-) N. condition in which blood lacks red corpuscles. The doctor ascribes his tiredness to *anemia.* anemic, ADJ.

anesthetic (-thĕt´-) N. substance that removes sensation with or without loss of consciousness. His monotonous voice acted like an *anesthetic;* his audience was soon asleep. anesthesia, N.

animadversion (-vêr´-) N. critical remark. He resented the *animadversions* of his critics, particularly because he realized they were true.

animated ADJ. lively. Her *animated* expression indicated a keenness of intellect.

animosity N. active enmity. He incurred the *animosity* of the ruling class because he advocated limitations of their power.

annals N. records; history. In the *annals* of this period, we find no mention of democratic movements.

annihilate (-nī´-ə-) V. destroy. The enemy in its revenge tried to *annihilate* the entire population.

annuity N. yearly allowance. The *annuity* he set up with the insurance company supplements his social security benefits so that he can live very comfortably without working.

annul (-nŭl´) V. make void. The parents of the eloped couple tried to *annul* the marriage.

anomalous (-nŏm´-) ADJ. abnormal; irregular. He was placed in the *anomalous* position of seeming to approve procedures which he despised.

anomaly N. irregularity. A bird that cannot fly is an *anomaly.*

anonymous (-nŏn´-) ADJ. having no name. He tried to ascertain the identity of the writer of the *anonymous* letter.

antagonism (-tăg´-) N. active resistance. We shall have to overcome the *antagonism* of the natives before our plans for settling this area can succeed.

antediluvian (-lōō´-) ADJ. antiquated; ancient. The *antediluvian* customs had apparently not changed for thousands of years. also N.

anthropoid (ăn´-) ADJ. manlike. The gorilla is the strongest of the *anthropoid* animals. also N.

anthropologist (-pŏl´-) N. a student of the history and science of mankind. *Anthropologists* have discovered several relics of prehistoric man in this area.

anticlimax (-klī´-) N. letdown in thought or emotion. After the fine performance in the first act, the rest of the play was an *anticlimax.* anticlimactic, ADJ.

antipathy (-tĭp´-) N. aversion; dislike. His extreme *antipathy* to dispute caused him to avoid argumentative discussions with his friends.

antiseptic N. substance that prevents infection. It is advisable to apply an *antiseptic* to any wound, no matter how slight or insignificant. also ADJ.

antithesis (-tĭth´-ə-) N. contrast; direct opposite of or to. This tyranny was the *antithesis* of all that he had hoped for, and he fought it with all his strength.

apathetic ADJ. indifferent. He felt *apathetic* about the conditions he had observed and did not care to fight against them. apathy, N.

aperture (ăp´-) N. opening; hole. He discovered a small *aperture* in the wall, through which the insects had entered the room.

apex N. tip; summit; climax. He was at the *apex* of his career.

aphorism (ăf´-ə-rĭzm) N. pithy maxim. An *aphorism* differs from an adage in that it is more philosophical or scientific. aphoristic, ADJ.

aplomb N. poise. His nonchalance and *aplomb* in times of trouble always encouraged his followers.

apocryphal (-pŏk´-) ADJ. not genuine; sham. His *apocryphal* tears misled no one.

apogee (ăp´-ə-jē) N. highest point. When the moon in its orbit is furthest away from the earth, it is at its *apogee.*

apostate (-pŏs´-) N. one who abandons his religious faith or political beliefs. Because he switched from one party to another, his former friends shunned him as an *apostate.*

apothecary (-pŏth´-) N. druggist. In the *apothecaries'* weight, twelve ounces equal one pound.

apothegm (ăp´-ə-thĕm) N. pithy, compact saying. Proverbs are *apothegms* that have become familiar sayings.

apotheosis (-thē-ŏ´-səs) N. deification; glorification. The *apotheosis* of a Roman emperor was designed to insure his eternal greatness.

apparition N. ghost; phantom. Hamlet was uncertain about the identity of the *apparition* that had appeared and spoken to him.

appease V. pacify; soothe. We have discovered that, when we

ā—ale; ă—add; ä—arm; à—ask; ē—eve; ĕ—end; ê—err, her; ə—allow; even; ī—ice; ĭ—ill; ō—oll; ŏ—odd; ô—orb; ōō—food; ŏŏ—foot, put; ou—out; th—thin; ū—use; ŭ—up; zh—pleasure

try to *appease* our enemies, we encourage them to make additional demands.

appellation N. name; title. He was amazed when the witches hailed him with his correct *appellation*.

append V. attach. I shall *append* this chart to my report.

apposite (*ăp´-*) ADJ. appropriate; fitting. He was always able to find the *apposite* phrase, the correct expression for every occasion.

appraise V. estimate value of. It is difficult to *appraise* the value of old paintings; it is easier to call them priceless. appraisal, N.

apprehend (*-hĕnd´*) V. arrest (a criminal); dread; perceive. The police will *apprehend* the culprit and convict him

before long.

apprehensive ADJ. fearful; discerning. His *apprehensive* glances at the people who were walking in the street revealed his nervousness.

apprise (*-prīz´*) V. inform. When he was *apprised* of the dangerous weather conditions, he decided to postpone his trip.

appurtenances N. subordinate possessions. He bought the estate and all its *appurtenances*.

aptitude N. fitness; talent. The counselor gave him an *aptitude* test before advising him about the career he should follow.

ETYMOLOGY 2

AMBI (both) prefix

ambidextrous skillful with both hands
ambiguous of double meaning
ambivalent possessing conflicting (both) emotions

AN (without) prefix

anarchy lack of government
anemic lack of blood
anesthetize deprive of feeling

ANIM (mind, soul)

animadvert cast criticism upon (turn one's mind)
unanimous of one mind
magnanimity greatness of mind or spirit

ANN, ENN (year)

annuity yearly remittance
biennial every two years
perennial flowering yearly; a yearly flowering plant

ANTE (before) prefix

antecedent preceding event or word
antediluvian ancient (before the flood)
ante-nuptial before the wedding

ANTHROP (man)

anthropology study of man
misanthrope recluse (hater of mankind)
philanthropy love of mankind; charity

TEST—WORD LIST 2—*Antonyms*

Each of the questions below consists of a word printed in italics, followed by five words or phrases numbered 1 to 5. Choose the numbered word or phrase which is most nearly opposite in meaning to the word in italics and write the number of your choice on your answer paper.

21. *alleviate* 1 endure 2 worsen 3 enlighten 4 maneuver 5 humiliate
22. *amalgamate* 1 equip 2 separate 3 generate 4 materialize 5 repress
23. *amass* 1 concentrate 2 rotate 3 concern 4 separate 5 recollect
24. *antediluvian* 1 transported 2 subtle 3 isolated 4 celebrated 5 modern
25. *antipathy* 1 profundity 2 objection 3 willingness 4 abstention 5 fondness
26. *appease* 1 agitate 2 qualify 3 display 4 predestine 5 interrupt
27. *apposite* 1 inappropriate 2 diagonal 3 exponential 4 unobtrusive 5 discouraging
28. *apprehend* 1 obviate 2 set free 3 shiver 4 understand 5 contrast
29. *aloof* 1 triangular 2 gregarious 3 comparable 4 honorable 5 savory
30. *amicable* 1 penetrating 2 compensating 3 unfriendly 4 zig-zag 5 unescapable
31. *amorphous* 1 nauseous 2 obscene 3 providential 4 definite 5 happy
32. *amplify* 1 distract 2 infer 3 publicize 4 decrease 5 pioneer
33. *antithesis* 1 velocity 2 maxim 3 similarity 4 acceleration 5 reaction
34. *anomaly* 1 desperation 2 requisition 3 registry 4 regularity 5 radiation
35. *aptitude* 1 sarcasm 2 inversion 3 adulation 4 lack of talent 5 gluttony
36. *anathematize* 1 locate 2 deceive 3 regulate 4 radiate 5 bless
37. *altruism* 1 good nature 2 height 3 descent 4 modernity 5 miserliness
38. *ambiguous* 1 salvageable 2 corresponding 3 responsible 4 clear 5 auxiliary
39. *anemic* 1 pallid 2 cruel 3 red-blooded 4 ventilating 5 hazardous
40. *anonymous* 1 desperate 2 signed 3 defined 4 expert 5 written

WORD LIST 3 aquiline - bantering

aquiline (ăk´-wə-lĭn) ADJ. curved, hooked. He can be recognized by his *aquiline* nose, curved like the beak of the eagle.

arable ADJ. fit for plowing. The land was no longer *arable;* erosion had removed the valuable topsoil.

arbiter (är´-) N. a person with power to decide a dispute; judge. As an *arbiter* in labor disputes, he has won the confidence of the workers and the employers.

arbitrary ADJ. fixed or decided; despotic. Any *arbitrary* action on your part will be resented by the members of the board whom you do not consult.

arcade N. a covered passageway, usually lined with shops. The *arcade* was popular with shoppers because it gave them protection from the summer sun and the winter rain.

archaeology (-kē-ŏl´-) N. study of artifacts and relics of early mankind. The professor of *archaeology* headed an expedition to the Gobi Desert in search of ancient ruins.

archaic (-kā´-ĭk) ADJ. antiquated. "Methinks," "thee," and "thou" are *archaic* words which are no longer part of our normal vocabulary.

archipelago (är-kə-pĕl´-) N. group of closely located islands. When he looked at the map and saw the *archipelagoes* in the South Seas, he longed to visit them.

ardor N. heat; passion; zeal. His *ardor* was contagious; soon everyone was eagerly working.

arduous ADJ. hard; strenuous. His *arduous* efforts had sapped his energy.

argot (är´-gət) N. slang. In the *argot* of the underworld, he "was taken for a ride."

aromatic ADJ. fragrant. Medieval sailing vessels brought *aromatic* herbs from China to Europe.

arraign (-rān´) V. charge in court; indict. After his indictment by the Grand Jury, the accused man was *arraigned* in the County Criminal Court.

arrant (är´-) ADJ. thorough; complete; unmitigated. "*Arrant* knave," an epithet found in books dealing with the age of chivalry, is a term of condemnation.

arrogance N. haughtiness. The *arrogance* of the nobility was resented by the middle class.

artifacts N. products of primitive culture. Archaeologists debated the significance of the *artifacts* discovered in the ruins of Asia Minor and came to no conclusion.

artifice N. deception; trickery. The Trojan War proved to the Greeks that cunning and *artifice* were often more effective than military might.

artisan N. a manually skilled worker. Artists and *artisans* alike are necessary to the development of a culture.

ascertain (-tān´) V. find out for certain. Please *ascertain* his present address.

ascetic (ă-sĕt´-) ADJ. practicing self-denial; austere. The cavalier could not understand the *ascetic* life led by the monks. also N.

asceticism N. doctrine of self-denial. We find *asceticism* carried on in many parts of the world.

ascribe (-skrīb´) V. refer; attribute; assign. I can *ascribe* no motiv~ for his acts.

ashen ADJ. ash-colored. His face was *ashen* with fear.

asinine ADJ. stupid. Your *asinine* remarks prove that you have not given this problem any serious consideration.

askance (-skăns´) ADV. with a sideways or indirect look. Looking *askance* at her questioner, she displayed her scorn.

askew (-skū´) ADV. crookedly; slanted; at an angle. When he placed his hat *askew* upon his head, his observers laughed.

asperity N. sharpness (of temper). These remarks, spoken with *asperity,* stung the boys to whom they had been directed.

aspersion N. slanderous remark. Do not cast *aspersions* on his character.

aspirant N. seeker after position or status. Although I am an *aspirant* for public office, I am not willing to accept the dictates of the party bosses. also ADJ.

aspiration N. noble ambition. Man's *aspirations* should be as lofty as the stars.

assail V. assault. He was *assailed* with questions after his lecture.

assay (-sā´) V. analyze; evaluate. When they *assayed* the ore, they found that they had discovered a very rich vein. also N.

asseverate (-sĕv´-) V. make a positive statement or solemn declaration. I will *asseverate* my conviction that he is guilty.

assiduous (-sĭj´-ə-wəs) ADJ. diligent. He worked *assiduously* at this task for weeks before he felt satisfied with his results. assiduity, N.

assuage (-swāj´) V. ease; lessen (pain). Your messages of cheer should *assuage* his suffering. assuagement, N.

asteroid N. small planet. *Asteroids* have become commonplace to the readers of interstellar travel stories in science fiction magazines.

astral ADJ. relating to the stars. He was amazed at the number of *astral* bodies the new telescope revealed.

astringent ADJ. binding; causing contraction. The *astringent* quality of the unsweetened lemon juice made swallowing difficult. also N.

astute ADJ. wise; shrewd. That was a very *astute* observation. I shall heed it.

atheistic ADJ. denying the existence of God. His *atheistic* remarks shocked the religious worshippers.

athwart PREP. across; in opposition. His tendency toward violence was *athwart* the philosophy of the peace movement. also ADV.

atrocity N. brutal deed. In time of war, many *atrocities* are committed by invading armies.

atrophy (ă´-) N. wasting away. Polio victims need physiotherapy to prevent the *atrophy* of affected limbs. also V.

attenuate V. make thin; weaken. By withdrawing their forces, the generals hoped to *attenuate* the enemy lines.

attest V. testify, bear witness. Having served as a member of the Grand Jury, I can *attest* that our system of indicting individuals is in need of improvement.

attribute (ă´-) N. essential quality. His outstanding *attribute* was his kindness.

attrition N. gradual wearing down. They decided to wage a war of *attrition* rather than to rely on an all-out attack.

atypical (ā-tĭp´-) ADJ. not normal. You have taken an *atypical* case. It does not prove anything.

audacity N. boldness. His *audacity* in this critical moment encouraged us.

audit N. examination of accounts. When the bank examiners a ived to hold their annual *audit,* they discovered the embezzlements of the chief cashier. also V.

augment V. increase. How can we hope to *augment* our forces when our allies are deserting us?

ā—ale; ă—add; ä—arm; à—ask, ē—eve; ĕ—end; ê—err, her; ə—allow; even; ī—ice; ĭ—ill; ō—oll; ŏ—odd; ô—orb; oo—food; oo—foot, put; ou—out; th—thin; ū—use; ù—up; zh—pleasure

augury (ô´-gyə-) N. omen; prophecy. He interpreted the departure of the birds as an *augury* of evil. augur, V.

auspicious ADJ. favoring success. With favorable weather conditions, it was an *auspicious* moment to set sail.

austere ADJ. strict, stern. His *austere* demeanor prevented us from engaging in our usual frivolous activities.

austerity N. sternness; severity. The *austerity* and dignity of the court were maintained by the new justices.

authenticate V. prove genuine. An expert was needed to *authenticate* the original Van Gogh painting from its imitation.

autocrat N. monarch with supreme power. The nobles tried to limit the powers of the *autocrat* without success. autocracy, N.

automaton (-tŏm´-) N. mechanism which imitates actions of humans. Long before science fiction readers became aware of robots, writers were presenting stories of *automatons* who could outperform men.

autonomous ADJ. self-governing. This island is a colony; however, in most matters, it is *autonomous* and receives no orders from the mother country. autonomy, N.

autopsy (ô´-tŏp-sē) N. examination of a dead body; postmortem. The medical examiner ordered an *autopsy* to determine the cause of death. also V.

auxiliary ADJ. helper, additional or subsidiary. To prepare for the emergency, they built an *auxiliary* power station. also N.

avarice N. greediness for wealth. King Midas's *avarice* has been famous for centuries. avaricious, ADJ.

aver (ə-vêr´) V. state confidently. I wish to *aver* that I am certain of success.

averse ADJ. reluctant. He was *averse* to revealing the sources of his information.

avid ADJ. greedy; eager for. He was *avid* for learning and read everything he could get. avidity, N.

avouch V. affirm; proclaim. I am willing to employ your friend if you will *avouch* his integrity.

avow V. declare openly. I must *avow* that I am innocent.

avuncular (-vŭn´-) ADJ. like an uncle. *Avuncular* pride did not prevent him from noticing his nephew's shortcomings.

awe N. solemn wonder. The tourists gazed with *awe* at the tremendous expanse of the Grand Canyon.

awry (-rī´) ADV. distorted; crooked. He held his head *awry*, giving the impression that he had caught cold in his neck during the night. also ADJ.

axiom N. self-evident truth requiring no proof. Before a student can begin to think along the lines of Euclidean geometry, he must accept certain principles or *axioms*.

azure ADJ. sky blue. *Azure* skies are indicative of good weather.

babble V. chatter idly. The little girl *babbled* about her doll. also N.

bacchanalian (băk-ə-nāl´-) ADJ. drunken. Emperor Nero attended the *bacchanalian* orgy.

badger V. pester; annoy. She was forced to change her telephone number because she was *badgered* by obscene phone calls.

baffle V. frustrate; perplex. The new code *baffled* the enemy agents.

baleful ADJ. deadly; destructive. The drought was a *baleful* omen.

balk (bôk) V. foil. When the warden learned that several inmates were planning to escape, he took steps to *balk* their attempt.

balmy ADJ. mild; fragrant. A *balmy* breeze refreshed us after the sultry blast.

banal (bə-nāl´-) ADJ. hackneyed; commonplace; trite. His frequent use of clichés made his essay seem *banal*. banality, N.

bandanna N. large, bright-colored handkerchief. She could be identified by the gaudy *bandanna* she wore as a head covering.

baneful ADJ. ruinous; poisonous. His *baneful* influence was feared by all.

bantering ADJ. good-natured ridiculing. They resented his *bantering* remarks because they thought he was being sarcastic.

ETYMOLOGY 3

AQUA, AQUE (water)

aqueduct a passageway for conducting water; a conduit
aquatic living in water
aqua fortis nitric acid (strong water)

ARCH (chief, first) prefix

archetype original model
archbishop chief bishop
archaeology study of antiquities (study of first things)

ARCH (government, ruler, first)

monarch sole ruler
anarchy lack of government
oligarchy government by the few

ASTER, ASTR (star)

astronomy study of the stars
asterisk starlike type character (*)
disaster catastrophe (contrary star)

AUD, AUDIT (to hear)

audible able to be heard
auditorium place where people may be heard
audience hearers

AUTO (self)

autocracy rule by self (one person)
automobile vehicle that moves by itself
autobiography story of a person's life written by himself

TEST—WORD LIST 3—*Synonyms and Antonyms*

Each of the following questions consists of a word printed in italics, followed by five words or phrases numbered 1 to 5. Choose the numbered word or phrase which is most nearly the same as or the opposite of the word in italics and write the number of your choice on your answer paper.

ā—ale; ȧ—add; ä—arm; a̦—ask, ē—eve; ĕ—end; ê—err, her; ə—allow; even; ī—ice; ĭ—ill; ō—oll; ŏ—odd; ô—orb; ōō—food; ŏŏ—foot, put; ou—out; th—thin; ū—use; ŭ—up; zh—pleasure

41. *aquiline* 1 watery 2 hooked 3 refined 4 antique 5 rodentlike
42. *archaic* 1 youthful 2 cautious 3 antiquated 4 placated 5 buttressed
43. *ardor* 1 zeal 2 paint 3 proof 4 group 5 excitement
44. *artifice* 1 spite 2 exception 3 anger 4 candor 5 loyalty
45. *artisan* 1 educator 2 decider 3 sculptor 4 discourser 5 unskilled laborer
46. *ascertain* 1 amplify 2 master 3 discover 4 retain 5 explode
47. *asteroid* 1 Milky Way 2 radiance 3 large planet 4 rising moon 5 setting moon
48. *asperity* 1 anguish 2 absence 3 innuendo 4 good temper 5 snake
49. *assuage* 1 stuff 2 describe 3 wince 4 worsen 5 introduce
50. *astute* 1 sheer 2 noisy 3 astral 4 unusual 5 foolish
51. *atrocity* 1 endurance 2 fortitude 3 session 4 heinous act 5 hatred

52. *atypical* 1 superfluous 2 booming 3 normal 4 clashing 5 lovely
53. *audacity* 1 boldness 2 asperity 3 strength 4 stature 5 anchorage
54. *avarice* 1 anxiety 2 generosity 3 statement 4 invoice 5 power
55. *balmy* 1 venturesome 2 dedicated 3 mild 4 fanatic 5 memorable
56. *awry* 1 recommended 2 commiserating 3 startled 4 straight 5 psychological
57. *banal* 1 philosophical 2 original 3 dramatic 4 heedless 5 discussed
58. *baleful* 1 doubtful 2 virtual 3 deadly 4 conventional 5 virtuous
59. *auxiliary* 1 righteous 2 prospective 3 assistant 4 archaic 5 mandatory
60. *baneful* 1 intellectual 2 thankful 3 decisive 4 nonpoisonous 5 remorseful

---

WORD LIST 4 barb - cadaverous

barb N. sharp projection from fishhook, etc. The *barb* from the fishhook caught in his finger as he grabbed the fish. barbed, ADJ.

baroque (-rōk´) ADJ. highly ornate. They found the *baroque* architecture amusing.

barrage (-äzh´) N. barrier laid down by artillery fire. The company was forced to retreat through the *barrage* of heavy cannons.

barrister (bar´-ə-) N. counselor-at-law. Galsworthy started as a *barrister*, but, when he found the practice of law boring, turned to writing.

barterer N. trader. The *barterer* exchanged trinkets for the natives' furs.

bate (bāt) V. let down; restrain. Until it was time to open the presents, the children had to *bate* their curiosity. bated, ADJ.

batten V. grow fat; thrive upon others. We cannot accept a system where a favored few can *batten* in extreme comfort while others toil.

bauble (bô´-) N. trinket; trifle. The child was delighted with the *bauble* she had won in the grab bag.

beatific (bē-ə-tĭf´) ADJ. giving bliss; blissful. The *beatific* smile on the child's face made us very happy.

bedizen (bĭ-dīz´-) V. dress with vulgar finery. The witch doctors were *bedizened* in all their gaudiest costumes.

bedraggle V. wet thoroughly. We were so *bedraggled* by the severe storm that we had to change into dry clothing. bedraggled, ADJ.

beguile (-gīl´) V. delude; cheat; amuse. He *beguiled* himself during the long hours by playing solitaire.

behoove V. suited to; incumbent upon. In this time of crisis, it *behooves* all of us to remain calm and await the instructions of our superiors.

belabor V. beat soundly; assail verbally. He was *belaboring* his opponent.

belated ADJ. delayed. He apologized for his *belated* note of condolence to the widow of his friend and explained that he had just learned of her husband's untimely death.

beleaguer V. besiege. As soon as the city was *beleaguered*, life became more subdued as the citizens began their long wait for outside assistance. beleaguered, ADJ.

bellicose ADJ. warlike. His *bellicose* disposition alienated his friends.

benediction N. blessing. The appearance of the sun after the many rainy days was like a *benediction*.

benefactor N. gift giver; patron. Scrooge later became Tiny Tim's *benefactor*.

beneficiary N. person entitled to benefits or proceeds of an insurance policy or will. You may change your *beneficiary* as often as you wish.

benevolent (-nĕv´-) ADJ. generous; charitable. His *benevolent* nature prevented him from refusing any beggar who accosted him.

benighted ADJ. overcome by darkness. In the *benighted* Middle Ages, intellectual curiosity was discouraged by the authorities.

benign (-nīn´) ADJ. kindly; favorable; not malignant. The old man was well liked because of his *benign* attitude toward friend and stranger alike.

berate V. scold strongly. He feared she would *berate* him for his forgetfulness.

bereft ADJ. deprived of; lacking. The foolish gambler soon found himself *bereft* of funds.

berserk (bêr-sêrk´) ADV. frenzied. Angered, he went *berserk* and began to wreck the room.

besmirch V. soil, defile. The scandalous remarks in the newspaper *besmirch* the reputations of every member of the society.

bestow V. confer. He wished to *bestow* great honors upon the hero.

bête noire (bĕt-nwär´) N. aversion; person or thing strongly disliked or avoided. Going to the opera was his personal *bête noire* because high-pitched sounds irritated him.

betroth (-trōth´) V. become engaged to marry. The announcement that they had become *betrothed* surprised their friends who had not suspected any romance. betrothal, N.

bicameral (bī-) ADJ. two-chambered, as a legislative body. The United States Congress is a *bicameral* body.

biennial (bī-) ADJ. every two years. The plant bore *biennial* flowers. also N.

bigotry N. stubborn intolerance. Brought up in a democratic atmosphere, the student was shocked by the *bigotry* and narrowness expressed by several of his classmates.

ā—ale; ă—add; ä—arm; à—ask, ē—eve; ĕ—end; ê—err, her; ə—allow; even; ī—ice; ĭ—ill; ō—oll; ŏ—odd; ô—orb; oo—food; oo—foot; put; ou—out; th—thin; ū—use; ŭ—up; zh—pleasure

bilious ADJ. suffering from indigestion; irritable. His *bilious* temperament was apparent to all who heard him rant about his difficulties.

bivouac (*bǐv'-ə-wăk*) N. temporary encampment. While in *bivouac*, we spent the night in our sleeping bags under the stars. also V.

bizarre (*bə-zär'*) ADJ. fantastic; violently contrasting. The plot of the novel was too *bizarre* to be believed.

bland ADJ. soothing; mild. She used a *bland* ointment for her sunburn.

blandishment N. flattery. Despite the salesperson's *blandishments*, the customer did not buy the outfit.

blasphemous (*blăs'-fə-*) ADJ. profane; impious. The people in the room were shocked by his *blasphemous* language.

blatant (*blāt'-*) ADJ. loudly offensive. I regard your remarks as *blatant* and ill-mannered. blatancy, N.

blazon (*blāz'-*) V. decorate with an heraldic coat of arms. *Blazoned* on his shield were the two lambs and the lion, the traditional coat of arms of his family. also N.

bleak ADJ. cold; cheerless. The Aleutian Islands are *bleak* military outposts.

blighted ADJ. suffering from a disease; destroyed. The extent of the *blighted* areas could be seen only when viewed from the air.

blithe ADJ. gay; joyous. Shelley called the skylark a "*blithe* spirit" because of its happy song.

bloated ADJ. swollen or puffed as with water or air. The *bloated* corpse was taken from the river.

bludgeon (*blŭj'-*) N. club; heavy-headed weapon. His walking stick served him as a *bludgeon* on many occasions. also V.

bode V. foreshadow; portend. The gloomy skies and the sulphurous odors from the mineral springs seemed to *bode* evil to those who settled in the area.

bogus ADJ. counterfeit; not authentic. The police quickly found the distributors of the *bogus* twenty-dollar bills.

boisterous ADJ. violent; rough; noisy. The unruly crowd became even more *boisterous* when he tried to quiet them.

bolster V. support; prop up. I do not intend to *bolster* your hopes with false reports of outside assistance; the truth is that we must face the enemy alone. also N.

bombastic ADJ. pompous; using inflated language. The orator spoke in a *bombastic* manner. bombast, N.

bootless ADJ. useless. I "trouble deaf heaven with my *bootless* cries."

bouillon (*bōol'-yän*) N. clear beef soup. The cup of *bouillon* served by the stewards was welcomed by those who had been chilled by the cold ocean breezes.

bountiful ADJ. generous; showing bounty. She distributed gifts in a *bountiful* and gracious manner.

bourgeois (*bŏorzh-wä'*) N. middle class. The French Revolution was inspired by the *bourgeois*. also ADJ.

braggadocio (*-dō'-shē-ō*) N. boasting. He was disliked because his manner was always full of *braggadocio*.

bravado (*-văd'-ō*) N. swagger; assumed air of defiance. The *bravado* of the young criminal disappeared when he was confronted by the victims of his brutal attack.

brazen (*brāz'-*) ADJ. insolent. Her *brazen* contempt for authority angered the officials.

brazier (*brā'-zhər*) N. open pan in which live coals are burned. On chilly nights, the room was warmed by coals burning in *braziers* set in the corners of the room.

breach N. breaking of contract or duty; fissure; gap. They found a *breach* in the enemy's fortifications and penetrated their lines. also V.

brevity N. conciseness. *Brevity* is essential when you send a telegram or cablegram; you are charged for every word.

bristling ADJ. rising like bristles; showing irritation. The dog stood there, *bristling* with anger.

broach V. open up. He did not even try to *broach* the subject of poetry.

brocade N. rich, figured fabric. The sofa was covered with expensive *brocade*.

brochure (*brō-shōor'*) N. pamphlet. This *brochure* on farming was issued by the Department of Agriculture.

brooch (*brōch*) N. ornamental clasp. She treasured the *brooch* because it was an heirloom.

brusque (*brŭsk*) ADJ. blunt; abrupt. She was offended by his *brusque* reply.

bucolic (*bū-kŏl'-*) ADJ. rustic; pastoral. The meadow was the scene of *bucolic* gaiety.

buffoonery N. clowning. Jimmy Durante's *buffoonery* was hilarious.

bullion (*bŏol'-yən*) N. gold and silver in the form of bars. Much *bullion* is stored in the vaults at Fort Knox.

bulwark (*bŏol'-*) N. earthwork or other strong defense; person who defends. The navy is our principal *bulwark* against invasion.

bumptious ADJ. self-assertive. His classmates called him a show-off because of his *bumptious* airs.

bungle V. spoil by clumsy behavior. I was afraid you would *bungle* this assignment but I had no one else to send.

burgeon (*bêr'-jən*) V. grow forth; send out buds. In the spring, the plants that burgeon are a promise of the beauty that is to come.

burlesque V. give an imitation that ridicules. In his caricature, he *burlesqued* the mannerisms of his adversary. also N.

burnish V. make shiny by rubbing; polish. The *burnished* metal reflected the lamplight.

buttress N. support or prop. The huge cathedral walls were supported by flying *buttresses*. also V.

buxom (*bŭk'-səm*) ADJ. plump; vigorous; jolly. The soldiers remembered the *buxom* nurse who had always been so pleasant to them.

cabal (*-băl'*) N. small group of persons secretly united to promote their own interests. The *cabal* was defeated when their scheme was discovered.

cache (*kăsh*) N. hiding place. The detectives followed the suspect until he led them to the *cache* where he had stored his loot. also V.

cacophony (*kă-kŏf'-*) N. discord. Some people seem to enjoy the *cacophony* of an orchestra that is tuning up.

cadaver (*kə-dăv'-*) N. corpse. In some states, it is illegal to dissect *cadavers*.

cadaverous ADJ. like a corpse; pale. By his *cadaverous* appearance, we could see how the disease had ravaged him.

ETYMOLOGY 4

BELLI (war)

bellicose inclined to fighting

belligerent engaged in war
rebellious warring against authority

BEN, BON (well, good) prefix

benefactor   one who does good
benevolence   charity (wishing good)
bonus   something extra above regular pay

BI (two) prefix

bicameral   legislature consisting of two houses
biennial   every two years
bicycle   two-wheeled vehicle

BIBLI (book)

bibliography   list of books
bibliophile   lover of books
Bible   the sacred scriptures ("The Book")

BIO (life)

biology   study of living things
biography   writing about a person's life
biochemist   a student of the chemistry of living things

BREV, BREVE (short)

brevity   briefness
abbreviate   shorten
breve   mark placed over a vowel to indicate that it is short
($\breve{a}$ as in h$\breve{a}$t)

CAD, CAS (to fall)

decadent   deteriorating
cadence   intonation, terminal musical phrase
cascade   waterfall

TEST—WORD LIST 4—*Synonyms*

Each of the questions below consists of a word printed in italics, followed by five words or phrases numbered 1 to 5. Choose the numbered word or phrase which is most nearly similar in meaning to the word in italics and write the number of your choice on your answer paper.

61. *baroque*   1 polished 2 constant 3 transformed 4 highly ornate 5 aglow
62. *benign*   1 tenfold 2 peaceful 3 blessed 4 wavering 5 favorable
63. *boisterous*   1 conflicting 2 noisy 3 testimonial 4 grateful 5 adolescent
64. *brazen*   1 shameless 2 quick 3 modest 4 pleasant 5 melodramatic
65. *barrister*   1 specialist 2 teacher 3 attorney 4 conductor 5 professor
66. *biennial*   1 yearly 2 every two years 3 favorable 4 impressive 5 celebrated
67. *bombastic*   1 sensitive 2 pompous 3 rapid 4 sufficient 5 expensive

68. *bucolic*   1 diseased 2 repulsive 3 rustic 4 twinkling 5 cold
69. *bauble*   1 mainstay 2 gas 3 soap 4 trifling piece of jewelry 5 expense
70. *bigotry*   1 arrogance 2 approval 3 mourning 4 promptness 5 intolerance
71. *bouillon*   1 insight 2 chowder 3 gold 4 clear soup 5 stew
72. *buxom*   1 voluminous 2 indecisive 3 convincing 4 plump 5 bookish
73. *beatific*   1 glorious 2 blissful 3 theatrical 4 crooked 5 handsome
74. *bland*   1 mild 2 meager 3 soft 4 uncooked 5 helpless
75. *braggadocio*   1 Cyrano 2 boasting 3 skirmish 4 encounter 5 position
76. *cache*   1 lock 2 hiding place 3 tide 4 automobile 5 grappling hook
77. *bellicose*   1 warlike 2 navel 3 amusing 4 piecemeal 5 errant
78. *blithe*   1 spiritual 2 profuse 3 gay 4 hybrid 5 comfortable
79. *brochure*   1 opening 2 pamphlet 3 censor 4 bureau 5 pin
80. *cacophony*   1 discord 2 dance 3 applause 4 type of telephone 5 rooster

---

WORD LIST   5   **cajole - churlish**

cajole   (-jōl´) V. coax; wheedle. I will not be *cajoled* into granting you your wish.

caliber   N. ability; capacity. A man of such *caliber* should not be assigned such menial tasks.

callous   ADJ. hardened; unfeeling. He had worked in the hospital for so many years that he was *callous* to the suffering in the wards. callus, N.

calorific   (kăl-ə-rĭf´-) ADJ. heat-producing. Coal is much more *calorific* than green wood.

calumniate   (-lŭm´-) V. slander. Shakespeare wrote that love and friendship were subject to envious and *calumniating* time.

calumny   (kăl´-) N. malicious misrepresentation; slander. He could endure his financial failure, but he could not bear the *calumny* that his foes heaped upon him.

cameo   N. shell or jewel carved in relief. Tourists are advised not to purchase *cameos* from the street peddlers of Rome

who sell poor specimens of the carver's art.

canard   (-närd´) N. unfounded rumor; exaggerated report. It is almost impossible to protect oneself from such a base *canard*.

candor   N. frankness. The *candor* and simplicity of his speech impressed all. candid, ADJ.

canker   N. any ulcerous sore; any evil. Poverty is a *canker* in the body politic; it must be cured.

canny   ADJ. shrewd; thrifty. The *canny* Scotsman was more than a match for the swindlers.

cant   N. jargon of thieves; pious phraseology. Many listeners were fooled by the *cant* and hypocrisy of his speech.

cantata   (-tät´-) N. story set to music, to be sung by a chorus. The choral society sang the new *cantata* composed by its leader.

canter   N. slow gallop. Because the racehorse had outdistanced its competition so easily, the reporter wrote that the

---

ā—ale; ă—add; ä—arm; à—ask; ē—eve; ĕ—end; ê—err, her, ə—allow; even; ī—ice; ĭ—ill; ō—oll; ŏ—odd; ô—orb; ōō—food;
ŏŏ—foot; put; ou—out; th—thin; ŭ—use; ŭ—up; zh—pleasure

race was won in a *canter.* also V.

canto N. division of a long poem. In *The Man without a Country,* Philip Nolan is upset when he reads one of Sir Walter Scott's *cantos.*

canvass V. determine votes, etc. After *canvassing* the sentiments of his constituents, the congressman was confident that he represented the majority opinion of his district. also N.

capacious ADJ. spacious. In the *capacious* areas of the railroad terminal, thousands of travelers lingered while waiting for their train.

caparison N, V. showy harness or ornamentation for a horse; put showy ornamentation on a horse. The audience admired the *caparison* of the horses as they made their entrance into the circus ring.

capitulate V. surrender. The enemy was warned to *capitulate* or face annihilation.

caprice (*-prēs´*) N. whim. Do not act on *caprice.* Study your problem.

capricious (*-prĭsh´-*) ADJ. fickle; incalculable. The storm was *capricious* and changed course constantly.

caption N. title; chapter heading; text under illustration. I find the *captions* which accompany these cartoons very clever and humorous. also V.

captious ADJ. faultfinding. His criticisms were always *captious* and frivolous, never offering constructive suggestions.

carat N. unit of weight for precious stones; measure of fineness of gold. He gave her a three-*carat* diamond mounted in an eighteen-*carat* gold band.

caricature N. distortion; burlesque. The *caricatures* he drew always emphasized a personal weakness of the people he burlesqued. also V.

carmine (*kär´-mən*) N. rich red. *Carmine* in her lipstick made her lips appear black in the photographs.

carnage N. destruction of life. The *carnage* that can be caused by atomic warfare adds to the responsibilities of our statesmen.

carnal ADJ. fleshly. The public was more interested in *carnal* pleasures than in spiritual matters.

carnivorous ADJ. meat-eating. The lion is a *carnivorous* animal. carnivore, N.

carousal (*-rou´-zəl*) N. drunken revel. The party degenerated into an ugly *carousal.*

carping ADJ. finding fault. A *carping* critic disturbs sensitive people.

carrion N. rotting flesh of a dead body. Buzzards are nature's scavengers; they eat the *carrion* left behind by other predators.

carte blanche (*kärt-blänsh´*) N. unlimited authority or freedom. Use your own discretion in this matter; I give you *carte blanche.*

cascade N. small waterfall. We could not appreciate the beauty of the many *cascades* as we were forced to make detours around each of them. also V.

castigate V. punish. He decided to *castigate* the culprit personally.

casualty N. serious or fatal accident. The number of *casualties* on this holiday weekend was high.

cataclysm N. deluge; upheaval. A *cataclysm* such as the French Revolution affects all countries. cataclysmic, ADJ.

catapult N. slingshot; a hurling machine. Airplanes are sometimes launched from battleships by *catapults.* also V.

catastrophe N. calamity. The Johnstown flood was a *catastrophe.*

catechism N. book for religious instruction; instruction by question and answer. He taught by engaging his pupils in a *catechism* until they gave him the correct answer.

cathartic N. purgative. Some drugs act as laxatives when taken in small doses but act as *cathartics* when taken in much larger doses.

catholic ADJ. broadly sympathetic; liberal. He was extremely *catholic* in his reading tastes.

caustic ADJ. burning; sarcastically biting. The critic's *caustic* remarks angered the hapless actors who were the subjects of his sarcasm.

cauterize (*kôt´-*) V. burn with hot iron or caustic. In order to prevent infection, the doctor *cauterized* the wound.

cavalcade N. procession; parade. As described by Chaucer, the *cavalcade* of Canterbury pilgrims was a motley group.

cavil (*kăv´-*) V. make frivolous objections. I respect your sensible criticisms, but I dislike the way you *cavil* about unimportant details. also N.

cede (*sēd*) V. transfer; yield title to. I intend to *cede* this property to the city.

celestial ADJ. heavenly. He wrote about the music of "*celestial* spheres."

celibate (*sĕl´-ə-bət*) ADJ. unmarried; abstaining from sexual intercourse. He vowed to remain *celibate.* celibacy, N.

censor N. overseer of morals; person who reads to eliminate inappropriate remarks. Soldiers dislike having their mail read by a *censor* but understand the need for this precaution. also V.

censure (*sĕn´-chər*) V. blame; criticize. He was *censured* for his ill-advised act. also N.

centaur (*sĕn´-tôr*) N. mythical figure, half man and half horse. I was particularly impressed by the statue of the *centaur* in the Roman Hall of the museum.

centigrade ADJ. measure of temperature used widely in Europe. On the *centigrade* thermometer, the freezing point of water is zero degrees.

centrifugal (*-trĭf´-*) ADJ. radiating; departing from the center. Many automatic drying machines remove excess moisture from clothing by *centrifugal* force.

centurion N. Roman army officer. Because he was in command of a company of one hundred soldiers, he was called a *centurion.*

cerebral (*sə-rē´-*) ADJ. pertaining to the brain or intellect. The content of philosophical works is *cerebral* in nature and requires much thought.

cerebration (*sĕr´-*) N. thought. Mathematics problems sometimes require much *cerebration.*

cessation N. stopping. The workers threatened a *cessation* of all activities if their demands were not met. cease, V.

cession N. yielding to another; ceding. The *cession* of Alaska to the United States is discussed in this chapter.

chafe (*chāf*) V. warm by rubbing; make sore by rubbing. The collar *chafed* his neck. also N.

chaffing ADJ. bantering; joking. Sometimes his flippant and *chaffing* remarks annoy us.

chagrin (*shə-grĭn´*) N. vexation; disappointment. His refusal to go with us filled us with *chagrin.*

chalice N. goblet; consecrated cup. In a small room adjoining the cathedral, many ornately decorated *chalices* made by the most famous European goldsmiths were on display.

chameleon (*kə-mēl´-yən*) N. lizard that changes color in different situations. Like the *chameleon,* he assumed the political thinking of every group he met.

champ V. chew noisily. His dining companions were amused by the way he *champed* his food.

chaotic (*kā-ŏt´-*) ADJ. in utter disorder. He tried to bring order into the *chaotic* state of affairs. chaos, N.

charisma (*kə-rĭz´-*) N. divine gift; great popular charm or appeal of a political leader. Political commentators have deplored the importance of a candidate's *charisma* in these days of television campaigning.

charlatan (*shär´-*) N. quack; pretender to knowledge. Be-

ā—ale; ă—add; ä—arm; à—ask; ē—eve; ĕ—end; ê—err, her; ə—allow; even; ī—ice; ĭ—ill; ō—oll; ŏ—odd; ô—orb; ōō—food; ŏŏ—foot, put; ou—out; th—thin; ū—use; ŭ—up; zh—pleasure

cause he was unable to substantiate his claim that he had found a cure for the dread disease, he was called a *charlatan* by his colleagues.

chary (*chăr´-ē*) ADJ. cautiously watchful. She was *chary* of her favors.

chasm (*kăzm*) N. abyss. They could not see the bottom of the *chasm*.

chassis (*shăs´-ē*) N. framework and working parts of an automobile. Examining the car after the accident, the owner discovered that the body had been ruined but that the *chassis* was unharmed.

chaste (*chāst*) ADJ. pure. Her *chaste* and decorous garb was appropriately selected for the solemnity of the occasion. chastity, N.

chastise V. punish. I must *chastise* you for this offense.

chattel N. personal property. When he bought his furniture on the installment plan, he signed a *chattel* mortgage.

chauvinist (*shō´-*) N. blindly devoted patriot. A *chauvinist* cannot recognize any faults in his country, no matter how flagrant they may be.

checkered ADJ. marked by changes in fortune. During his *checkered* career he had lived in palatial mansions and in dreary boardinghouses.

chicanery (*shĭk-ān´-*) N. trickery. Your deceitful tactics in this case are indications of *chicanery*.

chide V. scold. Grandma began to *chide* Steven for his lying.

chimerical (*kī-mēr´-*) ADJ. fantastic; highly imaginative. Poe's *chimerical* stories are sometimes too morbid for reading in bed. chimera, N.

chiropodist (*kə-rŏp´-*) N. one who treats disorders of the feet. The *chiropodist* treated the ingrown nail on the boy's foot.

choleric (*kŏl´-*) ADJ. hot-tempered. His flushed, angry face indicated a *choleric* nature.

chronic ADJ. long established as a disease. The doctors were able finally to attribute his *chronic* headaches and nausea to traces of formaldehyde gas in his apartment.

churlish ADJ. boorish; rude. Dismayed by his *churlish* manners at the party, the girls vowed never to invite him again.

ETYMOLOGY 5

CAP, CAPT, CEP, CIP (to take)

> *participate*   take part
> *precept*   a wise saying (originally, a command)
> *capture*   seize

CAP (head)

> *decapitate*   behead
> *captain*   chief
> *capital*   major city or site; first-rate

CATA (down) prefix

> *catastrophe*   disaster (turning down)
> *cataract*   waterfall
> *catapult*   hurl (throw down)

CED (to yield, to go)

> *recede*   go back, withdraw
> *antecedent*   that which goes before
> *concede*   yield, agree with

CENT (one hundred)

> *century*   one hundred years
> *centennial*   hundredth anniversary

CHRONOS (time)

> *chronology*   *timetable of events*
> *anachronism*   a thing out of time sequence, as Shakespeare's
> reference to clocks in *Julius Caesar*
> *chronicle*   register events in order

TEST—WORD LIST 5—*Antonyms*

Each of the questions below consists of a word printed in italics, followed by five words or phrases numbered 1 to 5. Choose the numbered word or phrase which is most nearly opposite in meaning to the word in italics and write the number of your choice on your answer paper.

81. *candid*   1 vague 2 secretive 3 experienced 4 anxious 5 sallow
82. *carnivorous*   1 gloomy 2 tangential 3 productive 4 weak 5 vegetarian
83. *celibate*   1 investing 2 married 3 retired 4 commodious 5 dubious
84. *chimerical*   1 developing 2 wonderful 3 disappearing 4 economical 5 realistic
85. *capacious*   1 warlike 2 cordial 3 curious 4 not spacious 5 not capable
86. *carousal*   1 awakening 2 sobriety 3 acceleration 4 direction 5 production
87. *censure*   1 process 2 enclose 3 interest 4 praise 5 penetrate
88. *choleric*   1 irascible 2 episodic 3 coolheaded 4 global 5 seasonal

89. *capricious*   1 satisfied 2 insured 3 photographic 4 scattered 5 steadfast
90. *catholic*   1 religious 2 pacific 3 narrow 4 weighty 5 funny
91. *cessation*   1 premium 2 gravity 3 beginning 4 composition 5 stoppage
92. *churlish*   1 marine 2 economical 3 polite 4 compact 5 young
93. *captious*   1 tolerant 2 capable 3 frivolous 4 winning 5 recollected
94. *carte blanche*   1 capitalistic 2 investment 3 importance 4 restriction 5 current
95. *chaste*   1 clean 2 clear 3 curt 4 wanton 5 outspoken
96. *chaffing*   1 achieving 2 serious 3 capitalistic 4 sneering 5 expensive
97. *carnal*   1 impressive 2 minute 3 spiritual 4 actual 5 private
98. *centrifugal*   1 centripetal 2 ephemeral 3 lasting 4 barometric 5 algebraic
99. *chide*   1 unite 2 fear 3 record 4 skid 5 praise
100. *carping*   1 acquiescent 2 mean 3 limited 4 farming 5 racing

ā—ale; ă—add; ä—arm; à—ask, ē—eve; ĕ—end; ê—err, her; ə—allow; even; ī—ice; ĭ—ill; ō—oll; ŏ—odd; ô—orb; oo—food; oo—foot, put; ou—out; th—thin; ū—use; ŭ—up; zh—pleasure

WORD LIST   6   **ciliated - concise**

ciliated ADJ. having minute hairs. The paramecium is a *ciliated,* one-celled animal.

circlet N. small ring; band. This tiny *circlet* is very costly because it is set with precious stones.

circuitous (*-kū´-*) ADJ. roundabout. Because of the traffic congestion on the main highways, he took a *circuitous* route. circuit, N.

circumscribe V. limit; confine. Although I do not wish to *circumscribe* your activities, I must insist that you complete this assignment before you start anything else.

circumspect ADJ. prudent; cautious. Investigating before acting, he tried always to be *circumspect.*

circumvent V. outwit; baffle. In order to *circumvent* the enemy, we will make two preliminary attacks in other sections before starting our major campaign.

citadel N. fortress. The *citadel* overlooked the city like a protecting angel.

cite V. quote; commend. He could *cite* passages in the Bible from memory. citation, N.

clairvoyant (*klăr-vôî´-*) ADJ., N. having foresight; fortuneteller. Cassandra's *clairvoyant* warning was not heeded by the Trojans. clairvoyance, N.

clamber V. climb by crawling. He *clambered* over the wall.

clandestine (*-dĕs´-tən*) ADJ. secret. After avoiding their chaperon, the lovers had a *clandestine* meeting.

clarion ADJ. shrill trumpetlike sound. We woke to the *clarion* call of the bugle. also N.

claustrophobia (*klô-*) N. fear of being locked in. His fellow classmates laughed at his *claustrophobia* and often threatened to lock him in his room.

clavicle N. collarbone. Even though he wore shoulder pads, the football player broke his *clavicle* during a practice scrimmage.

cleave V. split asunder. The lightning *cleaves* the tree in two. cleavage, N.

cleft N. split. There was a *cleft* in the huge boulder. also ADJ.

clemency N. disposition to be lenient; mildness, as of the weather. The lawyer was pleased when the case was sent to Judge Smith's chambers because Smith was noted for his *clemency* toward first offenders.

cliché (*klĭ-shā´*) N. phrase dulled in meaning by repetition. High school compositions are often marred by such *clichés* as "strong as an ox."

climactic ADJ. relating to the highest point. When he reached the *climactic* portions of the book, he could not stop reading. climax, N.

clique (*klēk*) N. small exclusive group. He charged that a *clique* had assumed control of school affairs.

cloister N. monastery or convent. The nuns lived in the *cloister.*

coadjutor (*kō-ə-jŏŏt´-*) N. assistant; colleague. He was assigned as *coadjutor* of the bishop.

coalesce V. combine; fuse. The brooks *coalesce* into one large river.

cockade N. decoration worn on hat. Members of that brigade can be recognized by the green and white *cockade* in their helmets.

coerce (*kō-êrs´*) V. force; repress. Do not *coerce* me into doing this; I hate force.

cog N. tooth projecting from a wheel. On steep slopes, *cog* railways are frequently used to prevent slipping.

cogent (*kō´-jənt*) ADJ. convincing. He presented *cogent* arguments to the jury.

cogitate V. think over. *Cogitate* on this problem; the solution will come.

cognate ADJ. allied by blood; of the same or kindred nature. In the phrase "die a thousand deaths," the word "death" is a *cognate* object.

cognizance (*kŏg´-*) N. knowledge. During the election campaign, the two candidates were kept in full *cognizance* of the international situation.

cognomen (*kŏg-nō´-*) N. family name. He asked the court to change his *cognomen* to a more American-sounding name.

cohere V. stick together. Solids have a greater tendency to *cohere* than liquids.

cohesion N. force which keeps parts together. In order to preserve our *cohesion,* we must not let minor differences interfere with our major purposes.

cohorts N. armed band. Caesar and his Roman *cohorts* conquered almost all of the known world.

coincident ADJ. occurring at the same time. Some people find the *coincident* events in Hardy's novels annoying.

collaborate V. work together. Two writers *collaborated* in preparing this book.

collate V. examine in order to verify authenticity; arrange in order. They *collated* the newly found manuscripts to determine their age.

collateral N. security given for loan. The sum you wish to borrow is so large that it must be secured by *collateral.*

collation N. a light meal. Tea sandwiches and cookies were offered at the *collation.*

collier N. worker in coal mine; ship carrying coal. The extended cold spell has prevented the *colliers* from delivering the coal to the docks as scheduled.

colloquy (*kŏl´-ə-kwē*) N. informal discussion. I enjoy our *colloquies,* but I sometimes wish that they could be made more formal and more searching.

collusion N. conspiring in a fraudulent scheme. The swindlers were found guilty of *collusion.*

colossal ADJ. huge. Radio City Music Hall has a *colossal* stage.

combustible ADJ. easily burned. After the recent outbreak of fires in private homes, the fire commissioner ordered that all *combustible* materials be kept in safe containers. also N.

comely (*kŭm´-*) ADJ. attractive; agreeable. I would rather have a *comely* wife than a rich one.

comestible (*-mĕs´-*) N. something fit to be eaten. The roast turkey and other *comestibles,* the wines, and the excellent service made this Thanksgiving dinner particularly memorable.

comity N. courtesy; civility. A spirit of *comity* should exist among nations.

commandeer V. to draft for military purposes; to take for public use. The policeman *commandeered* the first car that approached and ordered the driver to go to the nearest hospital.

commensurate ADJ. equal in extent. Your reward will be *commensurate* with your effort.

commiserate V. feel or express pity or sympathy for. Her friends *commiserated* with the widow.

commodious ADJ. spacious and comfortable. After sleeping in small roadside cabins, they found their hotel suite *commodious*.

compact N. agreement; contract. The signers of the Mayflower *Compact* were establishing a form of government.

compatible ADJ. harmonious; in harmony with. They were *compatible* neighbors, never quarreling over unimportant matters.

compilation N. listing of statistical information in tabular or book form. The *compilation* of available scholarships serves a very valuable purpose.

complacent (-*plās´*-) ADJ. self-satisfied. There was a *complacent* look on his face as he examined his paintings. complacency, N.

complaisant ADJ. trying to please; obliging. The courtier obeyed the king's orders in a *complaisant* manner.

complement N. that which completes. A predicate *complement* completes the meaning of the subject. also V.

compliant ADJ. yielding. He was *compliant* and ready to conform to the pattern set by his friends.

comport V. bear one's self; behave. He *comported* himself with great dignity.

compunction N. remorse. The judge was especially severe in his sentencing because he felt that the criminal had shown no *compunction* for his heinous crime.

compute V. reckon; calculate. He failed to *compute* the interest.

concatenate V. link as in a chain. It is difficult to understand how these events could *concatenate* as they did without outside assistance.

concentric ADJ. having a common center. The target was made of *concentric* circles.

conception N. beginning; forming of an idea. At the first *conception* of the work, he was consulted. conceive, V.

conciliate V. pacify; win over. She tried to *conciliate* me with a gift. conciliatory, ADJ.

concise ADJ. brief and compact. The essay was *concise* and explicit.

ETYMOLOGY 6

CID, CIS (to cut, to kill)

incision a cut (surgical)
homicide killing of a man
fratricide killing of a brother

CIRCUM (around) prefix

circumnavigate sail around the world
circumspect cautious (looking around)
circumscribe place a circle around

CIT, CITAT (to call, to start)

incite stir up, start up
excite stir up
recitation a recalling (or repeating) aloud

CIVI (citizen)

civilization society of citizens, culture
civilian member of a community
civil courteous

CLAM, CLAMAT (to cry out)

clamorous loud
declamation speech
acclamation shouted approval

CLAUD, CLAUS, CLOS, CLUD (to close)

claustrophobia fear of close places
enclose close in

conclude finish

CLE, CULE (small) noun suffix

molecule small mass
corpuscle blood cell
follicle small sac

COGNOSC, COGNIT (to learn)

agnostic lacking knowledge, skeptical
incognito traveling under an assumed identity (without knowledge)
cognition knowledge

COM (with, together) prefix

combine merge with
commerce trade with
communicate correspond with

Note: By assimilation,
coeditor associate editor
collateral connected
conference meeting
corroborate confirm

COMP (to fill)

complete filled out
complement that which completes something
comply fulfill

TEST—WORD LIST 6—*Synonyms and Antonyms*

Each of the following questions consists of a word printed in italics, followed by five words or phrases numbered 1 to 5. Choose the numbered word or phrase which is most nearly the same as or the opposite of the word in italics and write the number of your choice on your answer paper.

101. *clandestine* 1 abortive 2 secret 3 tangible 4 doomed 5 approved

102. *cognomen* 1 family name 2 dwarf 3 suspicion 4 kind of railway 5 pseudopod

103. *combustible* 1 flammable 2 industrious 3 waterproof 4 specific 5 plastic

104. *compliant* 1 numerous 2 veracious 3 soft 4 adamant 5 livid

105. *ciliated* 1 foolish 2 swift 3 early 4 constructed 5 hairy

ā—ale; ă—add; ä—arm; à—ask, ē—eve; ĕ—end; ê—err, her; ə—allow; even; ī—ice; ĭ —ill; ō—oll; ŏ—odd; ô—orb; ōō—food; ŏŏ—foot, put; ou—out; th—thin; ū—use; ŭ—up; zh—pleasure

106. *cleft* 1 split 2 waterfall 3 assembly 4 parfait 5 surplus
107. *cohesion* 1 independence 2 pedestrian 3 shift 4 pharmacy 5 climbing
108. *comestible* 1 vigorous 2 fit to be eaten 3 liquid 4 beautiful 5 circumvented
109. *circuitous* 1 direct 2 complete 3 obvious 4 aware 5 tortured
110. *cliché* 1 increase 2 vehicle 3 morale 4 original 5 pique
111. *coincidental* 1 simultaneous 2 changing 3 fortuitous 4 startling 5 trivial
112. *collation* 1 furor 2 emphasis 3 distillery 4 spree 5 lunch
113. *claustrophobia* 1 lack of confidence 2 fear of spiders 3 love of books 4 fear of grammar 5 fear of closed places
114. *cite* 1 galvanize 2 visualize 3 locate 4 quote 5 signal
115. *coerce* 1 recover 2 total 3 force 4 license 5 ignore
116. *cognizance* 1 policy 2 ignorance 3 advance 4 omission 5 examination
117. *colloquy* 1 dialect 2 diversion 3 announcement 4 discussion 5 expansion
118. *conciliate* 1 defend 2 activate 3 integrate 4 quarrel 5 react
119. *commiserate* 1 communicate 2 expand 3 repay 4 diminish 5 sympathize
120. *commodious* 1 numerous 2 accommodating 3 leisurely 4 limited 5 expensive

---

WORD LIST 7 conclave - crux

conclave N. private meeting. He was present at all their *conclaves* as a sort of unofficial observer.

concoct V. prepare by combining; make up in concert. How did you ever *concoct* such a strange dish? concoction, N.

concomitant N. that which accompanies. Culture is not always a *concomitant* of wealth. also ADJ.

concurrent ADJ. happening at the same time. In America, the colonists were resisting the demands of the mother country; at the *concurrent* moment in France, the middle class was sowing the seeds of rebellion.

condescend V. bestow courtesies with a superior air. The king *condescended* to grant an audience to the friends of the condemned man. condescension, N.

condign (-dīn´) ADJ. adequate; deservedly severe. The public approved the *condign* punishment.

condiments N. seasonings; spices. Spanish food is full of *condiments*.

condole V. express sympathetic sorrow. His friends gathered to *condole* with him over his loss. condolence, N.

condone V. overlook; forgive. We cannot *condone* your recent criminal cooperation with the gamblers.

confiscate V. seize; commandeer. The army *confiscated* all available supplies of uranium.

conformity N. harmony; agreement. In *conformity* with our rules and regulations, I am calling a meeting of our organization.

congeal (-jēl´) V. freeze; coagulate. His blood *congealed* in his veins as he saw the dread monster rush toward him.

congenital ADJ. existing at birth. His *congenital* deformity disturbed his parents.

conglomeration N. mass of material sticking together. In such a *conglomeration* of miscellaneous statistics, it was impossible to find a single area of analysis.

congruence N. correspondence of parts; harmonious relationship. The student demonstrated the *congruence* of the two triangles by using the hypotenuse-arm theorem.

conifer N. pine tree; cone-bearing tree. According to geologists, the *conifers* were the first plants to bear flowers.

conjugal ADJ. pertaining to marriage. Their dreams of *conjugal* bliss were shattered as soon as their temperaments clashed.

connivance N. pretense of ignorance of something wrong; assistance; permission to offend. With the *connivance* of his friends, he plotted to embarrass the teacher. connive, V.

connoisseur (kŏn-ə-sŭr´) N. person competent to act as a judge of art, etc.; a lover of an art. He had developed into a *connoisseur* of fine china.

connotation N. suggested or implied meaning of an expression. Foreigners frequently are unaware of the *connotations* of the words they use.

connubial (-nū´-) ADJ. pertaining to marriage or the matrimonial state. In his telegram, he wished the newlyweds a lifetime of *connubial* bliss.

consanguinity N. kinship. The lawsuit developed into a test of the *consanguinity* of the claimant to the estate.

consecrate V. dedicate; sanctify. We shall *consecrate* our lives to this noble purpose.

consensus N. general agreement. The *consensus* indicates that we are opposed to entering into this pact.

consort V. associate with. We frequently judge people by the company with whom they *consort*. also N.

constraint N. compulsion; repression of feelings. There was a feeling of *constraint* in the room because no one dared to criticize the speaker. constrain, V.

construe V. explain; interpret. If I *construe* your remarks correctly, you disagree with the theory already advanced.

consummate (-sŭm´-) ADJ. complete. I have never seen anyone who makes as many stupid errors as you do; you must be a *consummate* idiot. also V.

contaminate V. pollute. The sewage system of the city so *contaminated* the water that swimming was forbidden.

contemn V. regard with contempt; disregard. I will not tolerate those who *contemn* the sincere efforts of this group.

contentious ADJ. quarrelsome. We heard loud and *contentious* noises in the next room.

context N. writings preceding and following the passage quoted. Because these lines are taken out of *context*, they do not convey the message the author intended.

contiguous ADJ. adjacent to; touching upon. The two countries are *contiguous* for a few miles; then they are separated by the gulf.

continence N. self-restraint; sexual chastity. He vowed to lead a life of *continence*. continent, ADJ.

contingent ADJ. conditional. The continuation of this contract is *contingent* on the quality of your first output. contingency, N.

contortions N. twistings; distortions. As the effects of the opiate wore away, the *contortions* of the patient became more violent and demonstrated how much pain he was enduring.

contraband N, ADJ. illegal trade; smuggling. The Coast Guard tries to prevent traffic in *contraband* goods.

ā—ale; ă—add; ä—arm; à—ask; ē—eve; ĕ—end; ê—err, her; ə—allow; even; ī—ice; ĭ—ill; ō—oll; ŏ—odd; ô—orb; ōō—food; ŏŏ—foot, put; ou—out; th—thin; ū—use; ŭ—up; zh—pleasure

contravene V. contradict; infringe on. I will not attempt to *contravene* your argument for it does not affect the situation.

contrite ADJ. penitent. Her *contrite* tears did not influence the judge when he imposed sentence. contrition, N.

controvert V. oppose with arguments; contradict. To *controvert* your theory will require much time but it is essential that we disprove it.

contumacious ADJ. disobedient; resisting authority. The *contumacious* mob shouted defiantly at the police. contumacy, N.

contumely (*kŏn-tū-me-lē*) N. scornful insolence; insult. The "proud man's *contumely*" is distasteful to Hamlet.

contusion N. bruise. He was treated for *contusions* and abrasions.

convene V. assemble. Because much needed legislation had to be enacted, the governor ordered the legislature to *convene* in special session by January 15.

conversant (*-vərs´-*) ADJ. familiar with. The lawyer is *conversant* with all the evidence.

conveyance N. vehicle; transfer. During the transit strike, commuters used various kinds of *conveyances*.

convivial ADJ. festive; gay; characterized by joviality. The *convivial* celebrators of the victory sang their college songs.

convoke V. call together. Congress was *convoked* at the outbreak of the emergency. convocation, N.

copious ADJ. plentiful. He had *copious* reasons for rejecting the proposal.

coquette (*kō-kĕt´*) N. flirt. Because she refused to give him any answer to his proposal of marriage, he called her a *coquette*. also V.

cornice N. projecting molding on building (usually above columns). Because the *cornice* stones had been loosened by the storms, the police closed the building until repairs could be made.

corporeal (*-pôr´-ē-əl*) ADJ. bodily; material. He was not a churchgoer; he was interested only in *corporeal* matters.

corpulent ADJ. very fat. The *corpulent* man resolved to reduce. corpulence, N.

corroborate V. confirm. Unless we find a witness to *corroborate* your evidence, it will not stand up in court.

corrosive ADJ. eating away by chemicals or disease. Stainless steel is able to withstand the effects of *corrosive* chemicals.

corsair (*kôr´-*) N. pirate; pirate ship. The *corsairs*, preying on shipping in the Mediterranean, were often inspired by racial and religious hatreds as well as by the desire for money and booty.

cortege (*kôr-tĕzh´*) N. procession. The funeral *cortege* proceeded slowly down the avenue.

cosmic ADJ. pertaining to the universe; vast. *Cosmic* rays derive their name from the fact that they bombard the earth's atmosphere from outer space. cosmos, N.

coterie (*kōt´-*) N. group that meets socially; select circle. After his book had been published, he was invited to join the literary *coterie* that lunched daily at the hotel.

countermand V. cancel; revoke. The general *countermanded* the orders issued in his absence.

counterpart N. a thing that completes another; things very much alike. Night and day are *counterparts*.

covenant N. agreement. We must comply with the terms of the *covenant*.

covert (*kō´-*) ADJ. secret; hidden; implied. He could understand the *covert* threat in the letter.

covetous ADJ. avaricious; eagerly desirous of. The child was *covetous* by nature and wanted to take the toys belonging to his classmates. covet, V.

cower V. shrink quivering, as from fear. The frightened child *cowered* in the corner of the room.

coy ADJ. shy; modest; coquettish. She was *coy* in her answers to his offer.

crabbed (*krăb´-əd*) ADJ. sour; peevish. The *crabbed* old man was avoided by the children because he scolded them when they made noise.

crass ADJ. very unrefined; grossly insensible. The philosophers deplored the *crass* commercialism.

craven (*krā´-*) ADJ. cowardly. His *craven* behavior in this critical period was criticized.

credence (*krēd´-*) N. belief. Do not place any *credence* in his promises.

credulity (*krĭ-dū´-*) N. belief on slight evidence. The witch doctor took advantage of the *credulity* of the superstitious natives. credulous, ADJ.

creed N. system of religious or ethical belief. In any loyal American's *creed*, love of democracy must be emphasized.

crestfallen ADJ. dejected; dispirited. We were surprised at his reaction to the failure of his project; instead of being *crestfallen*, he was busily engaged in planning new activities.

crevice N. crack; fissure. The mountain climbers found footholds in the tiny *crevices* in the mountainside.

criterion N. standard used in judging. What *criterion* did you use when you selected this essay as the prizewinner? criteria, PL.

crone N. hag. The toothless *crone* frightened us when she smiled.

crux N. crucial point. This is the *crux* of the entire problem.

ETYMOLOGY 7

CONTRA (against) prefix

contradict disagree
controversy dispute (turning against)
contrary opposed

CORD (heart)

accord agreement (from the heart)
cordial friendly
discord lack of harmony

CORPOR (body)

incorporate organize into a body
corporeal pertaining to the body or physical mass
corpse dead body

CRED (to believe)

incredulous not believing, skeptical
credulity gullibility
credence belief

ā—ale; ă—add; ä—arm; à—ask; ē—eve; ĕ—end; ê—err, her; ə—allow; even; ī—ice; ĭ—ill; ō—oll; ŏ—odd; ô—orb; ōō—food; ŏŏ—foot, put; ou—out; th—thin; ū—use; ŭ—up; zh—pleasure

TEST—WORD LIST 7—*Synonyms*

Each of the questions below consists of a word printed in italics, followed by five words or phrases numbered 1 to 5. Choose the numbered word or phrase which is most nearly similar in meaning to the word in italics and write the number of your answer on your answer paper.

121. *condone* 1 stop 2 evaluate 3 pierce 4 infuriate 5 overlook
122. *consanguinity* 1 kinship 2 friendship 3 bloodletting 4 relief 5 understanding
123. *continence* 1 humanity 2 research 3 embryology 4 bodies of land 5 self-restraint
124. *confiscate* 1 discuss 2 discover 3 seize 4 exist 5 convey
125. *consensus* 1 general agreement 2 project 3 insignificance 4 sheaf 5 crevice
126. *conformity* 1 agreement 2 ambition 3 confinement 4 pride 5 restraint
127. *construe* 1 explain 2 promote 3 reserve 4 erect 5 block
128. *congenital* 1 slight 2 obscure 3 thorough 4 existing at birth 5 classified
129. *contaminate* 1 arrest 2 prepare 3 pollute 4 beam 5 inform
130. *connoisseur* 1 gourmand 2 lover of art 3 humidor 4 delinquent 5 interpreter
131. *contentious* 1 squealing 2 surprising 3 quarrelsome 4 smug 5 creative
132. *contraband* 1 purpose 2 rogue 3 rascality 4 difficulty 5 smuggling
133. *copious* 1 plentiful 2 cheating 3 dishonorable 4 adventurous 5 inspired
134. *contrite* 1 smart 2 penitent 3 restful 4 recognized 5 perspiring
135. *corpulent* 1 regenerate 2 obese 3 different 4 hungry 5 bloody
136. *controvert* 1 turn over 2 contradict 3 mind 4 explain 5 swing
137. *craven* 1 desirous 2 direct 3 cowardly 4 civilized 5 controlled
138. *contumely* 1 sensation 2 noise 3 silence 4 insult 5 classic
139. *crux* 1 acne 2 spark 3 events 4 crucial point 5 belief
140. *conversant* 1 ignorant 2 speaking 3 incorporated 4 familiar 5 pedantic

---

WORD LIST 8 cryptic - despoil

cryptic ADJ. mysterious; hidden; secret. His *cryptic* remarks could not be interpreted.

cuisine (kwĭ-zēn´) N. style of cooking. French *cuisine* is noted for its use of sauces and wines.

culinary (kŭl´-) ADJ. relating to cooking. Many chefs attribute their *culinary* skill to the wise use of spices.

cull V. pick out; reject. Every month the farmer *culls* the nonlaying hens from his flock and sells them to the local butcher. also N.

culmination N. attainment of highest point. His inauguration as President of the United States marked the *culmination* of his political career.

culpable ADJ. deserving blame. Corrupt politicians who condone the activities of the gamblers are equally *culpable*.

cupidity N. greed. The defeated people could not satisfy the *cupidity* of the conquerors, who demanded excessive tribute.

curry V. dress; treat leather; seek favor. The courtier *curried* favors of the king.

cursory ADJ. casual; hastily done. A *cursory* examination of the ruins indicates the possibility of arson; a more extensive study should be undertaken.

curtail V. shorten; reduce. During the coal shortage, we must *curtail* our use of this vital commodity.

cynic N. one who is skeptical or distrustful of human motives. A *cynic* at all times, he was suspicious of all altruistic actions of others. cynical, ADJ.

dais (dā´-əs) N. raised platform for guests of honor. When he approached the *dais*, he was greeted by cheers from the people who had come to honor him.

dally V. trifle with; procrastinate. Laertes told Ophelia that Hamlet could only *dally* with her affections.

dank ADJ. damp. The walls of the dungeon were *dank* and slimy.

dastard N. coward. This sneak attack is the work of a *dastard*. dastardly, ADJ.

daunt V. intimidate. Your threats cannot *daunt* me.

dauntless ADJ. bold. Despite the dangerous nature of the undertaking, the *dauntless* soldier volunteered for the assignment.

dawdle V. loiter; waste time. Inasmuch as we must meet a deadline, do not *dawdle* over this work.

dearth (dêrth) N. scarcity. The *dearth* of skilled labor compelled the employers to open trade schools.

debase V. reduce to lower state. Do not *debase* yourself by becoming maudlin.

debauch (-bôch´) V. corrupt; make intemperate. A vicious newspaper can *debauch* public ideals. debauchery, N.

debilitate V. weaken; enfeeble. Overindulgence *debilitates* character as well as physical stamina.

debonair ADJ. friendly; aiming to please. The *debonair* youth was liked by all who met him, because of his cheerful and obliging manner.

debutante (dĕb´-yŏŏ-) N. young woman making formal entrance into society. As a *debutante*, she was often mentioned in the society columns of the newspapers.

decadence (dĕk´-) N. decay. The moral *decadence* of the people was reflected in the lewd literature of the period.

decant (-kănt´) V. pour off gently. Be sure to *decant* this wine before serving it.

deciduous ADJ. falling off as of leaves. The oak is a *deciduous* tree.

declivity N. downward slope. The children loved to ski down the *declivity*.

decorous ADJ. proper. Her *decorous* behavior was praised by her teachers. decorum, N.

decoy (dē´-kŏĭ) N. lure or bait. The wild ducks were not fooled by the *decoy*. also V.

decrepit ADJ. worn out by age. The *decrepit* car blocked traffic on the highway.

decry V. disparage. Do not attempt to increase your stature by *decrying* the efforts of your opponents.

deducible ADJ. derived by reasoning. If we accept your premise, your conclusions are easily *deducible*.

ā—ale; ă—add; ä—arm; à—ask, ē—eve; ĕ—end; ê—err, her; ə—allow; even; ī—ice; ĭ—ill; ō—oll; ŏ—odd; ô—orb; ōō—food; ŏŏ—foot, put; ou—out; th—thin; ū—use; ŭ—up; zh—pleasure

defalcate (-făl´-) v. misuse money held in trust. Legislation was passed to punish brokers who *defalcated* their clients' funds.

defamation N. harming a person's reputation. Such *defamation* of character may result in a slander suit.

default N. failure to do. As a result of her husband's failure to appear in court, she was granted a divorce by *default*. also v.

defeatist ADJ. attitude of one who is ready to accept defeat as a natural outcome. If you maintain your *defeatist* attitude, you will never succeed. also N.

defection N. desertion. The children, who had made him an idol, were hurt most by his *defection* from our cause.

deference (def´-) N. courteous regard for another's wish. In *deference* to his desires, the employers granted him a holiday.

defile v. pollute; profane. The hoodlums *defiled* the church with their scurrilous writing.

definitive ADJ. final; complete. Carl Sandburg's *Abraham Lincoln* may be regarded as the *definitive* work on the life of the Great Emancipator.

deflect v. turn aside. His life was saved when his cigarette case *deflected* the bullet.

defunct ADJ. dead; no longer in use or existence. The lawyers sought to examine the books of the *defunct* corporation.

deign (dān) v. condescend. He felt that he would debase himself if he *deigned* to answer his critics.

delete v. erase; strike out. If you *delete* this paragraph, the composition will have more appeal.

deleterious (-tĭr´-) ADJ. harmful. Workers in nuclear research must avoid the *deleterious* effects of radioactive substances.

delineation N. portrayal. He is a powerful storyteller, but he is weakest in his *delineation* of character.

delirium N. mental disorder marked by confusion. The drunkard in his *delirium* saw strange animals.

delude v. deceive. Do not *delude* yourself into believing that he will relent.

delusion N. false belief; hallucination. This scheme is a snare and a *delusion*.

delusive ADJ. deceptive; raising vain hopes. Do not raise your hopes on the basis of his *delusive* promises.

demagogue N. person who appeals to people's prejudice; false leader of people. He was accused of being a *demagogue* because he made promises which aroused futile hopes in his listeners.

demean v. degrade; humiliate. He felt that he would *demean* himself if he replied to the scurrilous letter.

demeanor N. behavior; bearing. His sober *demeanor* quieted the noisy revelers.

demise (-mīz´) N. death. Upon the *demise* of the dictator, a bitter dispute about succession to power developed.

demolition N. destruction. One of the major aims of the air force was the complete *demolition* of all means of transportation by bombing of rail lines and terminals.

demoniac (-mō´-) ADJ. fiendish. The Spanish Inquisition devised many *demoniac* means of torture. demon, N.

demur v. delay; object. To *demur* at this time will only worsen the already serious situation; now is the time for action.

demure ADJ. grave; serious; coy. She was *demure* and reserved.

denizen (dĕn´-) N. inhabitant of. Ghosts are *denizens* of the land of the dead who return to earth.

depict v. portray. In this book, the author *depicts* the slave owners as kind and benevolent masters.

depilate (dĕp´-) v. remove hair. Many women *depilate* their legs.

deplete v. reduce; exhaust. We must wait until we *deplete* our present inventory before we order replacements.

deploy v. move troops so that the battle line is extended at the expense of depth. The general ordered the battalion to *deploy* in order to meet the offensive of the enemy.

deposition (dĕp´-) N. testimony under oath. He made his *deposition* in the judge's chamber.

depravity N. corruption; wickedness. The *depravity* of his behavior shocked all.

deprecate (dĕp´-) v. disapprove regretfully. I must *deprecate* your attitude and hope that you will change your mind.

deprecatory ADJ. disapproving. Your *deprecatory* criticism has offended the author.

depreciate v. lessen in value. If you neglect this property, it will *depreciate*.

depredation N. plundering. After the *depredations* of the invaders, the people were penniless.

deranged ADJ. insane. He was mentally *deranged*.

derelict ADJ. abandoned. The *derelict* craft was a menace to navigation. also N.

deride v. scoff at. The people *derided* his grandiose schemes.

derision N. ridicule. They greeted his proposal with *derision* and refused to consider it seriously.

dermatologist N. one who studies the skin and its diseases. I advise you to consult a *dermatologist* about your acne.

derogatory ADJ. expressing a low opinion. I resent your *derogatory* remarks.

descant (dĕs´-) v. discuss fully. He was willing to *descant* upon any topic of conversation, even when he knew very little about the subject under discussion. also N.

descry (-skrī´) v. catch sight of. In the distance, we could barely *descry* the enemy vessels.

desecrate v. profane; violate the sanctity of. The soldiers *desecrated* the temple.

desiccate v. dry up. A tour of this smokehouse will give you an idea of how the pioneers used to *desiccate* food in order to preserve it.

despicable (-spĭk´-) ADJ. contemptible. Your *despicable* remarks call for no reply.

despise v. scorn. I *despise* your attempts at a reconciliation at this time.

despoil v. plunder. If you do not yield, I am afraid the enemy will *despoil* the buildings.

ETYMOLOGY 8

CUR (to care)

curator person in charge
sinecure position without responsibility
secure safe

CURR, CURS (to run)

excursion journey

cursory brief
precursor forerunner

CY (state of being) noun suffix

democracy a democratic state
obstinacy state of being stubborn
accuracy state of being accurate

ā—ale; ă—add; ä—arm; à—ask, ē—eve; ĕ—end; ê—err, her; ə—allow; even; ī—ice; ĭ—ill; ō—oll; ŏ—odd; ô—orb; ōō—food; ŏŏ—foot, put; ou—out; th—thin; ū—use; ŭ—up; zh—pleasure

DA, DAT (to give)

data facts, statistics
mandate command
date given time

DE (down, away) prefix

debase lower in value
decadence deterioration
decant pour off

DEB, DEBIT (to owe)

debt something owed

indebtedness debt
debenture bond

DEMOS (people)

democracy rule of the people
demagogue (false) leader of the people
epidemic widespread disease (among the people)

DERM (skin)

epidermis skin
pachyderm thick-skinned quadruped
dermatology study of the skin and its disorders

TEST—WORD LIST 8—*Antonyms*

Each of the questions below consists of a word printed in italics, followed by five words or phrases numbered 1 to 5. Choose the numbered word or phrase which is most nearly opposite in meaning to the word in italics and write the number of your choice on your answer paper.

141. *cryptic* 1 tomblike 2 secret 3 famous 4 candid 5 coded
142. *dank* 1 dry 2 guiltless 3 warm 4 babbling 5 reserved
143. *cupidity* 1 anxiety 2 tragedy 3 generosity 4 entertainment 5 love
144. *dastard* 1 illegitimacy 2 hero 3 presence 4 warmth 5 idol
145. *curtail* 1 mutter 2 lengthen 3 express 4 burden 5 shore
146. *dauntless* 1 stolid 2 weak 3 irrelevant 4 peculiar 5 particular
147. *cynical* 1 trusting 2 effortless 3 conclusive 4 gallant 5 vertical
148. *debilitate* 1 bedevil 2 repress 3 strengthen 4 animate 5 deaden
149. *debonair* 1 awkward 2 windy 3 balmy 4 sporty

5 stormy
150. *declivity* 1 trap 2 quadrangle 3 quarter 4 activity 5 upward slope
151. *derogatory* 1 roguish 2 immediate 3 opinionated 4 praising 5 conferred
152. *decrepit* 1 momentary 2 emotional 3 suppressed 4 youthful 5 unexpected
153. *depravity* 1 goodness 2 sadness 3 heaviness 4 tidiness 5 seriousness
154. *defection* 1 determination 2 joining 3 invitation 4 affection 5 cancellation
155. *deranged* 1 sane 2 announced 3 neighborly 4 alphabetical 5 arranged
156. *defalcate* 1 abscond 2 elope 3 observe 4 panic 5 use money held in trust properly
157. *desecrate* 1 desist 2 integrate 3 confuse 4 intensify 5 consecrate
158. *defile* 1 manicure 2 ride 3 purify 4 assemble 5 order
159. *despicable* 1 steering 2 worthy of esteem 3 inevitable 4 featureless 5 incapable
160. *deleterious* 1 delaying 2 experimental 3 harmless 4 graduating 5 glorious

WORD LIST 9 **despotism - diverse**

despotism N. tyranny. The people rebelled against the *despotism* of the king.
destitute ADJ. extremely poor. The illness left the family *destitute*.
desuetude (dĕs´-wĭ-) N. disused condition. The machinery in the idle factory was in a state of *desuetude*.
desultory (dĕs´-) ADJ. aimless; jumping around. The animals' *desultory* behavior indicated that they had no awareness of their predicament.
detergent N. cleansing agent. Many new *detergents* have replaced soap.
detonation N. explosion. The *detonation* could be heard miles away.
detraction N. slandering; aspersion. He is offended by your frequent *detractions* of his ability as a leader.
detriment N. harm; damage. Your acceptance of his support will ultimately prove to be a *detriment* rather than an aid to your cause.
deviate (dē´-) V. turn away from. Do not *deviate* from the

truth.
devious ADJ. going astray; erratic. Your *devious* behavior in this matter puzzles me since you are usually direct and straightforward.
devoid ADJ. lacking. He was *devoid* of any personal desire for gain in his endeavor to secure improvement in the community.
devolve V. deputize; pass to others. It *devolved* upon us, the survivors, to arrange peace terms with the enemy.
devout ADJ. pious. The *devout* man prayed daily.
dexterous ADJ. skillful. The magician was so *dexterous* that we could not follow him as he performed his tricks.
diabolical ADJ. devilish. This scheme is so *diabolical* that I must reject it.
diadem (dī´-ə-) N. crown. The king's *diadem* was on display at the museum.
dialectic N. art of debate. I am not skilled in *dialectic* and, therefore, cannot answer your arguments as forcefully as I wish.

ā—ale; ă—add; ä—arm; à—ask; ē—eve; ĕ—end; ê—err, her; ə—allow; even; ī—ice; ĭ—ill; ō—oll; ŏ—odd; ô—orb; ōō—food; ŏŏ—foot, put; ou—out; th—thin; ū—use; ŭ—up; zh—pleasure

diaphanous (*dī-ăf´-*) ADJ. sheer; transparent. They admired her *diaphanous* and colorful dress.

dichotomy (*dī-kŏt´-*) N. branching into two parts. The *dichotomy* of our legislative system provides us with many safeguards.

dictum N. authoritative and weighty statement. He repeated the statement as though it were the *dictum* of the most expert worker in the group.

diffidence N. shyness. You must overcome your *diffidence* if you intend to become a salesperson.

diffusion N. wordiness; spreading in all directions like a gas. Your composition suffers from a *diffusion* of ideas; try to be more compact. diffuse, ADJ. and V.

digressive ADJ. wandering away from the subject. His book was marred by his many *digressive* remarks.

dilapidation N. ruin because of neglect. We felt that the *dilapidation* of the building could be corrected by several coats of paint.

dilate V. expand. In the dark, the pupils of your eyes *dilate*.

dilatory (*dĭl´-*) ADJ. delaying. Your *dilatory* tactics may compel me to cancel the contract.

dilemma N. problem; choice of two unsatisfactory alternatives. In this *dilemma*, he knew no one to whom he could turn for advice.

dilettante (*-tänt´*) N. aimless follower of the arts; amateur; dabbler. He was not serious in his painting; he was rather a *dilettante*.

diminution N. lessening; reduction in size. The blockaders hoped to achieve victory as soon as the *diminution* of the enemy's supplies became serious.

dint N. means; effort. By *dint* of much hard work, the volunteers were able to place the raging forest fire under control.

dipsomaniac N. one who has a strong craving for intoxicating liquor. The picture *The Lost Weekend* was an excellent portrayal of the struggles of the *dipsomaniac*.

dire ADJ. disastrous. People ignored his *dire* predictions of an approaching depression.

dirge N. lament with music. The funeral *dirge* stirred us to tears.

disavowal N. denial; disclaiming. His *disavowal* of his part in the conspiracy was not believed by the jury.

discernible ADJ. distinguishable; perceivable. The ships in the harbor were not *discernible* in the fog.

discerning ADJ. mentally quick and observant; having insight. Because he was considered the most *discerning* member of the firm, he was assigned the most difficult cases.

disclaim V. disown; renounce claim to. If I grant you this privilege, will you *disclaim* all other rights?

discomfit V. put to rout; defeat; disconcert. This ruse will *discomfit* the enemy. discomfiture, N.

disconcert V. confuse; upset; embarrass. The lawyer was *disconcerted* by the evidence produced by his adversary.

disconsolate ADJ. sad. The death of his wife left him *disconsolate*.

discordant ADJ. inharmonious; conflicting. He tried to unite the *discordant* factions.

discrete ADJ. separate; unconnected. The universe is composed of *discrete* bodies.

discretion N. prudence; ability to adjust actions to circumstances. Use your *discretion* in this matter.

discursive ADJ. digressing; rambling. They were annoyed and bored by his *discursive* remarks.

disdain V. treat with scorn or contempt. You make enemies of all you *disdain*. also N.

disgruntle V. make discontented. The passengers were *disgruntled* by the numerous delays.

disheveled (*dĭsh-ĕv´-*) ADJ. untidy. Your *disheveled* appearance will hurt your chances in this interview.

disingenuous ADJ. not naive; sophisticated. Although he was young, his remarks indicated that he was *disingenuous*.

disinterested ADJ. unprejudiced. The only *disinterested* person in the room was the judge.

disjointed ADJ. disconnected. His remarks were so *disjointed* that we could not follow his reasoning.

dismember V. cut into small parts. When the Austrian Empire was *dismembered*, several new countries were established.

disparage V. belittle. Do not *disparage* anyone's contribution; these little gifts add up to large sums.

disparate ADJ. basically different; unrelated. It is difficult, if not impossible, to organize these *disparate* elements into a coherent whole.

disparity N. difference; condition of inequality. The *disparity* in their ages made no difference at all.

dispersion N. scattering. The *dispersion* of this group throughout the world may be explained by their expulsion from their homeland.

dispirited ADJ. lacking in spirit. The coach used all the tricks at his command to buoy up the enthusiasm of his team, which had become *dispirited* at the loss of the star player.

disport V. amuse. The popularity of Florida as a winter resort is constantly increasing; each year, thousands more *disport* themselves at Miami and Palm Beach.

disputatious (*-ta´-*) ADJ. argumentative; fond of argument. People avoided discussing contemporary problems with him because of his *disputatious* manner.

disquisition N. a formal systematic inquiry; an explanation of the results of a formal inquiry. In his *disquisition*, he outlined the steps he had taken in reaching his conclusions.

dissection (*dĭs-ĕk´-*) N. analysis; cutting apart in order to examine. The *dissection* of frogs in the laboratory is particularly unpleasant to some students.

dissemble V. disguise; pretend. Even though you are trying to *dissemble* your motive in joining this group, we can see through your pretense.

disseminate V. scatter (like seeds). The invention of the radio has helped propagandists to *disseminate* their favorite doctrines very easily.

dissertation N. formal essay. In order to earn a graduate degree from many of our universities, a candidate is frequently required to prepare a *dissertation* on some scholarly subject.

dissimulate V. pretend; conceal by feigning. She tried to *dissimulate* her grief by her gay attitude.

dissipate V. squander. The young man quickly *dissipated* his inheritance.

dissolute ADJ. loose in morals. The *dissolute* life led by these people is indeed shocking.

dissonance N. discord. Some contemporary musicians deliberately use *dissonance* to achieve certain effects.

dissuade (*dĭs-wād´*) V. advise against. He could not *dissuade* his friend from joining the conspirators.

dissuasion N. advice against. All his powers of *dissuasion* were useless.

distend V. expand; swell out. I can tell when he is under stress by the way the veins *distend* on his forehead.

distortion N. twisting out of shape. It is difficult to believe the newspaper accounts of this event because of the *distortions* and exaggerations written by the reporters.

distrait (*-strā´*) ADJ. absentminded. Because of his concentration on the problem, the professor often appeared *distrait* and unconcerned about routine.

distraught ADJ. upset; distracted by anxiety. The *distraught* parents searched the ravine for their lost child.

ā—ale; ă—add; ä—arm; à—ask, ē—eve; ĕ—end; ê—err, her; ə—allow; even; ī—ice; ĭ—ill; ō—oll; ŏ—odd; ô—orb; oo—food; oŏ—foot, put; ou—out; th—thin; ū—use; ŭ—up; zh—pleasure

diurnal (dī-êrn´-) ADJ. daily. A farmer cannot neglect his *diurnal* tasks at any time; cows, for example, must be milked regularly.

diva (dē´-) N. operatic singer; prima donna. Although world famous as a *diva,* she did not indulge in fits of temperament.

diverge (də-vêrj´-) V. vary; go in different directions from the same point. The spokes of the wheel *diverge* from the hub.

divers (dī´-) ADJ. several; differing. We could hear *divers* opinions of his ability.

diverse ADJ. differing in some characteristics; various. There are *diverse* ways of approaching this problem.

ETYMOLOGY 9

DI, DIURN (day)

diary daybook
diurnal pertaining to daytime
journey day's travel

DIA (across) prefix

diagonal across a figure
diameter across a circle
diagram outline drawing (writing across)

DIC, DICT (to say)

abdicate renounce
diction speech
verdict statement of jury

DIS, DIF (not) prefix

discord lack of harmony
differ disagree (carry apart)
distrust lack of trust

TEST—WORD LIST 9—*Synonyms and Antonyms*

Each of the questions below consists of a word printed in italics, followed by five words or phrases numbered 1 to 5. Choose the numbered word or phrase which is most nearly the same as or the opposite of the word in italics and write the number of your choice on your answer paper.

161. *disingenuous* 1 uncomfortable 2 eventual 3 naïve 4 complex 5 enthusiastic
162. *destitute* 1 reckless 2 dazzling 3 wanton 4 characteristic 5 explanatory
163. *dilate* 1 procrastinate 2 expand 3 conclude 4 participate 5 divert
164. *devout* 1 quiet 2 dual 3 impious 4 loyal 5 faithless
165. *diminution* 1 expectation 2 context 3 validity 4 appreciation 5 difficulty
166. *devoid* 1 latent 2 eschewed 3 full of 4 suspecting 5 evident
167. *disconsolate* 1 examining 2 thankful 3 theatrical 4 joyous 5 prominent
168. *diabolical* 1 mischievous 2 lavish 3 seraphic 4 azure 5 red
169. *disheveled* 1 recognized 2 unkempt 3 short 4 written 5 witty
170. *diffidence* 1 sharpness 2 boldness 3 malcontent 4 dialogue 5 catalog
171. *dissonance* 1 admonition 2 splendor 3 discord 4 reflection 5 consonance
172. *distrait* 1 clever 2 industrial 3 absentminded 4 narrow crooked
173. *disinterested* 1 prejudiced 2 horrendous 3 affected 4 arbitrary 5 bored
174. *dissipate* 1 economize 2 clean 3 accept 4 anticipate 5 withdraw
175. *disjointed* 1 satisfied 2 carved 3 understood 4 connected 5 evicted
176. *distend* 1 bloat 2 adjust 3 exist 4 materialize 5 finish
177. *dispirited* 1 current 2 dented 3 drooping 4 removed 5 dallying
178. *diurnal* 1 containing 2 daily 3 weekly 4 monthly 5 annual
179. *disparity* 1 resonance 2 elocution 3 relief 4 difference 5 symbolism
180. *dilatory* 1 narrowing 2 procrastinating 3 enlarging 4 portentous 5 sour

WORD LIST 10 **diversity - enigma**

diversity N. variety; dissimilitude. The *diversity* of colleges in this country indicates that many levels of ability are being cared for.

divest (dī-věst´) V. strip; deprive. He was *divested* of his power to act.

divination N. foreseeing the future with aid of magic. I base my opinions not on any special gift of *divination* but on the laws of probability.

divulge V. reveal. I will not tell you this news because I am sure you will *divulge* it prematurely.

docile ADJ. obedient; easily managed. As *docile* as he seems today, that old lion was once a ferocious, snarling beast.

docket N. program as for trial; book where such entries are made. The case of Smith vs. Jones was entered in the *docket* for July 15. also V.

doff V. take off. He *doffed* his hat to the lady.

doggerel N. poor verse. Although we find occasional snatches of genuine poetry in his work, most of his writing is mere *doggerel.*

dogmatic ADJ. positive; arbitrary. Do not be so *dogmatic* about that statement; it can be easily refuted.

dolorous (dōl´-) ADJ. sorrowful. He found the *dolorous* lamentations of the bereaved family emotionally disturbing and he left as quickly as he could.

dolt N. stupid person. I thought I was talking to a mature audience; instead, I find myself addressing a pack of *dolts* and idiots.

domicile N. home. Although his legal *domicile* was in New York City, his work kept him away from his residence for many years. also V.

dormant ADJ. sleeping; lethargic; torpid. Sometimes *dormant* talents in our friends surprise those of us who never realized how gifted our acquaintances really are. dormancy, N.

dorsal ADJ. relating to the back of an animal. A shark may be identified by its *dorsal* fin, which projects above the surface of the ocean.

dotage (*dōt´-*) N. senility. In his *dotage*, the old man bored us with long tales of events in his childhood.

doughty (*dout´-*) ADJ. courageous. Many folk tales have sprung up about this *doughty* pioneer who opened up the New World for his followers.

dour (*dour*) ADJ. sullen; stubborn. The man was *dour* and taciturn.

dregs N. sediment; worthless residue. The *dregs* of society may be observed in this slum area of the city.

droll (*drōl*) ADJ. queer and amusing. He was a popular guest because his *droll* anecdotes were always amusing.

dross (*drŏs*) N. waste matter; worthless impurities. Many methods have been devised to separate the valuable metal from the *dross*.

drudgery N. menial work. Cinderella's fairy godmother rescued her from a life of *drudgery*.

dubious ADJ. doubtful. He has the *dubious* distinction of being the lowest man in his class.

duplicity N. double-dealing; hypocrisy. People were shocked and dismayed when they learned of his *duplicity* in this affair for he had always seemed honest and straightforward.

duress (*-rĕs´*) N. forcible restraint, especially unlawfully. The hostages were held under *duress* until the prisoners' demands were met.

earthy ADJ. unrefined; coarse. His *earthy* remarks often embarrassed the women in his audience.

ebullient (*-bŏol´-*) ADJ. showing excitement; overflowing with enthusiasm. His *ebullient* nature could not be repressed; he was always laughing and gay. ebullience, N.

eccentricity N. oddity; idiosyncrasy. Some of his friends tried to account for his rudeness to strangers as the *eccentricity* of genius. eccentric, ADJ.

ecclesiastic ADJ. pertaining to the church. The minister donned his *ecclesiastic* garb and walked to the pulpit. also N.

ecstasy N. rapture; joy; any overpowering emotion. The announcement that the war had ended brought on an *ecstasy* of joy that resulted in many uncontrolled celebrations.

edify V. instruct; correct morally. Although his purpose was to *edify* and not to entertain his audience, many of his listeners were amused and not enlightened.

educe (*ĭ-dūs´*) V. draw forth; elicit. He could not *educe* a principle that would encompass all the data.

eerie (*ĭ´-rē*) ADJ. weird. In that *eerie* setting, it was easy to believe in ghosts and other supernatural beings.

efface V. rub out. The coin had been handled so many times that its date had been *effaced*.

effectual ADJ. efficient. If we are to succeed in this endeavor, we must seek *effectual* means of securing our goals.

effeminate ADJ. having womanly traits. His voice was high-pitched and *effeminate*.

effervesce (*-vĕs´*) V. bubble over; show excitement. Some of us cannot stand the way she *effervesces* over trifles.

effete (*ĕ-fēt´*) ADJ. worn out; exhausted; barren. The literature of the age reflected the *effete* condition of the writers; no new ideas were forthcoming.

efficacy (*ĕf´-*) N. power to produce desired effect. The *efficacy* of this drug depends on the regularity of the dosage.

effigy (*ĕf´-ə-jē*) N. dummy. The mob showed its irritation by hanging the judge in *effigy*.

efflorescent ADJ. flowering. Greenhouse gardeners are concerned with the coinciding of the plants' *efflorescent* period with certain holidays.

effrontery N. shameless boldness. He had the *effrontery* to insult the guest.

effulgent (*-fŏol´-*) ADJ. brilliantly radiant. The *effulgent* rays of the rising sun lit the sky.

effusion N. pouring forth. The critics objected to his literary *effusion* because it was too flowery.

effusive ADJ. pouring forth; gushing. Her *effusive* manner of greeting her friends finally began to irritate them.

egoism N. excessive interest in one's self; belief that one should be interested in one's self rather than in others. His *egoism* prevented him from seeing the needs of his colleagues.

egotism N. conceit; vanity. We found his *egotism* unwarranted and irritating.

egregious (*ĭ-grē´-jəs*) ADJ. gross; shocking. He was an *egregious* liar.

egress (*ē´-*) N. exit. Barnum's sign "To the *Egress*" fooled many people who thought they were going to see an animal and instead found themselves in the street.

ejaculation N. exclamation. He could not repress an *ejaculation* of surprise when he heard the news.

elation N. a rise in spirits; exaltation. She felt no *elation* at finding the purse.

elegiacal (*ĕl-ə-jī´-*) ADJ. like an elegy; mournful. The essay on the lost crew was *elegiacal* in mood. elegy, N.

elicit (*-lĭs´-ət*) V. draw out by discussion. The detectives tried to *elicit* where he had hidden his loot.

elucidate V. explain; enlighten. He was called upon to *elucidate* the disputed points in his article.

elusive ADJ. evasive; baffling; hard to grasp. His *elusive* dreams of wealth were costly to those of his friends who supported him financially.

elusory ADJ. tending to deceive expectations; elusive. He argued that the project was an *elusory* one and would bring disappointment to all.

emaciated ADJ. thin and wasted. His long period of starvation had left him wan and *emaciated*.

emanate V. issue forth. A strong odor of sulphur *emanated* from the spring.

emancipate V. set free. At first, the attempts of the Abolitionists to *emancipate* the slaves were unpopular in New England as well as in the South.

embellish V. adorn. His handwriting was *embellished* with flourishes.

embezzlement N. stealing. The bank teller confessed his *embezzlement* of the funds.

emblazon V. deck in brilliant colors. *Emblazoned* on his shield was his family coat of arms.

embroil V. throw into confusion; involve in strife; entangle. He became *embroiled* in the heated discussion when he tried to arbitrate the dispute.

emend V. correct; correct by a critic. The critic *emended* the book by selecting the passages which he thought most appropriate to the text.

emetic (*-mĕt´-*) N. substance causing vomiting. The use of

ā—ale; ă—add; ä—arm; à—ask; ē—eve; ĕ—end; ê—err, her; ə—allow; even; ī—ice; ĭ—ill; ō—oll; ŏ—odd; ô—orb; ŏŏ—food; ŏŏ—foot, put; ou—out; th—thin; ū—use; ŭ—up; zh—pleasure

an *emetic* like mustard is useful in cases of poisoning.

eminent ADJ. high; lofty. After his appointment to this *eminent* position, he seldom had time for his former friends.

emolument (*-mŏl'-*) N. salary; compensation. In addition to the *emolument* this position offers, you must consider the social prestige it carries with it.

emulate (*ĕm´-*) V. rival; imitate. As long as our political leaders *emulate* the virtues of the great leaders of this country, we shall flourish.

enamored (*-ăm´-*) ADJ. in love. Narcissus became *enamored* of his own beauty.

enclave (*ĕn´-klāv*) N. territory enclosed within an alien land. The Vatican is an independent *enclave* in Italy.

encomiastic ADJ. praising; eulogistic. Some critics believe that his *encomiastic* statements about Napoleon were inspired by his desire for material advancement rather than by an honest belief in the Emperor's genius. encomium, N.

encompass V. surround. Although we were *encompassed* by enemy forces, we were cheerful for we were well stocked and could withstand a siege until our allies joined us.

encroachment N. gradual intrusion. The *encroachment* of the factories upon the neighborhood lowered the value of the real estate.

encumber V. burden. Some people *encumber* themselves with too much luggage when they take short trips.

endearment N. fond statement. Your gifts and *endearments* cannot make me forget your earlier insolence.

endive (*ĕn´-dīv*) N. species of leafy plant used in salads. The salad contained *endive* in addition to the ingredients she usually used.

endue V. provide with some quality; endow. He was *endued* with a lion's courage.

energize V. invigorate; make forceful and active. We shall have to re-*energize* our activities by getting new members to carry on.

enervate V. weaken. The hot days of August are *enervating*.

engender V. cause; produce. This editorial will *engender* racial intolerance unless it is denounced.

engross V. occupy fully. John was so *engrossed* in his studies that he did not hear his mother call.

enhance V. advance; improve. Your chances for promotion in this department will be *enhanced* if you take some more courses in evening school.

enigma (*-nĭg´-*) N. puzzle. Despite all attempts to decipher the code, it remained an *enigma*. enigmatic, ADJ.

ETYMOLOGY 10

DOC, DOCT (to teach)

docile meek (teachable)
document something that provides evidence
doctor learned man (originally, teacher)

DOM, DOMIN (to rule)

dominate having power over
domain land under rule
dominant prevailing

DUC, DUCT (to lead)

viaduct arched roadway

aqueduct artificial waterway
education training (leading out)

DYNAM (power, strength)

dynamic powerful
dynamite powerful explosive
dynamo engine to make electrical power

EGO (I, self)

egoist person who is self-interested
egotist self-centered person
egocentric revolving about self

TEST—WORD LIST 10—*Synonyms*

Each of the questions below consists of a word printed in italics, followed by five words or phrases numbered 1 to 5. Choose the numbered word or phrase which is most nearly similar in meaning to the word in italics and write the number of your choice on your answer paper.

181. *elusive* 1 deadly 2 eloping 3 evasive 4 simple 5 petrified
182. *edify* 1 mystify 2 suffice 3 improve 4 erect 5 entertain
183. *dormant* 1 active 2 absurd 3 hibernating 4 unfortunate 5 permanent
184. *egress* 1 entrance 2 bird 3 exit 4 double 5 progress
185. *dubious* 1 external 2 straight 3 sincere 4 doubtful 5 filling in
186. *dogmatic* 1 benign 2 canine 3 impatient 4 petulant 5 arbitrary
187. *elated* 1 debased 2 respectful 3 drooping 4 gay 5 charitable
188. *droll* 1 rotund 2 amusing 3 fearsome 4 tiny 5 strange

189. *doff* 1 withdraw 2 take off 3 remain 4 control 5 start
190. *effigy* 1 requisition 2 organ 3 charge 4 accordion 5 dummy
191. *dour* 1 sullen 2 ornamental 3 grizzled 4 lacking speech 5 international
192. *divulge* 1 look 2 refuse 3 deride 4 reveal 5 harm
193. *efface* 1 countenance 2 encourage 3 recognize 4 blackball 5 rub out
194. *dotage* 1 senility 2 silence 3 sensitivity 4 interest 5 generosity
195. *emaciated* 1 garrulous 2 primeval 3 vigorous 4 disparate 5 thin
196. *enhance* 1 improve 2 doubt 3 scuff 4 gasp 5 agree
197. *embellish* 1 doff 2 don 3 balance 4 adorn 5 equalize
198. *enervate* 1 weaken 2 sputter 3 arrange 4 scrutinize 5 agree
199. *emend* 1 cherish 2 repose 3 correct 4 assure 5 worry
200. *eminent* 1 purposeful 2 high 3 delectable 4 curious 5 urgent

---

ā—ale; ă—add; ä—arm; à—ask, ē—eve; ĕ—end; ê—err, hẹr; ə—allow; evẹn; ī—ice; ĭ—ill; ō—oll; ŏ—odd; ô—orb; ōō—food; ŏŏ—foot, pụt; ou—out; th—thin; ū—use; ŭ—up; zh—pleasure

WORD LIST 11 ennui - extrovert

ennui (ŏn-wē´) N. boredom. The monotonous routine of hospital life induced a feeling of *ennui* which made him moody and irritable.

enormity N. hugeness (in a bad sense). He did not realize the *enormity* of his crime until he saw what suffering he had caused.

enrapture V. please intensely. The audience was *enraptured* by the freshness of the voices and the excellent orchestration.

ensconce (-skŏns´) V. settle comfortably. The parents thought that their children were *ensconced* safely in the private school and decided to leave for Europe.

enthrall V. capture; enslave. From the moment he saw her picture, he was *enthralled* by her beauty.

entity N. real being. As soon as the Charter was adopted, the United Nations became an *entity* and had to be considered as a factor in world diplomacy.

entree (ŏn´-trā) N. entrance. Because of his wealth and social position, he had *entree* into the most exclusive circles.

entrepreneur (än-trə-prə-nər´) N. businessman; contractor. Opponents of our present tax program argue that it discourages *entrepreneurs* from trying new fields of business activity.

environ (-vī´-) V. enclose; surround. In medieval days, Paris was *environed* by a wall. environs, N.

ephemeral (-fĕm´-) ADJ. short-lived; fleeting. The mayfly is an *ephemeral* creature.

epicure N. connoisseur of food and drink. *Epicures* frequent this restaurant because it features exotic wines and dishes.

epicurean N. person who devotes himself to pleasures of the senses, especially to food. This restaurant is famous for its menu, which can cater to the most exotic whim of the *epicurean*. also ADJ.

epigram N. witty thought or saying, usually short. Poor Richard's *epigrams* made Benjamin Franklin famous.

epilogue N. short speech at conclusion of dramatic work. The audience was so disappointed in the play that many did not remain to hear the *epilogue*.

epitaph N. inscription in memory of a dead person. In his will, he dictated the *epitaph* he wanted placed on his tombstone.

epithet N. descriptive word or phrase. Homer's writings were featured by the use of such *epithets* as "rosy-fingered dawn."

epitome (ĭ-pĭt´-ə-mē) N. summary; concise abstract. This final book is the *epitome* of all his previous books. epitomize, V.

epoch N. period of time. The glacial *epoch* lasted for thousands of years.

equable (ĕk´-) ADJ. tranquil; steady; uniform. After the hot summers and cold winters of New England, he found the climate of the West Indies *equable* and pleasant.

equanimity N. calmness of temperament. In his later years, he could look upon the foolishness of the world with *equanimity* and humor.

equestrian N. rider on horseback. These paths in the park are reserved for *equestrians* and their steeds. also ADJ.

equinox N. period of equal days and nights; the beginning of Spring and Autumn. The vernal *equinox* is usually marked by heavy rainstorms.

equipage (ĕk´-wə-pĭj) N. horse-drawn carriage. The *equip-age* drew up before the inn.

equity N. fairness; justice. Our courts guarantee *equity* to all.

equivocal (-kwĭv´-) ADJ. doubtful; ambiguous. Macbeth was misled by the *equivocal* statements of the witches.

equivocate V. lie; mislead; attempt to conceal the truth. The audience saw through his attempts to *equivocate* on the subject under discussion and ridiculed his remarks.

erode V. eat away. The limestone was *eroded* by the dripping water.

errant ADJ. wandering. Many a charming tale has been written about the knights-*errant* who helped the weak and punished the guilty during the Age of Chivalry.

erudite (ĕr´-yə-dīt) ADJ. learned; scholarly. His *erudite* writing was difficult to read because of the many allusions which were unfamiliar to most readers. erudition, N.

escapade (ĕs´-kə-pād) N. prank; flighty conduct. The headmaster could not regard this latest *escapade* as a boyish joke and expelled the young man.

eschew (ĭs-chōō´) V. avoid. He tried to *eschew* all display of temper.

escutcheon (-kŭch´-) N. shield-shaped surface on which coat of arms is placed. His traitorous acts placed a shameful blot on the family *escutcheon*.

esoteric (-tĕr´-) ADJ. known only to the chosen few. Those students who had access to his *esoteric* discussions were impressed by the scope of his thinking.

espionage (ĕs´-pē-) N. spying. In order to maintain its power, the government developed a system of *espionage* which penetrated every household.

esprit de corps (ĭs-prēd-ə-kōr´) N. comradeship; spirit. West Point cadets are proud of their *esprit de corps*.

estranged (-trānj'd) ADJ. separated. The *estranged* wife sought a divorce.

ethereal ADJ. light; heavenly; fine. Visitors were impressed by her *ethereal* beauty, her delicate charm.

ethnic ADJ. relating to races. Intolerance between *ethnic* groups is deplorable and usually is based on lack of information. ethnology, N.

eulogistic ADJ. praising. To everyone's surprise, the speech was *eulogistic* rather than critical in tone.

eulogy N. praise. All the *eulogies* of his friends could not remove the sting of the calumny heaped upon him by his enemies.

euphemism N. mild expression in place of an unpleasant one. The expression "He passed away" is a *euphemism* for "He died."

euphonious ADJ. pleasing in sound. Italian and Spanish are *euphonious* languages and therefore easily sung.

evanescent ADJ. fleeting; vanishing. For a brief moment, the entire skyline was bathed in an orange-red hue in the *evanescent* rays of the sunset.

evasive ADJ. not frank; eluding. Your *evasive* answers convinced the judge that you were withholding important evidence. evade, V.

evince V. show clearly. When he tried to answer the questions, he *evinced* his ignorance of the subject matter.

evoke V. call forth. He *evoked* much criticism by his hostile manner.

ewer N. water pitcher. The primitive conditions of the period were symbolized by the porcelain *ewer* and basin in the bedroom.

exaction N. exorbitant demand; extortion. The colonies re-

ā—ale; ă—add; ä—arm; à—ask, ē—eve; ĕ—end; ê—err, her; ə—allow; even; ī—ice; ĭ—ill; ō—oll; ä—odd; ô—orb; ōō—food; ŏŏ—foot, put; ou—out; th—thin; ū—use; ŭ—up; zh—pleasure

belled against the *exactions* of the mother country.

exasperate V. vex. Johnny often *exasperates* his mother with his pranks.

exchequer N. treasury. He had been Chancellor of the *Exchequer* before his promotion to the high office he now holds.

exculpate V. clear from blame. He was *exculpated* of the crime when the real criminal confessed.

execrable (ĕk´-sĭ-) ADJ. very bad. The anecdote was in *execrable* taste.

exemplary (-zĕm´-) ADJ. serving as a model; outstanding. Her *exemplary* behavior was praised at Commencement.

exhort (ĭg-zôrt´) V. urge. The evangelist will *exhort* all sinners in his audience to reform.

exhume V. dig out of the ground; remove from a grave. Because of the rumor that he had been poisoned, his body was *exhumed* in order that an autopsy might be performed.

exigency (ĕk´-sə-) N. urgent situation. In this *exigency*, we must look for aid from our allies.

exiguous (-zĭg´-) ADJ. small; minute. Grass grew there, an *exiguous* outcropping among the rocks.

exodus N. departure. The *exodus* from the hot and stuffy city was particularly noticeable on Friday evenings.

exonerate V. acquit; exculpate. I am sure this letter will *exonerate* you.

exorbitant ADJ. excessive. The people grumbled at his *exorbitant* prices but paid them because he had a monopoly.

exotic ADJ. not native; strange. Because of his *exotic* headdress, he was followed in the streets by small children who laughed at his strange appearance.

expatiate (ĕk-spā´-) V. talk at length. At this time, please give us a brief resumé of your work; we shall permit you to *expatiate* later.

expatriate N. exile; someone who has withdrawn from his native land. Henry James was an American *expatriate* who settled in England.

expediency N. that which is advisable or practical. He was guided by *expediency* rather than by ethical considerations.

expeditiously ADV. rapidly and efficiently. Please adjust this matter as *expeditiously* as possible as it is delaying important work.

expiate (ĕk´-spē-āt) V. make amends for (a sin). He tried to *expiate* his crimes by a full confession to the authorities.

expostulation N. remonstrance. Despite the teacher's scoldings and *expostulations*, the class remained unruly.

expunge V. cancel; remove. If you behave, I will *expunge* this notation from your record.

expurgate V. clean; remove offensive parts of a book. The editors felt that certain passages in the book had to be *expurgated* before it could be used in the classroom.

extant (ĕk´-) ADJ. still in existence. Although the authorities suppressed the book, many copies are *extant* and may be purchased at exorbitant prices.

extemporaneous ADJ. not planned; impromptu. Because his *extemporaneous* remarks were misinterpreted, he decided to write all his speeches in advance.

extenuate V. weaken; mitigate. It is easier for us to *extenuate* our own shortcomings than those of others.

extirpate (ĕk´-) V. root up. We must *extirpate* and destroy this monstrous philosophy.

extol V. praise; glorify. The astronauts were *extolled* as the pioneers of the Space Age.

extort V. wring from; get money by threats, etc. The blackmailer *extorted* money from his victim.

extradition N. surrender of prisoner by one state to another. The lawyers opposed the *extradition* of their client on the grounds that for more than five years he had been a model citizen.

extraneous ADJ. not essential; external. Do not pad your paper with *extraneous* matters; stick to essential items only.

extricate V. free; disentangle. He found that he could not *extricate* himself from the trap.

extrinsic ADJ. external; not inherent; foreign. Do not be fooled by *extrinsic* causes. We must look for the intrinsic reason.

extrovert N. person interested mostly in external objects and actions. A good salesman is usually an *extrovert*, who likes to mingle with people.

ETYMOLOGY 11

ERG, URG (work)

energy power
ergatocracy rule of the workers
metallurgy art of working in metal

ERR (to wander)

error mistake
erratic not reliable, not constant
knight-errant wandering knight

EU (good, well, beautiful) prefix

eulogize praise
euphemism substitution of pleasant way of saying something blunt or unpleasant
eupeptic having good digestion

EX (out) prefix

expel drive out
exit way out
extirpate root out

EXTRA (beyond, outside) prefix

extraordinary exceptional
extracurricular beyond the items in the curriculum
extraterritorial beyond the territory of a nation

TEST—WORD LIST 11—*Antonyms*

Each of the following questions consists of a word printed in italics, followed by five words or phrases numbered 1 to 5. Choose the numbered word or phrase which is most nearly opposite in meaning to the word in italics and write the number of your choice on your answer paper.

ā—ale; ă—add; ä—arm; à—ask, ē—eve; ĕ—end; ê—err, her; ə—allow; even; ī—ice; ĭ—ill; ō—oll; ŏ—odd; ô—orb; ōō—food; ŏŏ—foot, pŭt; ou—out; th—thin; ū—use; ŭ—up; zh—pleasure

201. *exodus* 1 neglect 2 consent 3 entry 4 gain 5 retreat
202. *exasperate* 1 confide 2 formalize 3 placate 4 betray 5 bargain
203. *equivocal* 1 mistaken 2 quaint 3 azure 4 clear 5 universal
204. *exhume* 1 decipher 2 dig 3 integrate 4 admit 5 inter
205. *evasive* 1 frank 2 correct 3 empty 4 fertile 5 watchful
206. *equanimity* 1 agitation 2 stirring 3 volume 4 identity 5 luster
207. *ephemeral* 1 sensuous 2 passing 3 popular 4 distasteful 5 eternal
208. *euphonious* 1 strident 2 lethargic 3 literary 4 significant 5 musical
209. *equable* 1 flat 2 decisive 3 stormy 4 rough 5 scanty
210. *execrable* 1 innumerable 2 philosophic 3 physical 4 excellent 5 meditative
211. *eulogistic* 1 pretty 2 critical 3 brief 4 stern 5 free
212. *ennui* 1 hate 2 excitement 3 seriousness 4 humility 5 kindness
213. *exculpate* 1 accuse 2 prevail 3 acquit 4 ravish 5 accumulate
214. *erudite* 1 professorial 2 stately 3 short 4 unknown 5 ignorant
215. *exonerate* 1 forge 2 accuse 3 record 4 doctor 5 reimburse
216. *extrovert* 1 clown 2 hero 3 ectomorph 4 neurotic 5 introvert
217. *exorbitant* 1 moderate 2 partisan 3 military 4 barbaric 5 expensive
218. *extrinsic* 1 reputable 2 inherent 3 swift 4 ambitious 5 cursory
219. *extraneous* 1 needless 2 decisive 3 essential 4 effective 5 expressive
220. *extemporaneous* 1 rehearsed 2 hybrid 3 humiliating 4 statesmanlike 5 picturesque

---

WORD LIST 12 extrude - fluster

extrude V. force or push out. Much pressure is required to *extrude* these plastics.

exuberant ADJ. abundant; effusive; lavish. His speeches were famous for his *exuberant* language and vivid imagery.

exude V. discharge; give forth. The maple syrup is obtained from the sap that *exudes* from the trees in early spring. exudation, N.

fabricate V. build; lie. If we pre*fabricate* the buildings in this project, we can reduce the cost considerably.

facade (*fə-säd´*) N. front of the building. The *facade* of the church had often been photographed by tourists.

facet (*făs´-ət*) N. small plane surface (of a gem); a side. The stonecutter decided to improve the rough diamond by providing it with several *facets*.

facetious ADJ. humorous; jocular. Your *facetious* remarks are not appropriate at this serious moment.

facile (*făs´-əl*) ADJ. easy; expert. Because he was a *facile* speaker, he never refused a request to address an organization.

facilitate V. make less difficult. He tried to *facilitate* matters at home by getting a part-time job.

faction N. party; clique; dissension. The quarrels and bickering of the two small *factions* within the club disturbed the majority of the members.

factious ADJ. inclined to form factions; causing dissension. Your statement is *factious* and will upset the harmony that now exists.

factitious ADJ. artificial; sham. Hollywood actresses often create *factitious* tears by using glycerine.

factotum (*-tōt´-*) N. handyman; person who does all kinds of work. Although we had hired him as a messenger, we soon began to use him as a general *factotum* around the office.

fain ADV. gladly. The knight said, "I would *fain* be your protector."

fallacious (*-lā´-*) ADJ. misleading. Your reasoning must be *fallacious* because it leads to a ridiculous answer.

fallible ADJ. liable to err. I know I am *fallible*, but I feel confident that I am right this time.

fallow ADJ. plowed but not sowed; uncultivated. Farmers have learned that it is advisable to permit land to lie *fallow* every few years.

fanaticism N. excessive zeal. The leader of the group was held responsible even though he could not control the *fanaticism* of his followers.

fancied ADJ. imagined; unreal. You are resenting *fancied* insults. No one has ever said such things about you.

fancier N. breeder or dealer of animals. The dog *fancier* exhibited his prize collie at the annual Kennel Club show.

fanciful ADJ. whimsical; visionary. This is a *fanciful* scheme because it does not consider the facts.

fantastic ADJ. unreal; grotesque; whimsical. Your fears are *fantastic* because no such animal as you have described exists.

fastidious ADJ. difficult to please; squeamish. The waitresses disliked serving him dinner because of his very *fastidious* taste.

fatalism N. belief that events are determined by forces beyond one's control. With fatalism, he accepted the hardships which beset him. fatalistic, ADJ.

fatuous ADJ. foolish; inane. He is far too intelligent to utter such *fatuous* remarks.

fauna (*fôn´-*) N. animals of a period or region. The scientist could visualize the *fauna* of the period by examining the skeletal remains and the fossils.

faux pas (*fō-pä´*) N. an error or slip (in manners or behavior). Your tactless remarks during dinner were a *faux pas*.

fawning ADJ. courting favor by cringing and flattering. He was constantly surrounded by a group of *fawning* admirers who hoped to win some favor.

fealty (*fē´-əl-*) N. loyalty; faithfulness. The feudal lord demanded *fealty* of his vassals.

feasible ADJ. practical. This is an entirely *feasible* proposal. I suggest we adopt it.

fecundity N. fertility; fruitfulness. The *fecundity* of his mind is illustrated by the many vivid images in his poems.

feign (*fān*) V. pretend. Lady Macbeth *feigned* illness in the courtyard.

feint (*fānt*) N. trick; shift; sham blow. The boxer was fooled by his opponent's *feint* and dropped his guard. also V.

felicitous ADJ. apt; suitably expressed; well chosen. He was famous for his *felicitous* remarks and was called upon to serve as master-of-ceremonies at many a banquet.

fell ADJ. cruel; deadly. Henley writes of the "*fell* clutch of

---

ā—ale; ă—add; ä—arm; à—ask, ē—eve; ĕ—end; ê—err, her; ə—allow; even; ī—ice; ĭ—ill; ō—oll; ŏ—odd; ô—orb; ōō—food; ŏŏ—foot, put; ou—out; th—thin; ü—use; ŭ—up; zh—pleasure

circumstance" in his poem "Invictus."

ferment (*fĕr´-*) N. agitation; commotion. The entire country was in a state of *ferment.*

ferret V. drive or hunt out of hiding. He *ferreted* out their secret.

fervent ADJ. ardent; hot. He felt that the *fervent* praise was excessive and somewhat undeserved.

fervid ADJ. ardent. His *fervid* enthusiasm inspired all of us to undertake the dangerous mission.

fervor N. glowing ardor. Their kiss was full of the *fervor* of first love.

fester V. generate pus. When his finger began to *fester,* the doctor lanced it and removed the splinter which had caused the pus to form.

fete (*fā t*) V. honor at a festival. The returning hero was *feted* at a community supper and dance. also N.

fetid (*fĕt´-əd*) ADJ. malodorous. The neglected wound became *fetid.*

fetish (*fĕt´-*) N. object supposed to possess magical powers; an object of special devotion. The native wore a *fetish* around his neck to ward off evil spirits.

fetter V. shackle. The prisoner was *fettered* to the wall.

fiasco (*fē-ŏs´-kō*) N. total failure. Our ambitious venture ended in a *fiasco.*

fiat (*fē´-*) N. command. I cannot accept government by *fiat;* I feel that I must be consulted.

fickle ADJ. changeable; faithless. He discovered she was *fickle.*

fictitious ADJ. imaginary. Although this book purports to be a biography of George Washington, many of the incidents are *fictitious.*

fidelity N. loyalty. A dog's *fidelity* to its owner is one of the reasons why that animal is a favorite household pet.

figment N. invention; imaginary thing. That incident is a *figment* of your imagination.

filch V. steal. The boys *filched* apples from the fruit stand.

filial ADJ. pertaining to a son or daughter. Many children forget their *filial* obligations and disregard the wishes of their parents.

finale (*fə-năl´-ē*) N. conclusion. It is not until we reach the *finale* of this play that we can understand the author's message.

finesse (*fə-nĕs´*) N. delicate skill. The *finesse* and adroitness of the surgeon impressed the observers in the operating room.

finicky ADJ. too particular; fussy. The old lady was *finicky* about her food.

finite (*fī´-nīt*) ADJ. limited. It is difficult for humanity with its *finite* existence to grasp the infinite.

fissure (*fĭsh´-ər*) N. crevice. The mountain climbers secured footholds in tiny *fissures* in the rock.

fitful ADJ. spasmodic; intermittent. After several *fitful* at-tempts, he decided to postpone the start of the project until he felt more energetic.

flaccid (*flăk´-səd*) ADJ. flabby. His sedentary life had left him with *flaccid* muscles.

flagellate (*flăj´-ə-*) V. flog; whip. The Romans used to *flagellate* criminals with a whip that had three knotted strands.

flagging ADJ. weak; drooping. The encouraging cheers of the crowd lifted the team's *flagging* spirits.

flagrant (*flā´-*) ADJ. conspicuously wicked. We cannot con-done such *flagrant* violations of the rules.

flail V. thresh grain by hand; strike or slap. In medieval times, warriors *flailed* their foe with a metal ball attached to a handle.

flair N. talent. He has an uncanny *flair* for discovering new artists before the public has become aware of their exis-tence.

flamboyant (*-bôī´-*) ADJ. ornate. Modern architecture has discarded the *flamboyant* trimming on buildings and em-phasizes simplicity of line.

flaunt V. display ostentatiously. She is not one of those actresses who *flaunt* their physical charms; she can act.

flay V. strip off skin; plunder. The criminal was condemned to be *flayed* alive.

fleck V. spot. Her cheeks, *flecked* with tears, were testimony to the hours of weeping.

fledgling ADJ. inexperienced. While it is necessary to provide these *fledgling* poets with an opportunity to present their work, it is not essential that we admire everything they write. also N.

flick N. light stroke as with a whip. The horse needed no encouragement; only one *flick* of the whip was all the jockey had to apply to get the animal to run at top speed.

flippancy N. trifling gaiety. Your *flippancy* at this serious moment is offensive.

flora N. plants of a region or era. Because she was a botanist, she spent most of her time studying the *flora* of the desert.

florid ADJ. flowery; ruddy. His complexion was even more *florid* than usual because of his anger.

flotilla (*-tĭl´-*) N. small fleet. It is always an exciting and interesting moment when the fishing *flotilla* returns to port.

flotsam (*flŏt´-*) N. drifting wreckage. Beachcombers eke out a living by salvaging the *flotsam* and jetsam of the sea.

flout V. reject; mock. The headstrong youth *flouted* all au-thority; he refused to be curbed.

fluctuation N. wavering. Meteorologists watch the *fluctua-tions* of the barometer in order to predict the weather.

fluency N. smoothness of speech. He spoke French with *fluency* and ease.

fluster V. confuse. The teacher's sudden question *flustered* him and he stammered his reply.

ETYMOLOGY 12

FAC, FIC, FEC, FECT (to make, to do)

factory   place where things are made
fiction   manufactured story
affect   cause to change

FALL, FALS (to deceive)

fallacious   faulty
infallible   not prone to error, perfect
falsify   lie

FER, LAT (to bring, to bear)

transfer   bring from one place to another
translate   bring from one language to another
coniferous   bearing cones, as pine trees

FIC (making, causing) adjective suffix

terrific   causing fear or awe
soporific   making sleepy

ā—ale; ă—add; ä—arm; à—ask; ē—eve; ĕ—end; ê—err, her; ə—allow; even; ī—ice; ĭ—ill; ō—oll; ŏ—odd; ô—orb; ōō—food; ŏŏ—foot, put; ou—out; th—thin; ū—use; ŭ—up; zh—pleasure

TEST—WORD LIST 12—*Synonyms and Antonyms*

Each of the questions below consists of a word printed in italics, followed by five words or phrases numbered 1 to 5. Choose the numbered word or phrase which is most nearly the same as or the opposite of the word in italics and write the number of your choice on your answer paper.

221. *finite*   1 bounded 2 established 3 affirmative 4 massive 5 finicky
222. *fiasco*   1 cameo 2 mansion 3 pollution 4 success 5 gamble
223. *flair*   1 conflagration 2 inspiration 3 bent 4 egregiousness 5 magnitude
224. *flamboyant*   1 old-fashioned 2 restrained 3 impulsive 4 cognizant 5 eloquent
225. *fanciful*   1 imaginative 2 knowing 3 elaborate 4 quick 5 lusty
226. *fecundity*   1 prophecy 2 futility 3 fruitfulness 4 need 5 dormancy

227. *fell*   1 propitious 2 illiterate 3 catastrophic 4 futile 5 inherent
228. *fiat*   1 motor 2 degree 3 lesion 4 suture 5 order
229. *fledgling*   1 weaving 2 bobbing 3 beginning 4 studying 5 flaying
230. *factitious*   1 genuine 2 magnificent 3 polished 4 puny 5 ridiculous
231. *fidelity*   1 brotherhood 2 parentage 3 treachery 4 conscience 5 consistency
232. *flail*   1 succeed 2 harvest 3 knife 4 strike 5 resent
233. *florid*   1 ruddy 2 rusty 3 ruined 4 patient 5 poetic
234. *fatuous*   1 fatal 2 natal 3 terrible 4 sensible 5 tolerable
235. *ferment*   1 stir up 2 fill 3 ferret 4 mutilate 5 banish
236. *fickle*   1 fallacious 2 tolerant 3 loyal 4 hungry 5 stupid
237. *exude*   1 prevent 2 ooze 3 manage 4 protrude 5 insure
238. *feasible*   1 theoretical 2 impatient 3 constant 4 present 5 impractical
239. *feign*   1 deserve 2 condemn 3 condone 4 attend 5 pretend
240. *filch*   1 milk 2 purloin 3 itch 4 cancel 5 resent

WORD LIST   13   flux - gloat

flux   N. flowing; series of changes. While conditions are in such a state of *flux*, I do not wish to commit myself too deeply in this affair.

foible   N. weakness; slight fault. We can overlook the *foibles* of our friends.

foist   V. insert improperly; palm off. I will not permit you to *foist* such ridiculous ideas upon the membership of this group.

foment   (-*mĕnt´*) V. stir up; instigate. This report will *foment* dissension in the club.

foolhardy   ADJ. rash. Don't be *foolhardy*. Get the advice of experienced people before undertaking this venture.

foppish   ADJ. vain about dress and appearance. He tried to imitate the *foppish* manner of the young men of the court.

foray   (*fŏ´-*) N. raid. The company staged a midnight *foray* against the enemy outpost.

forbearance   N. patience. We must use *forbearance* in dealing with him because he is still weak from his illness.

foreboding   N. premonition of evil. Caesar ridiculed his wife's *forebodings* about the Ides of March.

forensic   (-*rĕn´-sĭk*) ADJ. suitable to debate or courts of law. In his best *forensic* manner, the lawyer addressed the jury.

formidable   (*fŏr´-*) ADJ. menacing; threatening. We must not treat the battle lightly for we are facing a *formidable* foe.

forte   (*fŏr´-tā*) N. strong point or special talent. I am not eager to play this rather serious role, for my *forte* is comedy.

fortitude   N. bravery; courage. He was awarded the medal for his *fortitude* in the battle.

fortuitous   ADJ. accidental; by chance. There is no connection between these two events; their timing is extremely *fortuitous*.

foster   V. rear; encourage. According to the legend, Romulus and Remus were *fostered* by a she-wolf. also ADJ.

fractious   (*frăk´-shəs*) ADJ. unruly. The *fractious* horse unseated its rider.

frailty   N. weakness. Hamlet says, "*Frailty*, thy name is woman."

franchise   N. right granted by authority. The city issued a *franchise* to the company to operate surface transit lines on the streets for ninety-nine years. also V.

frantic   ADJ. wild. At the time of the collision, many people became *frantic* with fear.

fraudulent   ADJ. cheating; deceitful. The government seeks to prevent *fraudulent* and misleading advertising.

fraught   (*frôt*) ADJ. filled. Since this enterprise is *fraught* with danger, I will ask for volunteers who are willing to assume the risks.

fray   N. brawl. The three musketeers were in the thick of the *fray*.

freebooter   N. buccaneer. This town is a rather dangerous place to visit as it is frequented by pirates, *freebooters*, and other plunderers.

frenetic   ADJ. frenzied; frantic. His *frenetic* activities convinced us that he had no organized plan of operation.

frenzied   ADJ. madly excited. As soon as they smelled smoke, the *frenzied* animals milled about in their cages.

fresco   N. painting on plaster (usually fresh). The cathedral is visited by many tourists who wish to admire the *frescoes* by Giotto.

freshet   N. sudden flood. Motorists were warned that spring *freshets* had washed away several small bridges and that long detours would be necessary.

friction   N. clash in opinion; rubbing against. At this time when harmony is essential, we cannot afford to have any *friction* in our group.

frieze   (*frēz*) N. ornamental band on a wall. The *frieze* of the church was adorned with sculpture.

frigid   ADJ. intensely cold. Alaska is in the *frigid* zone.

fritter   V. waste. He could not apply himself to any task and *frittered* away his time in idle conversation.

frolicsome   ADJ. prankish; gay. The *frolicsome* puppy tried to lick the face of its master.

froward   (*frō´-*) ADJ. disobedient; perverse; stubborn. Your

ā—ale; ă—add; ä—arm; à—ask, ē—eve; ĕ—end; ê—err, her; ə—allow; even; ī—ice; ĭ—ill; ō—oll; ŏ—odd; ô—orb; ōō—food; ŏŏ—foot, put; ou—out; th—thin; ū—use; ŭ—up; zh—pleasure

froward behavior has alienated many of us who might have been your supporters.

frowzy ADJ. slovenly; unkempt; dirty. Her *frowzy* appearance and her cheap decorations made her appear ludicrous in this group.

fructify V. bear fruit. This tree should *fructify* in three years.

frugality N. thrift. In these difficult days, we must live with *frugality.*

fruition (*froō-ĭsh´-*) N. bearing of fruit; fulfillment; realization. This building marks the *fruition* of all our aspirations and years of hard work.

frustrate V. thwart; defeat. We must *frustrate* this dictator's plan to seize control of the government.

fulminate V. thunder; explode. The people against whom he *fulminated* were innocent of any wrongdoing.

fulsome ADJ. disgustingly excessive. His *fulsome* praise of the dictator annoyed his listeners.

functionary N. official. As his case was transferred from one *functionary* to another, he began to despair of ever reaching a settlement.

funereal (*-nĭr´-ē-əl*) ADJ. sad; solemn. I fail to understand why there is such a *funereal* atmosphere; we have lost a battle, not a war.

furor (*fūr´-ôr*) N. frenzy; great excitement. The story of his embezzlement of the funds created a *furor* on the Stock Exchange.

furtive (*fẽrt´-*) ADJ. stealthy. The boy gave a *furtive* look at his classmate's test paper.

fusion N. union; coalition. The opponents of the political party in power organized a *fusion* of disgruntled groups and became an important element in the election.

fustian (*fŭs´-*) ADJ. pompous; bombastic. Several in the audience were deceived by his *fustian* style; they mistook pomposity for erudition.

gadfly N. animal-biting fly; an irritating person. Like a *gadfly,* he irritated all the guests at the hotel; within forty-eight hours, everyone regarded him as an annoying busybody.

gaff N. hook; barbed fishing spear. When he attempted to land the sailfish, he was so nervous that he dropped the *gaff* into the sea. also V.

gainsay (*-sā´*) V. deny. He could not *gainsay* the truth of the report.

galleon N. large sailing ship. The Spaniards pinned their hopes on the *galleon,* the large warship; the British, on the smaller and faster pinnace.

galvanize V. stimulate by shock; stir up. The entire nation was *galvanized* into strong military activity by the news of the attack on Pearl Harbor.

gambol V. skip; leap playfully. Watching children *gamboling* in the park is a pleasant experience. also N.

gamester (*gām´-stər*) N. gambler. An inveterate *gamester,* he was willing to wager on the outcome of any event, even one which involved the behavior of insects.

gamut (*găm´-*) N. entire range. In this performance, the leading lady was able to demonstrate the complete *gamut* of her acting ability.

gape (*gāp*) V. open widely. The huge pit *gaped* before him; if he stumbled, he would fall in.

garbled ADJ. mixed up; based on false or unfair selection. The *garbled* report confused many readers who were not familiar with the facts. garble, V.

garish (*găr´-*) ADJ. gaudy. She wore a *garish* rhinestone necklace.

garner V. gather; store up. He hoped to *garner* the world's literature in one library.

garnish V. decorate. Parsley was used to *garnish* the boiled potato. also N.

garrulity (*-roō´-*) N. talkativeness. The man who married a dumb wife asked the doctor to make him deaf because of his wife's *garrulity* after her cure. garrulous, ADJ.

gauntlet N. leather glove. Now that we have been challenged, we must take up the *gauntlet* and meet our adversary fearlessly.

gazette N. official periodical publication. He read the *gazettes* regularly for the announcement of his promotion.

generality N. vague statement. This report is filled with *generalities;* you must be more specific in your statements.

geniality N. cheerfulness; kindliness; sympathy. This restaurant is famous and popular because of the *geniality* of the proprietor who tries to make everyone happy.

genre (*zhän´-rə*) N. style of art illustrating scenes of common life. His painting of fisher folk at their daily tasks is an excellent illustration of *genre* art.

genteel (*-tēl´*) ADJ. well-bred; elegant. We are looking for a man with a *genteel* appearance who can inspire confidence by his cultivated manner.

gentility N. those of gentle birth; refinement. Her family was proud of its *gentility.*

gentry N. people of standing; class of people just below nobility. The local *gentry* did not welcome the visits of the summer tourists and tried to ignore their presence in the community.

germane (*-mān´*) ADJ. pertinent; bearing upon the case at hand. The lawyer objected that the testimony being offered was not *germane* to the case at hand.

gesticulation (*jĕ-stĭk-yə-lā´-*)N. motion; gesture. Operatic performers are trained to make exaggerated *gesticulations* because of the large auditoriums in which they appear.

ghastly ADJ. horrible. The murdered man was a *ghastly* sight.

gibber (*jĭb´-*) V. speak foolishly. The demented man *gibbered* incoherently.

gibbet (*jĭb´-*) N. gallows. The bodies of the highwaymen were left dangling from the *gibbet* as a warning to other would-be transgressors.

gibe (*jīb*) V. mock. As you *gibe* at their superstitious beliefs, do you realize that you, too, are guilty of similarly foolish thoughts?

gig (*gĭg*) N. two-wheeled carriage. As they drove down the street in their new *gig,* drawn by the dappled mare, they were cheered by the people who recognized them.

gist (*jĭst*) N. essence. She was asked to give the *gist* of the essay in two sentences.

glaze V. cover with a thin and shiny surface. The freezing rain *glazed* the streets and made driving hazardous. also N.

glean V. gather leavings. After the crops had been harvested by the machines, the peasants were permitted to *glean* the wheat left in the fields.

glib ADJ. fluent. He is a *glib* speaker.

gloaming N. twilight. The snow began to fall in the *gloaming* and continued all through the night.

gloat V. express evil satisfaction; view malevolently. As you *gloat* over your ill-gotten wealth, do you think of the many victims you have defrauded?

ā—ale; ă—add; ä—arm; à—ask, ē—eve; ĕ—end; ê—err, her; ə—allow; even; ī—ice; ĭ—ill; ō—oll; ŏ—odd; ô—orb; oō—food; ŏŏ—foot, put; ou—out; th—thin; ū—use; ŭ—up; zh—pleasure

ETYMOLOGY 13

FY (to make) verb suffix

magnify   make greater
petrify   make into stone
beautify   make beautiful

GAM (marriage)

monogamy   marriage to one person

bigamy   marriage to two people at the same time
polygamy   having many spouses at the same time

GEN, GENER (class, race)

genus   group of biological species with similar characteristics
generic   characteristic of a class
gender   class organized according to sex

TEST—WORD LIST 13—*Synonyms*

Each of the questions below consists of a word printed in italics, followed by five words or phrases numbered 1 to 5. Choose the numbered word or phrase which is most nearly similar in meaning to the word in italics and write the number of your choice on your answer paper.

241. *garnish*   1 paint 2 garner 3 adorn 4 abuse 5 banish
242. *frugality*   1 foolishness 2 extremity 3 indifference 4 enthusiasm 5 economy
243. *foray*   1 excursion 2 contest 3 ranger 4 intuition 5 fish
244. *gadfly*   1 humorist 2 nuisance 3 scholar 4 bum 5 thief
245. *foolhardy*   1 strong 2 unwise 3 brave 4 futile 5 erudite
246. *glib*   1 slippery 2 fashionable 3 antiquated 4 articulate 5 anticlimactic
247. *franchise*   1 subway 2 kiosk 3 license 4 reason 5 fashion
248. *furtive*   1 underhanded 2 coy 3 blatant 4 quick 5 abortive
249. *garner*   1 prevent 2 assist 3 collect 4 compute 5 consult

250. *gist*   1 chaff 2 summary 3 expostulation 4 expiation 5 chore
251. *foster*   1 speed 2 fondle 3 become infected 4 raise 5 roll
252. *foppish*   1 scanty 2 radical 3 orthodox 4 dandyish 5 magnificent
253. *furor*   1 excitement 2 worry 3 flux 4 anteroom 5 lover
254. *germane*   1 bacteriological 2 middle European 3 prominent 4 warlike 5 relevant
255. *fritter*   1 sour 2 chafe 3 dissipate 4 cancel 5 abuse
256. *garish*   1 sordid 2 flashy 3 prominent 4 lusty 5 thoughtful
257. *formidable*   1 dangerous 2 outlandish 3 grandiloquent 4 impenetrable 5 vulnerable
258. *garrulity*   1 credulity 2 senility 3 loquaciousness 4 speciousness 5 artistry
259. *foment*   1 spoil 2 instigate 3 interrogate 4 settle 5 maintain
260. *galleon*   1 liquid measure 2 ship 3 armada 4 company 5 printer's proof

---

WORD LIST 14   glossy - homily

glossy ADJ. smooth and shining. I want this photograph printed on *glossy* paper.

glut V. overstock; fill to excess. The many manufacturers *glutted* the market and could not find purchasers for the many articles they had produced. also N.

glutinous (*glōōt´-*) ADJ. sticky; viscous. Molasses is a *glutinous* substance.

gluttonous ADJ. greedy for food. The *gluttonous* boy ate all the cookies.

gnarled (*närld*) ADJ. twisted. The *gnarled* oak tree had been a landmark for years and was mentioned in several deeds.

gnome (*nōm*) N. dwarf; underground spirit. In medieval mythology, *gnomes* were the special guardians and inhabitants of subterranean mines.

goad V. urge on. He was *goaded* by his friends until he yielded to their wishes. also N.

gorge V. stuff oneself. The gluttonous guest *gorged* himself with food as though he had not eaten for days.

gory ADJ. bloody. The audience shuddered as they listened to the details of the *gory* massacre.

gossamer (*gŏs´-*) ADJ. sheer; like cobwebs. Nylon can be woven into *gossamer* or thick fabrics. also N.

gouge (*gouj*) V. tear out. In that fight, all the rules were forgotten; the adversaries bit, kicked, and tried to *gouge* each other's eyes out.

gourmand (*gŏŏr´-mänd*) N. epicure; person who takes excessive pleasure in food and drink. The *gourmand* liked the French cuisine.

gourmet (*gŏŏr-mā´*) N. connoisseur of food and drink. The *gourmet* stated that this was the best onion soup he had ever tasted.

granary (*grăn´-*) N. storehouse for grain. We have reason to be thankful, for our crops were good and our *granaries* are full.

grandiloquent ADJ. pompous; bombastic; using high-sounding language. The politician could never speak simply; he was always *grandiloquent*.

grandiose (*grăn´-dē-ōs*) ADJ. imposing; impressive. His *grandiose* manner impressed those who met him for the first time.

granulate V. form into grains. Sugar that has been *granulated* dissolves more readily than lump sugar. granule, N.

graphic ADJ. pertaining to the art of delineating; vividly described. I was particularly impressed by the *graphic* presentation of the storm.

gratis (*grăt´-*) ADJ. free. The company offered to give one package *gratis* to every purchaser of one of their products. also ADJ.

gratuitous (*-tū´-*) ADJ. given freely; unwarranted. I resent your *gratuitous* remarks because no one asked for them. gratuity, N.

gregarious (*grĭ-găr´-*) ADJ. sociable. He was not *gregarious* and preferred to be alone most of the time.

grisly ADJ. ghastly. She shuddered at the *grisly* sight.

grotto N. small cavern. The Blue *Grotto* in Capri can be entered only by small boats rowed by natives through a

ā—ale; ă—add; ä—arm; à—ask, ē—eve; ĕ—end; ê—err, hẽr; ə—allow; evən; ī—ice; ĭ—ill; ō—oll; ŏ—odd; ô—orb; ōō—food; ŏŏ—foot, pŭt; ou—out; th—thin; ū—use; ŭ—up; zh—pleasure

natural opening in the rocks.

gruel N. liquid food made by boiling oatmeal, etc., in milk or water. Our daily allotment of *gruel* made the meal not only monotonous but also unpalatable.

grueling ADJ. exhausting. The marathon is a *grueling* race.

gruesome ADJ. grisly. People screamed when his *gruesome* appearance was flashed on the screen.

gruff ADJ. rough-mannered. Although he was blunt and *gruff* with most people, he was always gentle with children.

guffaw (gə-fô´) N. boisterous laughter. The loud *guffaws* that came from the closed room indicated that the members of the committee had not yet settled down to serious business. also V.

guile (gīl) N. deceit; duplicity. He achieved his high position by *guile* and treachery.

guileless ADJ. without deceit. He is naive, simple, and *guileless;* he cannot be guilty of fraud.

guise N. appearance; costume. In the *guise* of a plumber, the detective investigated the murder case.

gullible ADJ. easily deceived. He preyed upon *gullible* people, who believed his stories of easy wealth.

gustatory ADJ. affecting the sense of taste. This food is particularly *gustatory* because of the spices it contains.

gusto N. enjoyment; enthusiasm. He accepted the assignment with such *gusto* that I feel he would have been satisfied with a smaller salary.

gusty ADJ. windy. The *gusty* weather made sailing precarious.

guttural ADJ. pertaining to the throat. *Guttural* sounds are produced in the throat or in the back of the tongue and palate.

habiliments (-bĭl´-ə-) N. garb; clothing. Although not a minister, David Belasco used to wear clerical *habiliments*.

hackneyed ADJ. commonplace; trite. The English teacher criticized his story because of its *hackneyed* plot.

haggard ADJ. wasted away; gaunt. After his long illness, he was pale and *haggard*.

haggle V. argue about prices. I prefer to shop in a store that has a one-price policy because, whenever I *haggle* with a shopkeeper, I am never certain that I paid a fair price for the articles I purchased.

halcyon (hăl´-sē-) ADJ. calm; peaceful. In those *halcyon* days, people were not worried about sneak attacks and bombings.

hallowed ADJ. blessed; consecrated. He was laid to rest in *hallowed* ground.

hallucination N. delusion. I think you were frightened by a *hallucination* which you created in your own mind.

hamper V. obstruct. The minority party agreed not to hamper the efforts of the leaders to secure a lasting peace.

hap N. chance; luck. In his poem *Hap*, Thomas Hardy objects to the part chance plays in our lives.

haphazard ADJ. random; by chance. His *haphazard* reading left him unacquainted with authors of the books.

hapless ADJ. unfortunate. This *hapless* creature had never known a moment's pleasure.

harangue (-răng´) N. noisy speech. In his lengthy *harangue,* the principal berated the offenders. also V.

harass (-răs´) V. to annoy by repeated attacks. When he could not pay his bills as quickly as he had promised, he was *harassed* by his creditors.

harbinger (här´-bən-jər) N. forerunner. The crocus is an early *harbinger* of spring.

harping N. tiresome dwelling on a subject. After he had reminded me several times about what he had done for me, I told him to stop *harping* on my indebtedness to him. harp, V.

harridan N. shrewish hag. Most people avoided the *harridan* because they feared her abusive and vicious language.

harrow V. break up ground after plowing; torture. I don't want to *harrow* you at this time by asking you to recall the details of your unpleasant experience.

harry V. raid. The guerrilla band *harried* the enemy nightly.

haughtiness N. pride; arrogance. I resent his *haughtiness* because he is no better than we are.

hauteur (hô-tər´) N. haughtiness. His snobbishness is obvious to all who witness his *hauteur* when he talks to those whom he considers his social inferiors.

hawser N. large rope. The ship was tied to the pier by a *hawser*.

hazardous ADJ. dangerous. Your occupation is too *hazardous* for insurance companies to consider your application.

hazy ADJ. slightly obscure. In *hazy* weather, you cannot see the top of this mountain.

hedonism (hēd´-) N. belief that pleasure is the sole aim in life. *Hedonism* and asceticism are opposing philosophies of human behavior.

heedless ADJ. not noticing; disregarding. He drove on, *heedless* of the warnings placed at the side of the road that it was dangerous.

heinous (hā´-) ADJ. atrocious; hatefully bad. Hitler's *heinous* crimes will never be forgotten.

heresy N. opinion contrary to popular belief; opinion contrary to accepted religion. He was threatened with excommunication because his remarks were considered to be pure *heresy*.

heretic (hĕr´-) N. person who maintains opinions contrary to the doctrines of the church. She was punished by the Spanish Inquisition because she was a *heretic*.

hermitage N. home of a hermit. Even in his remote *hermitage* he could not escape completely from the world.

heterogeneous (-jĕ´-nē-əs) ADJ. dissimilar. In *heterogeneous* groupings, we have an unassorted grouping, while in homogeneous groupings we have people or things which have common traits.

hiatus (hī-āt´-) N. gap; pause. There was a *hiatus* of twenty years in the life of Rip van Winkle.

hibernal (hī-bêrn´-) ADJ. wintry. Bears prepare for their long *hibernal* sleep by overeating.

hibernate V. sleep throughout the winter. Bears are one of the many species of animals that *hibernate*.

hierarchy N. body divided into ranks. It was difficult to step out of one's place in this *hierarchy*.

hieroglyphic N. picture writing. The discovery of the Rosetta Stone enabled scholars to read the ancient Egyptian *hieroglyphics*.

hilarity N. boisterous mirth. This *hilarity* is improper on this solemn day of mourning.

hindmost ADJ. furthest behind. The coward could always be found in the *hindmost* lines whenever a battle was being waged.

hireling N. one who serves for hire [usually contemptuously]. In a matter of such importance, I do not wish to deal with *hirelings;* I must meet with the chief.

hirsute (hêr´-sōot) ADJ. hairy. He was a *hirsute* individual with a heavy black beard.

histrionic ADJ. theatrical. He was proud of his *histrionic* ability and wanted to play the role of Hamlet. histrionics, N.

hoary ADJ. white with age. The man was *hoary* and wrinkled.

hogshead N. large barrel. On the trip to England, the ship carried munitions; on its return trip, *hogsheads* filled with French wines and Scotch liquors.

ā—ale; ă—add; ä—arm; à—ask; ē—eve; ĕ—end; ê—err, her; ə—allow; even; ī—ice; ĭ—ill; ō—oll; ŏ—odd; ô—orb; ōō—food; ŏŏ—foot, put; ou—out; th—thin; ū—use; ŭ—up; zh—pleasure

holocaust N. destruction by fire. Citizens of San Francisco remember that the destruction of the city was caused not by the earthquake but by the *holocaust* that followed.

holster N. pistol case. Even when he was not in uniform, he carried a *holster* and pistol under his arm.

homespun ADJ. domestic; made at home. *Homespun* wit like *homespun* cloth was often coarse and plain.

homily (hŏm´-) N. sermon; serious warning. His speeches were always *homilies,* advising his listeners to repent and reform.

ETYMOLOGY 14

GRAPH, GRAM (writing)

epigram   a pithy statement
telegram   an instantaneous message over great distances (*tele*—far off)
stenography   shorthand (writing narrowly)

GREG (flock, herd)

gregarious   tending to group together as in a herd

aggregate   group, total
egregious   out of the group; now used in a bad sense as wicked

HELI, HELIO (sun)

heliotrope   flower that faces the sun
heliograph   instrument that uses the sun's rays to send signals
helium   element abundant in the sun's atmosphere

TEST—WORD LIST 14—*Antonyms*

Each of the questions below consists of a word printed in italics, followed by five words or phrases numbered 1 to 5. Choose the numbered word or phrase which is most nearly opposite in meaning to the word in italics and write the number of your choice on your answer paper.

261. *grandiose*   1 false 2 ideal 3 proud 4 simple 5 functional
262. *hibernal*   1 wintry 2 summerlike 3 local 4 seasonal 5 springlike
263. *gregarious*   1 antisocial 2 anticipatory 3 glorious 4 horrendous 5 similar
264. *gratuitous*   1 warranted 2 frank 3 ingenuous 4 frugal 5 pithy
265. *hapless*   1 cheerful 2 consistent 3 fortunate 4 considerate 5 shapely
266. *heterogeneous*   1 orthodox 2 pagan 3 unlike 4 similar 5 banished
267. *gusto*   1 noise 2 panic 3 fancy 4 gloom 5 distaste
268. *gusty*   1 calm 2 noisy 3 fragrant 4 routine 5 gloomy
269. *haphazard*   1 fortuitous 2 indifferent 3 deliberate 4 accidental 5 conspiring
270. *hirsute*   1 scaly 2 bald 3 erudite 4 quiet 5 long
271. *gullible*   1 incredulous 2 fickle 3 tantamount 4 easy 5 stylish
272. *granulate*   1 crystallize 2 store 3 crush 4 magnify 5 sweeten
273. *gourmet*   1 cook 2 maitre d' 3 glutton 4 epicure 5 author
274. *halcyon*   1 pacific 2 prior 3 subsequent 4 puerile 5 martial
275. *gnome*   1 fairy 2 giant 3 pygmy 4 native 5 alien
276. *hilarity*   1 gloom 2 heartiness 3 weakness 4 casualty 5 paucity
277. *hackneyed*   1 carried 2 original 3 banal 4 timely 5 oratorical
278. *heretic*   1 sophist 2 believer 3 interpreter 4 pacifist 5 owner
279. *grisly*   1 unsavory 2 doubtful 3 untidy 4 pleasant 5 bearish
280. *haggard*   1 shrewish 2 inspired 3 plump 4 maidenly 5 vast

---

WORD LIST   15   **homogeneous - incarnate**

homogeneous (-jē´-nē-əs) ADJ. of the same kind. Educators try to put pupils of similar abilities into classes because they believe that this *homogeneous* grouping is advisable. homogeneity, N.

horticultural ADJ. pertaining to cultivation of gardens. When he bought his house, he began to look for flowers and decorative shrubs, and began to read books dealing with *horticultural* matters.

hostelry (hŏs´-) N. inn. Travelers interested in economy should stay at *hostelries* and pensions rather than fashionable hotels.

hubbub N. confused uproar. The marketplace was a scene of *hubbub* and excitement; in all the noise, we could not distinguish particular voices.

humane (-mān´) ADJ. kind. His *humane* and considerate

treatment of the unfortunate endeared him to all.

humdrum ADJ. dull; monotonous. After his years of adventure, he could not settle down to a *humdrum* existence.

humid ADJ. damp. He could not stand the *humid* climate and moved to a drier area.

humility N. humbleness of spirit. He spoke with a *humility* and lack of pride which impressed his listeners.

humus N. substance formed by decaying vegetable matter. In order to improve his garden, he spread *humus* over his lawn and flower beds.

hybrid N. mongrel; mixed breed. Mendel's formula explains the appearance of *hybrids* and pure species in breeding. also ADJ.

hypercritical (hī-pər-krĭt´-) ADJ. excessively exacting. You are *hypercritical* in your demands for perfection; we all

ā—ale; ă—add; ä—arm; à—ask; ē—eve; ĕ—end; ê—err, her; ə—allow; even; ī—ice; ĭ—ill; ō—oll; ò—odd; ô—orb; ōō—food; ŏŏ—foot; pụt; ou—out; th—thin; ū—use; ŭ—up; zh—pleasure

make mistakes.

hypochondriac (*hī-pə-kŏn´-*) N. person unduly worried about his health; worrier without cause about illness. The doctor prescribed chocolate pills for his patient who was a *hypochondriac.*

hypocritical (*hĭp-ə-*) ADJ. pretending to be virtuous; deceiving. I resent his *hypocritical* posing as a friend for I know he is interested only in his own advancement.

hypothetical (*hī-pə-thĕt´-*) ADJ. based on assumptions or hypotheses. Why do we have to consider *hypothetical* cases when we have actual case histories which we may examine? hypothesis, N.

iconoclastic ADJ. attacking cherished traditions. George Bernard Shaw's *iconoclastic* plays often startled people.

ideology N. ideas of a group of people. That *ideology* is dangerous to this country because it embraces undemocratic philosophies.

idiom N. special usage in language. I could not understand their *idiom* because literal translation made no sense.

idiosyncrasy N. peculiarity; eccentricity. One of his personal *idiosyncrasies* was his habit of rinsing all cutlery given him in a restaurant.

idolatry N. worship of idols; excessive admiration. Such *idolatry* of singers of popular ballads is typical of the excessive enthusiasm of youth.

igneous (*ĭg´-*) ADJ. produced by fire; volcanic. Lava, pumice, and other *igneous* rocks are found in great abundance around Mount Vesuvius near Naples.

ignoble (*ĭg-nō´-*) ADJ. of lowly origin; unworthy. This plan is inspired by *ignoble* motives and I must, therefore, oppose it.

ignominious (*-mĭn´-*) ADJ. disgraceful. The country smarted under the *ignominious* defeat and dreamed of the day when it would be victorious. ignominy, N.

illimitable ADJ. infinite. Man, having explored the far corners of the earth, is now reaching out into *illimitable* space.

illusion N. misleading vision. It is easy to create an optical *illusion* in which lines of equal length appear different. illusory, ADJ.

imbecility N. weakness of mind. I am amazed at the *imbecility* of the readers of these trashy magazines.

imbibe V. drink in. The dry soil *imbibed* the rain quickly.

imbroglio (*-brōl´-yō*) N. a complicated situation; perplexity; entanglement. He was called in to settle the *imbroglio* but failed to bring harmony into the situation.

imbue V. saturate, fill. His visits to the famous Gothic cathedrals *imbued* him with feelings of awe and reverence.

immaculate ADJ. pure; spotless. The West Point cadets were *immaculate* as they lined up for inspection.

imminent ADJ. impending; near at hand. The *imminent* battle will determine our success or failure in this conflict.

immobility N. state of being immovable. Modern armies cannot afford the luxury of *immobility,* as they are vulnerable to attack while standing still.

immolate V. offer as a sacrifice. The tribal king offered to *immolate* his daughter to quiet the angry gods.

immune ADJ. exempt. He was fortunately *immune* from the disease and could take care of the sick.

immutable ADJ. unchangeable. Scientists are constantly seeking to discover the *immutable* laws of nature.

impair V. worsen; diminish in value. This arrest will *impair* his reputation in the community.

impale V. pierce. He was *impaled* by the spear hurled by his adversary.

impasse N. predicament from which there is no escape. In this *impasse,* all turned to prayer as their last hope.

impassive ADJ. without feeling; not affected by pain. The American Indian has been incorrectly depicted as an *impassive* individual, undemonstrative and stoical.

impeach V. charge with crime in office; indict. The angry congressman wanted to *impeach* the President.

impeccable ADJ. faultless. He was proud of his *impeccable* manners.

impecunious ADJ. without money. Now that he was wealthy, he gladly contributed to funds to assist the *impecunious* and the disabled.

impending ADJ. nearing; approaching. The entire country was saddened by the news of his *impending* death.

impenitent ADJ. not repentant. We could see by his brazen attitude that he was *impenitent.*

imperious ADJ. domineering. His *imperious* manner indicated that he had long been accustomed to assuming command.

impermeable ADJ. impervious; not permitting passage through its substance. This new material is *impermeable* to liquids.

impertinent ADJ. insolent. I regard your remarks as *impertinent* and resent them.

imperturbability N. calmness. We are impressed by his *imperturbability* in this critical moment and are calmed by it.

impervious ADJ. not penetrable; not permitting passage through. You cannot change their habits for their minds are *impervious* to reasoning.

impetuous ADJ. violent; hasty; rash. We tried to curb his *impetuous* behavior because we felt that in his haste he might offend some people.

impetus (*im´-*) N. moving force. It is a miracle that there were any survivors since the two automobiles that collided were traveling with great *impetus.*

impiety (*-pī´-ət-ē*) N. irreverence; wickedness. We must regard your blasphemy as an act of *impiety.*

impious (*im-´pē-əs*) ADJ. irreverent. The congregation was offended by his *impious* remarks.

implacable (*-plăk´-*) ADJ. incapable of being pacified. Madame Defarge was the *implacable* enemy of the Evremonde family.

implication N. that which is hinted at or suggested. If I understand the *implications* of your remark, you do not trust our captain.

implicit ADJ. understood but not stated. It is *implicit* that you will come to our aid if we are attacked.

impolitic (*-pŏl´-*) ADJ. not wise. I think it is *impolitic* to raise this issue at the present time because the public is too angry.

import (*im´-*) N. significance. I feel that you have not grasped the full *import* of the message sent to us by the enemy.

importune V. beg earnestly. I must *importune* you to work for peace at this time. importunate, ADJ.

imprecate (*ĭm´-*) V. curse; pray that evil will befall. To *imprecate* Hitler's atrocities is not enough; we must insure against any future practice of genocide.

impregnable (*-prĕg´-nə-*) ADJ. invulnerable. Until the development of the airplane as a military weapon, the fort was considered *impregnable.*

impromptu (*-prŏmp´-*) ADJ. without previous preparation. His listeners were amazed that such a thorough presentation could be made in an *impromptu* speech.

impropriety (*-prī´-*) N. state of being inappropriate. Because of the *impropriety* of his costume, he was denied entrance into the dining room.

improvident ADJ. thriftless. He was constantly being warned to mend his *improvident* ways and begin to "save for a rainy day."

ā—ale; ă—add; ä—arm; à—ask, ē—eve; ĕ—end; ê—err, her; ə—allow; even; ī—ice; ĭ—ill, ō—oll; ŏ—odd; ô—orb; oo—food; oo—foot, put; ou—out; th—thin; ū—use; ŭ—up; zh—pleasure

improvise V. compose on the spur of the moment. He would sit at the piano and *improvise* for hours on themes from Bach and Handel.

impugn (-*pūn´*) V. doubt; challenge; gainsay. I cannot *impugn* your honesty without evidence.

impunity N. freedom from punishment. The bully mistreated everyone in the class with *impunity* for he felt that no one would dare retaliate.

imputation N. charge; reproach. You cannot ignore the *imputations* in his speech that you are the guilty party.

inadvertence N. oversight; carelessness. By *inadvertence,* he omitted two questions on the examination.

inalienable ADJ. not to be taken away; nontransferable. The Declaration of Independence mentions the *inalienable* rights that all of us possess.

inane (*ĭn-ān´*) ADJ. silly; senseless. Such comments are *inane* because they do not help us solve our problem. inanity, N.

inanimate ADJ. lifeless. She was asked to identify the still and *inanimate* body.

inarticulate ADJ. speechless; producing indistinct speech. He became *inarticulate* with rage and uttered sounds without meaning.

incapacitate V. disable. During the winter, many people were *incapacitated* by respiratory ailments.

incarcerate V. imprison. The warden will *incarcerate* the felon.

incarnate ADJ. endowed with flesh; personified. Your attitude is so fiendish that you must be a devil *incarnate*.

ETYMOLOGY 15

IL, ILE (pertaining to, capable of) adjective suffix

puerile pertaining to a child

ductile capable of being led
civil pertaining to a citizen

TEST—WORD LIST 15—*Synonyms and Antonyms*

Each of the questions below consists of a word printed in italics, followed by five words or phrases numbered 1 to 5. Choose the numbered word or phrase which is most nearly the same as or the opposite of the word in italics and write the number of your choice on your answer paper.

281. *immutable* 1 silent 2 changeable 3 articulate 4 loyal 5 varied
282. *incarcerate* 1 inhibit 2 acquit 3 account 4 imprison 5 force
283. *importune* 1 export 2 plead 3 exhibit 4 account 5 visit
284. *inalienable* 1 inherent 2 repugnant 3 closed to immigration 4 full 5 accountable
285. *impetuous* 1 rash 2 inane 3 just 4 flagrant 5 redolent
286. *impromptu* 1 prompted 2 appropriate 3 rehearsed 4 foolish 5 vast
287. *immolate* 1 debate 2 scour 3 sacrifice 4 sanctify 5 ratify
288. *impervious* 1 impenetrable 2 vulnerable 3 chaotic 4 cool 5 perfect
289. *impeccable* 1 unmentionable 2 quotable 3 blinding 4 faulty 5 hampering
290. *hypercritical* 1 intolerant 2 false 3 extreme 4 inarticulate 5 cautious
291. *impassive* 1 active 2 demonstrative 3 perfect 4 anxious 5 irritated
292. *impair* 1 separate 2 make amends 3 make worse 4 falsify 5 cancel
293. *immaculate* 1 chastened 2 chewed 3 sullied 4 angered 5 beaten
294. *impolitic* 1 campaigning 2 advisable 3 appropriate 4 legal 5 fortunate
295. *hubbub* 1 bedlam 2 fury 3 cap 4 axle 5 wax
296. *impecunious* 1 affluent 2 afflicted 3 affectionate 4 affable 5 afraid
297. *hypothetical* 1 logical 2 fantastic 3 wizened 4 assumed 5 axiomatic
298. *hybrid* 1 product 2 species 3 mixture 4 fish 5 genus
299. *impunity* 1 violation 2 liability 3 joke 4 play on words 5 canard
300. *inane* 1 passive 2 wise 3 intoxicated 4 mellow 5 silent

---

WORD LIST 16 **incendiary - intellect**

incendiary N. arsonist. The fire spread in such an unusual manner that the fire department chiefs were certain that it had been set by an *incendiary*. also ADJ.

incentive N. spur; motive. Students who dislike school must be given an *incentive* to learn.

incessant ADJ. uninterrupted. The crickets kept up an *incessant* chirping which disturbed our attempts to fall asleep.

inchoate (*ĭn´-kō-*) ADJ. recently begun; rudimentary; elementary. Before the Creation, the world was an *inchoate* mass.

incipient ADJ. beginning; in an early stage. I will go to sleep early for I want to break an *incipient* cold.

incisive (*-sī´-*) ADJ. cutting; sharp. His *incisive* remarks made us see the fallacy in our plans.

incite V. arouse to action. The demagogue *incited* the mob to take action into its own hands.

inclement ADJ. stormy; unkind. I like to read a good book in *inclement* weather.

inclusive ADJ. tending to include all. This meeting will run from January 10 to February 15 *inclusive*.

incognito (*-nēt´-*) ADV. with identity concealed; using an assumed name. The monarch enjoyed traveling through

ā—ale; ă—add; ä—arm; à—ask; ē—eve; ĕ—end; ê—err, her; ə—allow; even; ī—ice; ĭ—ill; ō—oll; ŏ—odd; ô—orb; o͞o—food; o͝o—foot, put; ou—out; th—thin; ū—use; ŭ—up; zh—pleasure

the town *incognito* and mingling with the populace. also ADJ.

incommodious (-*mōd´*-) ADJ. not spacious. In their *incommodious* quarters, they had to improvise for closet space.

incompatible ADJ. inharmonious. The married couple argued incessantly and finally decided to separate because they were *incompatible.*

incongruity (-*grōō´*-) N. lack of harmony; absurdity. The *incongruity* of his wearing sneakers with formal attire amused the observers.

inconsequential (-*kwĕn´*-) ADJ. of trifling significance. Your objections are *inconsequential* and may be disregarded.

incontrovertible (-*vêrt´*-) ADJ. indisputable. We must yield to the *incontrovertible* evidence which you have presented and free your client.

incorporeal (-*pôr´-ē-*) ADJ. immaterial; without a material body. We must devote time to the needs of our *incorporeal* mind as well as our corporeal body.

incorrigible (-*kôr´*-) ADJ. uncorrectable. Because he was an *incorrigible* criminal, he was sentenced to life imprisonment.

incredulity (-*dū´*-) N. a tendency to disbelief. Your *incredulity* in the face of all the evidence is hard to understand.

increment N. increase. The new contract calls for a 10 percent *increment* in salary for each employee for the next two years.

incriminate V. accuse. The evidence gathered against the racketeers *incriminates* some high public officials as well.

incubate V. hatch; scheme. Inasmuch as our supply of electricity is cut off, we shall have to rely on the hens to *incubate* these eggs.

incubus N. burden; mental care; nightmare. The *incubus* of financial worry helped bring on his nervous breakdown.

inculcate V. teach. In an effort to *inculcate* religious devotion, the officials ordered that the school day begin with the singing of a hymn.

incumbent N. officeholder. The newly elected public official received valuable advice from the present *incumbent.* also ADJ.

incursion N. temporary invasion. The nightly *incursions* and hit-and-run raids of our neighbors across the border tried the patience of the country to the point where we decided to retaliate in force.

indefatigable (-*făt´*-) ADJ. tireless. He was *indefatigable* in his constant efforts to raise funds for the Red Cross.

indemnify V. make secure against loss; compensate for loss. The city will *indemnify* all home owners whose property is spoiled by this project.

indenture V. bind as servant or apprentice to master. Many immigrants could come to America only after they had *indentured* themselves for several years. also N.

indict (-*dīt´*) V. charge. If the grand jury *indicts* the suspect, he will go to trial.

indigenous (-*dĭj´-ə-*) ADJ. native. Tobacco is one of the *indigenous* plants which the early explorers found in this country.

indigent (*ĭn´*-) ADJ. poor. Because he was *indigent,* he was sent to the welfare office.

indignity N. offensive or insulting treatment. Although he seemed to accept cheerfully the *indignities* heaped upon him, he was inwardly very angry.

indisputable (-*pūt´*-) ADJ. too certain to be disputed. In the face of these *indisputable* statements, I withdraw my complaint.

indite V. write; compose. Cyrano *indited* many letters for Christian.

indolence (*ĭn´*-) N. laziness. The sultry weather in the tropics encourages a life of *indolence.*

indomitable ADJ. unconquerable. The founders of our country had *indomitable* willpower.

indubitably ADV. beyond a doubt. Because his argument was *indubitably* valid, the judge accepted it.

indulgent ADJ. humoring; yielding; lenient. An *indulgent* parent may spoil a child by creating an artificial atmosphere of leniency.

ineffable ADJ. unutterable; cannot be expressed in speech. Such *ineffable* joy must be experienced; it cannot be described.

inept ADJ. unsuited; absurd; incompetent. The constant turmoil in the office proved that he was an *inept* administrator.

inexorable (-*ĕks´*-) ADJ. relentless; unyielding; implacable. After listening to the pleas for clemency, the judge was *inexorable* and gave the convicted man the maximum punishment allowed by law.

infallible ADJ. unerring. We must remember that none of us is *infallible.*

infamous (*ĭn´*-) ADJ. notoriously bad. Jesse James was an *infamous* outlaw.

inference N. conclusion drawn from data. I want you to check this *inference* because it may have been based on insufficient information.

infinitesimal ADJ. very small. In the twentieth century, physicists have made their greatest discoveries about the characteristics of *infinitesimal* objects like the atom and its parts.

infirmity N. weakness. His greatest *infirmity* was lack of willpower.

inflated ADJ. enlarged (with air or gas). After the balloons were *inflated,* they were distributed among the children.

influx N. flowing into. The *influx* of refugees into the country has taxed the relief agencies severely.

infraction N. violation. Because of his many *infractions* of school regulations, he was suspended by the dean.

infringe V. violate; encroach. I think your machine *infringes* on my patent.

ingenuous (-*jĕn´-ū-*) ADJ. naive; young; unsophisticated. These remarks indicate that you are *ingenuous* and unaware of life's harsher realities.

ingrate N. ungrateful person. You are an *ingrate* since you have treated my gifts with scorn.

ingratiate (-*grā´*-) V. become popular with. He tried to *ingratiate* himself into her parents' good graces.

inherent (-*hĭr´*-) ADJ. firmly established by nature or habit. His *inherent* love of justice compelled him to come to their aid.

inhibit V. prohibit; restrain. The child was not *inhibited* in his responses. inhibition, N.

inimical (*ĭn-ĭm´*-) ADJ. unfriendly; hostile. She felt that they were *inimical* and were hoping for her downfall.

iniquitous ADJ. unjust; wicked. I cannot approve of the *iniquitous* methods you used to gain your present position. iniquity, N.

inkling N. hint. This came as a complete surprise to me as I did not have the slightest *inkling* of your plans.

innate ADJ. inborn. His *innate* talent for music was soon recognized by his parents.

innocuous ADJ. harmless. Let him drink it; it is *innocuous.*

innovation N. change; introduction of something new. He loved *innovations* just because they were new.

innuendo (*ĭn-ū-ĕn´*-) N. hint; insinuation. I resent the *innuendos* in your statement more than the statement itself.

inordinate ADJ. unrestrained; excessive. She had an *inordi-*

ā—ale; ă—add; ä—arm; à—ask, ē—eve; ĕ—end; ê—err, her; ə—allow; even; ī—ice; ĭ—ill; ō—oll; ŏ—odd; ô—orb; ōō—food; ŏŏ—foot, put; ou—out; th—thin; ū—use; ŭ—up; zh—pleasure

nate fondness for candy.

insatiable ADJ. not easily satisfied; greedy. His thirst for knowledge was *insatiable;* he was always in the library.

inscrutable ADJ. incomprehensible; not to be discovered. I fail to understand the reasons for your outlandish behavior; your motives are *inscrutable.*

insensate (-sĕn´-) ADJ. without feeling. He lay there as *insensate* as a log.

insidious ADJ. treacherous; stealthy; sly. The fifth column is *insidious* because it works secretly within our territory for our defeat.

insinuate V. hint; imply. What are you trying to *insinuate* by that remark?

insipid ADJ. tasteless; dull. I am bored by your *insipid* talk.

insolent ADJ. haughty and contemptuous. I resent your *insolent* manner.

insolvency N. bankruptcy; lack of ability to repay debts. When rumors of his *insolvency* reached his creditors, they began to press him for payment of the money due them.

insomnia N. wakefulness; inability to sleep. He refused to join us in a midnight cup of coffee because he claimed it gave him *insomnia.*

instigate V. urge; start; provoke. I am afraid that this statement will *instigate* a revolt.

insular ADJ. like an island; narrow-minded. In an age of such rapid means of communication, we cannot afford to be hemmed in by such *insular* ideas.

insuperable ADJ. insurmountable; invincible. In the face of *insuperable* difficulties they maintained their courage and will to resist.

insurgent ADJ. rebellious. We will not discuss reforms until the *insurgent* troops have returned to their homes. also N.

integrate V. make whole; combine; make into one unit. He tried to *integrate* all their activities into one program.

integrity N. wholeness; purity; uprightness. He was a man of great *integrity.*

intellect N. higher mental powers. He thought college would develop his *intellect.*

ETYMOLOGY 16

IN (in, into, upon, toward) prefix

incursion invasion
insidious treacherous

IN (not, without) prefix
inconsequential not significant
inimical hostile, not friendly
insipid tasteless

TEST—WORD LIST 16—*Synonyms*

Each of the questions below consists of a word printed in italics, followed by five words or phrases numbered 1 to 5. Choose the numbered word or phrase which is most nearly similar in meaning to the word in italics and write the number of your choice on your answer paper.

301. *incentive* 1 objective 2 goad 3 stimulation 4 beginning 5 simulation
302. *indubitably* 1 flagrantly 2 doubtfully 3 carefully 4 carelessly 5 certainly
303. *inconsequential* 1 disorderly 2 insignificant 3 subsequent 4 insufficient 5 preceding
304. *insinuate* 1 resist 2 suggest 3 report 4 rectify 5 lecture
305. *incorrigible* 1 narrow 2 straight 3 inconceivable 4 unreliable 5 unreformable
306. *ingenuous* 1 clever 2 stimulating 3 naive 4 wily 5 cautious
307. *indolence* 1 sloth 2 poverty 3 latitude 4 aptitude 5 anger
308. *innocuous* 1 not capable 2 not dangerous 3 not eager 4 not frank 5 not peaceful

309. *insipid* 1 witty 2 flat 3 wily 4 talkative 5 lucid
310. *incompatible* 1 capable 2 reasonable 3 faulty 4 indifferent 5 alienated
311. *incriminate* 1 exacerbate 2 involve 3 intimidate 4 lacerate 5 prevaricate
312. *infirmity* 1 disability 2 age 3 inoculation 4 hospital 5 unity
313. *infallible* 1 final 2 unbelievable 3 perfect 4 inaccurate 5 inquisitive
314. *indigent* 1 lazy 2 pusillanimous 3 penurious 4 affluent 5 contrary
315. *inclement* 1 unfavorable 2 abandoned 3 kindly 4 selfish 5 active
316. *integrate* 1 tolerate 2 unite 3 flow 4 copy 5 assume
317. *inimical* 1 antagonistic 2 anonymous 3 fanciful 4 accurate 5 seldom
318. *inculcate* 1 exculpate 2 educate 3 exonerate 4 prepare 5 embarrass
319. *indignity* 1 pomposity 2 bombast 3 obeisance 4 insult 5 message
320. *insensate* 1 aggrieved 2 unconcerned 3 angered 4 patent 5 prehensile

WORD LIST 17 intelligentsia - levity

intelligentsia N. the intelligent and educated classes [often used derogatorily]. He preferred discussions about sports and politics to the literary conversations of the *intelligentsia*.

inter (-têr´) V. bury. They are going to *inter* the body tomorrow.

interim N. meantime. The company will not consider our proposal until next week; in the *interim*, let us proceed as we have in the past.

interment (-têr´-) N. burial. *Interment* will take place in the church cemetery at 2 P.M. Wednesday.

interminable ADJ. endless. Although his speech lasted for only twenty minutes, it seemed *interminable* to his bored audience.

intermittent ADJ. periodic; on and off. Our picnic was marred by *intermittent* rains.

intimate V. hint. She *intimated* rather than stated her preferences.

intimidation (-dā´-) N. fear. A ruler who maintains his power by *intimidation* is bound to develop clandestine resistance.

intransigent (-jənt) ADJ. refusing any compromise. The strike settlement has collapsed because both sides are *intransigent*.

intrepid (-trĕp´-) ADJ. fearless. For his *intrepid* conduct in battle, he was promoted.

intrinsic ADJ. belonging to a thing in itself; inherent. Although the *intrinsic* value of this award is small, I shall always cherish it.

introvert N. one who is introspective; inclined to think more about oneself. In his poetry, he reveals that he is an *introvert* by his intense interest in his own problems. also V.

intrude V. trespass; enter as an uninvited person. He hesitated to *intrude* on their conversation.

intuition N. power of knowing without reasoning. She claimed to know the truth by *intuition*. intuitive, ADJ.

inundate V. overflow; flood. The tremendous waves *inundated* the town.

inured ADJ. accustomed; hardened. He became *inured* to the Alaskan cold.

invective N. abuse. He had expected criticism but not the *invective* which greeted his proposal.

inveigle (-vā´-) V. lead astray; wheedle. He was *inveigled* into joining the club.

inverse ADJ. opposite. There is an *inverse* ratio between the strength of light and its distance.

inveterate ADJ. deep-rooted; habitual. He is an *inveterate* smoker.

invidious ADJ. designed to create ill will or envy. We disregarded her *invidious* remarks because we realized how jealous she was.

inviolability (-vī-ə-lə-bĭl´-) N. security from being destroyed, corrupted or profaned. They respected the *inviolability* of her faith and did not try to change her manner of living.

invulnerable ADJ. incapable of injury. Achilles was *invulnerable* except in his heel.

iota (ī-ōt´-ə) N. very small quantity. He hadn't an *iota* of common sense.

irascible (ĭr-ăs´-ə-bəl) ADJ. irritable; easily angered. His *irascible* temper frightened me.

iridescent (-dĕs´-) ADJ. exhibiting rainbowlike colors. He admired the *iridescent* hues of the oil that floated on the surface of the water.

ironical (-rŏn´-) ADJ. resulting in an unexpected and contrary manner. It is *ironical* that his success came when he least wanted it. irony, N.

irreconcilable ADJ. incompatible; not able to be resolved. Because the separated couple were *irreconcilable*, the marriage counselor recommended a divorce.

irrelevant (-rĕl´-) ADJ. not applicable; unrelated. This statement is *irrelevant* and should be disregarded by the jury.

irremediable (-mĕd´-) ADJ. incurable; uncorrectable. The error he made was *irremediable*.

irreparable (-rĕp´-) ADJ. not able to be corrected or repaired. Your apology cannot atone for the *irreparable* damage you have done to his reputation.

irreverent ADJ. lacking proper respect. The worshippers resented his *irreverent* remarks about their faith.

irrevocable (-rĕv´-) ADJ. unalterable. Let us not brood over past mistakes since they are *irrevocable*.

iterate (ĭt´-) V. utter a second time; repeat. I will *iterate* the warning I have previously given to you.

itinerant (ī-tĭn´-) ADJ. wandering; traveling. He was an *itinerant* peddler and traveled through Pennsylvania and Virginia selling his wares. also N.

jaded ADJ. fatigued; surfeited. He looked for exotic foods to stimulate his *jaded* appetite.

jargon N. language used by special group; gibberish. We tried to understand the *jargon* of the peddlers in the market-place but could not find any basis for comprehension.

jaundiced ADJ. yellowed; prejudiced; envious. He gazed at the painting with *jaundiced* eyes.

jeopardy (jĕp´-) N. exposure to death or danger. He cannot be placed in double *jeopardy*.

jettison V. throw overboard. In order to enable the ship to ride safely through the storm, the captain had to *jettison* much of his cargo.

jingoism N. extremely aggressive and militant patriotism. We must be careful to prevent a spirit of *jingoism* from spreading at this time; the danger of a disastrous war is too great.

jocose (jō-kōs´) ADJ. giving to joking. The salesman was so *jocose* that many of his customers suggested that he become a "stand-up" comic.

jocular (jŏk´-) ADJ. said or done in jest. Do not take my *jocular* remarks seriously.

jocund ADJ. merry. Santa Claus is always vivacious and *jocund*.

jubilation N. rejoicing. There was great *jubilation* when the armistice was announced.

judicious ADJ. wise; determined by sound judgment. I believe that this plan is not *judicious*; it is too risky.

junket N. a merry feast or picnic. The opposition claimed that his trip to Europe was merely a political *junket*.

junta (hŏŏn´-tə) N. group of men joined in political intrigue; cabal. As soon as he learned of its existence, the dictator ordered the execution of all of the members of the *junta*.

ken N. range of knowledge. I cannot answer your question since this matter is beyond my *ken*.

kiosk (kē´-ŏsk) N. summerhouse; open pavilion. She waited at the subway *kiosk*.

kismet N. fate. *Kismet* is the Arabic word for "fate."

kith N. familiar friends. He always helped both his *kith* and kin.

kleptomaniac N. person who has a compulsive desire to

ā—ale; ă—add; ä—arm; à—ask; ē—eve; ĕ—end; ê—err, her; ə—allow; even; ī—ice; ĭ—ill; ō—oll; ŏ—odd; ô—orb; ōō—food; ŏŏ—foot, put; ou—out; th—thin; ū—use; ŭ—up; zh—pleasure

steal. They discovered that the wealthy customer was a *kleptomaniac* when they caught her stealing some cheap trinkets.

knavery N. rascality. We cannot condone such *knavery* in public officials.

knell N. tolling of a bell at a funeral; sound of the funeral bell. "The curfew tolls the *knell* of parting day."

knoll N. little round hill. Robert Louis Stevenson's grave is on a *knoll* in Samoa.

labyrinth N. maze. Tom and Betty were lost in the *labyrinth* of secret caves.

lacerate (*lăs´-ə-*) V. mangle; tear. Her body was *lacerated* in the automobile crash.

lackadaisical ADJ. affectedly languid. He was *lackadaisical* and indifferent about his part in the affair.

lackey N. footman; toady. The duke was followed by his *lackeys.*

laconic ADJ. brief and to the point. Will Rogers' *laconic* comments on the news made him world famous.

laggard ADJ. slow; sluggish. The sailor had been taught not to be *laggard* in carrying out orders.

lagniappe (*lăn-yăp´*) N. trifling present given to a customer. The butcher threw in some bones for the dog as a *lagniappe.*

lagoon N. shallow body of water near a sea; lake. They enjoyed their swim in the calm *lagoon.*

laity (*lā´-ĭ-tē*) N. laymen; persons not connected with the clergy. The *laity* does not always understand the clergy's problems.

lambent ADJ. flickering; softly radiant. They sat quietly before the *lambent* glow of the fireplace.

laminated ADJ. made of thin plates or scales. Banded gneiss is a *laminated* rock.

lampoon V. ridicule. This article *lampoons* the pretensions of some movie moguls. also N.

languid ADJ. weary; sluggish; listless. Her siege of illness left her *languid* and pallid.

languish V. lose animation; lose strength. In stories, lovelorn damsels used to *languish* and pine away.

lapidary N. worker in precious stones. He employed a *lapidary* to cut the large diamond.

largess (*lär´-zhĕs*) N. generous gift. Lady Bountiful distributed *largess* to the poor.

lascivious ADJ. lustful. The *lascivious* books were confiscated and destroyed.

lassitude N. languor; weariness. The hot, tropical weather created a feeling of *lassitude* and encouraged drowsiness.

latent (*lāt´-*) ADJ. dormant; hidden. His *latent* talent was discovered by accident.

lateral ADJ. coming from the side. In order to get good plant growth, the gardener must pinch off all *lateral* shoots.

latitude N. freedom from narrow limitations. I think you have permitted your son too much *latitude* in this matter.

laudatory ADJ. expressing praise. The critics' *laudatory* comments helped to make her a star.

lave (*lāv*) V. wash. The running water will *lave* away all stains.

lavish ADJ. liberal; wasteful. The actor's *lavish* gifts pleased her. also V.

lecherous ADJ. impure in thought and act; lustful; unchaste. He is a *lecherous* and wicked old man.

lesion N. unhealthy change in structure; injury. Many *lesions* are the result of disease.

lethal ADJ. deadly. It is unwise to leave *lethal* weapons where children may find them.

lethargic (*lə-thär´-*) ADJ. drowsy; dull. The stuffy room made him *lethargic.*

levity N. lightness. Such *levity* is improper on this serious occasion.

ETYMOLOGY 17

INTER (between, among) prefix

intervene come between
international between nations
interjection a statement thrown in

IST (one who practices) noun suffix

humorist one who provides humor
specialist one who engages in a specialty
optimist one who is hopeful

IT, ITINER (journey, road)

exit way out
itinerary plan of journey
itinerant traveling from place to place

ITY (state of being) noun suffix

annuity state of being paid yearly
credulity state of being gullible
sagacity wisdom

IZE, ISE (to make) verb suffix

victimize make a victim
rationalize reason
harmonize make peaceful

JAC, JACT, JEC (to throw)

projectile missile; something thrown forward
trajectory path taken by thrown object
reject throw back

JUR, JURAT (to swear)

abjure renounce
perjure testify falsely
jury group of men sworn to seek the truth

LABOR, LABORAT (to work)

laboratory place where work is done
collaborate work together with others
laborious difficult

LEG, LECT (to choose, to read)

election choice
legible able to be read
eligible able to be selected

LEG (law)

legislature law-making body
legitimate lawful
gal lawful

TEST—WORD LIST 17—*Antonyms*

Each of the questions below consists of a word printed in italics, followed by five words or phrases numbered 1 to 5. Choose the numbered word or phrase which is most nearly opposite in meaning to the word in italics and write the number of your choice on your answer paper.

321. *intermittent* 1 heavy 2 fleeting 3 constant 4 fearless 5 responding
322. *irreverent* 1 related 2 mischievous 3 respecting 4 pious 5 violent
323. *inundate* 1 abuse 2 deny 3 swallow 4 treat 5 drain
324. *laconic* 1 milky 2 verbose 3 wicked 4 flagrant 5 derelict
325. *inter* 1 exhume 2 amuse 3 relate 4 frequent 5 abandon
326. *latent* 1 hidden 2 forbidding 3 execrable 4 early 5 obvious
327. *intransigent* 1 stationary 2 yielding 3 incorruptible 4 magnificent 5 grandiose
328. *jaded* 1 upright 2 stimulated 3 aspiring 4 applied 5 void
329. *levity* 1 bridge 2 dam 3 praise 4 blame 5 solemnity

330. *inveterate* 1 inexperienced 2 sophisticated 3 professional 4 wicked 5 ascetic
331. *lampoon* 1 darken 2 praise 3 abandon 4 sail 5 fly
332. *irrelevant* 1 lacking piety 2 fragile 3 congruent 4 pertinent 5 varied
333. *intrepid* 1 cold 2 hot 3 understood 4 callow 5 craven
334. *intrinsic* 1 extrinsic 2 abnormal 3 above 4 abandoned 5 basic
335. *lackadaisical* 1 monthly 2 possessing time 3 ambitious 4 pusillanimous 5 intelligent
336. *lethargic* 1 convalescent 2 beautiful 3 enervating 4 invigorating 5 interrogating
337. *inured* 1 accustomed 2 fitted 3 intestate 4 futile 5 inexperienced
338. *jaundiced* 1 whitened 2 inflamed 3 quickened 4 aged 5 unbiased
339. *kith* 1 outfit 2 strangers 3 brothers 4 ceramics tool 5 quality
340. *laudatory* 1 dirtying 2 disclaiming 3 defamatory 4 inflammatory 5 debased

WORD LIST 18 **lewd - mendicant**

lewd ADJ. lustful. They found his *lewd* stories objectionable.

lexicon N. dictionary. I cannot find this word in any *lexicon* in the library. lexicographer, N.

liaison (*lē´-ə-zän*) N. officer who acts as go-between for two armies. As the *liaison,* he had to avoid offending the leaders of the two armies. also ADJ.

libelous ADJ. defamatory; injurious to the good name of a person. He sued the newspaper because of its *libelous* story.

libertine N. debauched person, roué. Although she was aware of his reputation as a *libertine,* she felt she could reform him and help him break his dissolute way of life.

libidinous (*-bĭd´-*) ADJ. lustful. They objected to his *libidinous* behavior.

libretto N. text of an opera. The composer of an opera's music is remembered more frequently than the author of its *libretto.*

licentious ADJ. wanton; lewd; dissolute. The *licentious* monarch helped bring about his country's downfall.

lieu (*lōō*) N. instead of. They accepted his check in *lieu* of cash.

limn (*lĭm*) V. portray; describe vividly. He was never satisfied with his attempts to *limn* her beauty on canvas.

limpid ADJ. clear. A *limpid* stream ran through his property.

linguistic ADJ. pertaining to language. The modern tourist will encounter very little *linguistic* difficulty as English has become an almost universal language.

liquidate V. settle accounts; clear up. He was able to *liquidate* all his debts in a short period of time.

lithe (*līth*) ADJ. flexible; supple. Her figure was *lithe* and willowy.

litigation N. lawsuit. Try to settle this amicably; I do not want to start *litigation.*

livid ADJ. lead-colored; black and blue; enraged. His face was so *livid* with rage that we were afraid that he might have an attack of apoplexy.

loath (*lōth*) ADJ. averse; reluctant. They were both *loath* for him to go.

loathe V. detest. We *loathed* the wicked villain.

lode N. metal-bearing vein. If this *lode* which we have discovered extends for any distance, we have found a fortune.

longevity (*-jĕv´-*) N. long life. The old man was proud of his *longevity.*

lope V. gallop slowly. As the horses *loped* along, we had an opportunity to admire the ever-changing scenery.

loquacious ADJ. talkative. She is very *loquacious* and can speak on the telephone for hours.

lout N. clumsy person. The delivery boy is an awkward *lout.*

lucent ADJ. shining. The moon's *lucent* rays silvered the river.

lucid ADJ. bright; easily understood. His explanation was *lucid* and to the point.

lucrative ADJ. profitable. He turned his hobby into a *lucrative* profession.

lucre N. money. Preferring *lucre* to fame, he wrote stories of popular appeal.

lugubrious ADJ. mournful. The *lugubrious* howling of the dogs added to our sadness.

luminous ADJ. shining; issuing light. The sun is a *luminous* body.

lunar ADJ. pertaining to the moon. *Lunar* craters can be plainly seen with the aid of a small telescope.

lurid ADJ. wild; sensational. The *lurid* stories he told shocked his listeners.

luscious ADJ. pleasing to taste or smell. The ripe peach was *luscious.*

luster N. shine; gloss. The soft *luster* of the silk in the dim light was pleasing.

lustrous ADJ. shining. Her large and *lustrous* eyes gave a touch of beauty to an otherwise drab face.

luxuriant ADJ. fertile; abundant; ornate. Farming was easy in this *luxuriant* soil.

macabre (*-käb´-*) ADJ. gruesome; grisly. The city morgue is a *macabre* spot for the uninitiated.

macerate (*mas´-*) V. waste away. Cancer *macerated* his body.

ā—ale; ă—add; ä—arm; à—ask, ē—eve; ĕ—end; ê—err, her; ə—allow; even; ī—ice; ĭ—ill; ō—oll; ŏ—odd; ô—orb; ōō—food; ŏŏ—foot, put; ou—out; th—thin; ū—use; ŭ—up; zh—pleasure

Machiavellian (*măk-ē-ə-vĕl´-*) ADJ. crafty; double-dealing. I do not think he will be a good ambassador because he is not accustomed to the *Machiavellian* maneuverings of foreign diplomats.

machinations (*măk-ə-nā´-*) N. schemes. I can see through your wily *machinations*.

madrigal N. pastoral song. His program of folk songs included several *madrigals* which he sang to the accompaniment of a lute.

maelstrom (*māl´-*) N. whirlpool. The canoe was tossed about in the *maelstrom*.

magnanimous ADJ. generous. The philanthropist was most *magnanimous*.

magnate N. person of prominence or influence. The steel *magnate* decided to devote more time to city politics.

magniloquent ADJ. boastful, pompous. In their stories of the trial, the reporters ridiculed the *magniloquent* speeches of the defense attorney.

magnitude N. greatness; extent. It is difficult to comprehend the *magnitude* of his crime.

maim V. mutilate; injure. The hospital could not take care of all who had been wounded or *maimed* in the railroad accident.

malediction N. curse. The witch uttered *maledictions* against her captors.

malefactor N. criminal. We must try to bring these *malefactors* to justice.

malevolent ADJ. wishing evil. We must thwart his *malevolent* schemes.

malicious ADJ. dictated by hatred or spite. The *malicious* neighbor spread the gossip.

malign (*-līn´*) V. speak evil of; defame. Because of her hatred of the family, she *maligns* all who are friendly to them.

malignant (*-līg´-*) ADJ. having an evil influence; virulent. This is a *malignant* disease; we may have to use drastic measures to stop its spread.

malingerer (*-līng´-gər-*) N. one who feigns illness to escape duty. The captain ordered the sergeant to punish all *malingerers*.

mall N. public walk. The *Mall* in Central Park has always been a favorite spot for Sunday strollers.

malleable (*măl´-*) ADJ. capable of being shaped by pounding. Gold is a *malleable* metal.

mammoth ADJ. gigantic. The *mammoth* corporations of the twentieth century are a mixed blessing.

mandatory ADJ. obligatory. These instructions are *mandatory*; any violation will be severely punished.

maniacal (*-nī´-*) ADJ. raving mad. His *maniacal* laughter frightened us.

manifest ADJ. understandable; clear. His evil intentions were *manifest* and yet we could not stop him. also V.

manifesto N. declaration; statement of policy. This statement may be regarded as the *manifesto* of the party's policy.

manipulate V. operate with the hands. How do you *manipulate* these puppets?

marauder N. raider; intruder. The sounding of the alarm frightened the *marauders*.

marital ADJ. pertaining to marriage. After the publication of his book on *marital* affairs, he was often consulted by married people on the verge of divorce.

maritime ADJ. bordering on the sea; nautical. The *Maritime* Provinces depend on the sea for their wealth.

marrow N. soft tissue filling the bones. The frigid cold chilled the traveler to the *marrow*.

martial ADJ. warlike. The sound of *martial* music is always inspiring.

martinet N. strict disciplinarian. The commanding officer was a *martinet* who observed each regulation to the letter.

masticate V. chew. We must *masticate* our food carefully and slowly in order to avoid stomach disorders.

maternal ADJ. motherly. Many animals display *maternal* instincts only while their offspring are young and helpless.

matricide N. murder of a mother by a child. A crime such as *matricide* is inconceivable.

matrix (*mā´-*) N. mold or die. The cast around the *matrix* was cracked.

maudlin ADJ. effusively sentimental. I do not like such *maudlin* pictures. I call them tearjerkers.

mausoleum (*-lē´-*) N. monumental tomb. His body was placed in the family *mausoleum*.

mauve (*mōv*) ADJ. pale purple. The *mauve* tint in the lilac bush was another indication that Spring had finally arrived.

maxim N. proverb; a truth pithily stated. Aesop's fables illustrate moral *maxims*.

meander V. to wind or turn in its course. It is difficult to sail up this stream because of the way it *meanders* through the countryside.

meddlesome ADJ. interfering. He felt his marriage was suffering because of his *meddlesome* mother-in-law.

mediate V. settle a dispute through the services of an outsider. Let us *mediate* our differences rather than engage in a costly strike.

mediocre ADJ. ordinary; commonplace. We were disappointed because he gave a rather *mediocre* performance in this role.

meditation N. reflection; thought. She reached her decision only after much *meditation*.

medley N. mixture. The band played a *medley* of Gershwin tunes.

melee (*mā´-lā*) N. fight. The captain tried to ascertain the cause of the *melee* which had broken out among the crew members.

mellifluous ADJ. flowing smoothly; smooth. Italian is a *mellifluous* language.

memento N. token; reminder. Take this book as a *memento* of your visit.

memorialize V. commemorate. Let us *memorialize* his great contribution by dedicating this library in his honor.

mendacious (*-dā´-*) ADJ. lying; false. He was a pathological liar, and his friends learned to discount his *mendacious* stories.

mendicant N. beggar. From the moment we left the ship, we were surrounded by *mendicants* and peddlers.

ETYMOLOGY 18

LIB, LIBR, LIBER (book)

library collection of books
libretto the "book" of a musical play
libel slander (originally found in a little book)

LOQU, LOCUT (to talk)

soliloquy speech by one individual

ā—ale; ă—add; ä—arm; à—ask; ē—eve; ĕ—end; ê—err, her; ə—allow; even; ī—ice; ĭ—ill; ō—oll; ŏ—odd; ô—orb; ōō—food; ŏŏ—foot, put; ou—out; th—thin; ū—use; ŭ—up; zh—pleasure

loquacious talkative
elocution speech

LUC (light)

elucidate enlighten
lucid clear
translucent allowing some light to pass through

MAL (bad) prefix

malevolent evil (wishing bad)
malediction curse (state of saying evil)

malefactor evildoer

MAN (hand)

manufacture create (make by hand)
manuscript writing by hand
emancipate free (to let go from the hand)

MAR (sea)

maritime connected with seafaring
submarine undersea craft
mariner seaman

TEST—WORD LIST 18—*Synonyms and Antonyms*

Each of the questions below consists of a word printed in italics, followed by five words or phrases numbered 1 to 5. Choose the numbered word or phrase which is most nearly the same as or the opposite of the word in italics and write the number of your choice on your answer paper.

341. *magnitude*   1 realization 2 fascination 3 enormity 4 gratitude 5 interference
342. *maniacal*   1 demoniac 2 saturated 3 sane 4 sanitary 5 handcuffed
343. *loquacious*   1 taciturn 2 sentimental 3 soporific 4 soothing 5 sedate
344. *malefactor*   1 quail 2 lawbreaker 3 beneficiary 4 banker 5 female agent
345. *mellifluous*   1 porous 2 honeycombed 3 strong 4 strident 5 viscous
346. *limpid*   1 erect 2 turbid 3 tangential 4 timid 5 weary
347. *mediocre*   1 average 2 bitter 3 medieval 4 industrial 5 agricultural
348. *macabre*   1 musical 2 frightening 3 chewed 4 wicked 5 exceptional
349. *malign*   1 intersperse 2 vary 3 emphasize 4 frighten 5 eulogize
350. *lithe*   1 stiff 2 limpid 3 facetious 4 insipid 5 vast
351. *lurid*   1 dull 2 duplicate 3 heavy 4 grotesque 5 intelligent
352. *malevolent*   1 kindly 2 vacuous 3 ambivalent 4 volatile 5 primitive
353. *manifest*   1 limited 2 obscure 3 faulty 4 varied 5 vital
354. *loath*   1 loose 2 evident 3 deliberate 4 eager 5 tiny
355. *malediction*   1 misfortune 2 hap 3 fruition 4 correct pronunciation 5 benediction
356. *magniloquent*   1 loquacious 2 bombastic 3 rudimentary 4 qualitative 5 minimizing
357. *lugubrious*   1 frantic 2 cheerful 3 burdensome 4 oily 5 militant
358. *malleable*   1 brittle 2 blatant 3 brilliant 4 brownish 5 basking
359. *martial*   1 bellicose 2 celibate 3 divorced 4 quiescent 5 planetary
360. *livid*   1 alive 2 mundane 3 positive 4 purplish 5 vast

---

WORD LIST 19   menial - nadir

menial ADJ. suitable for servants; low. I cannot understand why a person of your ability and talent should engage in such *menial* activities. also N.

mentor N. teacher. During this very trying period, he could not have had a better *mentor,* for the teacher was sympathetic and understanding.

mercantile ADJ. concerning trade. I am more interested in the opportunities available in the *mercantile* field than I am in those in the legal profession.

mercenary ADJ. interested in money or gain. I am certain that your action was prompted by *mercenary* motives. also N.

mercurial ADJ. fickle; changing. He was of a *mercurial* temperament and therefore unpredictable.

meretricious (*mĕr-ə-trĭsh´-*) ADJ. flashy; tawdry. Her jewels were inexpensive but not *meretricious.*

meringue (*mə-răng´*) N. a pastry decoration made of white of eggs. The lemon *meringue* pie is one of our specialties.

mesa (*mā-sə*) N. high, flat-topped hill. The *mesa,* rising above the surrounding countryside, was the most conspicuous feature of the area.

metallurgical ADJ. pertaining to the art of removing metals from ores. During the course of his *metallurgical* research, the scientist developed a steel alloy of tremendous strength.

metamorphosis N. change of form. The *metamorphosis* of caterpillar to butterfly is typical of many such changes in animal life.

metaphysical ADJ. pertaining to speculative philosophy. The modern poets have gone back to the fanciful poems of the *metaphysical* poets of the seventeenth century for many of their images. metaphysics, N.

mete (*mēt*) V. measure; distribute. He tried to be impartial in his efforts to *mete* out justice.

meticulous ADJ. excessively careful. He was *meticulous* in checking his accounts.

metropolis N. large city. Every evening this terminal is filled with the thousands of commuters who are going from this *metropolis* to their homes in the suburbs.

mettle N. courage; spirit. When challenged by the other horses in the race, the thoroughbred proved its *mettle* by its determination to hold the lead.

mews N. group of stables built around a courtyard. Let us

ā—ale; ă—add; ä—arm; à—ask, ē—eve; ĕ—end; ê—err, her; ə—allow; even; ī—ice; ĭ—ill; ō—oll; ŏ—odd; ô—orb; ōo—food; ŏŏ—foot, put; ou—out; th—thin; ū—use; ŭ—up; zh—pleasure

visit the *mews* to inspect the newly purchased horse.

mien (*mēn*) N. demeanor; bearing. She had the gracious *mien* of a queen.

migrant ADJ. changing its habitat; wandering. These *migrant* birds return every spring. also N.

migratory ADJ. wandering. The return of the *migratory* birds to the northern sections of this country is a harbinger of spring.

militate V. work against. Your record of lateness and absence will *militate* against your chances of promotion.

mincing ADJ. affectedly dainty. Yum-Yum walked across the stage with *mincing* steps.

mirage (*-räzh´*) N. unreal reflection; optical illusion. The lost prospector was fooled by a *mirage* in the desert.

misadventure N. mischance; ill luck. The young explorer met death by *misadventure.*

misanthrope N. one who hates mankind. We thought the hermit was a *misanthrope* because he shunned our society.

misapprehension N. error; misunderstanding. To avoid *misapprehension*, I am going to ask all of you to repeat the instructions I have given.

miscegenation N. intermarriage between races. Some states passed laws against *miscegenation.*

miscellany N. mixture of writings on various subjects. This is an interesting *miscellany* of nineteenth-century prose.

mischance N. ill luck. By *mischance,* he lost his week's salary.

miscreant N. wretch; villain. His kindness to the *miscreant* amazed all of us who had expected to hear severe punishment pronounced.

misdemeanor N. minor crime. The culprit pleaded guilty to a *misdemeanor* rather than face trial for a felony.

misgivings N. doubts. Hamlet described his *misgivings* to Horatio but decided to fence with Laertes despite his foreboding of evil.

mishap (*mĭs´-*) N. accident. With a little care you could have avoided this *mishap.*

misnomer N. wrong name; incorrect designation. His tyrannical conduct proved to all that his nickname, King Eric the Just, was a *misnomer.*

misogynist N. hater of women. She accused him of being a *misogynist* because he had been a bachelor all his life.

missile N. object to be thrown or projected. Scientists are experimenting with guided *missiles.*

mite N. very small object or creature; small coin. The criminal was so heartless that he even stole the widow's *mite.*

mitigate V. appease. Nothing he did could *mitigate* her wrath; she was unforgiving.

mobile ADJ. movable; not fixed. The *mobile* blood bank operated by the Red Cross visited our neighborhood today. mobility, N.

mode (*mōd*) N. prevailing style. She was not used to their lavish *mode* of living.

modicum (*mŏd´-*) N. limited quantity. Although his story is based on a *modicum* of truth, most of the events he describes are fictitious.

modish ADJ. fashionable. She always discarded all garments which were no longer *modish.*

modulation N. toning down; changing from one key to another. When she spoke, it was with quiet *modulation* of voice.

moiety (*môĭ´-ət-ē*) N. half; part. There is a slight *moiety* of the savage in her personality which is not easily perceived by those who do not know her well.

mollify V. soothe. We tried to *mollify* the hysterical child by promising her many gifts.

molt V. shed or cast off hair or feathers. The male robin

molted in the spring.

molten ADJ. melted. The city of Pompeii was destroyed by volcanic ash rather than by *molten* lava flowing from Mount Vesuvius.

momentous ADJ. very important. On this *momentous* occasion, we must be very solemn.

monetary ADJ. pertaining to money. She was in complete charge of all *monetary* matters affecting the household.

monotheism (*mŏn´-*) N. belief in one God. Abraham was the first to proclaim his belief in *monotheism.*

moodiness N. fits of depression or gloom. We could not discover the cause of his recurrent *moodiness.*

moot (*mōot*) ADJ. debatable. Our tariff policy is a *moot* subject.

morbid ADJ. given to unwholesome thought; gloomy. These *morbid* speculations are dangerous; we must lighten our thinking by emphasis on more pleasant matters.

mordant ADJ. biting; sarcastic; stinging. Actors feared the critic's *mordant* pen.

mores (*môr´-āz*) N. customs. The *mores* of Mexico are those of Spain with some modifications.

moribund ADJ. at the point of death. The doctors called the family to the bedside of the *moribund* patient.

morose (*-rōs´*) ADJ. ill-humored; sullen. When we first meet Hamlet, we find him *morose* and depressed.

mortician N. undertaker. The *mortician* prepared the corpse for burial.

mortify V. humiliate; punish the flesh. She was so *mortified* by her blunder that she ran to her room in tears.

mote N. small speck. The tiniest *mote* in the eye is very painful.

motif (*mō-tēf´*) N. theme. This simple *motif* runs throughout the entire score.

motley ADJ. parti-colored; mixed. The captain had gathered a *motley* crew to sail the vessel.

mountebank N. charlatan; boastful pretender. The patent medicine man was a *mountebank.*

muddle V. confuse; mix up. His thoughts were *muddled* and chaotic. also N.

muggy ADJ. warm and damp. August in New York City is often *muggy.*

mulct (*mŭlkt*) V. defraud a person of something. The lawyer was accused of trying to *mulct* the boy of his legacy.

multiform ADJ. having many forms. Snowflakes are *multiform* but always hexagonal.

multilingual ADJ. having many languages. Because they are bordered by so many countries, the Swiss people are *multilingual.*

multiplicity N. state of being numerous. He was appalled by the *multiplicity* of details he had to complete before setting out on his mission.

mundane ADJ. worldly as opposed to spiritual. He was concerned only with *mundane* matters, especially the daily stock market quotations.

munificent ADJ. very generous. The *munificent* gift was presented to the bride.

murkiness N. darkness; gloom. The *murkiness* and fog of the waterfront that evening depressed me.

muse V. ponder. For a moment he *mused* about the beauty of the scene, but his thoughts soon changed as he recalled his own personal problems. also N.

musky ADJ. having the odor of musk. She left a trace of *musky* perfume behind her.

musty ADJ. stale; spoiled by age. The attic was dark and *musty.*

mutable ADJ. changing in form; fickle. His opinions were *mutable* and easily influenced by anyone who had any

ā—ale; ă—add; ä—arm; å—ask; ē—eve; ĕ—end; ê—err, her; ə—allow; even; ī—ice; ĭ—ill; ō—oll; ŏ—odd; ô—orb; ōo—food; ŏo—foot, put; ou—out; th—thin; ū—use; ŭ—up; zh—pleasure

powers of persuasion.

mutilate V. maim. The torturer threatened to *mutilate* his victim.

mutinous ADJ. unruly; rebellious. The captain had to use force to quiet his *mutinous* crew.

myriad N. very large number. *Myriads* of mosquitoes from the swamps invaded our village every twilight. also ADJ.

nadir (*nā´-*) N. lowest point. Although few people realized it, the Dow-Jones averages had reached their *nadir* and would soon begin an upward surge.

ETYMOLOGY 19

MITT, MISS (to send)

missile projectile
admit allow in
dismiss send away
transmit send across

MON, MONIT (to warn)

admonish warn
premonition foreboding
monitor watcher (warner)

MORI, MORT (to die)

mortuary funeral parlor
moribund dying
immortal not dying

TEST—WORD LIST 19—*Synonyms*

Each of the questions below consists of a word printed in italics, followed by five words or phrases numbered 1 to 5. Choose the numbered word or phrase which is most nearly similar in meaning to the word in italics and write the number of your choice on your answer paper.

361. *modish* 1 sentimental 2 stylish 3 vacillating 4 contrary 5 adorned
362. *mordant* 1 dying 2 trenchant 3 fabricating 4 controlling 5 avenging
363. *mollify* 1 avenge 2 attenuate 3 attribute 4 mortify 5 appease
364. *menial* 1 intellectual 2 clairvoyant 3 servile 4 arrogant 5 laudatory
365. *moribund* 1 dying 2 appropriate 3 leather bound 4 answering 5 undertaking
366. *mirage* 1 dessert 2 illusion 3 water 4 mirror 5 statement
367. *mischance* 1 opportunity 2 ordinance 3 aperture 4 anecdote 5 adversity
368. *mundane* 1 global 2 futile 3 spiritual 4 heretic 5 worldly

369. *multilingual* 1 variegated 2 polyglot 3 multilateral 4 polyandrous 5 multiplied
370. *moot* 1 visual 2 invisible 3 controversial 4 anticipatory 5 obsequious
371. *motley* 1 active 2 disguised 3 variegated 4 somber 5 sick
372. *mulct* 1 swindle 2 hold 3 record 4 print 5 fertilize
373. *munificent* 1 grandiose 2 puny 3 philanthropic 4 poor 5 gracious
374. *monetary* 1 boring 2 fascinating 3 fiscal 4 stationary 5 stationery
375. *misanthrope* 1 benefactor 2 philanderer 3 hermit 4 aesthete 5 epicure
376. *mentor* 1 guide 2 genius 3 talker 4 philosopher 5 stylist
377. *meticulous* 1 steadfast 2 remiss 3 quaint 4 painstaking 5 overt
378. *muggy* 1 attacking 2 fascinating 3 humid 4 characteristic 5 gelid
379. *musty* 1 flat 2 necessary 3 indifferent 4 nonchalant 5 vivid
380. *misdemeanor* 1 felony 2 peccadillo 3 indignity 4 fiat 5 illiteracy

---

WORD LIST 20 naiveté - optometrist

naiveté (*nä-ē-və-tā´*) N. quality of being unsophisticated. I cannot believe that such *naiveté* is unassumed in a person of her age and experience.

natal (*nāt´-*) ADJ. pertaining to birth. He refused to celebrate his *natal* day because it reminded him of the few years he could look forward to.

natation N. swimming. The Red Cross emphasizes the need for courses in *natation*.

nauseate V. cause to become sick; fill with disgust. The foul smells began to *nauseate* him.

nave N. main body of a church. The *nave* of the cathedral was empty at this hour.

nebulous ADJ. cloudy; hazy. Your theories are too *nebulous;* please clarify them.

necrology N. obituary notice; list of the dead. The *necrology*

of those buried in this cemetery is available in the office.

necromancy N. black magic; dealings with the dead. Because he was able to perform feats of *necromancy,* the natives thought he was in league with the devil.

nefarious ADJ. very wicked. He was universally feared because of his many *nefarious* deeds.

negation N. denial. I must accept his argument since you have been unable to present any *negation* of his evidence.

nemesis (*nĕm´-*) N. revenging agent. Captain Bligh vowed to be Christian's *nemesis.*

neophyte N. recent convert; beginner. This mountain slope contains slides that will challenge experts as well as *neophytes.*

nepotism N. favoritism (to a relative). John left his position with the company because he felt that advancement was

ā—ale; ă—add; ä—arm; à—ask, ē—eve; ĕ—end; ê—err, her; ə—allow; even; ī—ice; ĭ—ill; ō—oll; ŏ—odd; ô—orb; ōō—food; ŏŏ—foot, put; ou—out; th—thin; ū—use; ŭ—up; zh—pleasure

based on *nepotism* rather than ability.

nettle   V. annoy; vex. Do not let him *nettle* you with his sarcastic remarks.

nexus   N. connection. I fail to see the *nexus* which binds these two widely separated events.

nib   N. beak; pen point. The *nibs* of fountain pens often became clotted and corroded.

nicety   (nī´-sət-ē) N. precision; minute distinction. I cannot distinguish between such *niceties* of reasoning.

niggardly   (nĭg´-) ADJ. meanly stingy; parsimonious. The *niggardly* pittance the widow receives from the government cannot keep her from poverty.

nocturnal   ADJ. done at night. Mr. Jones obtained a watchdog to prevent the *nocturnal* raids on his chicken coops.

noisome   ADJ. foul smelling; unwholesome. I never could stand the *noisome* atmosphere surrounding the slaughter houses.

nomadic   ADJ. wandering. Several *nomadic* tribes of Indians would hunt in this area each year.

nonchalance   N. indifference; lack of interest. Few people could understand how he could listen to the news of the tragedy with such *nonchalance;* the majority regarded him as callous and unsympathetic.

noncommittal   ADJ. neutral; unpledged; undecided. We were annoyed by his *noncommittal* reply for we had been led to expect definite assurances of his approval.

nonentity   N. nonexistence; person of no importance. Of course you are a *nonentity;* you will continue to be one until you prove your value to the community.

non sequitur   N. a conclusion that does not follow from the facts stated. Your term paper is full of *non sequiturs;* I cannot see how you reached the conclusions you state.

nosegay   N. fragrant bouquet. These spring flowers will make an attractive *nosegay.*

nostalgia   N. homesickness; longing for the past. The first settlers found so much work to do that they had little time for *nostalgia.*

notorious   ADJ. outstandingly bad; unfavorably known. Captain Kidd was a *notorious* pirate.

novice   N. beginner. Even a *novice* can do good work if he follows these simple directions.

noxious   ADJ. harmful. We must trace the source of these *noxious* gases before they asphyxiate us.

nugatory   ADJ. futile; worthless. This agreement is *nugatory* for no court will enforce it.

numismatist   (-mĭz´-) N. person who collects coins. The *numismatist* had a splendid collection of antique coins.

nurture   V. bring up; feed; educate. We must *nurture* the young so that they will develop into good citizens.

nutrient   ADJ. providing nourishment. During the convalescent period, the patient must be provided with *nutrient* foods. also N.

oaf   N. stupid, awkward person. He called the unfortunate waiter a clumsy *oaf.*

obdurate   ADJ. stubborn. He was *obdurate* in his refusal to listen to our complaints.

obeisance   (ō-bās´-) N. bow. She made an *obeisance* as the king and queen entered the room.

obelisk   N. tall column tapering and ending in a pyramid. Cleopatra's Needle is an *obelisk* in Central Park, New York City.

obese   (-bēs´) ADJ. fat. It is advisable that *obese* people try to lose weight.

obfuscate   V. confuse; muddle. Do not *obfuscate* the issues by dragging in irrelevant arguments.

obituary   ADJ. death notice. I first learned of his death when I read the *obituary* column in the newspaper. also N.

objurgate   V. scold; rebuke severely. I am afraid he will *objurgate* us publicly for this offense.

oblique   ADJ. slanting; deviating from the perpendicular or from a straight line. The sergeant ordered the men to march "*Oblique* Right."

obliquity   N. departure from right principles; perversity. His moral decadence was marked by his *obliquity* from the ways of integrity and honesty.

obliterate   V. destroy completely. The tidal wave *obliterated* several island villages.

oblivion   N. forgetfulness. His works had fallen into a state of *oblivion;* no one bothered to read them.

obloquy   (ŏb´-lə-kwē) N. slander; disgrace; infamy. I resent the *obloquy* that you are casting upon my reputation.

obnoxious   ADJ. offensive. I find your behavior *obnoxious;* please amend your ways.

obsequious   (-sē´-) ADJ. slavishly attentive; servile; sycophantic. Nothing is more disgusting to me than the *obsequious* demeanor of the people who wait upon you.

obsession   N. fixed idea; continued brooding. This *obsession* with the supernatural has made him unpopular with his neighbors.

obsolete   ADJ. outmoded. That word is *obsolete;* do not use it.

obtrude   V. push into prominence. The other members of the group object to the manner in which you *obtrude* your opinions into matters of no concern to you.

obtrusive   ADJ. pushing forward. I found him a very *obtrusive* person, constantly seeking the center of the stage.

obtuse   ADJ. blunt; stupid. Because he was so *obtuse,* he could not follow the teacher's reasoning and asked foolish questions.

obviate   V. make unnecessary; get rid of. I hope this contribution will *obviate* any need for further collections of funds.

occult   (-kŭlt´) ADJ. mysterious; secret; supernatural. The *occult* rites of the organization were revealed only to members. also N.

oculist   N. physician who specializes in treatment of the eyes. In many states, an *oculist* is the only one who may apply medicinal drops to the eyes for the purpose of examining them.

odious   ADJ. hateful. I find the task of punishing you most *odious.* odium, N.

odoriferous   ADJ. giving off an odor. The *odoriferous* spices stimulated his jaded appetite.

odorous   ADJ. having an odor. This variety of hybrid tea rose is more *odorous* than the one you have in your garden.

officious   ADJ. meddlesome; excessively trying to please. Browning informs us that the Duke resented the bough of cherries some *officious* fool brought to the Duchess.

ogle   (ōg´-əl) V. glance coquettishly at; make eyes at. Sitting for hours at the sidewalk cafe, the old gentleman would *ogle* the young girls and recall his youthful romances.

olfactory   ADJ. concerning the sense of smell. The *olfactory* organ is the nose.

oligarchy   N. government by a few. The feudal *oligarchy* was supplanted by an autocracy.

ominous   ADJ. threatening. These clouds are *ominous;* they portend a severe storm.

omnipotent   (-nĭp´-) ADJ. all-powerful. The monarch regarded himself as *omnipotent* and responsible to no one for his acts.

omniscient   (-nĭsh´-ənt) ADJ. all-knowing. I do not pretend to be *omniscient,* but I am positive about this item.

omnivorous   (-nĭv´-) ADJ. eating both plant and animal food; devouring everything. Some animals, including human beings, are *omnivorous* and eat both meat and vege-

---

ā—ale; ă—add; ä—arm; à—ask; ē—eve; ĕ—end; ê—err, her; ə—allow; even; ī—ice; ĭ—ill; ō—oll; ŏ—odd; ô—orb; o͞o—food; o͝o—foot, put; ou—out; th—thin; ū—use; ŭ—up; zh—pleasure

tables; others are either carnivorous or herbivorous.

onerous (ŏn´-) ADJ. burdensome. He asked for an assistant because his work load was too *onerous*. onus, N.

onomatopoeia (-pē´-yə) N. words formed in imitation of natural sounds. Words like "rustle" and "gargle" are illustrations of *onomatopoeia*.

onslaught N. vicious assault. We suffered many casualties during the unexpected *onslaught* of the enemy troops.

opalescent ADJ. iridescent. The Ancient Mariner admired the *opalescent* sheen on the water.

opaque ADJ. dark; not transparent. I want something *opaque* placed in this window so that no one will be able to watch me.

opiate N. sleep producer; deadener of pain. By such *opiates*, he made the people forget their difficulties and accept their unpleasant circumstances.

opportune ADJ. timely; well chosen. You have come at an *opportune* moment for I need a new secretary.

opprobrious ADJ. disgraceful. I find your conduct so *opprobrious* that I must exclude you from classes.

optician N. maker and seller of eyeglasses. The patient took the prescription given him by his oculist to the *optician*.

optometrist N. one who fits glasses to remedy visual defects. Although an *optometrist* is qualified to treat many eye disorders, he may not use medicines or surgery in his examinations.

ETYMOLOGY 20

NAV (ship)

navigate sail a ship
circumnavigate sail around the world
naval pertaining to ships

OMNI (all)

omniscient all knowing

omnipotent all powerful
omnivorous eating everything

OPER (to work)

operate work
cooperation working together
opera musical drama (specialized kind of work)

TEST—WORD LIST 20—*Antonyms*

Each of the questions below consists of a word printed in italics, followed by five words or phrases numbered 1 to 5. Choose the numbered word or phrase which is most nearly opposite in meaning to the word in italics and write the number of your choice on your answer paper.

381. *obsession* 1 whim 2 loss 3 phobia 4 delusion 5 feud
382. *nefarious* 1 wanton 2 lacking 3 benign 4 impious 5 futile
383. *obdurate* 1 yielding 2 fleeting 3 finite 4 fascinating 5 permanent
384. *obtuse* 1 sheer 2 transparent 3 tranquil 4 timid 5 shrewd
385. *nocturnal* 1 harsh 2 marauding 3 patrolling 4 daily 5 fallow
386. *obloquy* 1 praise 2 rectangle 3 circle 4 dialogue 5 cure
387. *neophyte* 1 veteran 2 satellite 3 aspirant 4 handwriting 5 violence
388. *opportune* 1 occasional 2 fragrant 3 fragile 4 awkward 5 neglected

389. *obese* 1 skillful 2 cadaverous 3 clever 4 unpredictable 5 lucid
390. *opiate* 1 distress 2 sleep 3 stimulant 4 laziness 5 despair
391. *notorious* 1 fashionable 2 renowned 3 infamous 4 intrepid 5 invincible
392. *odious* 1 fragrant 2 redolent 3 fetid 4 delightful 5 puny
393. *nebulous* 1 starry 2 clear 3 cold 4 fundamental 5 porous
394. *omniscient* 1 sophisticated 2 ignorant 3 essential 4 trivial 5 isolated
395. *obsolete* 1 heated 2 desolate 3 renovated 4 frightful 5 automatic
396. *niggardly* 1 protected 2 biased 3 prodigal 4 bankrupt 5 placated
397. *omnipotent* 1 weak 2 democratic 3 despotic 4 passionate 5 late
398. *negation* 1 postulation 2 hypothecation 3 affirmation 4 violation 5 anticipation
399. *noisome* 1 quiet 2 dismayed 3 fragrant 4 sleepy 5 inquisitive
400. *obsequious* 1 successful 2 democratic 3 supercilious 4 ambitious 5 lamentable

---

WORD LIST 21 opulence - perfunctory

opulence (ŏp´-yə-) N. wealth. Visitors from Europe are amazed at the *opulence* of this country.

oratorio N. dramatic poem set to music. The Glee Club decided to present an *oratorio* during their recital.

ordinance N. decree. Passing a red light is a violation of a city *ordinance*.

orifice (ôr´-) N. mouthlike opening; small opening. The Howe Caverns were discovered when someone observed

that a cold wind was issuing from an *orifice* in the hillside.

ornate (-nāt´-) ADJ. excessively decorated; highly decorated. Furniture of the Baroque period can be recognized by its *ornate* carvings.

ornithologist N. scientific student of birds. Audubon's drawings of American bird life have been of interest not only to the *ornithologists* but also to the general public.

oscillate (ŏs´-ə-) V. vibrate pendulumlike; waver. It is inter-

ā—ale; ă—add; ä—arm; à—ask, ē—eve; ĕ—end; ê—err, her; ə—allow; even; ī—ice; ĭ—ill; ō—oll; ŏ—odd; ô—orb; ōō—food; ŏŏ—foot; pụt; ou—out; th—thin; ū—use; ŭ—up; zh—pleasure

esting to note how public opinion *oscillates* between the extremes of optimism and pessimism.

ossify V. change or harden into bone. When he called his opponent a "bonehead," he implied that his adversary's brain had *ossified* and that he was not capable of clear thinking.

ostensible ADJ. apparent; professed; pretended. Although the *ostensible* purpose of this expedition is to discover new lands, we are really interested in finding new markets for our products.

ostentatious ADJ. showy; pretentious. The real hero is never *ostentatious*.

ostracize V. exclude from public favor; ban. As soon as the newspapers carried the story of his connection with the criminals, his friends began to *ostracize* him. ostracism, N.

overt (-vêrt´) ADJ. open to view. According to the United States Constitution, a person must commit an *overt* act before he may be tried for treason.

pacifist N. one opposed to force; antimilitarist. The *pacifists* urged that we reduce our military budget and recall our troops stationed overseas.

paean (pē´-) N. song of praise or joy. They sang *paeans* of praise.

palatable ADJ. agreeable; pleasing to the taste. Paying taxes can never be made *palatable*.

palatial ADJ. magnificent. He proudly showed us through his *palatial* home.

palaver (-lăv´-) N. discussion; misleading speech; chatter. In spite of all the *palaver* before the meeting, the delegates were able to conduct serious negotiations when they sat down at the conference table. also V.

palette N. board on which painter mixes pigments. At the present time, art supply stores are selling a paper *palette* which may be discarded after use.

pallet N. small, poor bed. The weary traveler went to sleep on his straw *pallet*.

palliate V. ease pain; make less guilty or offensive. Doctors must *pall.ate* that which they cannot cure.

pallid ADJ. pale; wan. Because his occupation required that he work at night and sleep during the day, he had an exceptionally *pallid* complexion.

palpable ADJ. tangible; easily perceptible. I cannot understand how you could overlook such a *palpable* blunder.

palpitate V. throb; flutter. As he became excited, his heart began to *palpitate* more and more erratically.

paltry (pôl´-) ADJ. insignificant; petty. This is a *paltry* sum to pay for such a masterpiece.

panacea (păn-ə-sē´-ə) N. cure-all; remedy for all diseases. There is no easy *panacea* that will solve our complicated international situation.

pandemonium N. wild tumult. When the ships collided in the harbor, *pandemonium* broke out among the passengers.

pander V. cater to the low desires of others. Books which *pander* to man's lowest instincts should be banned.

panegyric (-jĭr´-) N. formal praise. The modest hero blushed as he listened to the *panegyrics* uttered by the speakers about his valorous act.

panorama N. comprehensive view; unobstructed view in all directions. Tourists never forget the impact of their first *panorama* of the Grand Canyon.

pantomime N. acting without dialogue. Because he worked in *pantomime*, the clown could be understood wherever he appeared. also V.

papyrus (-pī´-) N. ancient paper made from stem of papyrus plant. The ancient Egyptians were among the first to write on *papyrus*.

parable N. short, simple story teaching a moral. Let us apply to our own conduct the lesson that this *parable* teaches.

paradox N. statement that looks false but is actually correct; a contradictory statement. Wordsworth's "The child is father to the man" is an example of *paradox*.

paragon N. model of perfection. The class disliked him because the teacher was always pointing to him as a *paragon* of virtue.

parallelism N. state of being parallel; similarity. There is a striking *parallelism* between the two ages.

paranoia (-nôĭ´-ə) N. chronic form of insanity marked by delusions of grandeur or persecution. The psychiatrists analyzed his ailment as *paranoia*.

paraphernalia (-nāl´-) N. equipment; odds and ends. His desk was cluttered with paper, pen, ink, dictionary and other *paraphernalia* of the writing craft.

paraphrase V. restate a passage in one's own words while retaining thought of author. In 250 words or less, *paraphrase* this article. also N.

parasite N. animal or plant living on another; toady; sycophant. The tapeworm is an example of the kind of *parasite* that may infest the human body.

paregoric N. medicine that eases pain. The doctor prescribed a *paregoric* to alleviate his suffering.

pariah (-rī´-) N. social outcast. I am not a *pariah* to be shunned and ostracized.

parlance N. language; idiom. All this legal *parlance* confuses me; I need an interpreter.

parley N. conference. The peace *parley* has not produced the anticipated truce. also V.

parody N. humorous imitation; travesty. We enjoyed the clever *parodies* of popular songs which the chorus sang.

paroxysm N. fit or attack of pain, laughter, rage. When he heard of his son's misdeeds, he was seized by a *paroxysm* of rage.

parricide N. person who murders his own father; murder of a father. The jury was shocked by the details of this vicious *parricide* and found the man who had killed his father guilty of murder in the first degree.

parry V. ward off a blow. He was content to wage a defensive battle and tried to *parry* his opponent's thrusts.

parsimonious ADJ. stingy; excessively frugal. His *parsimonious* nature did not permit him to enjoy any luxuries.

partiality N. inclination; bias. As a judge, not only must I be unbiased, but I must also avoid any evidence of *partiality* when I award the prize.

parvenu N. upstart; newly rich person. Although extremely wealthy, he was regarded as a *parvenu* by the aristocratic members of society.

passive ADJ. not active; acted upon. Mahatma Gandhi urged his followers to pursue a program of *passive* resistance as he felt that it was more effective than violence and acts of terrorism.

pastoral ADJ. rural. In these stories of *pastoral* life, we find an understanding of the daily tasks of country folk.

patent ADJ. open for the public to read; obvious. It was *patent* to everyone that the witness spoke the truth. also N.

pathetic ADJ. causing sadness, compassion, pity; touching. Everyone in the auditorium was weeping by the time he finished his *pathetic* tale about the orphaned boy.

pathos (pā´-thŏs) N. tender sorrow; pity; quality in art or literature that produces these feelings. The quiet tone of *pathos* that ran through the novel never degenerated into the maudlin or the overly sentimental.

patriarch (pā´-) N. father and ruler of a family or tribe. In many primitive tribes, the leader and lawmaker was the *patriarch*.

patricide N. person who murders his father; murder of a father. The words parricide and *patricide* have exactly the same meaning.

ā—ale; ă—add; ä—arm; à—ask; ē—eve; ĕ—end; ê—err, her; ə—allow; even; ī—ice; ĭ—ill; ō—oll; ŏ—odd; ô—orb; ōō—food;
ŏŏ—foot, put; ou—out; th—thin; ū—use; ŭ—up; zh—pleasure

patrimony N. inheritance from father. As predicted by his critics, he spent his *patrimony* within two years of his father's death.

paucity N. scarcity. The poor test papers indicate that the members of this class have a *paucity* of intelligence.

peccadillo N. slight offense. If we examine these escapades carefully, we will realize that they are mere *peccadilloes* rather than major crimes.

peculate V. steal; embezzle. His crime of *peculating* public funds entrusted to his care is especially damnable.

pecuniary ADJ. pertaining to money. I never expected a *pecuniary* reward for my work in this activity.

pedagogue N. teacher; dull and formal teacher. He could never be a stuffy *pedagogue;* his classes were always lively and filled with humor.

pedantic ADJ. showing off learning; bookish. What you say is *pedantic* and reveals an unfamiliarity with the realities of life. pedant, N.

pediatrician N. expert in children's diseases. The family doctor advised the parents to consult a *pediatrician* about their child's ailment.

pelf N. stolen property; money or wealth [in a contemptuous sense]. Your possessions are only *pelf;* they will give you no lasting pleasure.

pell-mell ADV. in confusion; disorderly. The excited students dashed *pell-mell* into the stadium to celebrate the victory.

pellucid (-lōō´-səd) ADJ. transparent; limpid; easy to understand. After reading these stodgy philosophers, I find his *pellucid* style very enjoyable.

penance N. self-imposed punishment for sin. The Ancient Mariner said, "I have *penance* done and *penance* more will do," to atone for the sin of killing the albatross.

penchant (pĕn´-chənt) N. strong inclination; liking. He had a strong *penchant* for sculpture.

pendant ADJ. hanging down from something. Her *pendant* earrings glistened in the light.

pendent ADJ. suspended; jutting; pending. The *pendent* rock hid the entrance to the cave.

penitent ADJ. repentant. When he realized the enormity of his crime, he became remorseful and *penitent*. also N.

pensive ADJ. dreamily thoughtful; thoughtful with a hint of sadness. The *pensive* youth gazed at the painting for a long time and then sighed.

penumbra (-nŭm´-) N. partial shadow (in an eclipse). During an eclipse, we can see an area of total darkness and a lighter area which is the *penumbra*.

penurious (-yŏor´-) ADJ. stingy; parsimonious. He was a *penurious* man, averse to spending money even for the necessities of life.

penury (pĕn´-) N. extreme poverty. We find much *penury* and suffering in this slum area.

percussion ADJ. striking one object against another sharply. The drum is a *percussion* instrument.

perdition N. damnation; complete ruin. He was damned to eternal *perdition*.

peremptory (pə-rĕmp´-) ADJ. demanding and leaving no choice. I resent your *peremptory* attitude.

perennial (-rĕn´-) N. lasting. These plants are hardy *perennials* and will bloom for many years. also ADJ.

perfidious (-fĭd´-) ADJ. basely false. Your *perfidious* gossip is malicious and dangerous.

perfidy (pêr´-) N. violation of a trust. When we learned of his *perfidy*, we were shocked and dismayed.

perforce (-fôrs´) ADV. of necessity. I must *perforce* leave, as my train is about to start.

perfunctory ADJ. superficial; listless; not thorough. He overlooked many weaknesses when he inspected the factory in his *perfunctory* manner.

ETYMOLOGY 21

PAC (peace)

pacify make peaceful
pacific peaceful
pacifist person opposed to war

PEL, PULS (to drive)

compulsion a forcing to do
repel drive back
expel drive out, banish

TEST—WORD LIST 21—*Synonyms and Antonyms*

Each of the following questions consists of a word printed in italics, followed by five words or phrases numbered 1 to 5. Choose the numbered word or phrase which is most nearly the same as or the opposite of the word in italics and write the number of your choice on your answer paper.

401. *ostentatious* 1 occasional 2 flashy 3 intermittent 4 authentic 5 hospitable

402. *palliate* 1 smoke 2 quicken 3 substitute 4 alleviate 5 sadden

403. *pandemonium* 1 calm 2 frustration 3 efficiency 4 impishness 5 sophistication

404. *pariah* 1 village 2 suburb 3 outcast 4 disease 5 benefactor

405. *papyrus* 1 mountain 2 peninsula 3 paper 4 animal 5 pyramid

406. *penchant* 1 distance 2 imminence 3 dislike 4 attitude 5 void

407. *perennial* 1 flowering 2 recurring 3 centennial 4 partial 5 deciduous

408. *pellucid* 1 logistical 2 philandering 3 limpid 4 vagrant 5 warranted

409. *paucity* 1 pouch 2 peace 3 quickness 4 abundance 5 nuisance

410. *panegyric* 1 medication 2 panacea 3 rotation 4 vacillation 5 praise

411. *paean* 1 serf 2 pealing 3 lien 4 lament 5 folly

412. *opulence* 1 pessimism 2 patriotism 3 potency 4 passion 5 poverty

413. *pallet* 1 bed 2 pigment board 3 bench 4 spectrum 5 quality

414. *parable* 1 equality 2 allegory 3 frenzy 4 folly 5 cuticle

415. *paranoia*   1 fracture 2 statement 3 quantity
    4 benefaction 5 sanity
416. *parsimonious*   1 grammatical 2 syntactical 3 effective
    4 extravagant 5 esoteric
417. *penurious*   1 imprisoned 2 captivated 3 parsimonious
    4 vacant 5 abolished
418. *perfunctory*   1 official 2 thorough 3 insipid 4 vicarious
    5 distinctive
419. *orifice*   1 altar 2 gun 3 guitar 4 device 5 opening
420. *paradox*   1 exaggeration 2 contradiction 3 hyperbole
    4 invective 5 poetic device

WORD LIST 22 perimeter - precedent (n)

perimeter   N. outer boundary. To find the *perimeter* of any quadrilateral, we add the four sides.

peripatetic   (*-tĕt´-*) ADJ. walking about; moving. The *peripatetic* school of philosophy derives its name from the fact that Aristotle walked with his pupils while discussing philosophy with them.

periphery   (*-rĭf´-*) N. edge, especially of a round surface. He sensed that there was something just beyond the *periphery* of his vision.

perjury   N. false testimony while under oath. When several witnesses appeared to challenge his story, he was indicted for *perjury*.

permeable   (*pêr´-*) ADJ. porous; allowing passage through. Glass is *permeable* to light.

permeate   V. pass through; spread. The odor of frying onions *permeated* the air.

pernicious   ADJ. very destructive. He argued that these books had a *pernicious* effect on young and susceptible minds.

perpetrate   V. commit an offense. Only an insane person could *perpetrate* such a horrible crime.

perpetual   ADJ. everlasting. Ponce de Leon hoped to find *perpetual* youth.

persiflage   (*pêr´-sĭ-fläzh*) N. flippant conversation; banter. This *persiflage* is not appropriate when we have such serious problems to discuss.

perspicacious   ADJ. having insight; penetrating; astute. We admired his *perspicacious* wisdom and sagacity.

pert   ADJ. impertinent; forward. I think your *pert* and impudent remarks call for an apology.

pertinacious   ADJ. stubborn; persistent. He is bound to succeed because his *pertinacious* nature will not permit him to quit.

pertinent   ADJ. suitable; to the point. The lawyer wanted to know all the *pertinent* details.

perturb   V. disturb greatly. I am afraid this news will *perturb* him.

perturbation   N. agitation. I fail to understand why such an innocent remark should create such *perturbation*.

perusal   (*-roo´-*) N. reading. I am certain that you have missed important details in your rapid *perusal* of this document. peruse, V.

pervade   V. spread throughout. As the news of the defeat *pervaded* the country, a feeling of anger directed at the rulers who had been the cause of the disaster grew.

perverse   ADJ. stubborn; intractable. Because of your *perverse* attitude, I must rate you as deficient in cooperation.

perversion   N. corruption; turning from right to wrong. Inasmuch as he had no motive for his crimes, we could not understand his *perversion*.

perversity   N. stubborn maintenance of a wrong cause. I cannot forgive your *perversity* in repeating such an impossible story.

pervious   ADJ. penetrable. He has a *pervious* mind and readily accepts new ideas.

pessimism   N. belief that life is basically bad or evil; gloominess. The good news we have been receiving lately indicates that there is little reason for your *pessimism*.

pestilential   ADJ. causing plague; baneful. People were afraid to explore the *pestilential* swamp. pestilence, N.

petrify   V. turn to stone. His sudden and unexpected appearance seemed to *petrify* her.

petulant   (*pĕch´-ə-*) ADJ. touchy; peevish. The feverish patient was *petulant* and restless.

phial   N. small bottle. Even though it is small, this *phial* of perfume is expensive.

philander   V. make love lightly; flirt. Do not *philander* with my affections because love is too serious.

philanthropist   N. lover of mankind; doer of good. As he grew older, he became famous as a *philanthropist* and benefactor of the needy.

philistine   (*fĭl´-ə-*) N. narrow-minded person, uncultured and exclusively interested in material gain. We need more men of culture and enlightenment; we have too many *philistines* among us.

philology   N. study of language. The professor of *philology* advocated the use of Esperanto as an international language.

phlegmatic   (*flĕg-măt´-*) ADJ. calm; not easily disturbed. The nurse was a cheerful but *phlegmatic* person.

physiognomy   N. face. He prided himself on his ability to analyze a person's character by studying his *physiognomy*.

pied   (*pīd*) ADJ. variegated; multicolored. The *Pied* Piper of Hamelin got his name from the multicolored clothing he wore.

pillage   (*pĭl´-ĭj*) V. plunder. The enemy *pillaged* the quiet village and left it in ruins.

pillory   V. punish by placing in a wooden frame and subjecting to ridicule. Even though he was mocked and *pilloried*, he maintained that he was correct in his beliefs. also N.

pinion   V. restrain. They *pinioned* his arms against his body but left his legs free so that he could move about. also N.

pinnacle   N. peak. We could see the morning sunlight illuminate the *pinnacle* while the rest of the mountain lay in shadow.

pious   ADJ. devout. The *pious* parents gave their children a religious upbringing.

piquant   (*pē´-kənt*) ADJ. pleasantly tart-tasting; stimulating. The *piquant* sauce added to our enjoyment of the meal. piquancy, N.

pique   (*pēk*) N. irritation; resentment. She showed her *pique* by her refusal to appear with the other contestants at the end of the contest.

piscatorial   ADJ. pertaining to fishing. He spent many happy hours in his *piscatorial* activities.

pithy   ADJ. concise; meaty. I enjoy reading his essays because they are always compact and *pithy*.

pittance   N. a small allowance or wage. He could not live on the *pittance* he received as a pension and had to look for

---

ā—ale; ă—add; ä—arm; à—ask, ē—eve; ĕ—end; ê—err, her; ə—allow; even; ī—ice; ĭ—ill; ō—oll; ŏ—odd; ô—orb; ōō—food;
ŏŏ—foot, put; ou—out; th—thin; ū—use; ŭ—up; zh—pleasure

an additional source of revenue.

placate V. pacify; conciliate. The teacher tried to *placate* the angry mother.

placid ADJ. peaceful; calm. After his vacation in this *placid* section, he felt soothed and rested.

plagiarism N. theft of another's ideas or writings passed off as original. The editor recognized the *plagiarism* and rebuked the culprit who had presented the manuscript as original.

plaintive ADJ. mournful. The dove has a *plaintive* and melancholy call.

platitude N. trite remark; commonplace statement. The *platitudes* in his speech were applauded by the vast majority in his audience; only a few people perceived how trite his remarks were.

plauditory ADJ. approving; applauding. The theatrical company reprinted the *plauditory* comments of the critics in its advertisement.

plebeian (-*bē´*-) ADJ. common; pertaining to the common people. His speeches were aimed at the *plebeian* minds and emotions; they disgusted the more refined.

plenary (*plē´*-) ADJ. complete; full. The union leader was given *plenary* power to negotiate a new contract with the employers.

plenipotentiary ADJ. fully empowered. Since he was not given *plenipotentiary* powers by his government, he could not commit his country without consulting his superiors. also N.

plethora (*plĕth´*-) N. excess; overabundance. She offered a *plethora* of reasons for her shortcomings.

plumb ADJ. checking perpendicularity; vertical. Before hanging wallpaper it is advisable to drop a *plumb* line from the ceiling as a guide. also N. and V.

podiatrist (-*dī´*-) N. doctor who treats ailments of the feet. He consulted a *podiatrist* about his fallen arches.

podium N. pedestal; raised platform. The audience applauded as the conductor made his way to the *podium*.

poignant (*pôi´-nyənt*) ADJ. keen; piercing; severe. Her *poignant* grief left her pale and weak.

politic ADJ. expedient; prudent; well devised. Even though he was disappointed, he did not think it *politic* to refuse this offer.

poltroon (-*trōōn´*) N. coward. Only a *poltroon* would so betray his comrades at such a dangerous time.

polygamist (-*lĭg´*-) N. one who has more than one spouse at a time. He was arrested as a *polygamist* when his two wives' filed complaints about him.

polyglot ADJ. speaking several languages. New York City is a *polyglot* community because of the thousands of immigrants who settle there.

pommel V. beat. The severity with which he was *pommeled* was indicated by the bruises he displayed on his head and face.

portend V. foretell; presage. The king did not know what these omens might *portend* and asked his soothsayers to interpret them.

portent N. sign; omen; forewarning. He regarded the black cloud as a *portent* of evil.

portentous (-*tĕnt´*-) ADJ. ominous; serious. I regard our present difficulties and dissatisfactions as *portentous* omens of future disaster.

portly ADJ. stately; stout. The overweight gentleman wore suits in special sizes for portly figures.

posterity N. descendants; future generations. We hope to leave a better world to *posterity*.

posthumous (*pŏs´-chə-*) ADJ. after death (as of child born after father's death or book published after author's death). The critics ignored his works during his lifetime; it was only after the *posthumous* publication of his last novel that they recognized his great talent.

postulate N. self-evident truth. We must accept these statements as *postulates* before pursuing our discussions any further. also V.

potentate (*pŏt´*-) N. monarch; sovereign. The *potentate* spent more time at Monte Carlo than he did at home with his people.

potential ADJ. expressing possibility; latent. This juvenile delinquent is a *potential* murderer. also N.

potion N. dose (of liquid). Tristan and Isolde drink a love *potion* in the first act of the opera.

potpourri (*pō-pŏo-rē´*) N. heterogeneous mixture; medley. He offered a *potpourri* of folk songs from many lands.

poultice (*pōl´*-) N. soothing application applied to sore and inflamed portions of the body. He was advised to apply a flaxseed *poultice* to the inflammation.

practicable ADJ. feasible. The board of directors decided that the plan was *practicable* and agreed to undertake the project.

practical ADJ. based on experience; useful. He was a *practical* man, opposed to theory.

pragmatic ADJ. practical; concerned with practical values. This test should provide us with a *pragmatic* analysis of the value of this course.

prate V. speak foolishly; boast idly. Let us not *prate* about our qualities; rather, let our virtues speak for themselves.

prattle V. babble. The little girl *prattled* endlessly about her dolls. also N.

preamble N. introductory statement. In the *Preamble* to the Constitution, the purpose of the document is set forth.

precarious ADJ. uncertain; risky. I think this stock is a *precarious* investment and advise against its purchase.

precedent (*prĕs´*-) N. something preceding in time which may be used as an authority or guide for future action. This decision sets a *precedent* for future cases of a similar nature.

ETYMOLOGY 22

PET, PETIT (to seek)

petition request
appetite craving, desire
compete vie with others

PON, POSIT (to place)

postpone place after

preposition that which goes before
positive definite, unquestioned (definitely placed)

PORT, PORTAT (to carry)

portable able to be carried
transport carry across
export carry out (of country)

TEST—WORD LIST 22—*Synonyms*

Each of the questions below consists of a word printed in italics, followed by five words or phrases numbered 1 to 5. Choose the numbered word or phrase which is most nearly similar in meaning to the word in italics and write the number of your choice on your answer paper.

421. *pillage*   1 hoard 2 plunder 3 versify 4 denigrate 5 confide
422. *petrify*   1 turn to water 2 refine 3 turn to stone 4 turn to gas 5 repeat
423. *pernicious*   1 practical 2 comparative 3 destructive 4 tangible 5 detailed
424. *physiognomy*   1 posture 2 head 3 physique 4 face 5 size
425. *pertinent*   1 understood 2 living 3 discontented 4 puzzling 5 relevant
426. *permeate*   1 enlarge 2 produce 3 prod 4 disfigure 5 spread
427. *phlegmatic*   1 calm 2 cryptic 3 practical 4 salivary 5 dishonest
428. *pertinacious*   1 sticking 2 consumptive 3 superficial 4 skilled 5 advertised
429. *permeable*   1 perishable 2 effective 3 plodding 4 porous 5 lasting
430. *philander*   1 flirt 2 quiz 3 decline 4 profit 5 quarrel
431. *pert*   1 impertinent 2 perishable 3 moral 4 deliberate 5 stubborn
432. *peripatetic*   1 worldly 2 moving 3 disarming 4 seeking 5 inherent
433. *petulant*   1 angry 2 moral 3 declining 4 underhanded 5 touchy
434. *perpetual*   1 eternal 2 standard 3 serious 4 industrial 5 interpretive
435. *plaintive*   1 mournful 2 senseless 3 persistent 4 rural 5 evasive
436. *pinion*   1 express 2 report 3 reveal 4 submit 5 restrain
437. *placate*   1 determine 2 transmit 3 pacify 4 allow 5 define
438. *pinnacle*   1 foothills 2 card game 3 pass 4 taunt 5 peak
439. *pique*   1 pyramid 2 revolt 3 resentment 4 struggle 5 inventory
440. *pious*   1 historic 2 devout 3 multiple 4 fortunate 5 authoritative

---

WORD LIST   23   **precedent (adj.) - purview**

precedent (-sēd´-) ADJ. preceding in time, rank, etc. Our discussions, *precedent* to this event, certainly did not give you any reason to believe that we would adopt your proposal.

precept N. practical rule guiding conduct. "Love thy neighbor as thyself" is a worthwhile *precept*.

precipitate (-sĭp´-ət-ət) ADJ. headlong; rash. Do not be *precipitate* in this matter; investigate further.

precipitate (-sĭp´-ə-tāt) V. throw headlong; hasten. We must be patient as we cannot *precipitate* these results.

precipitous ADJ. steep. This hill is difficult to climb because it is so *precipitous*.

preclude V. make impossible; eliminate. This contract does not *preclude* my being employed by others at the same time that I am working for you.

precocious ADJ. developed ahead of time. By his rather adult manner of discussing serious topics, the child demonstrated that he was *precocious*.

precursor N. forerunner. Gray and Burns were *precursors* of the Romantic Movement in English literature.

predatory ADJ. plundering. The hawk is a *predatory* bird.

predilection (-ĕk-) N. partiality; preference. Although the artist used various media from time to time, he had a *predilection* for watercolor.

preeminent (prē-ĕm´-) ADJ. outstanding; superior. The king traveled to Boston because he wanted the *preeminent* surgeon in the field to perform the operation.

prefatory (prĕf´-) ADJ. introductory. The chairman made a few *prefatory* remarks before he called on the first speaker.

prelude N. introduction; forerunner. I am afraid that this border raid is the *prelude* to more serious attacks.

premonition N. forewarning. We ignored these *premonitions*

of disaster because they appeared to be based on childish fears.

preponderate V. be superior in power; outweigh. I feel confident that the forces of justice will *preponderate* eventually in this dispute.

preposterous ADJ. absurd; ridiculous. The excuse he gave for his lateness was so *preposterous* that everyone laughed.

presage (prĕs´-) V. foretell. The vultures flying overhead *presaged* the discovery of the corpse in the desert.

presentiment (-zĕnt´-) N. premonition; foreboding. Hamlet felt a *presentiment* about his meeting with Laertes.

presumption N. arrogance; effrontery. She had the *presumption* to disregard our advice.

pretentious ADJ. ostentatious; ambitious. I do not feel that your limited resources will permit you to carry out such a *pretentious* program.

prevaricate V. lie. Some people believe that to *prevaricate* in a good cause is justifiable and regard the statement as a "white lie."

prim ADJ. very precise and formal; exceedingly proper. Many people commented on the contrast between the *prim* attire of the young lady and the inappropriate clothing worn by her escort.

primordial (prī-môrd´-) ADJ. existing at the beginning (of time); rudimentary. The Neanderthal Man is one of our *primordial* ancestors.

pristine ADJ. characteristic of earlier times; primitive; unspoiled. This area has been preserved in all its *pristine* wildness.

privy ADJ. secret; hidden; not public. We do not care for *privy* chamber government.

probity N. uprightness; incorruptibility. Everyone took his

ā—ale; ă—add; ä—arm; à—ask, ē—eve; ĕ—end; ê—err, her; ə—allow; even; ī—ice; ĭ—ill; ō—oll; ŏ—odd; ô—orb; oō—food; oŏ—foot, put; ou—out; th—thin; ū—use; ŭ—up; zh—pleasure

probity for granted; his defalcations, therefore, shocked us all.

proboscis (*-bŏs´-əs*) N. long snout; nose. The elephant uses his *proboscis* to handle things and carry them from place to place.

proclivity N. inclination; natural tendency. He has a *proclivity* to grumble.

procrastinate V. postpone; delay. It is wise not to *procrastinate;* otherwise, we find ourselves bogged down in a mass of work which should have been finished long ago.

prodigal ADJ. wasteful; reckless with money. The *prodigal* son squandered his inheritance. also N.

prodigious ADJ. marvelous; enormous. He marveled at her *prodigious* appetite.

profane V. violate; desecrate. Tourists are urged not to *profane* the sanctity of holy places by wearing improper garb. also ADJ.

profligate ADJ. dissipated; wasteful; licentious. In this *profligate* company, he lost all sense of decency. also N.

profusion N. lavish expenditure; overabundant condition. Seldom have I seen food and drink served in such *profusion.*

progenitor N. ancestor. We must not forget the teachings of our *progenitors* in our desire to appear modern.

progeny N. children; offspring. He was proud of his *progeny* but regarded George as the most promising of all his children.

prognosis N. forecasted course of a disease; prediction. If the doctor's *prognosis* is correct, the patient will be in a coma for at least twenty-four hours.

prognosticate V. predict. I *prognosticate* disaster unless we change our wasteful ways.

prolific ADJ. abundantly fruitful. He was a *prolific* writer and wrote as many as three books a year.

prolix ADJ. verbose; drawn out. His *prolix* arguments irritated the jury. prolixity, N.

promiscuous ADJ. mixed indiscriminately; haphazard; irregular. In the opera *La Boheme,* we get a picture of the *promiscuous* life led by the young artists of Paris.

promontory N. headland. They erected a lighthouse on the *promontory* to warn approaching ships of their nearness to the shore.

promulgate V. make known by official proclamation or publication. As soon as the Civil Service Commission *promulgates* the names of the successful candidates, we shall begin to hire members of our staff.

prone ADJ. inclined to; prostrate. She was *prone* to sudden fits of anger.

propagate V. multiply; spread. I am sure disease must *propagate* in such unsanitary and crowded areas.

propensity N. natural inclination. I dislike your *propensity* to belittle every contribution he makes to our organization.

propitiate V. appease. The natives offered sacrifices to *propitiate* the gods.

propitious ADJ. favorable; kindly. I think it is advisable that we wait for a more *propitious* occasion to announce our plans.

propound V. put forth for analysis. In your discussion, you have *propounded* several questions; let us consider each one separately.

propriety N. fitness; correct conduct. I want you to behave at this dinner with *propriety;* don't embarrass me.

propulsive ADJ. driving forward. The jet plane has a greater *propulsive* power than the engine-driven plane.

prorogue (*prə-rōg´*) V. dismiss parliament; end officially. It was agreed that the king could not *prorogue* parliament until it had been in session for at least fifty days.

prosaic (*prō-zā´-ĭk*) ADJ. commonplace; dull. I do not like this author because he is so unimaginative and *prosaic.*

proscribe V. ostracize; banish; outlaw. Antony, Octavius, and Lepidus *proscribed* all those who had conspired against Julius Caesar.

prosody (*prŏs´-*) N. the art of versification. This book on *prosody* contains a rhyming dictionary as well as samples of the various verse forms.

prostrate V. stretch out full on ground. He *prostrated* himself before the idol. also ADJ.

protégé (*prōt´-ə-zhā*) N. person under the protection and support of a patron. Cyrano de Bergerac refused to be a *protégé* of Cardinal Richelieu.

protocol N. diplomatic etiquette. We must run this state dinner according to *protocol* if we are to avoid offending any of our guests.

protract V. prolong. Do not *protract* this phone conversation as I expect an important business call within the next few minutes.

protrude V. stick out. His fingers *protruded* from the holes in his gloves.

provender (*prŏv´-*) N. dry food; fodder. I am not afraid of a severe winter because I have stored a large quantity of *provender* for the cattle.

provident ADJ. displaying foresight; thrifty; preparing for emergencies. In his usual *provident* manner, he had insured himself against this type of loss.

proviso (*-vī´-zō*) N. stipulation. I am ready to accept your proposal with the *proviso* that you meet your obligations within the next two weeks.

provocation N. cause for anger or retaliation. In order to prevent a sudden outbreak of hostilities, we must give our foe no *provocation.*

proximity N. nearness. The deer sensed the hunter's *proximity* and bounded away.

proxy N. authorized agent. Please act as my *proxy* and vote for this slate of candidates.

prurient ADJ. based on lascivious thoughts. The police attempted to close the theater where the *prurient* film was being presented.

pseudonym N. pen name. Samuel Clemens' *pseudonym* was Mark Twain.

psyche (*sī´-kē*) N. soul; mind. It is difficult to delve into the *psyche* of a human being.

psychiatrist N. a doctor who treats mental diseases. A *psychiatrist* often needs long conferences with his patient before a diagnosis can be made.

puerile (*pūr´-əl*) ADJ. childish. His *puerile* pranks sometimes offended his serious-minded friends.

pugnacious ADJ. combative; disposed to fight. As a child he was *pugnacious* and fought with everyone.

puissant (*pwĭs´-*) ADJ. powerful; strong; potent. We must keep his friendship for he will make a *puissant* ally.

pulchritude N. beauty; comeliness. I do not envy the judges who have to select this year's Miss America from this collection of female *pulchritude.*

pulmonary ADJ. pertaining to the lungs. In his researches on *pulmonary* diseases, he discovered many facts about the lungs of animals and human beings.

pulsate V. throb. We could see the blood vessels in his temple *pulsate* as he became more angry.

punctilious ADJ. laying stress on niceties of conduct, form; precise. We must be *punctilious* in our planning of this affair, for any error may be regarded as a personal affront.

pungent (*pŭn´-jənt*) ADJ. stinging; caustic. The *pungent* aroma of the smoke made me cough.

punitive (*pū´-*) ADJ. punishing. He asked for *punitive* mea-

---

ā—ale; ă—add; ä—arm; à—ask, ē—eve; ĕ—end; ê—err, her; ə—allow; even; ī—ice; ĭ—ill; ō—oll; ŏ—odd; ô—orb; ōō—food; ŏŏ—foot, put; ou—out; th—thin; ū—use; ŭ—up; zh—pleasure

sures against the offender.

puny ADJ. insignificant; tiny; weak. Our *puny* efforts to stop the flood were futile.

purgatory N. place of spiritual expiation. In this *purgatory,* he could expect no help from his comrades.

purge V. clean by removing impurities; to clear of charges. If you are to be *purged* of the charge of contempt of Congress, you must be willing to answer the questions previously asked. also N.

purloin V. steal. In the story, "The *Purloined* Letter," Poe

points out that the best hiding place is often the most obvious place.

purport N. intention; meaning. If the *purport* of your speech was to arouse the rabble, you succeeded admirably. also V.

purveyor N. furnisher of foodstuffs; caterer. As *purveyor* of rare wines and viands, he traveled through France and Italy every year in search of new products to sell.

purview N. scope. The sociological implications of these inventions are beyond the *purview* of this book.

ETYMOLOGY 23

PRAEDO, PREDA (prey)

predacious living by prey
predatory pillaging, plundering

PRE (before) prefix

precocious ahead of time
precursor forerunner

PRO (before, toward) prefix

prognosticate foretell
propulsive driving forward

TEST—WORD LIST 23—*Antonyms*

Each of the questions below consists of a word printed in italics, followed by five words or phrases numbered 1 to 5. Choose the numbered word or phrase which is most nearly opposite in meaning to the word in italics and write the number of your choice on your answer paper.

441. *precipitate* 1 fast 2 anticipatory 3 cautious 4 considerate 5 dry
442. *prim* 1 informal 2 prior 3 exterior 4 private 5 cautious
443. *protract* 1 make circular 2 shorten 3 further 4 retrace 5 involve
444. *prelude* 1 intermezzo 2 overture 3 aria 4 aftermath 5 duplication
445. *probity* 1 regret 2 assumption 3 corruptibility 4 extent 5 upswing
446. *pretentious* 1 ominous 2 calm 3 unassuming 4 futile 5 volatile
447. *prodigal* 1 wandering 2 thrifty 3 consistent 4 compatible 5 errant
448. *prosaic* 1 pacified 2 reprieved 3 pensive 4 imaginative 5 rhetorical

449. *propitious* 1 rich 2 induced 3 promoted 4 indicative 5 unfavorable
450. *puerile* 1 fragrant 2 adult 3 lonely 4 feminine 5 masterly
451. *pulchritude* 1 ugliness 2 notoriety 3 bestiality 4 masculinity 5 servitude
452. *prefatory* 1 outstanding 2 magnificent 3 conclusive 4 intelligent 5 predatory
453. *punctilious* 1 happy 2 active 3 vivid 4 careless 5 futile
454. *puissant* 1 pouring 2 fashionable 3 articulate 4 healthy 5 weak
455. *prolix* 1 stupid 2 indifferent 3 redundant 4 livid 5 pithy
456. *profane* 1 sanctify 2 desecrate 3 define 4 manifest 5 urge
457. *presumption* 1 assertion 2 activation 3 motivation 4 proposition 5 humility
458. *pristine* 1 cultivated 2 condemned 3 crude 4 cautious 5 critical
459. *prodigious* 1 infinitesimal 2 indignant 3 indifferent 4 indisposed 5 insufficient
460. *punitive* 1 large 2 vindictive 3 rewarding 4 restive 5 languishing

---

WORD LIST 24 **pusillanimous - reiterate**

pusillanimous ADJ. cowardly; fainthearted. You should be ashamed of your *pusillanimous* conduct during this dispute.

putrid ADJ. foul; rotten; decayed. The gangrenous condition of the wound was indicated by the *putrid* smell when the bandages were removed. putrescence, N.

pyromaniac N. person with an insane desire to set things on fire. The detectives searched the area for the *pyromaniac* who had set these costly fires.

quack N. charlatan; impostor. Do not be misled by the exorbitant claims of this *quack.*

quaff (*kwäf*) V. drink with relish. As we *quaffed* our ale, we

listened to the gay songs of the students in the tavern.

quail V. cower; lose heart. He was afraid that he would *quail* in the face of danger.

qualms N. misgivings. His *qualms* of conscience had become so great that he decided to abandon his plans.

quandary N. dilemma. When the two colleges to which he had applied accepted him, he was in a *quandary* as to which one he should attend.

quay (*kē*) N. dock; landing place. Because of the captain's carelessness, the ship crashed into the *quay.*

quell V. put down; quiet. The police used fire hoses and tear gas to *quell* the rioters.

ā—ale; ă—add; ä—arm; à—ask, ē—eve; ĕ—end; ê—err, her; ə—allow; even; ī—ice; ĭ—ill; ō—oll; ŏ—odd; ô—orb; ōō—food; ŏŏ—foot, put; ou—out; th—thin; ū—use; ŭ—up; zh—pleasure

querulous ADJ. fretful; whining. His classmates were repelled by his *querulous* and complaining statements.

quibble V. equivocate; play on words. Do not *quibble;* I want a straightforward and definite answer. also N.

quiescent (*kwī'-ĕs'-*) ADJ. at rest; dormant. After this geyser erupts, it will remain *quiescent* for twenty-four hours.

quietude (*kwī'-ə-tūd*) N. tranquillity. He was impressed by the air of *quietude* and peace that pervaded the valley.

quintessence N. purest and highest embodiment. These books display the *quintessence* of wit.

quip N. taunt. You are unpopular because you are too free with your *quips* and sarcastic comments. also V.

quirk N. startling twist; caprice. By a *quirk* of fate, he found himself working for the man whom he had discharged years before.

qui vive (*kē-vēv'*) N. wide awake; expectant. Let us be on the *qui vive.*

quixotic (*kwĭk-sŏt'-*) ADJ. idealistic but impractical. He is constantly presenting these *quixotic* schemes.

quizzical ADJ. bantering; comical; humorously serious. Will Rogers' *quizzical* remarks endeared him to his audiences.

rabid (*răb'-*) ADJ. like a fanatic; furious. He was a *rabid* follower of the Dodgers and watched them play whenever he could go to the ball park.

ragamuffin N. person wearing tattered clothes. He felt sorry for the *ragamuffin* who was begging for food and gave him money to buy a meal.

ramification N. branching out; subdivision. We must examine all the *ramifications* of this problem.

ramp N. slope; inclined plane. The house was built with *ramps* instead of stairs in order to enable the man in the wheelchair to move easily from room to room and floor to floor.

rampant ADJ. rearing up on hind legs; unrestrained. The *rampant* weeds in the garden killed all the flowers which had been planted in the spring.

rancid ADJ. having the odor of stale fat. A *rancid* odor filled the ship's galley.

rancor N. bitterness; hatred. Let us forget our *rancor* and cooperate in this new endeavor.

rant V. rave; speak bombastically. As we heard him *rant* on the platform, we could not understand his strange popularity with many people.

rapacious ADJ. excessively grasping; plundering. Hawks and *rapacious* birds play an important role in the "balance of nature;" therefore, they are protected from hunting throughout North America.

rapprochement (*răp-rōsh-män'*) N. reconciliation. Both sides were eager to effect a *rapprochement* but did not know how to undertake a program designed to bring about harmony.

rarefied ADJ. made less dense [of a gas]. The mountain climbers had difficulty breathing in the *rarefied* atmosphere.

ratiocination N. reasoning; act of drawing conclusions from premises. Poe's "The Gold Bug" is a splendid example of the author's use of *ratiocination.*

rationalize V. reason; justify an improper act. Do not try to *rationalize* your behavior by blaming your companions.

raucous ADJ. harsh and shrill. His *raucous* laughter irritated me.

ravage (*răv'-*) V. plunder; despoil. The marauding army *ravaged* the countryside.

ravening (*răv'-*) ADJ. rapacious; seeking prey. We kept our fires burning all night to frighten the *ravening* wolves.

ravenous (*răv'-*) ADJ. extremely hungry. The *ravenous* dog upset several garbage pails in its search for food.

raze (*rāz*) V. destroy completely. The owners intend to *raze* the hotel and erect an office building on the site.

realm N. kingdom; sphere. The *realm* of possibilities for the new invention was endless.

rebate N. discount. We offer a *rebate* of ten percent to those who pay cash.

recalcitrant ADJ. obstinately stubborn. Donkeys are reputed to be the most *recalcitrant* of animals.

recant V. repudiate; withdraw previous statement. Unless you *recant* your confession, you will be punished severely.

recapitulate V. summarize. Let us *recapitulate* what has been said thus far before going ahead.

recession N. withdrawal; retreat. The *recession* of the troops from the combat area was completed in an orderly manner.

recipient N. receiver. Although he had been the *recipient* of many favors, he was not grateful to his benefactor.

reciprocal ADJ. mutual; exchangeable; interacting. The two nations signed a *reciprocal* trade agreement.

reciprocate V. repay in kind. If they attack us, we shall be compelled to *reciprocate* and bomb their territory.

recluse (*rĕk'-lōōs*) N. hermit. The *recluse* lived in a hut in the forest.

reconcile V. make friendly after quarrel; correct inconsistencies. Each month we *reconcile* our checkbook with the bank statement.

recondite ADJ. abstruse; profound; secret. He read many *recondite* books in order to obtain the material for his scholarly thesis.

reconnaissance N. survey of enemy by soldiers; reconnoitering. If you encounter any enemy soldiers during your *reconnaissance,* capture them for questioning.

recourse N. resorting to help when in trouble. The boy's only *recourse* was to appeal to his father for aid.

recreant (*rĕk'-*) N. coward; betrayer of faith. The religious people ostracized the *recreant* who had abandoned their faith.

recrimination N. countercharges. Loud and angry *recriminations* were her answer to his accusations.

rectify V. correct. I want to *rectify* my error before it is too late.

rectitude N. uprightness. He was renowned for his *rectitude* and integrity.

recumbent ADJ. reclining; lying down completely or in part. The command "AT EASE" does not permit you to take a *recumbent* position.

recuperate (*rĭ-kū'-*) V. recover. The doctors were worried because the patient did not *recuperate* as rapidly as they had expected.

recurrent ADJ. occurring again and again. These *recurrent* attacks disturbed us and we consulted a physician.

redolent (*rĕd'-*) ADJ. fragrant; odorous; suggestive of an odor. Even though it is February, the air is *redolent* of spring.

redoubtable ADJ. formidable; causing fear. The neighboring countries tried not to offend the Russians because they could be *redoubtable* foes.

redress (*-drĕs'*) N. remedy; compensation. Do you mean to tell me that I can get no *redress* for my injuries? also V.

redundant ADJ. superfluous; excessively wordy; repetitious. Your composition is *redundant;* you can easily reduce its length.

reek V. emit (odor). The room *reeked* with stale tobacco smoke. also N.

refection N. slight refreshment. In our anxiety to reach our destination as rapidly as possible, we stopped on the road for only a quick *refection.*

refectory N. dining hall. In this huge *refectory,* we can feed

---

ā—ale; ă—add; ä—arm; à—ask; ē—eve; ĕ—end; ê—err, her; ə—allow; even; ī—ice; ĭ—ill; ō—oll; ŏ—odd; ô—orb; ōō—food; oŏ—foot, put; ou—out; th—thin; ū—use; ŭ—up; zh—pleasure

the entire student body at one sitting.

refraction N. bending of a ray of light. When you look at a stick inserted in water, it looks bent because of the *refraction* of the light by the water.

refractory ADJ. stubborn; unmanageable. The *refractory* horse was eliminated from the race.

refulgent ADJ. radiant. We admired the *refulgent* moon and watched it for a while.

refutation N. disproof of opponents' arguments. I will wait until I hear the *refutation* before deciding whom to favor.

regal ADJ. royal. He has a *regal* manner.

regale (-*gāl´*) V. entertain. John *regaled* us with tales of his adventures in Africa.

regatta (-*găt´-*) N. boat or yacht race. Many boating enthusiasts followed the *regatta* in their own yachts.

regeneration N. spiritual rebirth. Modern penologists strive for the *regeneration* of the prisoners.

regime (*rā-zhēm´*) N. method or system of government. When a Frenchman mentions the Old *Regime,* he refers to the government existing before the revolution.

regimen (*rĕj´-*) N. prescribed diet and habits. I doubt whether the results warrant our living under such a strict and inflexible *regimen.*

rehabilitate V. restore to proper condition. We must *rehabilitate* those whom we send to prison.

reimburse V. repay. Let me know what you have spent and I will *reimburse* you.

reiterate V. repeat. I shall *reiterate* this message until all have understood it.

ETYMOLOGY 24

PUT, PUTAT (to trim, to calculate)

computation a reckoning
amputate cut off
putative supposed (calculated)

QUAER, QUAESIT (to ask)

inquiry investigation
inquisitive questioning
query question

TEST—WORD LIST 24—*Synonyms and Antonyms*

Each of the questions below consists of a word printed in italics, followed by five words or phrases numbered 1 to 5. Choose the numbered word or phrase which is most nearly the same as or the opposite of the word in italics and write the number of your choice on your answer paper.

461. *regal* 1 oppressive 2 common 3 major 4 basic 5 entertaining
462. *rebate* 1 relinquish 2 settle 3 discount 4 cancel 5 elicit
463. *quandary* 1 quagmire 2 dilemma 3 epigram 4 enemy 5 finish
464. *refractory* 1 articulate 2 sinkable 3 vaunted 4 useless 5 manageable
465. *raze* 1 shave 2 heckle 3 finish 4 tear down 5 write
466. *putrid* 1 sick 2 lovely 3 aromatic 4 arrogant 5 humid
467. *recuperate* 1 reenact 2 engage 3 recapitulate 4 recover 5 encounter
468. *ravage* 1 rank 2 revive 3 plunder 4 pillory 5 age

469. *quaff* 1 drug 2 imbibe 3 seal 4 scale 5 joke
470. *rectify* 1 remedy 2 avenge 3 create 4 assemble 5 attribute
471. *raucous* 1 mellifluous 2 uncooked 3 realistic 4 veracious 5 anticipating
472. *pusillanimous* 1 poverty-stricken 2 chained 3 posthumous 4 cowardly 5 strident
473. *recreant* 1 vacationing 2 faithful 3 indifferent 4 obliged 5 reviving
474. *quixotic* 1 rapid 2 exotic 3 longing 4 timid 5 idealistic
475. *rehabilitate* 1 clothe 2 destroy 3 avenge 4 vanish 5 embarrass
476. *qui vive* 1 alive 2 fast 3 gloomy 4 vivid 5 awake
477. *reimburse* 1 remunerate 2 constitute 3 dip 4 demolish 5 patronize
478. *regatta* 1 impertinence 2 boat race 3 satisfaction 4 saturation 5 quiz
479. *reiterate* 1 gainsay 2 revive 3 revenge 4 repeat 5 return
480. *refulgent* 1 overflowing 2 effortless 3 dim 4 noisy 5 snoring

---

WORD LIST 25 **rejuvenate - rostrum**

rejuvenate V. make young again. The charlatan claimed that his elixir would *rejuvenate* the aged and weary.

relegate V. banish; consign to inferior position. If we *relegate* these experienced people to positions of unimportance because of their political persuasions, we shall lose the services of valuably trained personnel.

relevancy N. pertinence; reference to the case in hand. I was impressed by the *relevancy* of your remarks. relevant, ADJ.

relinquish V. abandon. I will *relinquish* my claims to this property if you promise to retain my employees.

relish V. savor; enjoy. I *relish* a good joke as much as anyone else. also N.

remediable (-*mĕd´-*) ADJ. reparable. Let us be grateful that the damage is *remediable.*

remedial ADJ. curative; corrective. Because he was a slow reader, he decided to take a course in *remedial* reading.

reminiscence N. recollection. Her *reminiscences* of her experiences are so fascinating that she ought to write a book.

remiss ADJ. negligent. He was accused of being *remiss* in his duty.

remnant N. remainder. I suggest that you wait until the store places the *remnants* of these goods on sale.

remonstrate (-*mŏn´-*) V. protest. I must *remonstrate* about the lack of police protection in this area.

ā—ale; ă—add; ä—arm; à—ask, ē—eve; ĕ—end; ê—err, her; ə—allow; even; ī—ice; ĭ—ill; ō—oll; ŏ—odd; ô—orb; ōō—food; ŏŏ—foot, put; ou—out; th—thin; ū—use; ŭ—up; zh—pleasure

remunerative ADJ. compensating; rewarding. I find my new work so *remunerative* that I may not return to my previous employment. remuneration, N.

rend V. split; tear apart. In his grief, he tried to *rend* his garments.

render V. deliver; provide; represent. He *rendered* aid to the needy and indigent.

rendezvous (rŏn´-dĭ-vōō) N. meeting place. The two fleets met at the *rendezvous* at the appointed time. also V.

renegade N. deserter; apostate. Because he refused to support his fellow members in their drive, he was shunned as a *renegade*.

renounce V. abandon; discontinue; disown; repudiate. Joan of Arc refused to *renounce* her statements even though she knew she would be burned at the stake as a witch.

renovate V. restore to good condition; renew. They claim that they can *renovate* worn shoes so that they look like new ones.

renunciation N. giving up; renouncing. Do not sign this *renunciation* of your right to sue until you have consulted a lawyer.

reparable (rĕp´-) ADJ. capable of being repaired. Fortunately, the damages we suffered in the accident were *reparable*.

reparation N. amends; compensation. At the peace conference, the defeated country promised to pay *reparations* to the victors.

repartee (rĕp-ər-tē´) N. clever reply. He was famous for his witty *repartee* and his sarcasm.

repellent ADJ. driving away; unattractive. Mosquitoes find the odor so *repellent* that they leave any spot where this liquid has been sprayed. also N.

repercussion N. rebound; reverberation; reaction. I am afraid that this event will have serious *repercussions*.

repertoire N. list of works of music, drama, etc., a performer is prepared to present. The opera company decided to include *Madame Butterfly* in its *repertoire* for the following season.

replenish V. fill up again. The end of rationing enabled us to *replenish* our supply of canned food.

replete (-plēt´) ADJ. filled to capacity; abundantly supplied. This book is *replete* with humorous situations.

replica N. copy. Are you going to hang this *replica* of the Declaration of Independence in the classroom or in the auditorium?

repository N. storehouse. Libraries are *repositories* of the world's best thoughts.

reprehensible ADJ. deserving blame. Your vicious conduct in this situation is *reprehensible*.

reprieve N. temporary stay. During the twenty-four-hour *reprieve*, the lawyers sought to make the stay of execution permanent. also V.

reprimand V. reprove severely. I am afraid that my parents will *reprimand* me when I show them my report card. also N.

reprisal N. retaliation. I am confident that we are ready for any *reprisals* the enemy may undertake.

reprobation N. severe disapproval. The students showed their *reprobation* of his act by refusing to talk with him.

repudiate V. disown; disavow. He announced that he would *repudiate* all debts incurred by his wife.

repugnance N. loathing. She looked at the snake with *repugnance*.

requiem N. mass for the dead; dirge. They played Mozart's *Requiem* at the funeral.

requisite N. necessary requirement. Many colleges state that a student must offer three years of a language as a *requisite*

for admission.

requite V. repay; revenge. The wretch *requited* his benefactors by betraying them.

rescind V. cancel. Because of public resentment, the king had to *rescind* his order.

rescission N. abrogation; annulment. The *rescission* of the unpopular law was urged by all political parties.

resonant (rĕz´-) ADJ. echoing; resounding; possessing resonance. His *resonant* voice was particularly pleasing.

respite (rĕs´-pət) N. delay in punishment; interval of relief; rest. The judge granted the condemned man a *respite* to enable his attorneys to file an appeal.

resplendent ADJ. brilliant; lustrous. The toreador wore a *resplendent* costume.

restitution N. reparation; indemnification. He offered to make *restitution* for the window broken by his son.

restive ADJ. unmanageable; fretting under control. We must quiet the *restive* animals.

resuscitate V. revive. The lifeguard tried to *resuscitate* the drowned child by applying artificial respiration.

retaliate V. repay in kind (usually for bad treatment). Fear that we will *retaliate* immediately deters our foe from attacking us.

retentive ADJ. holding; having a good memory. The pupil did not need to spend much time in study as he had a *retentive* mind.

reticence N. reserve; uncommunicativeness; inclination to be silent. Because of the *reticence* of the key witness, the case against the defendant collapsed.

retinue N. following; attendants. The queen's *retinue* followed her down the aisle.

retraction N. withdrawal. He dropped his libel suit after the newspaper published a *retraction* of its statement.

retribution N. vengeance; compensation; punishment for offenses. The evangelist maintained that an angry Deity would exact *retribution* from the sinners.

retrieve V. recover; find and bring in. The dog was intelligent and quickly learned to *retrieve* the game killed by the hunter.

retroactive ADJ. of a law which dates back to a period before its enactment. Because the law was *retroactive* to the first of the year, we found he was eligible for the pension.

retrograde V. going backwards; degenerating. Instead of advancing, our civilization seems to have *retrograded* in ethics and culture.

retrospective ADJ. looking back on the past. It is only when we become *retrospective* that we can appreciate the tremendous advances made during this century.

revelry N. boisterous merrymaking. New Year's Eve is a night of *revelry*.

reverberate V. echo; resound. The entire valley *reverberated* with the sound of the church bells.

reverie N. daydream; musing. He was awakened from his *reverie* by the teacher's question.

revile V. slander; vilify. He was avoided by all who feared that he would *revile* and abuse them if they displeased him.

revulsion N. sudden violent change of feeling; reaction. Many people in this country who admired dictatorships underwent a *revulsion* when they realized what Hitler and Mussolini were trying to do.

rhetoric N. art of effective communication; insincere language. All writers, by necessity, must be skilled in *rhetoric*. rhetorical, ADJ.

rheumy (rōō´-mē) ADJ. pertaining to a discharge from nose and eyes. His *rheumy* eyes warned us that he was coming down with a cold.

ribald (rĭb´-) ADJ. wanton; profane. He sang a *ribald* song

ā—ale; ă—add; ä—arm; à—ask; ē—eve; ĕ—end; ê—err, her; ə—allow; even; ī—ice; ĭ—ill; ō—oll; ŏ—odd; ô—orb; ōō—food; ŏŏ—foot, put; ou—out; th—thin; ū—use; ŭ—up; zh—pleasure

which offended many of us.

rife ADJ. abundant; current. In the face of the many rumors of scandal, which are *rife* at the moment, it is best to remain silent.

rift N. opening; break. The plane was lost in the stormy sky until the pilot saw the city through a *rift* in the clouds.

rigor N. severity. Many settlers could not stand the *rigors* of the New England winters.

rime N. white frost. The early morning dew had frozen and everything was covered with a thin coat of *rime*.

risible (*rĭz´-*) ADJ. inclined to laugh; ludicrous. His remarks were so *risible* that the audience howled with laughter. risibility, N.

risqué (*rĭ-skā´*) ADJ. verging upon the improper; off-color. Please do not tell your *risqué* anecdotes at this party.

roan ADJ. brown mixed with gray or white. You can distinguish this horse in a race because it is *roan* while all the others are bay or chestnut.

robust (*-bŭst´*) ADJ. vigorous; strong. The candidate for the football team had a *robust* physique.

rococo (*rə-kō´-kō*) ADJ. ornate; highly decorated. The *rococo* style in furniture and architecture, marked by scrollwork and excessive decoration, flourished during the middle of the eighteenth century.

roseate (*rō´-zē-ət*) ADJ. rosy; optimistic. I am afraid you will have to alter your *roseate* views in the light of the distressing news that has just arrived.

rostrum N. platform for speech-making; pulpit. The crowd murmured angrily and indicated that they did not care to listen to the speaker who was approaching the *rostrum*.

ETYMOLOGY 25

RID, RIS (to laugh)

derision scorn
risibility inclination to laughter
ridiculous deserving to be laughed at

ROG, ROGAT (to ask) ·

interrogate to question
prerogative privilege
derogatory disparaging (asking a question to belittle)

TEST—WORD LIST 25—*Synonyms*

Each of the questions below consists of a word printed in italics, followed by five words or phrases numbered 1 to 5. Choose the numbered word or phrase which is most nearly similar in meaning to the word in italics and write the number of your choice on your answer paper.

481. *restive* 1 buoyant 2 restless 3 remorseful 4 resistant 5 retiring
482. *replenish* 1 polish 2 repeat 3 reinstate 4 refill 5 refuse
483. *remonstrate* 1 display 2 restate 3 protest 4 resign 5 reiterate
484. *repugnance* 1 belligerence 2 tenacity 3 renewal 4 pity 5 loathing
485. *repercussion* 1 reverberation 2 restitution 3 resistance 4 magnificence 5 acceptance
486. *remiss* 1 lax 2 lost 3 foolish 4 violating 5 ambitious
487. *repudiate* 1 besmirch 2 appropriate 3 annoy 4 reject 5 avow
488. *repellent* 1 propulsive 2 unattractive 3 porous 4 stiff 5 elastic
489. *remedial* 1 therapeutic 2 corrective 3 traumatic
4 philandering 5 psychotic
490. *reprisal* 1 reevaluation 2 assessment 3 loss 4 retaliation 5 nonsense
491. *repartee* 1 witty retort 2 willful departure 3 spectator 4 monologue 5 sacrifice
492. *relish* 1 desire 2 nibble 3 savor 4 vindicate 5 avail
493. *replica* 1 museum piece 2 famous site 3 battle emblem 4 facsimile 5 replacement
494. *reparation* 1 result 2 compensation 3 alteration 4 retaliation 5 resistance
495. *robust* 1 vigorous 2 violent 3 vicious 4 villainous 5 voracious
496. *retinue* 1 continuation 2 attendants 3 application 4 beleaguer 5 assessment
497. *rife* 1 direct 2 scant 3 abundant 4 grim 5 mature
498. *reticence* 1 reserve 2 fashion 3 treachery 4 loquaciousness 5 magnanimity
499. *retrograde* 1 receding 2 inclining 3 evaluating 4 concentrating 5 directing
500. *retentive* 1 grasping 2 accepting 3 repetitive 4 avoiding 5 fascinating

WORD LIST **26 rote - silt**

rote N. repetition. He recited the passage by *rote* and gave no indication he understood what he was saying.

rotundity N. roundness; sonorousness of speech. Washington Irving emphasized the *rotundity* of the governor by describing his height and circumference.

rubble N. fragments. Ten years after World War II, some of the *rubble* left by enemy bombings could still be seen.

rubicund (*roo´-*) ADJ. having a healthy reddish color; ruddy; florid. His *rubicund* complexion was the result of an active

outdoor life.

ruddy ADJ. reddish; healthy-looking. His *ruddy* features indicated that he had spent much time in the open.

rudimentary ADJ. not developed; elementary. His dancing was limited to a few *rudimentary* steps.

rueful ADJ. regretful; sorrowful; dejected. The artist has captured the sadness of childhood in his portrait of the boy with the *rueful* countenance.

ruminate V. chew the cud; ponder. We cannot afford to wait

ā—ale; ă—add; ä—arm; à—ask; ē—eve; ĕ—end; ê—err, her; ə—allow; even; ī—ice; ĭ—ill; ō—oll; ŏ—odd; ô—orb; oo—food; oo—foot, put; ou—out; th—thin; ū—use; ŭ—up; zh—pleasure

while you *ruminate* upon these plans.

rummage V. ransack; thoroughly search. When we *rummaged* through the trunks in the attic, we found many souvenirs of our childhood days. also N.

ruse N. trick; stratagem. You will not be able to fool your friends with such an obvious *ruse.*

rusticate V. banish to the country; dwell in the country. I like city life so much that I can never understand how people can *rusticate* in the suburbs.

ruthless ADJ. pitiless. The escaped convict was a dangerous and *ruthless* murderer.

sacerdotal (săs-ər-dōt´-) ADJ. priestly. The priest decided to abandon his *sacerdotal* duties and enter the field of politics.

sacrilegious (-lĭj-) ADJ. desecrating; profane. His stealing of the altar cloth was a very *sacrilegious* act.

sacrosanct (săk´-) ADJ. most sacred; inviolable. The brash insurance salesman invaded the *sacrosanct* privacy of the office of the president of the company.

sadistic (-dĭs´-) ADJ. inclined to cruelty. If we are to improve conditions in this prison, we must first get rid of the *sadistic* warden.

saffron ADJ. orange-colored; colored like the autumn crocus. The Halloween cake was decorated with *saffron*-colored icing.

saga (säg´-) N. Scandinavian myth; any legend. This is a *saga* of the sea and the men who risk their lives on it.

sagacious ADJ. keen; shrewd; having insight. He is much too *sagacious* to be fooled by a trick like that.

salient (sā´-lyənt) ADJ. prominent. One of the *salient* features of that newspaper is its excellent editorial page.

saline (sā´-lēn) ADJ. salty. The slighty *saline* taste of this mineral water is pleasant.

sallow ADJ. yellowish; sickly in color. We were disturbed by his *sallow* complexion.

salubrious (-loō´-) ADJ. healthful. Many people with hay fever move to more *salubrious* sections of the country during the months of August and September.

salutary ADJ. tending to improve; beneficial; wholesome. The punishment had a *salutary* effect on the boy, as he became a model student.

salvage V. rescue from loss. All attempts to *salvage* the wrecked ship failed. also N.

sangfroid (sän´-frwä) N. coolness in a trying situation. The captain's *sangfroid* helped to allay the fears of the passengers.

sanguinary ADJ. bloody. The battle of Iwo Jima was unexpectedly *sanguinary.*

sanguine ADJ. cheerful; hopeful. Let us not be too *sanguine* about the outcome.

sapid (săp´-) ADJ. savory; tasty; relishable. This chef has the knack of making most foods more *sapid* and appealing.

sapient (sā´-) ADJ. wise; shrewd. The students enjoyed the professor's *sapient* digressions more than his formal lectures.

sardonic ADJ. disdainful; sarcastic; cynical. The *sardonic* humor of nightclub comedians who satirize or ridicule patrons in the audience strikes some people as amusing and others as rude.

sate V. satisfy to the full; cloy. Its hunger *sated,* the lion dozed.

satiate V. surfeit; satisfy fully. The guests, having eaten until they were *satiated,* now listened inattentively to the speakers.

satiety (-tī´-ət-ē) N. condition of being crammed full; glutted state; repletion. The *satiety* of the guests at the sumptuous feast became apparent when they refused the delicious dessert.

saturate V. soak. Their clothes were *saturated* by the rain.

saturnine (săt´-ər-nīn) ADJ. gloomy. Do not be misled by his *saturnine* countenance; he is not as gloomy as he looks.

saunter V. stroll slowly. As we *sauntered* through the park, we stopped frequently to admire the spring flowers.

savant (să-vänt´) N. scholar. Our faculty includes many world-famous *savants.*

savoir faire (săv-wär-fär´) N. tact; poise; sophistication. I envy his *savoir faire;* he always knows exactly what to do and say.

savor V. have a distinctive flavor, smell, or quality. I think your choice of a successor *savors* of favoritism.

scavenger N. collector and disposer of refuse; animal that devours refuse and carrion. The Oakland *Scavenger* Company is responsible for the collection and disposal of the community's garbage.

schism (sĭz´-əm) N. division; split. Let us not widen the *schism* by further bickering.

scintilla N. shred; least bit. You have not produced a *scintilla* of evidence to support your argument.

scintillate V. sparkle; flash. I enjoy her dinner parties because the food is excellent and the conversation *scintillates.*

scion (sī´-ən) N. offspring. The farm boy felt out of place in the school attended by the *scions* of the wealthy and noble families.

scourge (skêrj) N. lash; whip; severe punishment. They feared the plague and regarded it as a deadly *scourge.* also V.

scrupulous ADJ. conscientious; extremely thorough. I can recommend him for a position of responsibility for I have found him a very *scrupulous* young man.

scullion N. menial kitchen worker. Lynette was angry because she thought she had been given a *scullion* to act as her defender.

scurrilous ADJ. obscene; indecent. Your *scurrilous* remarks are especially offensive because they are untrue.

scuttle V. sink. The sailors decided to *scuttle* their vessel rather than surrender it to the enemy.

sebaceous (-bā´-) ADJ. oily; fatty. The *sebaceous* glands secrete oil to the hair follicles.

secession N. withdrawal. The *secession* of the Southern states provided Lincoln with his first major problem after his inauguration.

secular (sĕk´-) ADJ. worldly; not pertaining to church matters; temporal. The church leaders decided not to interfere in *secular* matters.

sedate ADJ. composed; grave. The parents were worried because they felt their son was too quiet and *sedate.*

sedentary (sĕd´-) ADJ. requiring sitting. Because he had a *sedentary* occupation, he decided to visit a gymnasium weekly.

sedulous ADJ. diligent. Stevenson said that he played the "*sedulous* ape" and diligently imitated the great writers of the past.

seethe V. be disturbed; boil. The nation was *seething* with discontent as the noblemen continued their arrogant ways.

seine (sān) N. net for catching fish. When the shad run during the spring, you may see fishermen with *seines* along the banks of our coastal rivers.

semblance N. outward appearance; guise. Although this book has a *semblance* of wisdom and scholarship, a careful examination will reveal many errors and omissions.

senility N. old age; feeblemindedness of old age. Most of the decisions are being made by the junior members of the company because of the *senility* of the president.

sensual ADJ. devoted to the pleasures of the senses; carnal; voluptuous. I cannot understand what caused him to drop

ā—ale; ă—add; ä—arm; à—ask; ē—eve; ĕ—end; ê—err, her; ə—allow; even; ī—ice; ĭ—ill; ō—oll; ŏ—odd; ô—orb; oō—food;
oŏ—foot, put; ou—out; th—thin; ū—use; ŭ—up; zh—pleasure

his *sensual* way of life and become so ascetic.

sententious ADJ. terse; concise; aphoristic. After reading so many redundant speeches, I find his *sententious* style particularly pleasing.

sepulcher N. tomb. Annabel Lee was buried in the *sepulcher* by the sea.

sequester V. retire from public life; segregate; seclude. Although he had hoped for a long time to *sequester* himself in a small community, he never was able to drop his busy round of activities in the city.

serendipity N. gift for finding valuable things not searched for. Many scientific discoveries are a matter of *serendipity*.

serenity N. calmness; placidity. The *serenity* of the sleepy town was shattered by a tremendous explosion.

serrated (sə-rā´-təd) ADJ. having a sawtoothed edge. The beech tree is one of many plants that have *serrated* leaves.

servile (sêr´-vəl) ADJ. slavish; cringing. Uriah Heep was a very *servile* individual.

severance N. division; partition; separation. The *severance* of church and state is a basic principle of our government.

shackle V. chain; fetter. The criminal's ankles were *shackled* to prevent his escape. also N.

shambles N. slaughterhouse; scene of carnage. By the time the police arrived, the room was a *shambles*.

sheaf N. bundle of stalks of grain; any bundle of things tied together. The lawyer picked up a *sheaf* of papers as he rose to question the witness.

sheathe V. place into a case. As soon as he recognized the approaching men, he *sheathed* his dagger and hailed them as friends.

sherbet N. flavored dessert ice. I prefer raspberry *sherbet* to ice cream since it is less fattening.

shibboleth (shĭb´-) N. watchword; slogan. We are often misled by *shibboleths*.

shimmer V. glimmer intermittently. The moonlight *shimmered* on the water as the moon broke through the clouds for a moment. also N.

shoal N. shallow place. The ship was stranded on a *shoal* and had to be pulled off by tugs.

shoddy ADJ. sham; not genuine; inferior. You will never get the public to buy such *shoddy* material.

sidereal (sī-dĭr´-) ADJ. relating to the stars. The study of *sidereal* bodies has been greatly advanced by the new telescope.

silt N. sediment deposited by running water. The harbor channel must be dredged annually to remove the *silt*.

ETYMOLOGY 26

RUPT (to break)

interrupt break into
bankrupt insolvent
rupture a break

SCI (to know)

science knowledge
omniscient knowing all
conscious aware

SCRIB, SCRIPT (to write)

transcribe copy
script writing
circumscribe enclose, limit (write around)

SED, SESS, SID (to sit)

sedentary inactive (sitting)
session meeting
residence place where one dwells

SENT, SENS (to think, to feel)

resent show indignation
sensitive showing feeling
consent agree

SEQUE, SECUT (to follow)

consecutive following in order
sequence arrangement
sequel that which follows

TEST—WORD LIST 26—*Antonyms*

Each of the questions below consists of a word printed in italics, followed by five words or phrases numbered 1 to 5. Choose the numbered word or phrase which is most nearly opposite in meaning to the word in italics and write the number of your choice on your answer paper.

501. *scurrilous* 1 savage 2 scabby 3 decent 4 volatile 5 major

502. *sagacious* 1 foolish 2 bitter 3 voracious 4 veracious 5 fallacious

503. *rudimentary* 1 pale 2 fundamental 3 asinine 4 developed 5 quiescent

504. *sanguine* 1 choleric 2 sickening 3 warranted 4 irritated 5 pessimistic

505. *sadistic* 1 happy 2 quaint 3 kindhearted 4 vacant 5 fortunate

506. *ruddy* 1 robust 2 witty 3 wan 4 exotic 5 creative

507. *salvage* 1 remove 2 outfit 3 burn 4 lose 5 confuse

508. *sacerdotal* 1 religious 2 frank 3 authoritative 4 violent 5 lay

509. *rubicund* 1 dangerous 2 pallid 3 remote 4 indicative 5 nonsensical

510. *salubrious* 1 salty 2 bloody 3 miasmic 4 maudlin 5 wanted

511. *ruthless* 1 merciful 2 majestic 3 mighty 4 militant 5 maximum

512. *rotundity* 1 promenade 2 nave 3 grotesqueness 4 slimness 5 impropriety

513. *sallow* 1 salacious 2 ruddy 3 colorless 4 permitted 5 minimum

514. *rueful* 1 sad 2 content 3 capable 4 capital 5 zealous

515. *secular* 1 vivid 2 clerical 3 punitive 4 positive 5 varying

516. *shoddy* 1 superior 2 incomplete 3 inadequate 4 querulous 5 garrulous

517. *sedentary* 1 vicarious 2 loyal 3 accidental 4 active 5 afraid

518. *servile* 1 menial 2 puerile 3 futile 4 lowly 5 haughty

ā—ale; ă—add; ä—arm; à—ask, ē—eve; ĕ—end; ê—err, her; ə—allow; even; ī—ice; ĭ—ill; ō—oll; ŏ—odd; ô—orb; ōō—food; ŏŏ—foot, put; ou—out; th—thin; ū—use; ŭ—up; zh—pleasure

519. *sententious* 1 paragraphed 2 positive 3 posthumous 4 pacific 5 wordy

520. *senility* 1 virility 2 loquaciousness 3 forgetfulness 4 youth 5 majority

---

WORD LIST 27 **simian - sultry**

simian ADJ. monkeylike. Lemurs are nocturnal mammals and have many *simian* characteristics, although they are less intelligent than monkeys.

simile (*sĭm´-ə-lē*) N. comparison of one thing with another, using the word *like* or *as*. We are constantly using *similes* and metaphors to convey our thoughts to others.

simulate V. feign. He *simulated* insanity in order to avoid punishment for his crime.

sinecure (*sī´-nĭ-kyŏor*) N. well-paid position with little responsibility. My job is no *sinecure;* I work long hours and have much responsibility.

sinister ADJ. evil. We must defeat the *sinister* forces that seek our downfall.

sinuous ADJ. winding; bending in and out; not morally honest. The snake moved in a *sinuous* manner.

skimp V. provide scantily; live very economically. They were forced to *skimp* on necessities in order to make their limited supplies last the winter.

skittish ADJ. lively; frisky. He is as *skittish* as a kitten playing with a piece of string.

skulk V. move furtively and secretly. He *skulked* through the less fashionable sections of the city in order to avoid meeting any of his former friends.

slake V. quench; sate. When we reached the oasis, we were able to *slake* our thirst.

sleazy ADJ. flimsy; unsubstantial. This is a *sleazy* material; it will not wear well.

sloth (*slôth*) N. laziness. Such *sloth* in a young person is deplorable.

slough (*slŭf*) V. cast off. Each spring, the snake *sloughs* off its skin.

slovenly (*slŭv´-*) ADJ. untidy; careless in work habits. Such *slovenly* work habits will never produce good products.

sluggard N. lazy person. "You are a *sluggard,* a drone, a parasite," the angry father shouted at his lazy son.

sobriety N. soberness. The solemnity of the occasion filled us with *sobriety.*

sojourn N. temporary stay. After his *sojourn* in Florida, he began to long for the colder climate of his native New England home.

solecism N. construction that is flagrantly incorrect grammatically. I must give this paper a failing mark because it contains many *solecisms.*

solicitous ADJ. worried; concerned. The employer was very *solicitous* about the health of his employees as replacements were difficult to get.

soliloquy N. talking to oneself. The *soliloquy* is a device used by the dramatist to reveal a character's innermost thoughts and emotions.

solstice N. point at which the sun is farthest from the equator. The winter *solstice* usually occurs on December 21.

solvent ADJ. able to pay all debts. By dint of very frugal living, he was finally able to become *solvent* and avoid bankruptcy proceedings.

somnambulist N. sleepwalker. The most famous *somnambulist* in literature is Lady Macbeth; her monologue in the sleepwalking scene is one of the highlights of Shakespeare's play.

somnolent ADJ. half asleep. The heavy meal and the overheated room made us all *somnolent* and indifferent to the speaker.

sonorous (*-nōr´-*) ADJ. resonant. His *sonorous* voice resounded through the hall.

soupçon (*soōp-sōn´*) N. suggestion; hint; taste. A *soupçon* of garlic will improve this dish.

spangle N. small metallic piece sewn to clothing for ornamentation. The thousands of *spangles* on her dress sparkled in the glare of the stage lights.

spasmodic ADJ. fitful; periodic. The *spasmodic* coughing in the auditorium annoyed the performers.

spatial ADJ. relating to space. It is difficult to visualize the *spatial* extent of our universe.

spawn V. lay eggs. Fish ladders had to be built in the dams to assist the salmon returning to *spawn* in their native streams. also N.

specious (*spē´-*) ADJ. seemingly reasonable but incorrect. Let us not be misled by such *specious* arguments.

spectral ADJ. ghostly. We were frightened by the *spectral* glow that filled the room.

splenetic (*splĭ-nĕt´-*) ADJ. spiteful; irritable; peevish. People shunned him because of his *splenetic* temper. spleen, N.

sporadic (*-răd´-*) ADJ. occurring irregularly. Although there are *sporadic* outbursts of shooting, we may report that the major rebellion has been defeated.

sportive ADJ. playful. Such a *sportive* attitude is surprising in a person as serious as you usually are.

spurious ADJ. false; counterfeit. He tried to pay the check with a *spurious* ten-dollar bill.

squalid (*skwŏl´-*) ADJ. dirty; neglected; poor. It is easy to see how crime can breed in such a *squalid* neighborhood.

squander V. waste. The prodigal son *squandered* the family estate.

stagnant ADJ. motionless; stale; dull. The *stagnant* water was a breeding ground for disease. stagnate, V.

staid ADJ. sober; sedate. His conduct during the funeral ceremony was *staid* and solemn.

stamina N. strength; staying power. I doubt that he has the *stamina* to run the full distance of the marathon race.

stanch (*stônch*) V. check flow of blood. It is imperative that we *stanch* the gushing wound before we attend to the other injuries.

statute N. law. We have many *statutes* in our law books which should be repealed.

stein N. beer mug. He thought of college as a place where one drank beer from *steins* and sang songs of lost lambs.

stellar ADJ. pertaining to the stars. He was the *stellar* attraction of the entire performance.

stentorian ADJ. extremely loud. The town crier had a *stentorian* voice.

stigmatize V. brand; mark as wicked. I do not want to *stigmatize* this young offender for life by sending him to prison.

stint N. supply; allotted amount; assigned portion of work. He performed his daily *stint* cheerfully and willingly. also, V.

stipend (*stī´-*) N. pay for services. There is a nominal *stipend*

ā—ale; ă—add; ä—arm; à—ask, ē—eve; ĕ—end; ê—err, her; ə—allow; even; ī—ice; ĭ—ill; ō—oll; ŏ—odd; ô—orb; ōo—food; ŏo—foot, put; ou—out; th—thin; ū—use; ŭ—up; zh—pleasure attached to this position.

stoic (*stō´-ĭk*) N. person who is indifferent to pleasure or pain. The doctor called her patient a *stoic* because he had borne the pain of the examination without whimpering. also ADJ.

stolid ADJ. dull; impassive. I am afraid that this imaginative poetry will not appeal to such a *stolid* person.

stratagem (*străt´-*) N. deceptive scheme. We saw through his clever *stratagem.*

striated (*strī´-āt-*) ADJ. marked with parallel bands. The glacier left many *striated* rocks.

stricture N. critical comments; severe and adverse criticism. His *strictures* on the author's style are prejudiced and unwarranted.

strident (*strīd´-*) ADJ. loud and harsh. She scolded him in a *strident* voice.

stringent (*strĭn´-jənt*) ADJ. binding; rigid. I think these regulations are too *stringent.*

stupor N. state of apathy; daze; lack of awareness. In his *stupor,* the addict was unaware of the events taking place around him.

stymie V. present an obstacle; stump. The detective was *stymied* by the contradictory evidence in the robbery investigation. also N.

suavity (*swäv´-*) N. urbanity; polish. He is particularly good in roles that require *suavity* and sophistication.

subaltern (*-bôl´-*) N. subordinate. The captain treated his *subalterns* as though they were children rather than commissioned officers.

subjugate V. conquer; bring under control. It is not our aim to *subjugate* our foe; we are interested only in establishing peaceful relations.

sublimate V. refine; purify. We must strive to *sublimate* these desires and emotions into worthwhile activities.

sublime ADJ. exalted; noble; uplifting. We must learn to recognize *sublime* truths.

sub rosa ADV. in strict confidence; privately. I heard of this *sub rosa* and I cannot tell you about it.

subsequent ADJ. following; later. In *subsequent* lessons, we shall take up more difficult problems.

subservient ADJ. behaving like a slave; servile; obsequious. He was proud and dignified; he refused to be *subservient*

to anyone.

subsidiary ADJ. subordinate; secondary. This information may be used as *subsidiary* evidence but is not sufficient by itself to prove your argument. also N.

subsistence N. existence; means of support; livelihood. In these days of inflated prices, my salary provides a mere *subsistence.*

substantiate V. verify; support. I intend to *substantiate* my statement by producing witnesses.

subterfuge N. pretense; evasion. As soon as we realized that you had won our support by a *subterfuge,* we withdrew our endorsement of your candidacy.

subtlety (*sŭt´-l-tē*) N. nicety; cunning; guile; delicacy. The *subtlety* of his remarks was unnoticed by most of his audience.

subversive ADJ. tending to overthrow or ruin. We must destroy such *subversive* publications.

succinct (*sŭk-sĭngkt´*) ADJ. brief; terse; compact. His remarks are always *succinct* and pointed.

succor N. aid; assistance; relief. We shall be ever grateful for the *succor* your country gave us when we were in need. also V.

succulent ADJ. juicy; full of richness. The citrus foods from Florida are more *succulent* to some people than those from California. also N.

suffuse V. spread over. A blush *suffused* her cheeks when we teased her about her love affair.

sully V. tarnish; soil. He felt that it was beneath his dignity to *sully* his hands in such menial labor.

sultry ADJ. sweltering. He could not adjust himself to the *sultry* climate of the tropics.

summation N. act of finding the total; summary. In his *summation,* the lawyer emphasized the testimony given by the two witnesses.

sumptuous ADJ. lavish; rich. I cannot recall when I have had such a *sumptuous* feast.

sunder V. separate; part. Northern and southern Ireland are politically and religiously *sundered.*

sundry ADJ. various; several. My suspicions were aroused when I read *sundry* items in the newspapers about your behavior.

ETYMOLOGY 27

SOLV, SOLUT (to loosen)

absolve free from blame
dissolute morally lax
absolute complete (not loosened)

SPEC, SPECT (to look at)

spectator observer
aspect appearance
circumspect cautious (looking around)

TEST—WORD LIST 27—*Synonyms and Antonyms*

Each of the following questions consists of a word printed in italics, followed by five words or phrases numbered 1 to 5. Choose the numbered word or phrase which is most nearly the same as or the opposite of the word in italics and write the number of your choice on your answer paper.

521. *squander* 1 fortify 2 depart 3 roam 4 preserve 5 forfeit
522. *somnolent* 1 stentorian 2 settled 3 half awake 4 soothed
5 ambulatory
523. *skittish* 1 tractable 2 inquiring 3 dramatic 4 vain 5 frisky
524. *sportive* 1 competing 2 playful 3 indignant 4 foppish 5 fundamental
525. *solvent* 1 enigmatic 2 bankrupt 3 fiducial 4 puzzling 5 gilded
526. *sloth* 1 penitence 2 filth 3 futility 4 poverty 5 industry
527. *spasmodic* 1 intermittent 2 fit 3 inaccurate 4 violent 5 physical

ā—ale; ă—add; ä—arm; à—ask, ē—eve; ĕ—end; ê—err, her; ə—allow; even; ī—ice; ĭ—ill; ō—oll; ŏ—odd; ô—orb; ōō—food; ŏŏ—foot, put; ou—out; th—thin; ū—use; ŭ—up; zh—pleasure

528. *sobriety* 1 inebriety 2 aptitude 3 scholasticism 4 monotony 5 aversion
529. *sleazy* 1 fanciful 2 creeping 3 substantial 4 uneasy 5 warranted
530. *solstice* 1 equinox 2 sunrise 3 pigsty 4 interstices 5 iniquity
531. *slovenly* 1 half-baked 2 loved 3 inappropriate 4 tidy 5 rapidly
532. *sinister* 1 unwed 2 ministerial 3 good 4 returned 5 splintered
533. *sonorous* 1 resonant 2 reassuring 3 repetitive 4 resinous 5 sisterly
534. *slough* 1 toughen 2 trap 3 violate 4 cast off 5 depart

535. *spurious* 1 genuine 2 angry 3 mitigated 4 interrogated 5 glorious
536. *stringent* 1 binding 2 reserved 3 utilized 4 lambent 5 indigent
537. *sublime* 1 unconscious 2 respected 3 exalted 4 sneaky 5 replaced
538. *stamina* 1 patience 2 pistils 3 weakness 4 fascination 5 patina
539. *sporadic* 1 seedy 2 latent 3 vivid 4 inconsequential 5 often
540. *suavity* 1 ingeniousness 2 indifference 3 urbanity 4 constancy 5 paucity

WORD LIST 28 superannuated - transcribe

superannuated ADJ. retired on pension because of age. The *superannuated* man was indignant because he felt that he could still perform a good day's work.

supercilious ADJ. contemptuous; haughty. I resent your *supercilious* and arrogant attitude.

superficial ADJ. trivial; shallow. Since your report gave only a *superficial* analysis of the problem, I cannot give you more than a passing grade.

superfluity (-*floo'-*) N. excess; overabundance. We have a definite lack of sincere workers and a *superfluity* of leaders.

supersede V. cause to be set aside; replace. This regulation will *supersede* all previous rules.

supine (-*pīn'*) ADJ. lying on back. The defeated pugilist lay *supine* on the canvas.

suppliant (*sŭp'-lē-*) ADJ. entreating; beseeching. He could not resist the dog's *suppliant* whimpering, and he gave it some food. also N.

supplicate V. petition humbly; pray to grant a favor. We *supplicate* your majesty to grant him amnesty.

supposititious ADJ. assumed; counterfeit; hypothetical. I find no similarity between your *supposititious* illustration and the problem we are facing.

surcease (-*sēs'*) N. cessation. He begged the doctors to grant him *surcease* from his suffering.

surfeit (*sêr'-fət*) V. cloy; overfeed. I am *surfeited* with the sentimentality of the average motion picture film.

surly (*sêr'-lē*) ADJ. rude; cross. Because of his *surly* attitude, many people avoided his company.

surmise (-*mīz'*) V. guess. I *surmise* that he will be late for this meeting. also N.

surreptitious ADJ. secret. News of their *surreptitious* meeting gradually leaked out.

surveillance (-*vā'-*) N. watching; guarding. The FBI kept the house under constant *surveillance* in the hope of capturing all the criminals at one time.

sustenance N. means of support, food, nourishment. In the tropics, the natives find *sustenance* easy to obtain.

swathe (*swäth*) V. wrap around; bandage. When I visited him in the hospital, I found him *swathed* in bandages.

swelter V. be oppressed by heat. I am going to buy an air conditioning unit for my apartment as I do not intend to *swelter* through another hot and humid summer.

sycophantic (*sĭk-ə-fănt'-*) ADJ. servilely flattering. The king enjoyed the *sycophantic* attentions of his followers.

sylvan ADJ. pertaining to the woods; rustic. His paintings of nymphs in *sylvan* backgrounds were criticized as overly sentimental.

synchronous (*sĭng'-*) ADJ. similarly timed; simultaneous with. We have many examples of scientists in different parts of the world who have made *synchronous* discoveries.

synthesis N. combining parts into a whole. Now that we have succeeded in isolating this drug, our next problem is to plan its *synthesis* in the laboratory.

synthetic ADJ. artificial; resulting from synthesis. During the twentieth century, many *synthetic* products have replaced the natural products. also N.

tacit ADJ. understood; not put into words. We have a *tacit* agreement.

taciturn ADJ. habitually silent; talking little. New Englanders are reputedly *taciturn* people.

tactile ADJ. pertaining to the organs or sense of touch. His calloused hands had lost their *tactile* sensitivity.

tainted ADJ. contaminated; corrupt. Health authorities are always trying to prevent the sale and use of *tainted* food.

talisman N. charm. She wore the *talisman* to ward off evil.

tantalize V. tease; torture with disappointment. Tom loved to *tantalize* his younger brother.

tantrum N. fit of petulance; caprice. The child learned that he could have almost anything if he went into *tantrums*.

tautological ADJ. needlessly repetitious. In the sentence "It was visible to the eye," the phrase "to the eye" is *tautological*.

tawdry ADJ. cheap and gaudy. He won a few *tawdry* trinkets in Coney Island.

tedium N. boredom; weariness. We hope this radio will help overcome the *tedium* of your stay in the hospital.

temerity (-*mĕr'-*) N. boldness; rashness. Do you have the *temerity* to argue with me?

tempo N. speed of music. I find the conductor's *tempo* too slow for such a brilliant piece of music.

temporal ADJ. not lasting forever; limited by time; secular. At one time in our history, *temporal* rulers assumed that they had been given their thrones by divine right.

temporize V. avoid committing oneself; gain time. I cannot permit you to *temporize* any longer; I must have a definite answer today.

tenacious ADJ. holding fast. I had to struggle to break his *tenacious* hold on my arm. tenacity, N.

tenet N. doctrine; dogma. I cannot accept the *tenets* of your faith.

tentative ADJ. provisional; experimental. Your *tentative* plans sound plausible.

tenuous ADJ. thin; rare; slim. The allegiance of our allies is held by rather *tenuous* ties.

ā—ale; ă—add; ä—arm; à—ask, ē—eve; ĕ—end; ê—err, her; ə—allow; even; ī—ice; ĭ—ill; ō—oll; ŏ—odd; ô—orb; ōō—food; ŏŏ—foot, put; ou—out; th—thin; ū—use; ŭ—up; zh—pleasure

tenure N. holding of an office; time during which such an office is held. He has permanent *tenure* in this position.

tepid (*tĕp´-*) ADJ. lukewarm. During the summer, I like to take a *tepid* bath.

terminus N. last stop of railroad. After we reached the railroad *terminus,* we continued our journey into the wilderness on saddle horses.

terrestrial ADJ. on the earth. We have been able to explore the *terrestrial* regions much more thoroughly than the aquatic or celestial regions.

terse ADJ. concise; abrupt; pithy. I admire his *terse* style of writing.

tertiary ADJ. third. He is so thorough that he analyzes *tertiary* causes where other writers are content with primary and secondary reasons.

testy ADJ. irritable; short-tempered. My advice is to avoid discussing this problem with him today as he is rather *testy.*

tether V. tie with a rope. Before we went to sleep, we *tethered* the horses to prevent their wandering off during the night.

theocracy N. government of a community by religious leaders. Some Pilgrims favored the establishment of a *theocracy* in New England.

therapeutic ADJ. curative. These springs are famous for their *therapeutic* qualities.

thermal ADJ. pertaining to heat. The natives discovered that the hot springs gave excellent *thermal* baths and began to develop their community as a health resort. also N.

thrall N. slave; bondage. The captured soldier was held in *thrall* by the conquering army.

threnody N. song of lamentation; dirge. When he died, many poets wrote *threnodies* about his passing.

throes N. violent anguish. The *throes* of despair can be as devastating as the spasms accompanying physical pain.

throttle V. strangle. The criminal tried to *throttle* the old man.

thwart V. baffle; frustrate. He felt that everyone was trying to *thwart* his plans.

timidity N. lack of self-confidence or courage. If you are to succeed as a salesman, you must first lose your *timidity.*

tipple V. drink (alcoholic beverages) frequently. He found that his most enjoyable evenings occurred when he *tippled* with his friends at the local pub.

tirade N. extended scolding; denunciation. Long before he had finished his *tirade,* we were sufficiently aware of the seriousness of our misconduct.

titanic ADJ. gigantic. *Titanic* waves beat against the shore during the hurricane.

tithe (*tīth*) N. tax of one-tenth. Because he was an agnostic, he refused to pay his *tithes* to the clergy. also V.

titular (*tĭch´-*) ADJ. nominal holding of title without obligations. Although he was the *titular* head of the company, the real decisions were made by his general manager.

toady V. flatter for favors. I hope you see through those who are *toadying* you for special favors. also N.

toga N. Roman outer robe. Marc Antony pointed to the slashes in Caesar's *toga.*

tome N. large volume. He spent much time in the libraries poring over ancient *tomes.*

topography N. physical features of a region. Before the generals gave the order to attack, they ordered a complete study of the *topography* of the region.

torpid ADJ. dormant; dull; lethargic. The *torpid* bear had just come out of his cave after his long hibernation.

torso N. trunk of statue with head and limbs missing; human trunk. This *torso,* found in the ruins of Pompeii, is now on exhibition in the museum in Naples.

tortuous ADJ. winding; full of curves. Because this road is so *tortuous,* it is unwise to go faster than twenty miles an hour on it.

touchy ADJ. sensitive; irascible. Do not discuss this phase of the problem as he is very *touchy* about it.

toxic ADJ. poisonous. We must seek an antidote for whatever *toxic* substance he has eaten.

tract N. pamphlet; a region of indefinite size. The King granted William Penn a *tract* of land in the New World.

tractable ADJ. docile. You will find the children in this school very *tractable* and willing to learn.

traduce V. expose to slander. His opponents tried to *traduce* the candidate's reputation by spreading rumors about his past.

tranquillity N. calmness; peace. After the commotion and excitement of the city, I appreciate the *tranquillity* of these fields and forests.

transcend V. exceed; surpass. This accomplishment *transcends* all our previous efforts. transcendental, ADJ.

transcribe V. copy. When you *transcribe* your notes, please send a copy to Mr. Smith and keep the original for our files. transcription, N.

ETYMOLOGY 28

TANG, TACT (to touch)

tangent   touching
contact   touching with, meeting
contingent   depending upon

TEMPOR (time)

contemporary   at the same time
extemporaneous   impromptu
temporize   to delay

TEN, TENT (to hold)

tenable   able to be held
tenacity   retention
tenure   holding of office

TERR (land)

terrestrial   pertaining to earth
subterranean   underground

TEST—WORD LIST 28—*Synonyms*

Each of the following questions consists of a word printed in italics, followed by five words or phrases numbered 1 to 5. Choose the numbered word or phrase which is most nearly similar in meaning to the word in italics and write the number of your choice on your answer paper.

ā—ale; ă—add; ä—arm; à—ask, ē—eve; ĕ—end; ê—err, her; ə—allow; even; ī—ice; ĭ—ill; ō—oll; ŏ—odd; ô—orb; ōō—food; ŏŏ—foot, put; ou—out; th—thin; ū—use; ŭ—up; zh—pleasure

541. *superannuated* 1 senile 2 experienced 3 retired 4 attenuated 5 accepted
542. *surfeit* 1 belittle 2 cloy 3 drop 4 estimate 5 claim
543. *tacit* 1 spoken 2 allowed 3 neural 4 understood 5 unwanted
544. *supercilious* 1 haughty 2 highbrow 3 angry 4 subservient 5 philosophic
545. *surreptitious* 1 secret 2 snakelike 3 nightly 4 abstract 5 furnished
546. *talisman* 1 chief 2 juror 3 medicine man 4 amulet 5 gift
547. *superficial* 1 abnormal 2 portentous 3 shallow 4 angry 5 tiny
548. *swathed* 1 wrapped around 2 waved 3 gambled 4 rapt 5 mystified
549. *tawdry* 1 orderly 2 meretricious 3 reclaimed 4 filtered 5 proper
550. *suppliant* 1 intolerant 2 swallowing 3 beseeching 4 finishing 5 flexible

551. *sycophantic* 1 quiet 2 recording 3 servilely flattering 4 frolicsome 5 eagerly awaiting
552. *tenacious* 1 fast running 2 intentional 3 obnoxious 4 holding fast 5 collecting
553. *supposititious* 1 irreligious 2 experimental 3 subjunctive 4 hypothetical 5 grammatical
554. *synthetic* 1 simplified 2 doubled 3 tuneful 4 artificial 5 fiscal
555. *tepid* 1 boiling 2 lukewarm 3 freezing 4 gaseous 5 cold
556. *tantalize* 1 tease 2 wax 3 warrant 4 authorize 5 total
557. *tenuous* 1 vital 2 thin 3 careful 4 dangerous 5 necessary
558. *temerity* 1 timidity 2 resourcefulness 3 boldness 4 tremulousness 5 caution
559. *tentative* 1 prevalent 2 certain 3 mocking 4 wry 5 experimental
560. *temporal* 1 priestly 2 scholarly 3 secular 4 sleepy 5 sporadic

---

WORD LIST 29 transgression - veer

transgression N. violation of a law; sin. Forgive us our *transgressions.*

transient ADJ. fleeting; quickly passing away; staying for a short time. This hotel caters to a *transient* trade.

transition N. going from one state of action to another. During the period of *transition* from oil heat to gas heat, the furnace will have to be shut off.

translucent ADJ. partly transparent. We could not recognize the people in the next room because of the *translucent* curtains which separated us.

transmute V. change; convert to something different. He was unable to *transmute* his dreams into actualities.

transparent ADJ. permitting light to pass through freely; easily detected. Your scheme is so *transparent* that it will fool no one.

transpire V. exhale; become known; happen. In spite of all our efforts to keep the meeting a secret, news of our conclusions *transpired.*

travail (*trə-vāl´*) N. painful labor. How long do you think a man can endure such *travail* and degradation without rebelling?

traverse V. go through or across. When you *traverse* this field, be careful of the bull.

travesty N. comical parody; treatment aimed at making something appear ridiculous. The decision the jury has arrived at is a *travesty* of justice.

treatise N. article treating a subject systematically and thoroughly. He is preparing a *treatise* on the Elizabethan playwrights for his graduate degree.

trek V. travel; migrate. The tribe *trekked* further north that summer in search of available game. also N.

tremor N. trembling; slight quiver. She had a nervous *tremor* in her right hand.

tremulous ADJ. trembling; wavering. She was *tremulous* more from excitement than from fear.

trenchant ADJ. cutting; keen. I am afraid of his *trenchant* wit for it is so often sarcastic.

trepidation N. fear; trembling agitation. We must face the enemy without *trepidation* if we are to win this battle.

tribulation N. distress; suffering. After all the trials and *tribulations* we have gone through, we need this rest.

tribunal N. court of justice. The decision of the *tribunal* was final.

tribute N. tax levied by a ruler; mark of respect. The colonists refused to pay *tribute* to a foreign despot.

trident (*trīd´-*) N. three-pronged spear. Neptune is usually depicted as rising from the sea, carrying his *trident* on his shoulder.

trilogy (*trĭl´-*) N. group of three works. Romain Rolland's novel *Jean Christophe* was first published as a *trilogy.*

trite ADJ. hackneyed; commonplace. The *trite* and predictable situations in many television programs alienate many viewers.

troth N. pledge of good faith especially in betrothal. He gave her his *troth* and vowed he would cherish her always.

truculent (*trŭk´-yə-*) ADJ. aggressive; savage. They are a *truculent* race, ready to fight at any moment.

truism N. self-evident truth. Many a *truism* is well expressed in a proverb.

trumpery N. objects that are showy, valueless, deceptive. All this finery is mere *trumpery.*

tryst (*trĭst*) N. meeting. The lovers kept their *tryst* even though they realized their danger.

tumbrel N. a farm tipcart. The *tumbrels* became the vehicles which transported the condemned people from the prisons to the guillotine.

tumid ADJ. swollen; pompous; bombastic. I especially dislike his *tumid* style; I prefer writing which is less swollen and bombastic.

turbid ADJ. muddy; having the sediment disturbed. The water was *turbid* after the children had waded through it.

turbulence N. state of violent agitation. We were frightened by the *turbulence* of the ocean during the storm.

turgid (*têr´-jəd*) ADJ. swollen; distended. The *turgid* river threatened to overflow the levees and flood the countryside.

turnkey N. jailer. By bribing the *turnkey,* the prisoner arranged to have better food brought to him in his cell.

turpitude N. depravity. A visitor may be denied admittance to this country if he has been guilty of moral *turpitude.*

tutelage N. guardianship; training. Under the *tutelage* of such masters of the instrument, he made rapid progress as a virtuoso.

tyro (*tī´-rō*) N. beginner; novice. For a mere *tyro,* you have produced some marvelous results.

ā—ale; ă—add; ä—arm; à—ask, ē—eve; ĕ—end; ê—err, her; ə—allow; even; ī—ice; ĭ—ill; ō—oll; ŏ—odd; ô—orb; ōō—food; ŏŏ—foot, put; ou—out; th—thin; ū—use; ŭ—up; zh—pleasure

ubiquitous ADJ. being everywhere; omnipresent. You must be *ubiquitous* for I meet you wherever I go.

ulterior ADJ. situated beyond; unstated. You must have an *ulterior* motive for your behavior.

ultimate ADJ. final; not susceptible to further analysis. Scientists are searching for the *ultimate* truths.

ultimatum (-*māt'*-) N. last demand; warning. Since they have ignored our *ultimatum,* our only recourse is to declare war.

umbrage (*ŭm'-brĭj*) N. resentment; anger; sense of injury or insult. She took *umbrage* at his remarks.

unanimity N. complete agreement. We were surprised by the *unanimity* with which our proposals were accepted by the different groups.

unassuaged ADJ. unsatisfied; not soothed. His anger is *unassuaged* by your apology.

unassuming ADJ. modest. He is so *unassuming* that some people fail to realize how great a man he really is.

unbridled ADJ. violent. He had a sudden fit of *unbridled* rage.

uncanny ADJ. strange; mysterious. You have the *uncanny* knack of reading my innermost thoughts.

unconscionable (-*kŏnch'*-) ADJ. unscrupulous; excessive. He found the loan shark's demands *unconscionable* and impossible to meet.

uncouth ADJ. outlandish; clumsy; boorish. Most biographers portray Lincoln as an *uncouth* and ungainly young man.

unction N. the act of anointing with oil. The anointing with oil of a person near death is called extreme *unction.*

unctuous ADJ. oily; bland; insincerely suave. Uriah Heep disguised his nefarious actions by *unctuous* protestations of his "'umility."

undulate V. move with a wavelike motion. The waters *undulated* in the breeze.

unearth V. dig up. When they *unearthed* the city, the archeologists found many relics of an ancient civilization.

unearthly ADJ. not earthly; weird. There is an *unearthly* atmosphere in his work which amazes the casual observer.

unequivocal ADJ. plain; obvious. My answer to your proposal is an *unequivocal* and absolute "No."

unfaltering ADJ. steadfast. She approached the guillotine with *unfaltering* steps.

unfeigned ADJ. genuine; real. I am sure her surprise was *unfeigned.*

ungainly ADJ. awkward. He is an *ungainly* young man.

unguent (*ŭng'-gwənt*) N. ointment. Apply this *unguent* to the sore muscles before retiring.

unimpeachable ADJ. blameless and exemplary. His conduct in office was *unimpeachable.*

unique ADJ. without an equal; single in kind. You have the *unique* distinction of being the first student whom I have had to fail in this course.

unison N. unity of pitch; complete accord. The choir sang in *unison.*

unkempt ADJ. disheveled; with uncared-for appearance. The beggar was dirty and *unkempt.*

unmitigated ADJ. harsh; severe; not lightened. I sympathize with you in your *unmitigated* sorrow.

unruly ADJ. disobedient; lawless. The only way to curb this *unruly* mob is to use tear gas.

unseemly ADJ. unbecoming; indecent. Your levity is *unseemly* at this time.

unsullied ADJ. untarnished. I am happy that my reputation is *unsullied.*

untenable ADJ. unsupportable. I find your theory *untenable* and must reject it.

unwitting ADJ. unintentional; not knowing. He was the *unwitting* tool of the swindlers.

unwonted ADJ. unaccustomed. He hesitated to assume the *unwonted* role of master of ceremonies at the dinner.

upbraid V. scold; reproach. I must *upbraid* him for his misbehavior.

urbane (-*bān'*) ADJ. suave; refined; elegant. The courtier was *urbane* and sophisticated. urbanity, N.

usury N. lending money at illegal rates of interest. The loan shark was found guilty of *usury.*

uxorious (*ŭk-sōr'*-) ADJ. excessively devoted to one's wife. His friends laughed at him because he was so *uxorious* and submissive to his wife's desires.

vacillation N. fluctuation; wavering. His *vacillation* when confronted with a problem annoyed all of us who had to wait until he made his decision.

vacuous ADJ. empty; inane. The *vacuous* remarks of the politician annoyed the audience, who had hoped to hear more than empty platitudes.

vagary (*vā'*-) N. caprice; whim. She followed every *vagary* of fashion.

vainglorious ADJ. boastful; excessively conceited. He was a *vainglorious* and arrogant individual.

validate V. confirm; ratify. I will not publish my findings until I *validate* my results.

vanguard N. forerunners; advance forces. We are the *vanguard* of a tremendous army that is following us.

vantage N. position giving an advantage. They fired upon the enemy from behind trees, walls and any other point of *vantage* they could find.

vapid (*văp'*-) ADJ. insipid; inane. He delivered an uninspired and *vapid* address.

variegated ADJ. many-colored. He will not like this blue necktie as he is addicted to *variegated* clothing.

vaunted ADJ. boasted; bragged; highly publicized. This much *vaunted* project proved a disappointment when it collapsed.

veer V. change in direction. After what seemed an eternity, the wind *veered* to the east and the storm abated.

ETYMOLOGY 29

URB (city)

urban pertaining to the city

urbane polished, sophisticated (pertaining to a city dweller)

suburban outside of the city

TEST—WORD LIST 29—*Antonyms*

Each of the following questions consists of a word printed in italics, followed by five words or phrases

ā—ale; ă—add; ä—arm; à—ask, ē—eve; ĕ—end; ê—err, her; ə—allow; even; ī—ice; ĭ—ill; ō—oll; ŏ—odd; ô—orb; ōō—food; ŏŏ—foot, put; ou—out; th—thin; ū—use; ŭ—up; zh—pleasure

numbered 1 to 5. Choose the numbered word or phrase which is most nearly opposite in meaning to the word in italics and write the number of your choice on your answer paper.

561. *unimpeachable*   1 fruitful 2 rampaging 3 faulty 4 pensive 5 thorough

562. *ulterior*   1 tipped 2 stated 3 sparking 4 uncompromising 5 corrugated

563. *transient*   1 carried 2 close 3 permanent 4 removed 5 certain

564. *ungainly*   1 ignorant 2 graceful 3 detailed 4 dancing 5 pedantic

565. *tyro*   1 infant 2 rubber 3 personnel 4 idiot 5 expert

566. *unfeigned*   1 pretended 2 fashionable 3 wary 4 switched 5 colonial

567. *turbulence*   1 reaction 2 approach 3 impropriety 4 calm 5 hostility

568. *unearth*   1 conceal 2 gnaw 3 clean 4 fling 5 reach

569. *turbid*   1 clear 2 improbable 3 invariable 4 honest 5 turgid

570. *ultimate*   1 competing 2 throbbing 3 poisonous 4 incipient 5 powerful

571. *trite*   1 correct 2 original 3 distinguished 4 premature 5 certain

572. *vaunted*   1 unvanquished 2 fell 3 belittled 4 exacting 5 believed

573. *unkempt*   1 bombed 2 washed 3 neat 4 shabby 5 tawdry

574. *unsullied*   1 tarnished 2 countless 3 soggy 4 papered 5 homicidal

575. *vacillation*   1 remorse 2 relief 3 respect 4 steadfastness 5 inoculation

576. *unruly*   1 chatting 2 obedient 3 definite 4 lined 5 curious

577. *untenable*   1 supportable 2 tender 3 sheepish 4 tremulous 5 adequate

578. *vanguard*   1 regiment 2 rear 3 echelon 4 protection 5 loyalty

579. *unseemly*   1 effortless 2 proper 3 conducive 4 pointed 5 informative

580. *unwitting*   1 clever 2 intense 3 sensitive 4 freezing 5 intentional

---

WORD LIST   30   vegetate - zephyr

vegetate   V. live in a monotonous way. I do not understand how you can *vegetate* in this quiet village after the adventurous life you have led.

vehement   ADJ. impetuous; with marked vigor. He spoke with *vehement* eloquence in defense of his client.

vellum   N. parchment. Bound in *vellum* and embossed in gold, this book is a beautiful example of the binder's craft.

venal   (*vēn´-*) ADJ. capable of being bribed. The *venal* policeman accepted the bribe offered him by the speeding motorist whom he had stopped.

veneer   N. thin layer; cover. Casual acquaintances were deceived by his *veneer* of sophistication and failed to recognize his fundamental shallowness.

venerable   ADJ. deserving high respect. We do not mean to be disrespectful when we refuse to follow the advice of our *venerable* leader.

venerate   V. revere. In China, the people *venerate* their ancestors.

venial   (*vē´-nē-*) ADJ. forgivable; trivial. We may regard a hungry man's stealing as a *venial* crime.

vent   N. a small opening; outlet. The wine did not flow because the air *vent* in the barrel was clogged.

vent   V. express; utter. He *vented* his wrath on his class.

ventral   V. abdominal. We shall now examine the *ventral* plates of this serpent.

venturous   ADJ. daring. The five *venturous* young men decided to look for a new approach to the mountain top.

veracious   ADJ. truthful. I can recommend him for this position because I have always found him *veracious* and reliable.

verbiage   N. pompous array of words. After we had waded through all the *verbiage,* we discovered that the writer had said very little.

verbose   (*-bōs´*) ADJ. wordy. This article is too *verbose;* we must edit it.

verdant   ADJ. green; fresh. The *verdant* meadows in the spring are always an inspiring sight.

verdigris   N. a green coating on copper which has been exposed to the weather. Despite all attempts to protect the statue from the elements, it became coated with *verdigris.*

verity   N. truth; reality. The four *verities* were revealed to Buddha during his long meditation.

vernal   ADJ. pertaining to spring. We may expect *vernal* showers all during the month of April.

versatile   ADJ. having many talents; capable of working in many fields. He was a *versatile* athlete; at college he had earned varsity letters in baseball, football, and track.

vertex   N. summit. Let us drop a perpendicular line from the *vertex* of the triangle to the base.

vertigo   (*vêr´-*) N. dizziness. We test potential plane pilots for susceptibility to spells of *vertigo.*

vestige   N. trace; remains. We discovered *vestiges* of early Indian life in the cave.

viand   (*vī´-*) N. food. There was a variety of *viands* at the feast.

vicarious   ADJ. acting as a substitute; done by a deputy. Many people get a *vicarious* thrill at the movies by imagining they are the characters on the screen.

vicissitude   N. change of fortune. I am accustomed to life's *vicissitudes,* having experienced poverty and wealth, sickness and health, and failure and success.

victuals   (*vĭt´-lz*) N. food. I am very happy to be able to provide you with these *victuals.*

vie   V. contend; compete. When we *vie* with each other for his approval, we are merely weakening ourselves and strengthening him.

vigilance   N. watchfulness. Eternal *vigilance* is the price of liberty.

vilify   V. slander. Why is he always trying to *vilify* my reputation?

vindicate   V. clear of charges. I hope to *vindicate* my client and return him to society as a free man.

vindictive   ADJ. revengeful. He was very *vindictive* and never forgave an injury.

viper   N. poisonous snake. The habitat of the horned *viper,* a particularly venomous snake, is in sandy regions like the Sahara or the Sinai peninsula.

virago   (*-räg´-ō*) N. shrew. Rip Van Winkle's wife was a

ā—ale; ă—add; ä—arm; à—ask, ē—eve; ĕ—end; ê—err, her; ə—allow; even; ī—ice; ĭ—ill; ō—oll; ŏ—odd; ô—orb; oo—food; oo—foot, put; ou—out; th—thin; ū—use; ŭ—up; zh—pleasure

veritable *virago.*

virile ADJ. manly. I do not accept the premise that a man is *virile* only when he is belligerent.

virtuoso N. highly skilled artist. Heifetz is a violin *virtuoso.*

virulent (*vĭr´-*) ADJ. extremely poisonous. The virus is highly *virulent* and has made many of us ill for days.

virus (*vī´-*) N. disease communicator. The doctors are looking for a specific medicine to control this *virus.*

visage (*vĭz´-*) N. face; appearance. The stern *visage* of the judge indicated that he had decided to impose a severe penalty.

viscid (*vĭs´-əd*) ADJ. sticky; adhesive. This is a *viscid* liquid.

viscous (*vĭs´-kŭs*) ADJ. sticky; gluey. Melted tar is a *viscous* substance.

visionary ADJ. produced by imagination; fanciful; mystical. He was given to *visionary* schemes which never materialized. also N.

vitiate (*vĭsh´-ē-āt*) V. spoil the effect of; make inoperative. Fraud will *vitiate* the contract.

vitriolic ADJ. corrosive; sarcastic. Such *vitriolic* criticism is uncalled for.

vituperative ADJ. abusive; scolding. He became more *vituperative* as he realized that we were not going to grant him his wish.

vivacious ADJ. animated; gay. She had always been *vivacious* and sparkling.

vociferous ADJ. clamorous; noisy. The crowd grew *vociferous* in its anger and threatened to take the law into its own hands.

vogue N. popular fashion. Slacks became the *vogue* on many college campuses.

volatile (*vŏl´-*) ADJ. evaporating rapidly; lighthearted; mercurial. Ethyl chloride is a very *volatile* liquid.

volition N. act of making a conscious choice. She selected this dress of her own *volition.*

voluble ADJ. fluent; glib. He was a *voluble* speaker, always ready to talk.

voluptuous ADJ. gratifying the senses. The nobility during the Renaissance led *voluptuous* lives.

voracious (*-rā´-*) ADJ. ravenous. The wolf is a *voracious* animal.

votary N. follower of a cult. He was a *votary* of every new movement in literature and art.

vouchsafe V. grant condescendingly; guarantee. I can safely *vouchsafe* you a fair return on your investment.

vulnerable ADJ. susceptible to wounds. Achilles was *vulnerable* only in his heel.

vying V. contending. Why are we *vying* with each other for his favors? vie, V.

waggish ADJ. mischievous; humorous; tricky. He was a prankster who, unfortunately, often overlooked the damage he could cause with his *waggish* tricks.

waive V. give up temporarily; yield. I will *waive* my rights in this matter in order to expedite our reaching a proper decision.

wan ADJ. having a pale or sickly color; pallid. Suckling asked, "Why so pale and *wan,* fond lover?"

wane V. grow gradually smaller. From now until December 21, the winter equinox, the hours of daylight will *wane.*

wanton ADJ. unruly; unchaste; excessive. His *wanton* pride cost him many friends.

wary ADJ. very cautious. The spies grew *wary* as they approached the sentry.

wheedle V. cajole; coax; deceive by flattery. She knows she can *wheedle* almost anything she wants from her father.

whet V. sharpen; stimulate. The odors from the kitchen are *whetting* my appetite; I will be ravenous by the time the meal is served.

whimsical ADJ. capricious; fanciful; quaint. *Peter Pan* is a *whimsical* play.

whit N. smallest speck. There is not a *whit* of intelligence or understanding in your observations.

wily ADJ. cunning; artful. He is as *wily* as a fox in avoiding trouble.

winsome ADJ. agreeable; gracious; engaging. By her *winsome* manner, she made herself liked by everyone who met her.

witless ADJ. foolish; idiotic. Such *witless* and fatuous statements will create the impression that you are an ignorant individual.

witticism N. witty saying; facetious remark. What you regard as *witticisms* are often offensive to sensitive people.

wizardry N. sorcery; magic. Merlin amazed the knights with his *wizardry.*

wizened (*wĭz´-*) ADJ. withered; shriveled. The *wizened* old man in the home for the aged was still active and energetic.

wont (*wônt*) N. custom; habitual procedure. As was his *wont,* he jogged two miles every morning before going to work.

worldly ADJ. engrossed in matters of this earth; not spiritual. You must leave your *worldly* goods behind you when you go to meet your Maker.

wraith (*rāth*) N. ghost; phantom of a living person. It must be a horrible experience to see a ghost; it is even more horrible to see the *wraith* of a person we know to be alive.

wreak V. inflict. I am afraid he will *wreak* his wrath on the innocent as well as the guilty.

wrest V. pull away; take by violence. With only ten seconds left to play, our team *wrested* victory from their grasp.

zealot (*zĕl´-*) N. fanatic; person who shows excessive zeal. It is good to have a few *zealots* in our group for their enthusiasm is contagious.

zenith N. point directly overhead in the sky; summit. When the sun was at its *zenith,* the glare was not as strong as at sunrise and sunset.

zephyr N. gentle breeze; west wind. When these *zephyrs* blow, it is good to be in an open boat under a full sail.

ETYMOLOGY 30

VENI, VENT (to come)

intervene come between
prevent stop
convention meeting

VIA (way)

deviation departure from way
viaduct roadway (arched)

trivial trifling (small talk at crossroads)

VID, VIS (to see)

vision sight
evidence things seen
vista view

ā—ale; ă—add; ä—arm; à—ask; ē—eve; ĕ—end; ê—err, her; ə—allow; even; ī—ice; ĭ—ill; ō—oll; ŏ—odd; ô—orb; ōō—food; ŏŏ—foot, put; ou—out; th—thin; ū—use; ŭ—up; zh—pleasure

VINC, VICT, VANQU (to conquer)

invincible unconquerable
victory winning
vanquish defeat

VOC, VOCAT (to call)

avocation calling, minor occupation

provocation calling or rousing the anger of
invocation calling in prayer

VOLV, VOLUT (to roll)

revolve roll around
evolve roll out, develop
convolution coiled state

TEST—WORD LIST 30 — *Synonyms and Antonyms*

Each of the questions below consists of a word printed in italics, followed by five words or phrases numbered 1 to 5. Choose the numbered word or phrase which is most nearly the same as or the opposite of the word in italics and write the number of your choice on your answer paper.

581. *vestige* 1 trek 2 trail 3 trace 4 trial 5 tract
582. *venturous* 1 timorous 2 confiscatory 3 lethal 4 tubercular 5 dorsal
583. *vehement* 1 substantial 2 regular 3 calm 4 cautious 5 sad
584. *verdant* 1 poetic 2 green 3 red 4 autumnal 5 frequent
585. *venerate* 1 revere 2 age 3 reject 4 reverberate 5 degenerate
586. *verity* 1 sanctity 2 reverence 3 falsehood 4 rarity 5 household
587. *venial* 1 unforgivable 2 unforgettable 3 unmistaken 4 fearful 5 fragrant
588. *vicarious* 1 substitutional 2 aggressive 3 sporadic 4 reverent 5 internal
589. *venal* 1 springlike 2 honest 3 angry 4 indifferent 5 going
590. *veracious* 1 worried 2 slight 3 alert 4 truthful 5 instrumental
591. *vellum* 1 schedule 2 scenario 3 parchment 4 monastery 5 victim
592. *visage* 1 doubt 2 personality 3 hermitage 4 face 5 armor
593. *vertex* 1 whirlpool 2 drift 3 vehicle 4 base 5 context
594. *virulent* 1 sensuous 2 malignant 3 masculine 4 conforming 5 approaching
595. *viand* 1 wand 2 gown 3 food 4 orchestra 5 frock
596. *viscid* 1 talkative 2 affluent 3 sticky 4 sweet 5 embarrassed
597. *vigilance* 1 bivouac 2 guide 3 watchfulness 4 mob rule 5 posse
598. *vindictive* 1 revengeful 2 fearful 3 divided 4 literal 5 convincing
599. *vilify* 1 erect 2 eulogize 3 better 4 magnify 5 horrify
600. *vindicate* 1 point out 2 blame 3 declare 4 evict 5 menace

---

ā—ale; ă—add; ä—arm; à—ask, ē—eve; ĕ—end; ê—err, her; ə—allow; even; ī—ice; ĭ—ill; ō—oll; ŏ—odd; ô—orb; ōō—food; ŏŏ—foot, put; ou—out; th—thin; ū—use; ŭ—up; zh—pleasure

aberration N. wandering or staying away; in optics, failure of rays to focus. In designing a good lens for a camera, the problem of correcting chromatic and rectilinear *aberration* was a serious one. aberrant, ADJ. and N.

abnegation N. repudiation; self-sacrifice. No act of *abnegation* was more pronounced than his refusal of any rewards for his discovery.

abut V. border upon; adjoin. Where our estates *abut*, we must build a fence.

abysmal (*-bĭz´-*) ADJ. bottomless. His arrogance is exceeded only by his *abysmal* ignorance.

accede (*ăk-sēd´*) V. agree. If I *accede* to this demand for blackmail, I am afraid that I will be the victim of future demands.

acclimate (*-klī´-*) V. adjust to climate. One of the difficulties of our present air age is the need of travelers to *acclimate* themselves to their new and often strange environments.

acephalous (*-sĕf´-*) ADJ. headless. Because the country was in a state of anarchy and lacked a leader, it was described as an *acephalous* monstrosity.

acerbity (*-sêr´-*) N. bitterness of speech and temper. The meeting of the United Nations Assembly was marked with such *acerbity* that little hope of reaching any useful settlement of the problem could be held.

acquiescence (*ăk-wē-ĕs´-*) N. submission; compliance. It is impossible to obtain their *acquiescence* to the proposal because it is abhorrent to their philosophy.

adjunct N. something attached to but holding an inferior position. I will entertain this concept as an *adjunct* to the main proposal.

adjure V. request solemnly. I must *adjure* you to consider this matter carefully as it is of utmost importance to all of us.

admonition N. warning. After repeated rejections of its *admonitions*, the country was forced to issue an ultimatum.

advert V. refer to. Since you *advert* to this matter so frequently, you must regard it as important.

adulterated ADJ. made impure or spoiled by the addition of inferior materials. The health authorities ordered the sale of the meat stopped because they found it *adulterated*.

advent N. arrival. Most Americans were unaware of the *advent* of the Nuclear Age until the news of Hiroshima reached them.

aegis (*ē´jəs*) N. shield; defense. Under the *aegis* of the Bill of Rights, we enjoy our most treasured freedoms.

aeon (*ē´-*) N. long period of time; an age. It has taken *aeons* for our civilization to develop.

affable ADJ. courteous. Although he held a position of responsibility, he was an *affable* individual and could be reached by anyone with a complaint.

afferent (*ăf´-*) ADJ. carrying toward the center. The nerves that carry stimuli to the brain are called *afferent;* those that convey messages from the brain, efferent.

affidavit N. written statement made under oath. The court refused to accept his statement unless he presented it in the form of an *affidavit*.

afflatus (*-flāt´-*) N. inspiration. The poet boasted of his divine *afflatus* as the source of his greatness.

agenda (*-jĕn´-*) N. items of business at a meeting. We had so much difficulty agreeing upon an *agenda* that there was very little time for the meeting.

agitation N. strong feeling; excitement. We felt that he was responsible for the *agitation* of the mob because of the inflammatory report he had issued.

agrarian ADJ. pertaining to land or its cultivation. The country is gradually losing its *agrarian* occupation and turning more and more to an industrial point of view.

agronomist N. scientist engaged in the management of land. Because the country failed to heed the warnings of its *agronomists*, it was faced with serious famine.

alliteration N. repetition of beginning sound in poetry. "The furrow followed free" is an example of *alliteration*.

amazon N. female warrior. Ever since the days of Greek mythology we refer to strong and aggressive women as *amazons*.

amoral ADJ. nonmoral. The *amoral* individual lacks a code of ethics; he should not be classified as immoral.

amortization N. act of reducing a debt through partial payments. Your monthly payments to the bank include provisions for taxes, interest on the principal, and *amortization* of the mortgage.

anachronism (*-năk´-*) N. an error involving time in a story. The reference to clocks in *Julius Caesar* is an *anachronism*.

analgesic (*-jē´-*) ADJ. causing insensitivity to pain. The *analgesic* qualities of this lotion will provide temporary relief.

animus N. hostile feeling or intent. The *animus* of the speaker became obvious to all when he began to indulge in sarcastic and insulting remarks.

anneal V. reduce brittleness and improve toughness by heating and cooling. After the glass is *annealed*, it will be less subject to shipping and cracking.

annotate V. comment; make explanatory notes. In the appendix to the novel, the critic sought to *annotate* many of the more esoteric references.

anthropomorphic ADJ. having human form or characteristics. Primitive religions often have deities with *anthropomorphic* characteristics.

aphasia (*-fā´-zhyə*) N. loss of speech due to injury. After the automobile accident, the victim had periods of *aphasia* when he could not speak at all or could only mumble incoherently.

apiary (*ā´-*) N. a place where bees are kept. Although he spent many hours daily in the *apiary*, he was very seldom stung by a bee.

apocalyptic (*-pŏk-ə-lĭp´-*) ADJ. prophetic; pertaining to revelations. His *apocalyptic* remarks were dismissed by his audience as wild surmises.

apologue N. moral fable. Aesop's *Fables* are classic examples of the *apologue*.

apropos (*ăp-rə-pō´*) PREP. with reference to; properly. I find your remarks *apropos* of the present situation timely and pertinent. also ADJ. and ADV.

archetype (*är´-kĭ-*) N. prototype; primitive pattern. The Brooklyn Bridge was the *archetype* of the many spans that now connect Manhattan with Long Island and New Jersey.

archives (*är´-kīvs*) N. public records; place where public records are kept. These documents should be part of the *archives* so that historians may be able to evaluate them in the future.

arrogate V. claim without reasonable grounds. I am afraid that the manner in which he *arrogates* power to himself indicates that he is willing to ignore Constitutional limitations.

arroyo (*-rôĭ´-ə*) N. gully. Until the heavy rains of the past spring, this *arroyo* had been a dry bed.

aseptic ADJ. preventing putrefaction or blood poisoning by killing bacteria. Hospitals succeeded in lowering the mortality rate as soon as they introduced *aseptic* conditions.

assimilate V. absorb; cause to become homogeneous. The manner in which the United States was able to *assimilate* the hordes of immigrants during the nineteenth and the early part of the twentieth centuries will always be a source of pride.

astigmatism N. eye defect which prevents proper focus. As soon as his parents discovered that the boy suffered from *astigmatism,* they took him to the optometrist for corrective glasses.

atavism N. resemblance to remote ancestors rather than to parents; deformity returning after passage of two or more generations. The doctors ascribed the child's deformity to an *atavism.*

atelier (*-yā´*) N. workshop; studio. Stories of Bohemian life in Paris are full of tales of artists' starving or freezing in their *ateliers.*

aureole (*ôr´-ē-ōl*) N. sun's corona; halo. Many medieval paintings depict saintly characters with *aureoles* around their heads.

auroral ADJ. pertaining to the aurora borealis. The *auroral* display was particularly spectacular that evening.

auscultation (*ô-skəl-tā´-*) N. act of listening to the heart or lungs to discover abnormalities. The science of *auscultation* was enhanced with the development of the stethoscope.

avatar N. incarnation. In Hindu mythology, the *avatar* of Vishnu is thoroughly detailed.

avocation N. secondary or minor occupation. His hobby proved to be so fascinating and profitable that gradually he abandoned his regular occupation and concentrated on his *avocation.*

TEST—WORD LIST 31—*Synonyms*

Each of the following questions consists of a word printed in italics, followed by five words or phrases numbered 1 to 5. Choose the numbered word or phrase which is most nearly similar in meaning to the word in italics and write the number of your choice on your answer paper.

601. *acerbity*   1 sweetness 2 bitterness 3 speed 4 slowness 5 shock
602. *admonition*   1 weapon 2 preamble 3 warning 4 alarm 5 hysteria
603. *animus*   1 pterodactyl 2 bastion 3 giraffe 4 grimace 5 bias
604. *aberration*   1 deviation 2 abhorrence 3 dislike 4 absence 5 anecdote
605. *aphasia*   1 loss of speech 2 necessity 3 pain 4 crack 5 loss of mobility
606. *amoral*   1 unusual 2 religious 3 unmoral 4 suave 5 firm
607. *abysmal*   1 bottomless 2 eternal 3 meteoric 4 diabolic 5 internal

608. *apologue*   1 facade 2 fable 3 novel 4 hymn 5 prayer
609. *abnegation*   1 blackness 2 self-denial 3 selfishness 4 cause 5 effect
610. *accede*   1 fail 2 compromise 3 correct 4 consent 5 mollify
611. *aegis*   1 shield 2 nave 3 swindle 4 bargain 5 fiasco
612. *arrogate*   1 swindle 2 balance 3 claim 4 perjure 5 effect
613. *acephalous*   1 moneyed 2 current 3 headless 4 modest 5 hungry
614. *arroyo*   1 crevice 2 gully 3 value 4 food 5 fabric
615. *afflatus*   1 rival 2 trance 3 reserve 4 inspiration 5 opposite
616. *avatar*   1 hedge 2 hypnosis 3 incarnation 4 perfume 5 disaster
617. *affable*   1 rude 2 ruddy 3 needy 4 useless 5 courteous
618. *abut*   1 stimulate 2 grasp 3 oppose 4 widen 5 adjoin
619. *amortization*   1 litigation 2 reduction 3 response 4 thrift 5 basis
620. *amazon*   1 native 2 gigantic warrior 3 female warrior 4 myrmidon 5 labyrinth

WORD LIST   32   **bassoon - crotchety**

bassoon N. reed instrument of the woodwind family. In the orchestra, the *bassoon* is related to the oboe and the clarinet.

beholden ADJ. obligated; indebted. Since I do not wish to be *beholden* to anyone, I cannot accept this favor.

belittle V. disparage; depreciate. Although I do not wish to *belittle* your contribution, I feel we must place it in its proper perspective.

benignity (*-nĭg´-*) N. state of being kind, benign, gracious. We have endowed our Creator with a *benignity* which permits forgiveness of our sins and transgressions.

benison N. blessing. Let us pray that the *benison* of peace once more shall prevail among the nations of the world.

bereavement N. state of being deprived of something valuable or beloved. His friends gathered to console him upon his sudden *bereavement.*

bestial ADJ. beastlike; brutal. We must suppress our *bestial* desires and work for peaceful and civilized ends.

bifurcated ADJ. divided into two branches; forked. With a *bifurcated* branch and a piece of elastic rubber, he made a crude but effective slingshot.

billingsgate N. vituperation; abusive language. His attempts at pacifying the mob were met by angry hoots and *billingsgate.*

ā—ale; ă—add; ä—arm; à—ask, ē—eve; ĕ—end; ê—err, her; ə—allow; even; ī—ice; ĭ—ill; ō—oll; ŏ—odd; ô—orb; ōō—food; ŏŏ—foot, put; ou—out; th—thin; ū—use; ŭ—up; zh—pleasure

blanch V. bleach; whiten. Although age had *blanched* his hair, he was still vigorous and energetic.

blasé (*blä-zā´*) ADJ. bored with pleasure or dissipation. Your *blasé* attitude gives your students an erroneous impression of the joys of scholarship.

boorish ADJ. rude; clownish. Your *boorish* remarks to the driver of the other car were not warranted by the situation and served merely to enrage him.

bowdlerize (*bōd´-*) V. expurgate. After the film editors had *bowdlerized* the language in the script, the motion picture's rating was changed from "R" to "PG."

brackish ADJ. somewhat saline. He found the only wells in the area were *brackish;* drinking the water made him nauseated.

breviary (*brē´-*) N. book containing the daily prayers. The religious sect demanded daily recitals of the *breviary* as well as formal Sabbath services.

brindled ADJ. tawny or grayish with streaks or spots. He was disappointed in the litter because the puppies were *brindled;* he had hoped for animals of a uniform color.

bugaboo N. bugbear; object of baseless terror. If we become frightened by such *bugaboos,* we are no wiser than the birds who fear scarecrows.

bureaucracy N. government by bureaus. Many people fear that the constant introduction of federal agencies will create a government by *bureaucracy.*

buskin N. thick-soled half boot worn by actors of Greek tragedy. Wearing the *buskin* gave the Athenian tragic actor a larger-than-life appearance and enhanced the intensity of the play.

calligraphy N. beautiful writing; excellent penmanship. As we examine ancient manuscripts, we become impressed with the *calligraphy* of the scribes.

callow ADJ. unfledged; youthful. In that youthful movement, the leaders were only a little less *callow* than their immature followers.

capillary ADJ. having a very fine bore. The changes in surface tension of liquids in *capillary* vessels is of special interest to physicists. also N.

carafe (*kə-rãf´*) N. glass water bottle; decanter. With each dinner, the patron receives a *carafe* of red or white wine.

carillon N. a set of bells capable of being played. The *carillon* in the bell tower of the Coca Cola pavilion at the New York World's Fair provided musical entertainment every hour.

cartographer (*-tŏg´-*) N. maker of maps or charts. *Cartographers* are unable to provide accurate maps of legal boundaries in the Near East because of the unsettled political situation in that part of the world following the recent military actions.

caryatid (*-ãt´-*) N. sculptured column of a female figure. The *caryatids* supporting the entablature reminded the onlooker of the columns he had seen in the Acropolis at Athens.

caste (*kãst*) N. one of the hereditary classes in Hindu society. The differences created by *caste* in India must be eradicated if true democracy is to prevail in that country.

casuistry (*kãzh´-wə-strē*) N. subtle or sophisticated reasoning resulting in minute distinctions. You are using *casuistry* to justify your obvious violation of decent behavior.

catalyst N. agent which brings about a chemical change while it remains unaffected and unchanged. Many chemical reactions cannot take place without the presence of a *catalyst.*

catharsis N. purging or cleansing of any passage of the body. Aristotle maintained that tragedy created a *catharsis* by purging the soul of base concepts.

caucus N. private meeting of members of a party to select officers or determine policy. At the opening of Congress, the members of the Democratic Party held a *caucus* to elect the Majority Leader of the House and the Party Whip.

celerity N. speed; rapidity. Hamlet resented his mother's *celerity* in remarrying within a month after his father's death.

centripetal (*-trĭp´-*) ADJ. tending toward the center. Does *centripetal* force or the force of gravity bring orbiting bodies to the earth's surface?

chiromancy (*kī´-*) N. art of telling fortunes by reading the hand; palmistry. The charlatans along the Midway claimed the ability to analyze character and predict the future by such means as handwriting analysis, phrenology and *chiromancy.*

choreography (*kō-rē-ŏg´-*) N. art of dancing. Martha Graham introduced a form of *choreography* which seemed awkward and alien to those who had been brought up on classic ballet.

circumlocution N. indirect or roundabout expression. He was afraid to call a spade a spade and resorted to *circumlocutions* to avoid direct reference to his subject.

codicil N. supplement to the body of a will. This *codicil* was drawn up five years after the writing of the original will.

colander N. utensil with perforated bottom used for straining. Before serving the spaghetti, place it in a *colander* to drain it.

colloquial ADJ. pertaining to conversational or common speech. Your use of *colloquial* expressions in a formal essay such as the one you have presented spoils the effect you hope to achieve.

comatose ADJ. in a coma; extremely sleepy. The long-winded orator soon had his audience in a *comatose* state.

compendium N. brief comprehensive summary. This text can serve as a *compendium* of the tremendous amount of new material being developed in this field.

complicity N. participation; involvement. You cannot keep your *complicity* in this affair secret very long; you would be wise to admit your involvement immediately.

compromise V. adjust; endanger the interests or reputation of. Your presence at the scene of the dispute *compromises* our claim to neutrality in this matter. also N.

conch N. large seashell. In this painting we see a Triton blowing on his *conch.*

concordat N. agreement, usually between the papal authority and the secular. One of the most famous of the agreements between a Pope and an emperor was the *Concordat* of Worms in 1122.

conduit (*kŏn´-dū-ət*) N. aqueduct; passageway for fluids. Water was brought to the army in the desert by an improvised *conduit* from the adjoining mountain.

conjecture N. surmise; guess. I will end all your *conjectures;* I admit I am guilty as charged. also V.

convoluted ADJ. coiled around; involved; intricate. His argument was so *convoluted* that few of us could follow it intelligently.

cordon N. extended line of men or fortifications to prevent access or egress. The police *cordon* was so tight that the criminals could not leave the area. also V.

cormorant (*kôrm´-*) N. greedy, rapacious bird. The *cormorants* spend their time eating the fish which they catch by diving. also ADJ.

correlation N. mutual relationship. He sought to determine the *correlation* that existed between ability in algebra and ability to interpret reading exercises.

coruscate V. glitter; scintillate. His wit is the kind that *coruscates* and startles all his listeners.

ā—ale; ă—add; ä—arm; à—ask, ē—eve; ĕ—end; ê—err, her; ə—allow; even; ī—ice; ĭ—ill; ō—oll; ŏ—odd; ô—orb; ōō—food; ŏŏ—foot, put; ou—out; th—thin; ū—use; ŭ—up; zh—pleasure

cozen (*kŭz´-*) v. cheat; hoodwink; swindle. He was the kind of individual who would *cozen* his friends in a cheap card game but remain eminently ethical in all his business dealings.

credo N. creed. I believe we may best describe his *credo* by saying that it approximates the Golden Rule.

crepuscular ADJ. pertaining to twilight. Bats are *crepuscular* creatures since they begin their flights as soon as the sun begins to sink below the horizon.

crescendo (*-shĕn´-*) N. increase in the volume of sound in a musical passage. The overture suddenly changed from a quiet pastoral theme to a *crescendo* featured by blaring trumpets and clashing cymbals.

crotchety ADJ. eccentric; whimsical. Although he was reputed to be a *crotchety* old gentleman, I found his ideas substantially sound and sensible.

TEST—WORD LIST 32—*Antonyms*

Each of the questions below consists of a word printed in italics, followed by five words or phrases numbered 1 to 5. Choose the numbered word or phrase which is most nearly opposite in meaning to the word in italics and write the number of your choice on your answer paper.

621. *brackish* 1 careful 2 sweetish 3 chosen 4 tough 5 wet
622. *comatose* 1 quiet 2 restrained 3 alert 4 asleep 5 grim
623. *callow* 1 sophisticated 2 naive 3 mild 4 colored 5 seated
624. *benignity* 1 fragility 2 diction 3 volition 4 evilness 5 grace
625. *centripetal* 1 average 2 median 3 normal 4 thrifty 5 centrifugal
626. *blanch* 1 bleach 2 scatter 3 darken 4 analyze 5 subdivide
627. *bestial* 1 animated 2 noble 3 zoological 4 clear 5 dusky
628. *benison* 1 curse 2 bachelor 3 wedding 4 orgy 5 tragedy

629. *conjecture* 1 certainty 2 guess 3 position 4 form 5 place
630. *billingsgate* 1 disguise 2 debt 3 fiction 4 settlement 5 acclaim
631. *brindled* 1 roan 2 pathetic 3 hasty 4 of uniform color 5 mild tasting
632. *blasé* 1 fiery 2 clever 3 intriguing 4 slim 5 ardent
633. *celerity* 1 assurance 2 state 3 acerbity 4 delay 5 infamy
634. *conviviality* 1 discourse 2 view 3 drunkenness 4 friendship 5 animosity
635. *calligraphy* 1 scribbling 2 sculpture 3 embarrassment 4 brevity 5 telegraphy
636. *colloquial* 1 burnt 2 polished 3 political 4 gifted 5 problematic
637. *boorish* 1 suave 2 oafish 3 rustic 4 speedy 5 dry
638. *crescendo* 1 fallacy 2 angular 3 diminution 4 full 5 macabre
639. *cozen* 1 cheat 2 treat honestly 3 prate 4 shackle 5 vilify
640. *belittle* 1 disobey 2 forget 3 magnify 4 extol 5 envy

WORD LIST 33 **cruet - exacerbate**

cruet N. small glass bottle for vinegar, oil, etc. The waiter preparing the salad poured oil and vinegar from two *cruets* into the bowl.

crypt N. secret recess or vault, usually used for burial. Until recently, only bodies of rulers and leading statesmen were interred in this *crypt.*

cubicle N. small chamber used for sleeping. After his many hours of intensive study in the library, he retired to his *cubicle.*

cul-de-sac N. blind alley; trap. The soldiers were unaware that they were marching into a *cul-de-sac* when they entered the canyon.

culvert N. artificial channel for water. If we build a *culvert* under the road at this point, we will reduce the possibility of the road's being flooded during the rainy season.

curator N. superintendent; manager. The members of the board of trustees of the museum expected the new *curator* to plan events and exhibitions which would make the museum more popular.

curmudgeon N. churlish, miserly individual. Although he was regarded by many as a *curmudgeon,* a few of us were aware of the many kindnesses and acts of charity which he secretly performed.

cursive ADJ. flowing, running. In normal writing we run our letters together in *cursive* form; in printing, we separate the letters.

cynosure (*sī´-*) N. the object of general attention. As soon as the movie star entered the room, she became the *cynosure* of all eyes.

debacle (*-băk´-əl*) N. breaking up; downfall. This *debacle* in the government can only result in anarchy.

debenture (*-bĕn´-*) N. bond issued to secure a loan. The manager of the company urged that the company try to raise money by issuing *debentures* rather than to try to sell stock.

decimate (*dĕs´-*) v. kill, usually one out of ten. We do more to *decimate* our population in automobile accidents than we do in war.

decolleté (*dā-kŏl-ə-tā´*) ADJ. having a low-necked dress. Current fashion decrees that evening gowns be *decolleté* this season; bare shoulders are again the vogue.

decrepitude N. state of collapse caused by illness or old age. I was unprepared for the state of *decrepitude* in which I had found my old friend; he seemed to have aged twenty years in six months.

degraded ADJ. lowered in rank; debased. The *degraded* wretch spoke only of his past glories and honors.

deliquescent (*dĕl-ĭ-kwĕs´-*) ADJ. capable of absorbing moisture from the air and becoming liquid. Since this powder is extremely *deliquescent,* it must be kept in a hermetically sealed container until it is used.

demesne (*dĭ-mān´*) N. domain; land over which a person has full sovereignty. Keats is referring to epic poetry when he mentions Homer's "proud *demesne.*"

demotic ADJ. pertaining to the people. He lamented the passing of aristocratic society and maintained that a *demotic* society would lower the nation's standards.

denigrate (*dĕn´-*) v. blacken. All attempts to *denigrate* the

---

ā—ale; ă—add; ä—arm; à—ask, ē—eve; ĕ—end; ê—err, her; ə—allow; even; ī—ice; ĭ—ill; ō—oll; ŏ—odd; ô—orb; ōō—food; ŏŏ—foot; pŭt; ou—out; th—thin; ū—use; ŭ—up; zh—pleasure

character of our late President have failed; the people still love him and cherish his memory.

denotation N. meaning; distinguishing by name. A dictionary will always give us the *denotation* of a word; frequently, it will also give us its connotation.

denouement (*dā-nōō-män´*) N. outcome; final development of the plot of a play. The play was childishly written; the *denouement* was obvious to sophisticated theatergoers as early as the middle of the first act.

desideratum (*-rät´-*) N. that which is desired. Our first *desideratum* must be the establishment of peace; we can then attempt to remove the causes of the present conflict.

diatribe (*dī´-ə-*) N. bitter scolding; invective. During the lengthy *diatribe* delivered by his opponent he remained calm and self-controlled.

didactic ADJ. teaching; instructional. The *didactic* qualities of his poetry overshadow its literary qualities; the lesson he teaches is more memorable than the lines.

disabuse V. correct a false impression; undeceive. I will attempt to *disabuse* you of your impression of my client's guilt; I know he is innocent.

dishabille (*dĭs-ə-bēl´*) N. in a state of undress. Because he was certain that he would have no visitors, he lounged around the house in a state of *dishabille*, wearing only his pajamas and a pair of old bedroom slippers.

dispassionate ADJ. calm; impartial. In a *dispassionate* analysis of the problem, he carefully examined the causes of the conflict and proceeded to suggest suitable remedies.

distaff ADJ. female. His ancestors on the *distaff* side were equally as famous as his father's progenitors; his mother's father and grandfather were both famous judges.

doddering ADJ. shaky; infirm from old age. Although he is not as yet a *doddering* and senile old man, his ideas and opinions no longer can merit the respect we gave them years ago.

duenna (*dū-ĕn´-*) N. attendant of young female; chaperone. Their romance could not flourish because of the presence of her *duenna*.

dulcet (*-sət*) ADJ. sweet sounding. The *dulcet* sounds of the birds at dawn were soon drowned out by the roar of traffic passing our motel.

durance N. restraint; imprisonment. The lecturer spoke of a "*durance* vile" to describe his years in the prison camp.

dynamic ADJ. active; efficient. A *dynamic* government is necessary to meet the demands of a changing society.

eclat (*ā-klä´*) N. brilliance; glory. To the delight of his audience, he completed his task with *eclat* and consummate ease.

eclecticism N. selection of elements from various sets of opinions or systems. The *eclecticism* of the group was demonstrated by their adoption of principles and practices of many forms of government.

effluvium N. noxious smell. Air pollution has become a serious problem in our major cities; the *effluvium* and the poisons in the air are hazards to life.

embryonic (*-ŏn´-*) ADJ. undeveloped; rudimentary. The evil of class and race hatred must be eliminated while it is still in an *embryonic* state; otherwise, it may grow to dangerous proportions.

emendation N. correction of errors; improvement. Please initial all the *emendations* you have made in this contract.

emeritus ADJ. retired but retained in an honorary capacity. As professor *emeritus*, he retained all his honors without having to meet the obligations of daily assignments.

emollient N. soothing or softening remedy. He applied an *emollient* to the inflamed area. Also ADJ.

empirical ADJ. based on experience. He distrusted hunches and intuitive flashes; he placed his reliance entirely on *empirical* data.

empyreal (*-pī´-rē-əl*) ADJ. celestial; fiery. The scientific advances of the twentieth century have enabled man to invade the *empyreal* realm of the eagle.

encomium (*-kō´-mē-əm*) N. praise; eulogy. He was sickened by the *encomiums* and panegyrics expressed by speakers who had previously been among the first to vilify the man they were now honoring.

endemic (*-dĕm´-*) ADJ. prevailing among a specific group of people or in a specific area or country. This disease is *endemic* in this part of the world; more than 80 percent of the population are at one time or another affected by it.

enigmatic ADJ. obscure; puzzling. Many have sought to fathom the *enigmatic* smile of the *Mona Lisa*.

enjoin V. command; order; forbid. The owners of the company asked the court to *enjoin* the union from picketing the plant.

ensue V. follow. The evils that *ensued* were the direct result of the miscalculations of the leaders.

entomology N. study of insects. I found *entomology* the least interesting part of my course in biology; studying insects bored me.

equitable ADJ. fair; impartial. I am seeking an *equitable* solution to this dispute, one which will be fair and acceptable to both sides.

erotic ADJ. pertaining to passionate love. The *erotic* passages in this novel should be removed as they are merely pornographic.

erudition N. high degree of knowledge and learning. Although they respected his *erudition*, the populace refused to listen to his words of caution and turned to less learned leaders.

ethnology N. study of man. Sociology is one aspect of the science of *ethnology*.

etymology N. study of derivation, structure and development of words. To the student of *etymology*, the dictionary is a tremendous source of information.

eugenic ADJ. pertaining to the improvement of race. It is easier to apply *eugenic* principles to the raising of race-horses or prize cattle than to the development of human beings.

eviscerate V. disembowel; remove entrails. The medicine man *eviscerated* the animal and offered the entrails to the angry gods.

exacerbate V. worsen; embitter. This latest arrest will *exacerbate* the already existing discontent of the people and enrage them.

TEST—WORD LIST 33—*Synonyms*

Each of the following questions consists of a word printed in italics, followed by five words or phrases numbered 1 to 5. Choose the numbered word or phrase which is most nearly similar in meaning to the word in italics and write the number of your choice on your answer paper.

ā—ale; ă—add; ä—arm; à—ask, ē—eve; ĕ—end; ê—err, her; ə—allow; even; ī—ice; ĭ—ill; ō—oll; ŏ—odd; ô—orb; ōō—food; ŏŏ—foot, put; ou—out; th—thin; ū—use; ŭ—up; zh—pleasure

641. *cynosure*   1 midway 2 attrition 3 circle 4 hardihood 5 center of attention
642. *degraded*   1 surprised 2 lowered 3 ascended 4 learned 5 prejudged
643. *diatribe*   1 mass 2 range 3 discourse 4 harangue 5 starvation
644. *cul-de-sac*   1 blind alley 2 avenue 3 point 4 rage 5 gambit
645. *dipsomaniac*   1 realist 2 thief 3 sot 4 pyromaniac 5 swimmer
646. *decolleté*   1 flavored 2 demure 3 flowery 4 low-necked 5 sweet
647. *duenna*   1 baby-sitter 2 relative 3 partner 4 young noblewoman 5 chaperon
648. *cursive*   1 deprecatory 2 avowing 3 running 4 flashy 5 lewd
649. *emendation*   1 correction 2 interpretation 3 exhumation 4 inquiry 5 fault
650. *denigrate*   1 refuse 2 blacken 3 terrify 4 lighten 5 review

651. *dulcet*   1 hidden 2 demanding 3 soothing 4 downy 5 tempestuous
652. *disabuse*   1 crash 2 violate 3 renege 4 control 5 undeceive
653. *debacle*   1 progress 2 collapse 3 masque 4 cowardice 5 traffic
654. *dispassionate*   1 sensual 2 immoral 3 inhibited 4 impartial 5 scientific
655. *decrepitude*   1 feebleness 2 disease 3 coolness 4 melee 5 crowd
656. *decimate*   1 kill 2 disgrace 3 search 4 collide 5 deride
657. *distaff*   1 wholesome 2 graceful 3 female 4 masculine 5 parental
658. *denouement*   1 action 2 scenery 3 resort 4 character 5 solution
659. *didactic*   1 mystic 2 titillating 3 chemical 4 instructing 5 chaotic
660. *crypt*   1 stone 2 vault 3 stove 4 tradition 5 monument

---

WORD LIST   34   **excision - imperturbable**

excision   N. act of cutting away. With the *excision* of the dead and dying limbs of this tree, you have not only improved its appearance but you have enhanced its chances of bearing fruit.

excoriate   V. flay; abrade. These shoes are so ill-fitting that they will *excoriate* the feet and create blisters.

execrate   V. curse; express abhorrence for. The world *execrates* the memory of Hitler and hopes that genocide will never again be the policy of any nation.

exegesis   (-jē´-) N. explanation, especially of Biblical passages. I can follow your *exegesis* of this passage to a limited degree; some of your reasoning eludes me.

ex officio   (-fĭsh´-) ADJ. by virtue of one's office. The Mayor was *ex officio* chairman of the committee that decided the annual tax rate. also ADV.

exorcise   V. drive out evil spirits. By incantation and prayer, the medicine man sought to *exorcise* the evil spirits which had taken possession of the young warrior.

expletive   (ĕk´-) N. interjection; profane oath. The sergeant's remarks were filled with *expletives* which reflected on the intelligence and character of the new recruits.

explicit   ADJ. definite; open. Your remarks are *explicit;* no one can misinterpret them.

fanfare   N. call by bugles or trumpets. The exposition was opened with a *fanfare* of trumpets and the firing of cannon.

febrile   ADJ. feverish. In his *febrile* condition, he was subject to nightmares and hallucinations.

fiduciary   ADJ. pertaining to a position of trust. In his will, he stipulated that the bank act in a *fiduciary* capacity and manage his estate until his children became of age. also N.

flinch   V. hesitate; shrink. He did not *flinch* in the face of danger but fought back bravely.

floe   N. mass of floating ice. The ship made slow progress as it battered its way through the ice *floes.*

fluted   ADJ. having vertical parallel grooves (as in a pillar). All that remained of the ancient building were the *fluted* columns.

fracas   (frā k´-) N. brawl, melee. The military police stopped the *fracas* in the bar and arrested the belligerents.

frond   N. fern leaf; palm or banana leaf. After the storm the beach was littered with the *fronds* of palm trees.

fulcrum   N. support on which a lever rests. If we use this stone as a *fulcrum* and the crowbar as a lever, we may be able to move this boulder.

fulgent   ADJ. beaming; radiant. In the *fulgent* glow of the early sunrise everything seemed bright and gleaming.

galaxy   N. the Milky Way; any collection of brilliant personalities. The deaths of such famous actors as Clark Gable, Gary Cooper and Spencer Tracy demonstrate that the *galaxy* of Hollywood superstars is rapidly disappearing.

gambit   N. opening in chess in which a piece is sacrificed. The player was afraid to accept his opponent's *gambit* because he feared a trap which as yet he could not see.

gargoyle   N. waterspout carved in grotesque figures on building. The *gargoyles* adorning the Cathedral of Notre Dame in Paris are amusing in their grotesqueness.

garrulous   ADJ. loquacious; wordy. Many members avoided the company of the *garrulous* old gentleman because his constant chatter on trivial matters bored them.

gasconade   (-nād´) N. bluster; boastfulness. Behind his front of *gasconade* and pompous talk, he tried to hide his inherent uncertainty and nervousness. also V.

gastronomy   N. science of preparing and serving good food. One of the by-products of his trip to Europe was his interest in *gastronomy;* he enjoyed preparing and serving foreign dishes to his friends.

gauche   (gōsh) ADJ. clumsy; boorish. Such remarks are *gauche* and out of place; you should apologize for making them.

genealogy   N. record of descent; lineage. He was proud of his *genealogy* and constantly referred to the achievements of his ancestors.

generic   ADJ. characteristic of a class or species. You have made the mistake of thinking that his behavior is *generic;* actually, very few of his group behave the way he does.

genuflect   V. bend the knee as in worship. A proud democrat, he refused to *genuflect* to any man.

germinal   ADJ. pertaining to a germ; creative. Such an idea is *germinal;* I am certain that it will influence thinkers and philosophers for many generations.

germinate   V. cause to sprout; sprout. After the seeds *germinate* and develop their permanent leaves, the plants may be removed from the cold frames and transplanted to the garden.

ā—ale; ă—add; ä—arm; à—ask; ē—eve; ĕ—end; ê—err, her; ə—allow; even; ī—ice; ĭ—ill; ō—oll; ŏ—odd; ô—orb; ōō—food; ŏŏ—foot, put; ou—out; th—thin; ū—use; ŭ—up; zh—pleasure

gerrymander V. change voting district lines in order to favor a political party. The illogical pattern of the map of this congressional district is proof that the State Legislature *gerrymandered* this area in order to favor the majority party. also N.

gestate *(jĕs´-)* V. evolve, as in prenatal growth. While this scheme was being *gestated* by the conspirators, they maintained complete silence about their intentions.

glossary N. brief explanation of words used in the text. I have found the *glossary* in this book very useful; it has eliminated many trips to the dictionary.

gratuity N. tip. Many service employees rely more on *gratuities* than on salaries for their livelihood.

grimace *(grĭm´-)* N. a facial distortion to show feeling such as pain, disgust, etc. Even though he remained silent, his *grimace* indicated his displeasure. also V.

grovel V. crawl or creep on ground; remain prostrate. Even though we have been defeated, we do not have to *grovel* before our conquerors.

hackles N. hairs on back and neck of a dog. The dog's *hackles* rose and he began to growl as the sound of footsteps grew louder.

hegira *(-jĭ´-rə)* flight, especially Mohammed's flight from Mecca to Medina. Mohammed began his *hegira* when he was 53 years old.

hermetically ADV. sealed by fusion so as to be airtight. After these bandages are sterilized, they are placed in *hermetically* sealed containers.

hew V. cut to pieces with ax or sword. The cavalry rushed into the melee and *hewed* the enemy with their swords.

hoax N. trick; practical joke. Embarrassed by the *hoax*, he reddened and left the room. also V.

hoodwink V. deceive; delude. Having been *hoodwinked* once by the fast-talking salesman, he was extremely cautious when he went to purchase a used car.

hortatory ADJ. encouraging; exhortive. The crowd listened to his *hortatory* statements with ever growing excitement; finally they rushed from the hall to carry out his suggestions.

hoyden N. boisterous girl. Although she is now a *hoyden,* I am sure she will outgrow her tomboyish ways and quiet down.

hummock N. small hill. The ascent of the *hummock* is not difficult and the view from the hilltop is ample reward for the effort.

husbandry N. frugality; thrift; agriculture. He accumulated his small fortune by diligence and *husbandry*.

hustings *(hŭs´-)* N. meetings particularly to choose candidates. Congress adjourned so that the members could attend to their political *hustings*.

hyperbole *(-pêr´-bə-lē)* N. exaggeration; overstatement. This salesman is guilty of *hyperbole* in describing his product; it is wise to discount his claims.

hyperborean ADJ. situated in extreme north; arctic; cold. The *hyperborean* blasts brought snow and ice to the countryside.

hypothecate V. mortgage; pledge as security. I have no authority to *hypothecate* this property as security for the loan.

idiosyncratic ADJ. private; peculiar to an individual. Such behavior is *idiosyncratic;* it is as easily identifiable as a signature.

illusive ADJ. deceiving. This mirage is an illusion; let us not be fooled by its *illusive* effect.

imbrue V. drench, stain, especially with blood. As the instigator of this heinous murder, he is as much *imbrued* in blood as the actual assassin.

immure V. imprison; shut up in confinement. For the two weeks before the examination, the student *immured* himself in his room and concentrated upon his studies.

impalpable ADJ. imperceptible; intangible. The ash is so fine that it is *impalpable* to the touch but it can be seen as a fine layer covering the window ledge.

imperturbable ADJ. calm; placid. He remained *imperturbable* and in full command of the situation in spite of the hysteria and panic all around him.

TEST—WORD LIST 34—*Antonyms*

Each of the questions below consists of a word printed in italics, followed by five words or phrases numbered 1 to 5. Choose the numbered word or phrase which is most nearly opposite in meaning to the word in italics and write the number of your choice on your answer paper.

661. *hortatory* 1 inquiring 2 denying 3 killing 4 frantic 5 dissuading

662. *execrate* 1 disobey 2 enact 3 perform 4 acclaim 5 fidget

663. *husbandry* 1 sportsmanship 2 dishonesty 3 wastefulness 4 friction 5 cowardice

664. *gasconade* 1 transparency 2 cleanliness 3 modesty 4 imposture 5 seizure

665. *illusive* 1 not deceptive 2 not certain 3 not obvious 4 not coherent 5 not brilliant

666. *genuflect* 1 falsify 2 trick 3 project 4 stand erect 5 pronounce correctly

667. *gratuity* 1 ingratitude 2 idea 3 suggestion 4 stipend 5 prerequisite

668. *hyperborean* 1 sultry 2 pacific 3 noteworthy 4 western 5 wooded

669. *imperturbable* 1 calm 2 swift 3 arable 4 hysterical 5 solemn

670. *fulgent* 1 dizzy 2 empty 3 diverse 4 shining 5 dull

671. *hummock* 1 hillock 2 scorn 3 elevation 4 vale 5 vestment

672. *impalpable* 1 obvious 2 combined 3 high 4 connecting 5 lost

673. *hegira* 1 return 2 harem 3 oasis 4 panic 5 calm

674. *garrulous* 1 arid 2 hasty 3 sociable 4 quaint 5 taciturn

675. *hyperbole* 1 exaggeration 2 climax 3 curve 4 understatement 5 expansion

676. *gauche* 1 rigid 2 graceful 3 swift 4 tacit 5 needy

677. *hoyden* 1 burden 2 lighter 3 demure girl 4 gamin 5 traffic

678. *germinal* 1 fully developed 2 excused 3 sterilized 4 primitive 5 strategic

679. *immure* 1 inter 2 liberate 3 exhume 4 exit 5 incarcerate

680. *excoriate* 1 scandalize 2 encourage 3 avoid 4 praise 5 vanquish

WORD LIST 35 **implement - mammal**

implement V. supply what is needed; furnish with tools. I am unwilling to *implement* this plan until I have assurances that it has the full approval of your officials. also N.

imply V. suggest a meaning not expressed; signify. Even though your statement does not declare that you are at war with that country, your actions *imply* that that is the actual situation.

imponderable ADJ. weightless. I can evaluate the data gathered in this study; the *imponderable* items are not so easily analyzed.

importunate ADJ. urging; demanding. He tried to hide from his *importunate* creditors until his allowance arrived.

impotent (*ĭm´-*) ADJ. weak; ineffective. Although he wished to break the nicotine habit, he found himself *impotent* in resisting the craving for a cigarette.

imprimatur N. permission to print or publish a book. The publication of the book was delayed until the *imprimatur* of the State Education Committee was granted.

impute V. attribute; ascribe. If I wished to *impute* blame to the officers in charge of this program, I would come out and state it definitely and without hesitation.

incantation N. singing or chanting of magic spells; magical formula. Uttering *incantations* to make the brew more potent, the witch doctor stirred the liquid in the caldron.

incarnadine V. stain crimson or blood-color. After killing Duncan, Macbeth cries that his hands are so bloodstained that they would "the multitudinous seas *incarnadine.*"

incarnation N. act of assuming a human body and human nature. The *incarnation* of Jesus Christ is a basic tenet of Christian theology.

incidence N. falling on a body; a casual occurrence. We must determine the angle of *incidence* of the rays of light.

incongruous ADJ. not fitting; absurd. These remarks do not have any relationship to the problem at hand; they are *incongruous* and should be stricken from the record.

incontinent ADJ. lacking self-restraint; licentious. His *incontinent* behavior off stage shocked many people and they refused to attend the plays and movies in which he appeared.

incredulous ADJ. withholding belief; skeptical. The *incredulous* judge refused to accept the statement of the defendant.

inductive ADJ. pertaining to induction or proceeding from the specific to the general. The discovery of the planet Pluto is an excellent example of the results that can be obtained from *inductive* reasoning.

inebriety (*-brī´-*) N. habitual intoxication. Because of his *inebriety,* he was discharged from his position as family chauffeur.

ineluctable ADJ. irresistible; not to be escaped. He felt that his fate was *ineluctable* and refused to make any attempt to improve his lot.

inertia N. state of being inert or indisposed to move. Our *inertia* in this matter may prove disastrous; we must move to aid our allies immediately.

infer V. deduce; conclude. We must be particularly cautious when we *infer* that a person is guilty on the basis of circumstantial evidence.

ingenue N. an artless girl; an actress who plays such parts. Although she was forty, she still insisted that she be cast as an *ingenue* and refused to play more mature roles.

insouciant ADJ. indifferent; without concern or care. Your *insouciant* attitude at such a critical moment indicates that you do not understand the gravity of the situation.

integument N. outer covering or skin. The turtle takes advantage of its hard *integument* and hides within its shell when threatened.

interdict V. prohibit; forbid. Civilized nations must *interdict* the use of nuclear weapons if we expect our society to live.

interlocutory ADJ. conversational; intermediate, not final. This *interlocutory* decree is only a temporary setback; the case has not been settled.

internecine ADJ. mutually destructive. The rising death toll on both sides indicates the *internecine* nature of this conflict.

interstices (*-têr´-stə-sēz*) N. chinks; crevices. The mountain climber sought to obtain a foothold in the *interstices* of the cliff.

intractable ADJ. unruly; refractory. The horse was *intractable* and refused to enter the starting gate.

intransigence N. state of stubborn unwillingness to compromise. The *intransigence* of both parties in the dispute makes an early settlement almost impossible to obtain.

invalidate V. weaken; destroy. The relatives who received little or nothing sought to *invalidate* the will by claiming that the deceased had not been in his right mind when he had signed the document.

inveigh V. denounce; utter censure or invective. He *inveighed* against the demagoguery of the previous speaker and urged that the audience reject his philosophy as dangerous.

irksome ADJ. repetitious; tedious. He found working on the assembly line *irksome* because of the monotony of the operation he had to perform.

irony N. hidden sarcasm or satire; use of words that convey a meaning opposite to the literal meaning. Gradually his listeners began to realize that the excessive praise he was lavishing was merely *irony;* he was actually denouncing his opponent.

irrefragable (*-rĕf´-*) ADJ. not to be disproved; indisputable. The testimonies of the witnesses provide *irrefragable* proof that my client is innocent; I demand that he be released at once.

isotope (*ī´-*) N. varying form of an element. The study of the *isotopes* of uranium led to the development of the nuclear bomb.

itinerary N. plan of a trip. Before leaving for his first visit to France and England, he discussed his *itinerary* with people who had been there and with his travel agent.

jejune (*jĭ-jōōn´*) ADJ. lacking interest; barren; meager. The plot of the play is *jejune* and fails to capture the interest of the audience.

jeremiad (*jĕr-ə-mī´-əd*) N. lament; complaint. His account of the event was a lengthy *jeremiad,* unrelieved by any light moments.

juncture N. crisis; joining point. At this critical *juncture,* let us think carefully before determining the course we shall follow.

jurisprudence N. science of law. He was more a student of *jurisprudence* than a practitioner of the law.

juxtapose V. place side by side. Comparison will be easier if you *juxtapose* the two objects.

kaleidoscope N. tube in which patterns made by the reflection in mirrors of colored pieces of glass, etc., produce interesting symmetrical effects. People found a new source of entertainment while peering through Sir David Brewster's invention, the *kaleidoscope;* they found the ever-changing patterns fascinating.

kinetic ADJ. producing motion. Designers of the electric automobile find that their greatest obstacle lies in the development of light and efficient storage batteries, the source of the *kinetic* energy needed to propel the vehicle.

lachrymose (*lăk´-*) ADJ. producing tears. His voice has a *lachrymose* quality which is more appropriate at a funeral than a class reunion.

languor N. lassitude; depression. His friends tried to overcome the *languor* into which he had fallen by taking him to parties and to the theater.

larceny N. theft. Because of the prisoner's record, the district attorney refused to reduce the charge from grand *larceny* to petit larceny.

laudable ADJ. praiseworthy; commendable. His *laudable* deeds will be remembered by all whom he aided.

lechery N. gross lewdness; lustfulness. In his youth he led a life of *lechery* and debauchery; he did not mend his ways until middle age.

lectern N. reading desk. The chaplain delivered his sermon from a hastily improvised *lectern*.

lexicographer N. compiler of a dictionary. The new dictionary is the work of many *lexicographers* who spent years compiling and editing the work.

libido N. emotional urges behind human activity. The psychiatrist maintained that suppression of the *libido* often resulted in maladjustment and neuroses.

limbo N. region near heaven or hell where certain souls are kept; a prison (slang). Among the divisions of Hell are Purgatory and *Limbo*.

lissom ADJ. agile; lithe. As a young boy, he was *lissom* and graceful; he gave promise of developing into a fine athlete.

litany N. supplicatory prayer. On this solemn day, the congregation responded to the prayers of the priest during the *litany* with fervor and intensity.

litotes (*lī´-ə-tēz*) N. understatement for emphasis. To say, "He little realizes," when we mean that he does not realize at all, is an example of the kind of understatement we call *litotes*.

lubricity N. slipperiness; evasiveness. He exasperated the reporters by his *lubricity;* they could not pin him down to a definite answer.

ludicrous ADJ. laughable; trifling. Let us be serious; this is not a *ludicrous* issue.

maladroit ADJ. clumsy; bungling. In his usual *maladroit* way, he managed to upset the cart and spill the food.

malcontent N. person dissatisfied with existing state of affairs. He was one of the few *malcontents* in Congress; he constantly voiced his objections to the Presidential program. also ADJ.

mammal N. a vertebrate animal whose female suckles its young. Many people regard the whale as a fish and do not realize that it is a *mammal*.

TEST—WORD LIST 35—*Synonyms*

Each of the questions below consists of a word printed in italics, followed by five words or phrases numbered 1 to 5. Choose the numbered word or phrase which is most nearly similar in meaning to the word in italics and write the number of your choice on your answer paper.

681. *intractable*   1 incorrigible 2 flexible 3 unruly 4 efficient 5 base
682. *jeremiad*   1 prophecy 2 proposition 3 complaint 4 overture 5 explanation
683. *inebriety*   1 revelation 2 drunkenness 3 felony 4 starvation 5 gluttony
684. *lachrymose*   1 tearful 2 smooth 3 passionate 4 curt 5 tense
685. *maladroit*   1 malicious 2 starving 3 thirsty 4 tactless 5 artful
686. *jejune*   1 youthful 2 ancient 3 superb 4 fictional 5 meager
687. *intransigence*   1 lack of training 2 stubbornness 3 novelty 4 timidity 5 cupidity
688. *imponderable*   1 weightless 2 candid 3 unthinking 4 uneasy 5 fraught
689. *limbo*   1 hopelessness 2 limitation 3 devilishness 4 ostracism 5 dwelling place of lost souls
690. *ingenue*   1 shrew 2 actress 3 character 4 artless girl 5 understudy
691. *kinetic*   1 cinematic 2 polar 3 pertaining to motion 4 foreign 5 motivated
692. *inveigh*   1 speak violently 2 orate 3 disturb 4 apply 5 whisper
693. *incarnadine*   1 blacken 2 imprison 3 bleach 4 redden 5 powder
694. *jurisprudence*   1 caution 2 law 3 misdemeanor 4 grand jury 5 haste
695. *languor*   1 faintness 2 length 3 embarrassment 4 wine 5 avarice
696. *interdict*   1 acclaim 2 dispute 3 prohibit 4 decide 5 fret
697. *irksome*   1 tedious 2 lazy 3 tireless 4 few 5 too many
698. *importunate*   1 unlucky 2 demanding 3 refusing 4 urgent 5 vital
699. *lechery*   1 trust 2 compulsion 3 zeal 4 addiction 5 lust
700. *incontinent*   1 insular 2 complaisant 3 crass 4 wanton 5 false

---

WORD LIST 36 **mandate - paddock**

mandate N. order; charge. In his inaugural address, the President stated that he had a *mandate* from the people to seek an end to social evils such as poverty, poor housing, etc. also V.

manifold ADJ. numerous; varied. I cannot begin to tell you how much I appreciate your *manifold* kindnesses.

manumit V. emancipate; free from bondage. Enlightened slave owners were willing to *manumit* their slaves and thus put an end to the evil of slavery in the country.

marsupial N. one of a family of mammals that nurse their offspring in a pouch. The most common *marsupial* in North America is the opossum.

ā—ale; ă—add; ä—arm; à—ask, ē—eve; ĕ—end; ê—err, her; ə—allow; even; ī—ice; ĭ—ill; ō—oll; ŏ—odd; ô—orb; oo—food; oo—foot, put; ou—out; th—thin; ū—use; ŭ—up; zh—pleasure

maunder V. talk incoherently; utter drivel. You do not make sense; you *maunder* and garble your words.

mawkish ADJ. sickening; insipid. Your *mawkish* sighs fill me with disgust.

mayhem N. injury to body. The riot was marked not only by *mayhem* with its attendant loss of life and limb but also by arson and pillage.

mélange (*mā-länzh´*) N. medley; miscellany. This anthology provides a *mélange* of the author's output in the fields of satire, criticism and political analysis.

mesmerize V. hypnotize. The incessant drone seemed to *mesmerize* him and place him in a hypnotic trance.

metaphor N. implied comparison. "He soared like an eagle" is an example of a simile; "He is an eagle in flight," a *metaphor*.

miasma N. swamp gas; odor of decaying matter. I suspect that this area is infested with malaria as I can readily smell the *miasma*.

microcosm N. small world. In the *microcosm* of our small village, we find illustrations of all the evils that beset the universe.

milieu N. environment; means of expression. His *milieu* is watercolor although he has produced excellent oil paintings and lithographs.

militant ADJ. combative; bellicose. Although at this time he was advocating a policy of neutrality, one could usually find him adopting a more *militant* attitude. also N.

millennium N. thousand-year period; period of happiness and prosperity. I do not expect the *millennium* to come during my lifetime.

minaret N. slender tower attached to a mosque. From the balcony of the *minaret* we obtained an excellent view of the town and the neighboring countryside.

minatory ADJ. threatening. All abusive and *minatory* letters received by the mayor and other public officials were examined by the police.

minion N. a servile dependent. He was always accompanied by several of his *minions* because he enjoyed their subservience and flattery.

molecule N. the smallest part of a homogeneous substance. In chemistry, we study how atoms and *molecules* react to form new substances.

momentum N. quantity of motion of a moving body; impetus. The car lost *momentum* as it tried to ascend the steep hill.

moor N. marshy wasteland. These *moors* can only be used for hunting; they are too barren for agriculture.

moratorium N. legal delay of payment. If we declare a *moratorium* and delay collection of debts for six months, I am sure the farmers will be able to meet their bills.

morganatic ADJ. describing a marriage between a member of a royal family and a commoner in which it is agreed that any children will not inherit title, etc. Refusing the suggestion of a *morganatic* marriage, the king abdicated from the throne when he could not marry the woman he loved.

mugwump N. defector from a party. When he refused to support his party's nominees, he was called a *mugwump* and deprived of his seniority privileges in Congress.

murrain N. plague; cattle disease. "A *murrain* on you" was a common malediction in that period.

myopic ADJ. nearsighted. In thinking only of your present needs and ignoring the future, you are being rather *myopic*.

nascent ADJ. incipient; coming into being. If we could identify these revolutionary movements in their *nascent* state, we would be able to eliminate serious trouble in later years.

nautical ADJ. pertaining to ships or navigation. The Maritime Museum contains many models of clipper ships, log-

books, anchors and many other items of a *nautical* nature.

neap ADJ. lowest. We shall have to navigate very cautiously over the reefs as we have a *neap* tide this time of the month.

nirvana N. in Buddhist teachings, the ideal state in which the individual loses himself in the attainment of an impersonal beatitude. He tried to explain the concept of *nirvana* to his skeptical students.

nonplus V. bring to a halt by confusion. In my efforts to correct this situation I felt *nonplussed* by the stupidity of my assistants.

nuance (*nū´-äns*) N. shade of difference in meaning or color. The unskilled eye of the layman has difficulty in discerning the *nuances* of color in the paintings.

nubile ADJ. marriageable. Mrs. Bennet, in *Pride and Prejudice* by Jane Austen, was worried about finding suitable husbands for her five *nubile* daughters.

objurgation N. severe rebuke; scolding. *Objurgations* and even threats of punishment did not deter the young hoodlums.

oblation N. the Eucharist; pious donation. The wealthy man offered *oblations* so that the Church might be able to provide for the needy.

obligatory ADJ. binding; required. It is *obligatory* that books borrowed from the library be returned within two weeks.

obsidian N. black volcanic rock. The deposits of *obsidian* on the mountain slopes were an indication that the volcano had erupted in ancient times.

obstetrician N. physician specializing in delivery of babies. In modern times, the delivery of children has passed from the midwife to the more scientifically trained *obstetrician*.

obstreperous ADJ. boisterous; noisy. The crowd became *obstreperous* and shouted their disapproval of the proposals made by the speaker.

Occident N. the West. It will take time for the *Occident* to understand the ways and customs of the Orient.

odium N. repugnance; dislike. I cannot express the *odium* I feel at your heinous actions.

offal N. waste; garbage. In America, we discard as *offal* that which could feed families in less fortunate parts of the world.

offertory N. collection of money at religious ceremony; part of the Mass during which offerings are made. The donations collected during the *offertory* will be assigned to our mission work abroad.

omnipresent ADJ. universally present; ubiquitous. On Christmas Eve, Santa Claus is *omnipresent*.

onus (*ō´-*) N. burden; responsibility. The emperor was spared the *onus* of signing the surrender papers; instead, he relegated the assignment to his generals.

opportunist N. individual who sacrifices principles for expediency by taking advantage of circumstances. I do not know how he will vote on this question as he is an *opportunist*.

opprobrium N. infamy; vilification. He refused to defend himself against the slander and *opprobrium* hurled against him by the newspapers; he preferred to rely on his record.

optimum ADJ. most favorable. If you wait for the *optimum* moment to act, you may never begin your project. also N.

opus N. work. Although many critics hailed his Fifth Symphony as his major work, he did not regard it as his major *opus*.

orientation N. act of finding oneself in society. Freshman *orientation* provides the incoming students with an opportunity to learn about their new environment and their place in it.

orison (*ŏr´-ə-sən*) N. prayer. Hamlet greets Ophelia with the request, "Nymph, in thy *orisons*, be all my sins remembered."

ornithology N. study of birds. Audubon's studies of American birds greatly influenced the course of *ornithology* in this country.

orotund ADJ. having a round, resonant quality; inflated speech. The politician found that his *orotund* voice was an asset when he spoke to his constituents.

orthography N. correct spelling. Many of us find English *orthography* difficult to master because so many of our words are not written phonetically.

overweening ADJ. presumptuous; arrogant. His *overweening* pride in his accomplishments was not justified.

pachyderm N. thick-skinned animal. The elephant is probably the best-known *pachyderm*.

paddock N. saddling enclosure at race track; lot for exercising horses. The *paddock* is located directly in front of the grandstand so that all may see the horses being saddled and the jockeys mounted.

TEST—WORD LIST 36—*Antonyms*

Each of the questions below consists of a word printed in italics, followed by five words or phrases numbered 1 to 5. Choose the numbered word or phrase which is most nearly opposite in meaning to the word in italics and write the number of your choice on your answer paper.

701. *nascent* 1 fading 2 reoccurring 3 loyal 4 treacherous 5 unnamed

702. *orotund* 1 not reddish 2 not resonant 3 loud 4 pompous 5 not eager

703. *mugwump* 1 disease 2 loyal member 3 atheist 4 defector 5 scribbler

704. *manumit* 1 print 2 impress 3 enslave 4 endeavor 5 fail

705. *omnipresent* 1 taxing 2 total 3 limited 4 ignorant 5 magnificent

706. *odium* 1 noise 2 liking 3 dominant 4 hasty 5 atrium

707. *myopic* 1 visionary 2 farsighted 3 moral 4 glassy 5 blind

708. *opprobrium* 1 delineation 2 aptitude 3 majesty 4 freedom 5 praise

709. *overweening* 1 humble 2 impotent 3 avid 4 acrimonious 5 exaggerated

710. *opportunist* 1 man of destiny 2 man of principle 3 changeling 4 adversary 5 colleague

711. *odium* 1 shame 2 aptitude 3 anachronism 4 affection 5 futility

712. *minion* 1 master 2 quorum 3 majority 4 host 5 beneficiary

713. *obstreperous* 1 turbid 2 quiet 3 remote 4 obnoxious 5 active

714. *obligatory* 1 demanding 2 optional 3 facile 4 available 5 required

715. *militant* 1 combative 2 dramatic 3 religious 4 quaint 5 pacific

716. *maunder* 1 gibber 2 masticate 3 talk intelligently 4 wander 5 succeed

717. *objurgation* 1 elegy 2 rebuke 3 model 4 praise 5 approval

718. *optimum* 1 pessimistic 2 knowledgeable 3 worst 4 minimum 5 opprobrious

719. *miasma* 1 fragrant aroma 2 noxious fumes 3 scenario 4 quantity 5 total

720. *mawkish* 1 sentimental 2 sweet 3 certain 4 intelligent 5 carefree

---

WORD LIST 37 **palimpsest - prophylactic**

palimpsest N. parchment used for second time after original writing has been erased. Using chemical reagents, scientists have been able to restore the original writings on many *palimpsests*.

palliation N. act of making less severe or violent. If we cannot find a cure for this disease at the present time, we can, at least, endeavor to seek its *palliation*.

panoply N. full set of armor. The medieval knight in full *panoply* found his movements limited by the weight of his armor.

paramour N. illicit lover. She sought a divorce on the grounds that her husband had a *paramour* in another town.

paranoiac N. mentally unsound person suffering from delusions. Although he is obviously suffering from delusions, I hesitate to call him a *paranoiac*.

parapet N. low wall at edge of roof or balcony. The best way to attack the soldiers fighting behind the *parapets* on the roof is by bombardment from the air.

parity N. equality; close resemblance. I find your analogy inaccurate because I do not see the *parity* between the two illustrations.

parlous ADJ. dangerous; perilous. In these *parlous* times, we must overcome the work of saboteurs and propagandists.

parturition N. delivery; childbirth. The difficulties anticipated by the obstetricians at *parturition* did not materialize; it was a normal delivery.

passé (-sā´) ADJ. old-fashioned; past the prime. His style is *passé* and reminiscent of the Victorian era.

pastiche (-tēsh´) N. imitation of another's style in musical composition or in writing. We cannot even say that his music is a *pastiche* of this composer or that; it is, rather, reminiscent of many musicians.

pathological ADJ. pertaining to disease. As we study the *pathological* aspects of this disease, we must not overlook the psychological elements.

patina N. green crust on old bronze works; tone slowly taken by varnished painting. Judging by the *patina* on this bronze statue, we can conclude that this is the work of a medieval artist.

patois (pă-twä´) N. local or provincial dialect. His years of study of the language at the university did not enable him to understand the *patois* of the natives.

peculation N. embezzlement; theft. His *peculations* were not discovered until the auditors found discrepancies in the financial statements.

pedant N. scholar who overemphasizes book learning or technicalities. His insistence that the book be memorized

---

ā—ale; ă—add; ä—arm; à—ask, ē—eve; ĕ—end; ê—err, her; ə—allow; even; ī—ice; ĭ—ill; ō—oll; ŏ—odd; ô—orb; ōō—food; ŏŏ—foot, pŭt; ou—out; th—thin; ū—use; ŭ—up; zh—pleasure

marked the teacher as a *pedant* rather than a scholar.

pediment N. triangular part above columns in Greek buildings. The *pediment* of the building was filled with sculptures and adorned with elaborate scrollwork.

pejorative ADJ. having a deteriorating or depreciating effect on the meaning of a word. His use of *pejorative* language indicated his contempt for his audience.

pendulous ADJ. hanging; suspended. The *pendulous* chandeliers swayed in the breeze and gave the impression that they were about to fall from the ceiling.

pennate ADJ. having wings or feathers. The *pennate* leaves of the sumac remind us of feathers.

peregrination N. journey. His *peregrinations* in foreign lands did not bring understanding; he mingled only with fellow tourists and did not attempt to communicate with the native population.

perigee (*pĕr´-ə-jē*) N. point of moon's orbit when it is nearest the earth. The rocket which was designed to take photographs of the moon was launched as the moon approached its *perigee.*

peristyle N. series of columns surrounding a building or yard. The cloister was surrounded by a *peristyle* reminiscent of the Parthenon.

peroration N. conclusion of an oration. The *peroration* was largely hortatory and brought the audience to its feet clamoring for action at its close.

perquisite N. any gain above stipulated salary. The *perquisites* attached to this job make it even more attractive than the salary indicates.

personable ADJ. attractive. The man I am seeking to fill this position must be *personable* since he will be representing us before the public.

perspicuity (*-kū´-*) N. clearness of expression; freedom from ambiguity. One of the outstanding features of this book is the *perspicuity* of its author; his meaning is always clear.

perspicuous (*-spĭk´-*) ADJ. plainly expressed. His *perspicuous* comments eliminated all possibility of misinterpretation.

pharisaical (*făr-ə-sā´-ə-*) ADJ. pertaining to the Pharisees, who paid scrupulous attention to tradition; self-righteous; hypocritical. Walter Lippman has pointed out that moralists who do not attempt to explain the moral code they advocate are often regarded as *pharisaical* and ignored.

phobia N. morbid fear. His fear of flying was more than mere nervousness; it was a real *phobia.*

physiological ADJ. pertaining to the science of the function of living organisms. To understand this disease fully, we must examine not only its *physiological* aspects but also its psychological elements.

picaresque ADJ. pertaining to rogues in literature. *Tom Jones* has been hailed as one of the best *picaresque* novels in the English language.

piebald (*pī´-*) ADJ. mottled; spotted. You should be able to identify this horse easily as it is the only *piebald* horse in the race.

plangent (*-jənt*) ADJ. plaintive; resounding sadly. Although we could not understand the words of the song, we got the impression from the *plangent* tones of the singers that it was a lament of some kind.

platonic ADJ. purely spiritual; theoretical; without sensual desire. Although a member of the political group, he took only a *platonic* interest in its ideals and goals.

plausible ADJ. having a show of truth but open to doubt; specious. Even though your argument is *plausible,* I still would like to have more proof.

plebiscite (*plĕb´-*) N. expression of the will of a people by direct election. I think this matter is so important that it should be decided not by a handful of legislators but by a *plebiscite* of the entire nation.

polemic (*-lĕm´-*) N. controversy; argument in support of point of view. His essays were, for the main part, *polemics* in support of the party's policy.

polity N. form of government of nation or state. Our *polity* should be devoted to the concept that the government should strive for the good of all citizens.

porphyry (*pôr´-fə-rē*) N. igneous rock containing feldspar or quartz crystals. The *porphyry* used by the Egyptians in their buildings was purplish in color.

postprandial ADJ. after dinner. The most objectionable feature of these formal banquets is the *postprandial* speech.

potable (*pōt´-*) ADJ. suitable for drinking. The recent drought in the Middle Atlantic States has emphasized the need for extensive research in ways of making sea water *potable.* also N.

preciosity (*prĕsh-ē-ŏs´-*) N. overrefinement in art or speech. Roxane, in the play *Cyrano de Bergerac,* illustrates the extent to which *preciosity* was carried in French society.

preempt V. appropriate beforehand. Your attempt to *preempt* this land before it is offered to the public must be resisted.

prehensile ADJ. capable of grasping or holding. Monkeys use not only their arms and legs but also their *prehensile* tails in traveling through the trees.

premonitory (*-mŏn´-*) ADJ. serving to warn. You should have visited a doctor as soon as you felt these *premonitory* chest pains.

preponderance N. superiority of power, quantity, etc. The rebels sought to overcome the *preponderance* of strength of the government forces by engaging in guerrilla tactics.

prerogative N. privilege; unquestionable right. The President cannot levy taxes; that is the *prerogative* of the legislative branch of government.

prestige N. impression produced by achievements or reputation. The wealthy man sought to obtain social *prestige* by contributing to popular charities.

primogeniture N. seniority by birth. By virtue of *primogeniture,* the first-born child has many privileges denied his brothers and sisters.

probe V. explore with tools. The surgeon *probed* the wound for foreign matter before suturing it. also N.

prognathous ADJ. having projecting jaws. His *prognathous* face made him seem more determined than he actually was.

projectile N. missile. Man has always hurled *projectiles* at his enemy whether in the form of stones or of highly explosive shells.

proletarian N. member of the working class. The aristocrats feared mob rule and gave the right to vote only to the wealthy, thus depriving the *proletarians* of a voice in government. also ADJ.

propellants N. substances which propel or drive forward. The development of our missile program has forced our scientists to seek more powerful *propellants.*

prophylactic ADJ. used to prevent disease. Despite all *prophylactic* measures introduced by the authorities, the epidemic raged until cool weather set in. also N.

ā—ale; ă—add; ä—arm; ȧ—ask; ē—eve; ĕ—end; ê—err, her; ə—allow; even; ī—ice; ĭ—ill; ō—oll; ŏ—odd; ô—orb; ōō—food; ŏŏ—foot, put; ou—out; th—thin; ū—use; ŭ—up; zh—pleasure

TEST—WORD LIST 37—*Synonyms*

Each of the questions below consists of a word printed in italics, followed by five words or phrases numbered 1 to 5. Choose the numbered word or phrase which is most nearly similar in meaning to the word in italics and write the number of your choice on your answer paper.

721. *parlous* 1 accepted 2 difficult 3 organic 4 inherent 5 excessive
722. *postprandial* 1 after dark 2 on awakening 3 in summer 4 after dinner 5 in winter
723. *peculation* 1 noise 2 drunkenness 3 creation 4 embezzlement 5 party
724. *prognathous* 1 chewing 2 maxillary 3 projecting 4 belligerent 5 impacted
725. *pastiche* 1 imitation 2 glue 3 meter 4 greeting 5 family
726. *perquisite* 1 requirement 2 wage 3 information 4 fringe benefit 5 price
727. *perspicuity* 1 grace 2 feature 3 review 4 difficulty 5 lucidity
728. *prehensile* 1 curly 2 grasping 3 avaricious 4 curt 5 glamorous
729. *piebald* 1 motley 2 coltish 3 hairless 4 thoroughbred 5 delicious
730. *pejorative* 1 causing to deteriorate 2 causing to inundate 3 determining 4 delighting 5 declaiming
731. *paramour* 1 illicit lover 2 majority 3 wife 4 husband 5 clandestine affair
732. *polemic* 1 black 2 lighting 3 magnetism 4 controversy 5 grimace
733. *perigee* 1 eclipse 2 planet 3 apogee 4 point furthest from earth 5 point nearest to earth
734. *patois* 1 romance 2 child's game 3 dialect 4 song 5 medley
735. *prophylactic* 1 toxic 2 preventive of disease 3 antagonistic 4 brushing 5 favorable
736. *parity* 1 duplicate 2 miniature 3 golf tee 4 similarity 5 event
737. *patina* 1 green coat 2 shine 3 cover 4 black polish 5 white lid
738. *prerogative* 1 inquiry 2 caution 3 candor 4 gratitude 5 privilege
739. *palliation* 1 increase 2 ascent 3 decline 4 alleviation 5 desire
740. *passé* 1 overdone 2 rural 3 out-of-date 4 silly 5 barbaric

---

WORD LIST 38 propinquity - similitude

propinquity N. nearness; kinship. Their relationship could not be explained as being based on mere *propinquity;* they were more than relatives; they were true friends.

proscenium (-sē´-) N. part of stage in front of curtain. In the theater-in-the-round there can be no *proscenium* or *proscenium* arch.

proselytize (prŏs´-) V. convert to a religion or belief. In these interfaith meetings, there must be no attempt to *proselytize;* we must respect all points of view.

prototype N. original work used as a model by others. The crude typewriter on display in this museum is the *prototype* of the elaborate machines in use today.

provenance N. origin or source of something. I am not interested in its *provenance;* I am more concerned with its usefulness than with its source.

provincial ADJ. pertaining to a province; limited. We have to overcome their *provincial* attitude and get them to become more cognizant of world problems.

psychopathic ADJ. pertaining to mental derangement. The *psychopathic* patient suffers more frequently from a disorder of the nervous system than from a diseased brain.

psychosis (sī-kō´-) N. mental disorder. We must endeavor to find an outlet for the patient's repressed desires if we hope to combat this *psychosis.*

pterodactyl (tĕr-ə-dăk´-) N. extinct flying reptile. The remains of *pterodactyls* indicate that these flying reptiles had a wingspan of as much as twenty feet.

pundit N. learned Hindu; any learned man; authority on a subject. Even though he discourses on the matter like a *pundit,* he is actually rather ignorant about this topic.

purblind ADJ. dim-sighted; obtuse. In his *purblind* condition, he could not identify the people he saw.

putative ADJ. supposed; reputed. Although there are some doubts, the *putative* author of this work is Massinger.

quadruped N. four-footed animal. Most mammals are *quadrupeds.*

quagmire N. bog; marsh. Our soldiers who served in Vietnam will never forget the drudgery of marching through the *quagmires* of the delta country.

quarantine N. isolation of person or ship to prevent spread of infection. We will have to place this house under *quarantine* until we determine the exact nature of the disease. also V.

queasy ADJ. easily nauseated; squeamish. As the ship left the harbor, he became *queasy* and thought that he was going to suffer from seasickness.

quorum N. number of members necessary to conduct a meeting. The senator asked for a roll call to determine whether a *quorum* was present.

ramify V. divide into branches or subdivisions. When the plant begins to *ramify,* it is advisable to nip off most of the new branches.

rampart N. defensive mound of earth. "From the *ramparts* we watched" as the fighting continued.

rationalization N. bringing into conformity with reason. All attempts at *rationalization* at this time are doomed to failure; tempers and emotions run too high for intelligent thought to prevail.

reactionary ADJ. recoiling from progress; retrograde. His program was *reactionary* since it sought to abolish many of the social reforms instituted by the previous administration. also N.

recherché (rə-shĕr-shā´) ADJ. choice, sought after; rare. His language was peculiarly literary; he avoided common expressions and used *recherché* terminology as often as possible.

recidivism N. habitual return to crime. Prison reformers in the United States are disturbed by the high rate of *recidivism;* the number of men serving second and third terms in prison indicates the failure of the prisons to rehabilitate the inmates.

recrudescence N. reopening of a wound or sore. Keep this wound bandaged until it has completely healed to prevent its *recrudescence.*

ā—ale; ă—add; ä—arm; à—ask, ē—eve; ĕ—end; ê—err, her; ə—allow; even; ī—ice; ĭ—ill; ō—oll; ŏ—odd; ô—orb; ōō—food; ŏŏ—foot, put; ou—out; th—thin; ū—use; ŭ—up; zh—pleasure

recusant N. person who refuses to comply; applied specifically to those who refused to attend Anglican services. In that religious community, the *recusant* was shunned as a pariah.

refurbish V. renovate; make bright by polishing. The flood left a deposit of mud on everything; it was necessary to *refurbish* our belongings.

rendition N. translation; artistic interpretation of a song, etc. The audience cheered enthusiastically as she completed her *rendition* of the aria.

reprobate N. person hardened in sin, devoid of a sense of decency. I cannot understand why he has so many admirers if he is the *reprobate* you say he is.

reprove V. censure; rebuke. The principal *reproved* the students when they became unruly in the auditorium.

residue N. remainder; balance. In his will, he requested that after payment of debts, taxes, and funeral expenses, the *residue* be given to his wife.

resilient ADJ. elastic; having the power of springing back. Steel is highly *resilient* and therefore is used in the manufacture of springs.

resurgent ADJ. rising again after defeat, etc. The *resurgent* nation surprised everyone by its quick recovery after total defeat.

reticulated ADJ. covered with a network; having the appearance of a mesh. She wore the *reticulated* stockings so popular with teenagers at that time.

rood N. crucifix. "By the *rood*" used to be a strong oath.

rotunda N. circular building or hall covered with a dome. His body lay in state in the *rotunda* of the Capitol.

rustic ADJ. pertaining to country people; uncouth. The backwoodsman looked out of place in his *rustic* attire.

saltatory ADJ. relating to leaping. The male members of the ballet company were renowned for their *saltatory* exploits.

salver N. tray. The food was brought in on silver *salvers* by the waiters.

sanctimonious ADJ. displaying ostentatious or hypocritical devoutness. You do not have to be so *sanctimonious* to prove that you are devout.

sarcophagus N. stone coffin, often highly decorated. The display of the *sarcophagus* in the art museum impresses me as a morbid exhibition.

sartorial ADJ. pertaining to tailors. He was as famous for the *sartorial* splendor of his attire as he was for his acting.

satellite N. small body revolving around a larger one. During the first few years of the Space Age, hundreds of *satellites* were launched by Russia and the United States.

satire N. form of literature in which irony, sarcasm, and ridicule are employed to attack vice and folly. *Gulliver's Travels,* which is regarded by many as a tale for children, is actually a bitter *satire* attacking man's folly.

satrap (*sā'-*) N. petty ruler working for a superior despot. The monarch and his *satraps* oppressed the citizens of the country.

satyr (*sāt'-ər*) N. half-human, half-bestial being in the court of Dionysos, portrayed as wanton and cunning. He was like a *satyr* in his lustful conduct.

scarify V. make slight incisions in; scratch. He was not severely cut; the flying glass had merely *scarified* him.

sciolism (*sī'-ə-*) N. quackery; superficial information. His superficial scientific treatises were filled with *sciolisms* and outmoded data.

screed N. long, tiresome harangue. His letters were no more than *screeds* in which he listed his complaints.

senescence (*-něs'-*) N. state of growing old. He did not show any signs of *senescence* until he was well past seventy.

sensuous ADJ. pertaining to the physical senses; operating through the senses. He was stimulated by the sights, sounds and smells about him; he was enjoying his *sensuous* experience.

septic ADJ. putrid; producing putrefaction. The hospital was in such a filthy state that we were afraid that many of the patients would suffer from *septic* poisoning.

sequacious ADJ. eager to follow; ductile. The *sequacious* members of Parliament were only too willing to do the bidding of their leader.

seraph N. high-ranking, six-winged angel. In "Annabel Lee" Poe maintains that the "winged *seraphs* of Heaven" envied their great love.

serried ADJ. standing shoulder to shoulder; crowded. In these days of automatic weapons, it is suicidal for troops to charge in *serried* ranks against the foe.

sibylline ADJ. prophetic; oracular. Until their destruction by fire in 83 B.C., the *sibylline* books were often consulted by the Romans.

similitude N. similarity; using comparisons such as similes, etc. Although the critics deplored his use of mixed metaphors, he continued to write in *similitudes*.

TEST—WORD LIST 38—*Synonyms and Antonyms*

Each of the following questions consists of a word printed in italics, followed by five words or phrases numbered 1 to 5. Choose the numbered word or phrase which is most nearly the same as or the opposite of the word in italics and write the number of your choice on the answer paper.

741. *resilient*   1 pungent 2 foolish 3 worthy 4 insolent 5 unyielding

742. *serried*   1 worried 2 embittered 3 in close order 4 fallen 5 infantile

743. *provincial*   1 wealthy 2 crass 3 literary 4 aural 5 sophisticated

744. *pundit*   1 authority 2 humorist 3 undergraduate 4 thief 5 illiterate

745. *rustic*   1 peasant 2 recruit 3 tyrant 4 mercenary 5 civilian

746. *similitude*   1 gratitude 2 magnitude 3 likeness 4 aptitude 5 kindness

747. *queasy*   1 toxic 2 easily upset 3 chronic 4 choleric 5 false

748. *sanctimonious*   1 hypothetical 2 paltry 3 mercenary 4 pious 5 grateful

749. *recherché*   1 learned 2 tiresome 3 usual 4 studied 5 outrageous

750. *senescence*   1 youth 2 romance 3 doldrums 4 quintessence 5 friendship

751. *propinquity*   1 remoteness 2 uniqueness 3 health 4 virtue 5 simplicity

752. *reprove*   1 prevail 2 commend 3 ascertain 4 prove false 5 scarify

753. *seraph*   1 messenger 2 harbinger 3 demon 4 official 5 potentate

754. *psychotic*   1 dangerous 2 clairvoyant 3 criminal 4 soulful 5 suffering from mental disorder

755. *putative*   1 colonial 2 quarrelsome 3 undisputed

ā—ale; ă—add; ä—arm; à—ask, ē—eve; ĕ—end; ê—err, her; ə—allow; even; ī—ice; ĭ—ill; ō—old; ŏ—odd; ô—orb; ōō—food; ŏŏ—foot, put; ou—out; th—thin; ū—use; ŭ—up; zh—pleasure

4 powerful 5 unremarkable
756. *recusant* 1 nonconformer 2 deliberator 3 abstainer
    4 qualifier 5 patient
757. *screed* 1 belief 2 scolding 3 text 4 falsehood 5 pennant
758. *reactionary* 1 conservative retrograde 3 dramatist
    4 militant 5 chemical

759. *sartorial* 1 pertaining to clothes
    2 pertaining to the dance 3 tonsorial 4 hirsute
    5 masterful
760. *reprobate* 1 interior 2 retrial 3 acquisition
    4 qualification 5 profligate

WORD LIST 39   simpering - tergiversation

simpering ADJ. smirking. I can overlook his *simpering* manner, but I cannot ignore his stupidity.

sirocco N. warm, sultry wind blown from Africa to southern Europe. We can understand the popularity of the siesta in southern Spain; when the *sirocco* blows, the afternoon heat is unbearable.

skeptic N. doubter; person who suspends judgment until he has examined the evidence supporting a point of view. In this matter, I am a *skeptic;* I want proof.

slander N. defamation; utterance of false and malicious statements. Unless you can prove your allegations, your remarks constitute *slander.* also V.

slattern N. untidy or slovenly person. If you persist in wearing such sloppy clothes, people will call you a *slattern.*

sleight (*slīt*) N. dexterity. The magician amazed the audience with his *sleight* of hand.

slither V. slip or slide. During the recent ice storm, many people *slithered* down this hill as they walked to the station.

sluice N. artificial channel for directing or controlling the flow of water. This *sluice* gate is opened only in times of drought to provide water for irrigation.

smattering N. slight knowledge. I don't know whether it is better to be ignorant of a subject or to have a mere *smattering* of information about it.

sobriquet (*sō-brĭ-kā´*) N. nickname. Despite all his protests, his classmates continued to call him by that unflattering *sobriquet.*

solace N. comfort in trouble. I hope you will find *solace* in the thought that all of us share your loss.

somatic ADJ. pertaining to the body; physical. Why do you ignore the spiritual aspects and emphasize only the corporeal and the *somatic?*

sophist N. teacher of philosophy; quibbler; employer of fallacious reasoning. You are using all the devices of a *sophist* in trying to prove your case; your argument is specious.

sophistication N. artificiality; unnaturalness; act of employing sophistry in reasoning. *Sophistication* is an acquired characteristic, found more frequently among city dwellers than among residents of rural areas.

sophomoric ADJ. immature; shallow. Your *sophomoric* remarks indicate that you have not given much thought to the problem.

soporific N. sleep producer. I do not need a *soporific* when I listen to one of his speeches. also ADJ.

spate N. sudden flood. I am worried about the possibility of a *spate* if the rains do not diminish soon.

spatula N. broad-bladed instrument used for spreading or mixing. The manufacturers of this frying pan recommend the use of a rubber *spatula* to avoid scratching the specially treated surface.

spectrum N. colored band produced when beam of light passes through a prism. The visible portion of the *spectrum* includes red at one end and violet at the other.

spoliation N. pillaging; depredation. We regard this unwarranted attack on a neutral nation as an act of *spoliation* and we demand that it cease at once and that proper restitution be made.

spoonerism N. accidental transposition of sounds in successive words. When the radio announcer introduced the President as Hoobert Herver, he was guilty of a *spoonerism.*

spume N. froth; foam. The *spume* at the base of the waterfall extended for a quarter of a mile downriver.

staccato ADJ. played in an abrupt manner; marked by abrupt sharp sound. His *staccato* speech reminded one of the sound of a machine gun.

stalemate N. deadlock. Negotiations between the union and the employers have reached a *stalemate;* neither side is willing to budge from previously stated positions.

stalwart ADJ. strong, brawny; steadfast. His consistent support of the party has proved that he is a *stalwart* and loyal member. also N.

statutory ADJ. created by statute or legislative action. This is a *statutory* crime.

stereotyped ADJ. fixed and unvarying representation. My chief objection to the book is that the characters are *stereotyped.*

stertorous ADJ. having a snoring sound. He could not sleep because of the *stertorous* breathing of his roommates.

stigma N. token of disgrace; brand. I do not attach any *stigma* to the fact that you were accused of this crime; the fact that you were acquitted clears you completely.

stilted ADJ. bombastic; inflated. His *stilted* rhetoric did not impress the college audience; they were immune to bombastic utterances.

stratum (*strāt´-*) N. layer of earth's surface; layer of society. Unless we alleviate conditions in the lowest *stratum* of our society, we may expect grumbling and revolt.

stultify V. cause to appear foolish or inconsistent. By changing your opinion at this time, you will *stultify* yourself.

suave ADJ. smooth; bland. He is the kind of individual who is more easily impressed by a *suave* approach than by threats or bluster.

subjective ADJ. occurring or taking place within the subject; unreal. Your analysis is highly *subjective;* you have permitted your emotions and your opinions to color your thinking.

subliminal ADJ. below the threshold. We may not be aware of the *subliminal* influences which affect our thinking.

subsidy N. direct financial aid by government, etc. Without this *subsidy,* American ship operators would not be able to compete in world markets.

substantive ADJ. essential; pertaining to the substance. Although the delegates were aware of the importance of the problem, they could not agree on the *substantive* issues.

sudorific ADJ. pertaining to perspiration. Manufacturers of deodorants have made the public conscious of the need to avoid offending people with *sudorific* odors.

sumptuary ADJ. limiting or regulating expenditures. While no *sumptuary* law has been enacted, the public will never tolerate the expenditure of so large a sum.

superimpose V. place over something else. Your attempt to *superimpose* another agency in this field will merely increase the bureaucratic nature of our government.

supernal ADJ. heavenly; celestial. His tale of *supernal* beings was skeptically received.

supernumerary N. person or thing in excess of what is necessary; extra. His first appearance on the stage was as a *supernumerary* in a Shakespearean tragedy.

supple ADJ. flexible; pliant. The angler found a *supple* limb and used it as a fishing rod.

suppurate V. create pus. The surgeon refused to lance the abscess until it *suppurated.*

suture N. stitches sewn to hold the cut edges of a wound or incision; material used in sewing. We will remove the *sutures* as soon as the wound heals. also V.

syllogism N. logical formula utilizing a major premise, a minor premise and a conclusion. There must be a fallacy in this *syllogism;* I cannot accept the conclusion.

symmetry N. arrangement of parts so that balance is obtained; congruity. The addition of a second tower will give this edifice the *symmetry* which it now lacks.

talon N. claw of bird. The falconer wore a leather gauntlet to avoid being clawed by the hawk's *talons.*

tantamount ADJ. equal. Your ignoring their pathetic condition is *tantamount* to murder.

tarantula N. venomous spider. We need an antitoxin to counteract the bite of the *tarantula.*

tarn N. small mountain lake. This mountainous area is famous for its picturesque *tarns* and larger lakes.

tatterdemalion N. ragged fellow. Do you expect an army of *tatterdemalions* and beggars to put up a real fight?

taut ADJ. tight; ready. The captain maintained that he ran a *taut* ship.

tautology N. unnecessary repetition; pleonasm. "Joyful happiness" is an illustration of *tautology.*

teleology N. belief that a final purpose or design exists for the presence of individual beings or of the universe itself. The questions propounded by *teleology* have long been debated in religious and scientific circles.

temerarious ADJ. rash. Mountain climbing at this time of year is *temerarious* and foolhardy.

tenacity N. firmness; persistency; adhesiveness. It is extremely difficult to overcome the *tenacity* of a habit such as smoking.

tendentious ADJ. having an aim; designed to further a cause. The editorials in this periodical are *tendentious* rather than truth-seeking.

tenebrous (*tĕn´-*) ADJ. dark; gloomy. We were frightened as we entered the *tenebrous* passageways of the cave.

tergiversation (*-jĭv-ər-sā´-*) N. evasion; fickleness. I cannot understand your *tergiversation;* I was certain that you were devoted to our cause.

TEST—WORD LIST 39—*Synonyms and Antonyms*

Each of the questions below consists of a word printed in italics, followed by five words or phrases numbered 1 to 5. Choose the numbered word or phrase which is most nearly the same as or the opposite of the word in italics and write the number of your choice on the answer paper.

761. *tautology* 1 memory 2 repetition 3 tension 4 simile 5 lack of logic

762. *stilted* 1 candid 2 pompous 3 modish 4 acute 5 inarticulate

763. *tendentious* 1 biased 2 likely 3 absurd 4 festive 5 literary

764. *staccato* 1 musical 2 long 3 legato 4 sneezing 5 pounded

765. *stereotyped* 1 original 2 antique 3 modeled 4 repetitious 5 continued

766. *sophomoric* 1 unprecedented 2 mature 3 insipid 4 intellectual 5 illusionary

767. *supernumerary* 1 star 2 extra 3 associate 4 astronomer 5 inferiority

768. *somatic* 1 mental 2 menial 3 soporific 4 loyal 5 frantic

769. *suture* 1 stitch 2 reflection 3 knitting 4 tailor 5 past

770. *sobriquet* 1 ingenue 2 livelihood 3 bar 4 epitaph 5 nickname

771. *tantamount* 1 level 2 equivalent 3 cinematic 4 inadequate 5 professional

772. *tergiversation* 1 loyalty 2 conversation 3 altercation 4 swollen state 5 acquiescence

773. *soporific* 1 dining 2 caustic 3 memorial 4 awakening 5 springing

774. *subliminal* 1 radiant 2 unknown 3 obvious 4 domestic 5 horizontal

775. *simpering* 1 smirking 2 wincing 3 crying 4 quoting verbatim 5 extemporizing

776. *tatterdemalion* 1 confetti 2 crudity 3 stubborn individual 4 ragged fellow 5 artist

777. *spoliation* 1 exhumation 2 humidity 3 pillaging 4 exhortation 5 immunity

778. *temerarious* 1 contagious 2 plucky 3 prudent 4 discreet 5 lucky

779. *tenacity* 1 splendor 2 perseverance 3 tendency 4 ingratitude 5 decimation

780. *stertorous* 1 typical 2 working 3 northern 4 labored 5 lyrical

WORD LIST 40 **termagant - yokel**

termagant N. shrew; scolding, brawling woman. *The Taming of the Shrew* is one of many stories of the methods used in changing a *termagant* into a demure lady.

terminology N. terms used in a science or art. The special *terminology* developed by some authorities in the field has

done more to confuse the layman than to enlighten him.

terrapin N. American marsh tortoise. The flesh of the diamondback *terrapin* is considered by many epicures to be a delicacy.

tessellated ADJ. inlaid; mosaic. I recall seeing a table with a *tesselated* top of bits of stone and glass in a very interesting pattern.

testator N. maker of a will. The attorney called in his secretary and his partner to witness the signature of the *testator*.

thaumaturgist (*thô´-*) N. miracle worker; magician. I would have to be a *thaumaturgist* and not a mere doctor to find a remedy for this disease.

theosophy N. wisdom in divine things. *Theosophy* seeks to embrace the essential truth in all religions.

thyme N. aromatic plant used for seasoning. The addition of a little *thyme* will enhance the flavor of the clam chowder.

timbre N. quality of a musical tone produced by a musical instrument. We identify the instrument producing a musical sound by its *timbre*.

timorous ADJ. fearful; demonstrating fear. His *timorous* manner betrayed the fear he felt at the moment.

titillate V. tickle. I am here not to *titillate* my audience but to enlighten it.

tocsin N. alarm bell. Awakened by the sound of the *tocsin*, we rushed to our positions to await the attack.

tonsure N. shaving of the head, especially by person entering religious orders. His *tonsure*, even more than his monastic garb, indicated that he was a member of the religious order.

tortilla (*tôr-tē´-yə*) N. flat cake made of cornmeal, etc. As we traveled through Mexico, we became more and more accustomed to the use of *tortillas* instead of bread.

touchstone N. stone used to test the fineness of gold alloys; criterion. What *touchstone* can be used to measure the character of a person?

trajectory N. path taken by a projectile. The police tried to locate the spot from which the assassin had fired the fatal shot by tracing the *trajectory* of the bullet.

traumatic ADJ. pertaining to an injury caused by violence. In his nightmares, he kept on recalling the *traumatic* experience of being wounded in battle.

treacle N. syrup obtained in refining sugar. *Treacle* is more highly refined than molasses.

trencherman N. good eater. He is not finicky about his food; he is a *trencherman*.

triolet N. eight-line stanza with rhyme scheme *a b aaa b a b*. The *triolet* is a difficult verse pattern because it utilizes only two rhymes in its eight lines.

troglodyte N. cave dweller. We know that the first men in this area were *troglodytes* by the artifacts we have discovered in the caves.

trope (*trōp*) N. figure of speech. The poem abounds in *tropes* and alliterative expressions.

truckle V. curry favor; act in an obsequious way. If you *truckle* to the lord, you will be regarded as a sycophant; if you do not, you will be considered arrogant.

truncate V. cut the top off. The top of a cone which has been *truncated* in a plane parallel to its base is a circle.

tundra N. rolling, treeless plain in Siberia and arctic North America. Despite the cold, many geologists are trying to discover valuable mineral deposits in the *tundra*.

tureen N. deep table dish for holding soup. The waiters brought the soup to the tables in silver *tureens*.

tutelary ADJ. protective; pertaining to a guardianship. I am acting in my *tutelary* capacity when I refuse to grant you permission to leave the campus.

ukase (*ū-kās´*) N. official decree, usually Russian. It was easy to flaunt the *ukases* issued from St. Petersburg; there was no one to enforce them.

unilateral ADJ. one-sided. This legislation is *unilateral* since it binds only one party in the controversy.

untoward ADJ. unfortunate; annoying. *Untoward* circumstances prevent me from being with you on this festive occasion.

ursine (*êr´-sīn*) ADJ. bearlike; pertaining to a bear. Because of its *ursine* appearance, the great panda has been identified with the bears; actually, it is closely related to the raccoon.

usufruct N. right of enjoying things belonging to another. By contract, the tenant has the *usufruct* of all the livestock and machinery on the farm.

usurpation N. act of seizing power and rank of another. The revolution ended with the *usurpation* of the throne by the victorious rebel leader.

utopia N. imaginary land with perfect social and political system. Shangri-la was the name of James Hilton's Tibetan *utopia*.

valance N. short drapery hanging above window frame. The windows were curtainless; only the tops were covered with *valances*.

valedictory ADJ. pertaining to farewell. I found the *valedictory* address too long; leave-taking should be brief.

valetudinarian N. invalid. He enjoyed the attentions showered upon him while he was a *valetudinarian* and insisted that they be continued long after his recovery from his illness. also ADJ.

vampire N. ghostly being that sucks the blood of the living. Children were afraid to go to sleep at night because of the many legends of *vampires*.

vassal N. in feudalism, one who held land of a superior lord. The lord demanded that his *vassals* contribute more to his military campaign.

vendetta N. feud; private warfare. The *vendetta* continued for several generations despite all attempts by authorities to end the killings.

verbatim ADV. word for word. He repeated the message *verbatim*. also ADJ.

vermicular ADJ. pertaining to a worm. The *vermicular* burrowing in the soil helps to aerate it.

vertiginous (*-tĭj´-*) ADJ. giddy; causing dizziness. I do not like the rides in the amusement park because they have a *vertiginous* effect on me.

viable ADJ. capable of maintaining life. The infant, though prematurely born, is *viable* and has a good chance to survive.

vitreous ADJ. pertaining to or resembling glass. Although this plastic has many *vitreous* qualities such as transparency, it is unbreakable.

vivisection N. act of dissecting living animals. The Society for the Prevention of Cruelty to Animals opposed *vivisection* and deplored the practice of using animals in scientific experiments.

warranty N. guarantee; assurance by seller. The purchaser of this automobile is protected by the manufacturer's *warranty* that he will replace any defective part for five years or 50,000 miles.

wastrel N. profligate. He was denounced as a *wastrel* who had dissipated his inheritance.

welkin N. sky. They made the *welkin* ring with their shouts.

welter V. wallow. At the height of the battle, the casualties were so numerous that the victims *weltered* in their blood while waiting for medical attention.

whorl N. ring of leaves around stem; ring. Identification by fingerprints is based on the difference in shape and number of the *whorls* on the fingers.

yeoman (*yō´-*) N. man owning small estate; middle-class farmer. It was not the aristocrat but the *yeoman* who determined the nation's policies.

yokel N. country bumpkin. At school, his classmates regarded him as a *yokel* and laughed at his rustic mannerisms.

TEST—WORD LIST 40—*Synonyms and Antonyms*

Each of the questions below consists of a word printed in italics, followed by five words or phrases numbered 1 to 5. Choose the numbered word or phrase which is most nearly the same as or the opposite of the word in italics and write the number of your choice on the answer paper.

781. *warranty* 1 threat 2 guarantee 3 order for arrest 4 issue 5 fund
782. *thaumaturgist* 1 producer 2 dreamer 3 philosopher 4 thief 5 miracle worker
783. *tureen* 1 young lady 2 Irish stew 3 soup dish 4 bend 5 collision
784. *valetudinarian* 1 senile person 2 farewell speaker 3 healthy person 4 servant 5 agent
785. *utopia* 1 hades 2 sky 3 political paradise 4 subsidiary 5 cornucopia
786. *viable* 1 moribund 2 salable 3 useful 4 foolish 5 inadequate
787. *titillate* 1 hasten 2 fasten 3 stimulate 4 incorporate 5 enlarge
788. *wastrel* 1 trash 2 paragon 3 mortal 4 tolerance 5 song
789. *welkin* 1 bell 2 greeting 3 cloudy 4 pressure 5 sky
790. *tesselated* 1 striped 2 made of mosaics 3 piebald 4 uniform 5 trimmed
791. *yokel* 1 singer 2 humorist 3 urbane individual 4 farmer 5 young man
792. *tonsure* 1 shaved head 2 weight 3 impiety 4 hoarseness 5 mask
793. *yeoman* 1 masses 2 middle-class farmer 3 proletarian 4 indigent person 5 man of rank
794. *valedictory* 1 sad 2 collegiate 3 derivative 4 salutatory 5 promising
795. *truncate* 1 carry in valise 2 cut off top 3 ship 4 lighten 5 extirpolate
796. *tutelary* 1 sincere 2 protecting 3 early 4 timid 5 beneath
797. *triolet* 1 8-line poem 2 *3*-line poem 3 flower 4 stool 5 sermon
798. *vertiginous* 1 high 2 green 3 fascinating 4 nervous 5 causing dizziness
799. *ukase* 1 request 2 languor 3 police 4 edict 5 action
800. *trencherman* 1 finicky eater 2 infantryman 3 soldier 4 imbiber 5 epicure

---

ā—ale; ă—add; ä—arm; à—ask, ē—eve; ĕ—end; ê—err, her; ə—allow; even; ī—ice; ĭ—ill; ō—oll; ŏ—odd; ô—orb; ōō—food; ŏŏ—foot, put; ou—out; th—thin; ū—use; ŭ—up; zh—pleasure

Cumulative Etymology List

AB, ABS (from, away from) prefix
abduct   lead away, kidnap
abjure   renounce (swear away from)
abject   degraded (thrown away from)

ABLE, IBLE (capable of) adjective suffix
portable   able to be carried
legible   able to be read
interminable   unable to be ended

AC, IC (like, pertaining to) adjective suffix
cardiac   pertaining to heart
aquatic   pertaining to water
dramatic   pertaining to drama

ACR (sharp)
acrimonious   bitter
acerbity   bitterness of temper
acidulate   to make somewhat acidy or sour

AD (to, forward) prefix
adit   entrance
adjure   request earnestly
admit   allow entrance
  Note: by assimilation, the AD prefix is changed to
AC in accord
AF in affliction
AG in aggregation
AN in annexation
AP in apparition
AR in arraignment
AS in assumption
AT in attendance

AEV (age, era)
primeval   of the first age
coeval   of the same age or era
medieval   of the middle ages

AG, ACT (to do)
act   deed
agent   doer
retroactive   having a backward or reversed action

AGOG (leader)
demagogue   false leader of people
pedagogue   teacher (leader of children)
synagogue   house of worship (leading together of people)

AGRI, AGRARI (field)
agrarian   one who works in the fields; farmer
agriculture   cultivation of fields
peregrination   wandering; going through fields

ALI (another)
alias   assumed (another) name
alienate   estrange (divert from another)
inalienable   unable to be diverted from another

AMBI (both) prefix
ambidextrous   skilled with both hands (both right hands)
ambiguous   of double meaning
ambivalent   possessing conflicting (both) emotions

AN (without) prefix
anarchy   lack of government
anemia   lack of blood
anesthesia   without feeling

ANTE (before) prefix
antecedent   preceding event or word
antediluvian   ancient (before the flood)
ante-nuptial   before the wedding

ANIM (mind, soul)
animadvert   cast criticism upon (turn one's mind)
unanimous   of one mind
magnanimity   greatness of mind or spirit

ANN (year)
annuity   yearly remittance
biennial   every two years
perennial   flowering yearly; a yearly flowering plant

ANTHROP (man)
anthropology   study of man
misanthrope   recluse (hater of mankind)
philanthropy   love of mankind; charity

ARCH (chief, first) prefix
archetype   original model
archbishop   chief bishop
archeology   study of antiquities (study of first things)

ARCH (government, ruler, first)
monarch   sole ruler
anarchy   lack of government
archeology   study of first or ancient times

AQUA (water)
aqueduct   a passageway for conducting water; a conduit
aquatic   living in water
aqua fortis   nitric acid (strong water)

Cumulative Etymology List

AB, ABS (from, away from) prefix

abduct   lead away, kidnap
abjure   renounce (swear away from)
abject   degraded (thrown away from)

ABLE, IBLE (capable of) adjective suffix

portable   able to be carried
legible   able to be read
interminable   unable to be ended

AC, IC (like, pertaining to) adjective suffix

cardiac   pertaining to heart
aquatic   pertaining to water
dramatic   pertaining to drama

ACR (sharp)

acrimonious   bitter
acerbity   bitterness of temper
acidulate   to make somewhat acidy or sour

AD (to, forward) prefix

adit   entrance
adjure   request earnestly
admit   allow entrance
   Note: by assimilation, the AD prefix is changed to

AC in accord
AF in affliction
AG in aggregation
AN in annexation
AP in apparition
AR in arraignment
AS in assumption
AT in attendance

AEV (age, era)

primeval   of the first age
coeval   of the same age or era
medieval   of the middle ages

AG, ACT (to do)

act   deed
agent   doer
retroactive   having a backward or reversed action

AGOG (leader)

demagogue   false leader of people
pedagogue   teacher (leader of children)
synagogue   house of worship (leading together of people)

AGRI, AGRARI (field)

agrarian   one who works in the fields; farmer
agriculture   cultivation of fields
peregrination   wandering; going through fields

ALI (another)

alias   assumed (another) name
alienate   estrange (divert from another)
inalienable   unable to be diverted from another

AMBI (both) prefix

ambidextrous   skilled with both hands (both right hands)
ambiguous   of double meaning
ambivalent   possessing conflicting (both) emotions

AN (without) prefix

anarchy   lack of government
anemia   lack of blood
anesthesia   without feeling

ANTE (before) prefix

antecedent   preceding event or word
antediluvian   ancient (before the flood)
ante-nuptial   before the wedding

ANIM (mind, soul)

animadvert   cast criticism upon (turn one's mind)
unanimous   of one mind
magnanimity   greatness of mind or spirit

ANN (year)

annuity   yearly remittance
biennial   every two years
perennial   flowering yearly; a yearly flowering plant

ANTHROP (man)

anthropology   study of man
misanthrope   recluse (hater of mankind)
philanthropy   love of mankind; charity

ARCH (chief, first) prefix

archetype   original model
archbishop   chief bishop
archeology   study of antiquities (study of first things)

ARCH (government, ruler, first)

monarch   sole ruler
anarchy   lack of government
archeology   study of first or ancient times

AQUA (water)

aqueduct   a passageway for conducting water; a conduit
aquatic   living in water
aqua fortis   nitric acid (strong water)

ASTER (star)

astronomy   study of the stars
asterisk   star-like type character (*)
disaster   catastrophe (contrary star)

AUD, AUDIT (hear)

audible   able to be heard
auditorium   place where people may be heard
audience   hearers

AUTO (self)

autocracy   rule by self (one person)
automobile   vehicle that moves by itself
autobiography   story of a person's life written by himself

BELLI (war)

bellicose   inclined to fighting
belligerent   engaged in war
rebellious   warring against authority

BEN, BON (well, good)

benefactor   one who does good
benevolence   charity (wishing good)
bonus   something extra above regular pay

BI (two) prefix

bicameral   legislature consisting of two houses
biennial   every two years
bicycle   two-wheeled vehicle

BIBLIO (book)

bibliography   list of books
bibliophile   lover of books
Bible   The Book

BIO (life)

biology   study of living things
biography   writing about a person's life
biochemist   a student of the chemistry of living things

BREVE (short)

brevity   briefness
abbreviate   shorten
breve   mark placed over vowel to indicate that it is short
   (ă as in hăt)

CAD, CAS (to fall)

decadent   deteriorating
cadence   intonation, musical movement
accident   unexpected, chance event

CAP, CAPT, CEP (to take)

participate   to take part
precept   a wise saying (originally, a command)
capture   sieze

CAP, CIP (head)

decapitate   remove head
captain   chief
capital   major

CATA (down) prefix

catastrophe   disaster (turning down)
cataract   waterfall
catapult   hurl (throw down)

CED, CESS (to yield, to go)

recede   go back, withdraw
antecedent   that which goes before
concede   to yield, to agree with

CENT (one hundred)

century   one hundred years
centennial   hundredth anniversary
Centigrade   system of measuring by hundreds

CHRONOS (time)

chronology   time table of events
anachronism   a thing out of time sequence as Shakespeare's reference to clocks in *Julius Caesar*
chronicle   to register events in order

CID, CIS (to cut, to kill)

incision   a cut (surgical)
homicide   killing of a man
fratricide   killing of a brother

CIRCUM (around) prefix

circumnavigate   sail around world
circumspect   cautious (looking around)
circumscribe   place a circle around

CIT, CITAT (to call, to start)

incite   to stir up, to start up
excite   to stir up
recitation   a calling-back again

CIVI (citizen)

civilization   society of citizens, culture
civilian   a member of community
civil   courteous

CLAM, CLAMAT (to cry out)

clamorous   loud
declamation   a speech
acclamation   shouted approval

CLAUD, CLAUS (to close)

claustrophobia   fear of close places
enclose   to close in
conclude   to finish

CLE, CULE (small) noun suffix

molecule   small mass
corpuscle   blood cell
follicle   small sac

COGNOSC, COGNIT (to learn)

agnostic   lacking knowledge, skeptical
incognito   traveling under assumed name (without knowledge)
cognition   knowledge

COM (with, together) prefix

combine   merge with
commerce   trade with
communicate   correspond with
By assimilation
coeditor   associate editor
collateral   connected
conference   meeting
corroborate   confirm

COMP, COMPLETE (to fill)

complete   filled out
complement   that which completes something
comply   to fulfil

CONTRA (against)

contradict disagree
controversy dispute (turning against)
contrary opposed

CORD (heart)

accord agreement (from the heart)
cordial friendly
discord lack of harmony

CORPOR (body)

incorporate to organize into a body
corporeal pertaining to the body, fleshly
corpse a dead body

CRED, CREDIT (to believe)

incredulous not believing, skeptical
credulity gullibility
credence belief

CUR (to care)

curator person in charge
sinecure position without responsibility
secure safe

CURR, CURS (to run)

excursion journey
cursory brief
precursor forerunner

CY (state of being) noun suffix

democracy a democratic state
obstinacy state of being stubborn
accuracy state of being precise

DA, DAT (to give)

data facts, statistics
mandate command
date given time

DE (down, away) prefix

debase lower in value
decadence deterioration
decant pour off

DEB, DEBIT (to owe)

debt something owed
indebtedness debt
debenture bond

DEMOS (people)

democracy rule of the people
demagogue (false) leader of the people
epidemic wide spread disease (among the people)

DERM (skin)

epidermis skin
pachyderm thick skinned quadruped
dermatology study of skin and its disorders

DI, DIURN (day)

diary day book
diurnal pertaining to day time
journey day's travel

DIA (across) prefix

diagonal across a figure
diameter across a circle
diagram (writing across) outline drawing

DIC, DICT (to say)

abdicate renounce
diction speech
verdict statement of jury

DIS, DIF (not) prefix

discord lack of harmony
differ disagree (carry apart)
distrust lack of trust

DOC, DOCT (to teach)

docile meek (teachable)
document something that provides evidence
doctor learned man (originally, teacher)

DOMIN (to rule)

dominate having power over
domain land under rule
dominant prevailing

DUC, DUCT (to lead)

viaduct arched roadway
aqueduct artificial waterway
education training (leading out)

DYNAM (power, strength)

dynamic powerful
dynamite powerful explosive
dynamo engine to make electrical power

EGO (I)

egoist person who is self-interested
egotist selfish person
egocentric revolving about self

ERG (work)

energy power
ergatocracy rule of the workers
metallurgy art of working in metal

ERR (to wander)

error mistake
erratic not reliable, wandering
knight-errant wandering knight

EU (good, well, beautiful)

eulogize to praise
euphemism substitution of pleasant way of saying something blunt or unpleasant
eupeptic having good digestion

EX (out) prefix

expel drive out
exit way out
extirpate root out

EXTRA (beyond, outside) prefix

extraordinary exceptional
extracurricular beyond the items in the curriculum
extraterritorial beyond the territory of a nation

FAC, FIC, FEC, FECT (to make, to do)

factory place where things are made
fiction manufactured story
affect to cause to change

FALL, FALS (to deceive)

fallacious faulty
infallible not prone to error, perfect
falsify to lie

FER, LAT (to bring, to bear)

transfer to bring from one place to another
translate to bring from one language to another
coniferous bearing cones, as pine trees

FIC (making, doing) adjective suffix

terrific making terrible
soporific making sleepy
frantic made excited by pain, grief, etc.

FY (to make) verb suffix

magnify to make greater
petrify to make into stone
beautify to make beautiful

GAM (marriage)

monogamy marriage to one person
bigamy marriage to two people at same time
polygamy having many wives or husbands at same time

GEN, GENER (class, race)

genus group of animals with similar characteristics
generic characteristic of a class
gender class organized into sex

GRAPH, GRAM (writing)

epigram a pithy statement
telegram an instantaneous message over great distances (tele - far)
stenography shorthand (writing narrowly)

GREG (flock, herd)

gregarious tending to group together as in a herd
aggregate group, total
egregious out of the group; now used in a bad sense as wicked

HELIO (sun)

heliotrope flower that faces the sun
heliograph instrument that uses sun's rays to send signals
helium element abundant in sun's atmosphere

IL, ILE (pertaining to, capable of) adjective suffix

puerile pertaining to a child
ductile capable of being led; metal capable of being drawn into wire
civil pertaining to a citizen

INTER (between, among) prefix

intervene come between
international between nations
interjection a statement thrown in

IST (one who practices) noun suffix

humorist one who provides humor
specialist one who engages in a specialty
optimist one who is hopeful

IT, ITINER (journey, road)

exit way out
itinerary plan of journey
iterate repeat

ITY (state of being) noun suffix

annuity state of being yearly
credulity state of being gullible
sagacity wisdom

IZE, ISE (to make) verb suffix

victimize to make a victim
rationalize to reason
harmonize to make peaceful

JAC, JACT, JEC (to throw)

projectile missile; something thrown forward
trajectory path taken by thrown object
reject throw back

JUR, JURAT (to swear)

abjure renounce
perjure to testify falsely
jury group of men sworn to seek the truth

LABOR, LABORAT (to work)

laboratory place where work is done
collaborate work together with others
laborious difficult

LEG, LECT (to choose, to read)

election choice
legible able to be read
eligible able to be selected

LEG (law)

legislature law-making body
legitimate lawful
legal lawful

LIBER (book)

library collection of books
libretto the "book" of a musical play
libel slander (originally found in a little book)

LOQU, LOCUT (to talk)

soliloquy speech by one individual
loquacious talkative
elocution speech

LUC (light)

elucidate enlighten
lucid clear
translucent allowing some light to pass through

MAL (bad)

malevolent evil (wishing bad)
malediction curse (state of saying evil)
malefactor evil-doer

MAN (hand)

manufacture create (make by hand)
manuscript writing by hand
emancipate free (to let go from the hand)

MAR (sea)

maritime connected with seafaring
submarine undersea craft
mariner seaman

MITT, MISS (to send)

missile projectile
admit allow in
dismiss send away
transmit send across

MON, MONIT (to warn)

admonish warn
premonition foreboding
monitor watcher (warner)

MORI, MORT (to die)

mortuary funeral parlor
moribund dying
immortal not dying

NAV (ship)

navigate to sail a ship
circumnavigate sail around the world
naval pertaining to ships

OMNI (all)

omniscient all knowing
omnipotent all powerful
omniverous eating everything

OPER (to work)

operate to work
cooperation working together
opera Musical drama (specialized kind of work)

PAC (peace)

pacify to make peaceful
pacific peaceful
pacifist person opposed to war

PELL, PULS (to drive)

compulsion a forcing to do
repel drive back
expel drive out, banish

PET, PETIT (to seek)

petition request
appetite craving, desire
compete vie with others

PON, POSIT (to place)

postpone place after
preposition that which goes before
positive definite, unquestioned (definitely placed)

PORT, PORTAT (to carry)

portable able to be carried
transport carry across
export carry out (of country)

PUT, PUTAT (to trim, to calculate)

computation a reckoning
amputate cut off
putative supposed (calculated)

QUAER, QUAESIT (to ask)

inquiry investigation
inquisitive questioning
query question

RID, RIS (to laugh)

derision scorn
risibility inclination to laughter
ridiculous deserving to be laughed at

ROG, ROGAT (to ask)

interrogate to question
prerogative privilege
derogatory disparaging (asking a question to belittle)

RUMP, RUPT (to break)

interrupt to break into
bankrupt insolvent
rupture a break

SCRIB, SCRIPT (to write)

transcribe copy
script writing
circumscribe enclose, limit (write around)

SCI (to know)

science knowledge
omniscient knowing all
conscious aware

SED, SESS (to sit)

sedentary inactive (sitting)
session meeting
residence place where one dwells

SENT, SENS (to think, to feel)

resent show indignation
sensitive showing feeling
consent agree

SEQUI, SECUT (to follow)

consecutive following in order
sequence arrangement
sequel that which follows

SOLV, SOLUT (to loosen)

absolve free from blame
dissolute morally lax
absolute complete (not loosened)

SPEC, SPECT (to look at)

spectator observer
aspect appearance
circumspect cautious (looking around)

TANG, TACT (to touch)

tangent touching
contact touching with, meeting
contingent depending upon

TEMPOR (time)

contemporary at same time
extemporaneous impromptu
temporize to delay

TEN, TENT (to hold)

tenable able to be held.
tenacity retention
tenure holding of office

TERR (land)

terrestrial pertaining to earth
subterranean underground
Mediterranean Middle Land

URB (city)

urban pertaining to city
urbane polished, sophisticated (pertaining to city dweller)
suburban outside of city

VENI, VENT (to come)

intervene come between
prevent stop
convention meeting

VIA (way)

deviation departure from way
viaduct roadway (arched)
trivial trifling (small talk at crossroads)

VID, VIS (to see)

vision sight
evidence things seen
vista view

VINCT, VICT (to conquer)

invincible unconquerable
victory winning
vanquish to defeat

VOC, VOCAT (to call)

avocation calling, minor occupation
provocation calling or rousing the anger of
invocation calling in prayer

VOLV, VOLUT (to roll)

revolve roll around
evolve roll out, develop
convolution coiled state

TESTING YOUR KNOWLEDGE OF VOCABULARY

The synonym question and the antonym question
These tests are similar in nature to the questions which have appeared previously. Allow 15 minutes for each test.

Synonym Test A

Each of the questions below consists of a word printed in italics, followed by five words or phrases numbered 1 to 5. Choose the numbered word or phrase which is most nearly similar in meaning to the word in italics and write the number of your choice on your answer paper.

EXAMPLE

wily 1. willing 2. cunning 3. agile 4. sad 5. slow
Answer 2

1. *hirsute* 1. damp 2. bearded 3. humorous 4. formerly 5. sad
2. *panacea* 1. pancake 2. praise 3. inactivity 4. cure-all 5. talk
3. *celibate* 1. single 2. double 3. married 4. bald 5. hypocritical
4. *chasten* 1. discipline 2. pursue 3. sanctify 4. stop 5. start
5. *meretricious* 1. conspicuous 2. blonde 3. tawdry 4. angry 5. aping
6. *requiem* 1. recess 2. assignment 3. profanity 4. dirge 5. musing
7. *effigy* 1. proxy 2. profundity 3. boldness 4. exit 5. dummy
8. *blissful* 1. maudlin 2. dour 3. beatific 4. moot 5. modish
9. *homogeneous* 1. heterogeneous 2. motley 3. scrambled 4. different 5. similar
10. *wraith* 1. apparition 2. garland 3. Christmas decoration 4. anger 5. excitement
11. *disparity* 1. argumentation 2. difference 3. belittlement 4. harmony 5. discord
12. *variegate* 1. set type 2. multi-color 3. differ 4. reject 5. reply in kind

13. *filch* 1. pretend 2. dirty 3. embarrass 4. steal 5. honor
14. *infinite* 1. verbal 2. indefinite 3. endless 4. strange 5. vague
15. *demise* 1. residence 2. dismissal 3. accident 4. act 5. death
16. *frugality* 1. extravagance 2. ripening 3. thrift 4. resentment 5. miserliness
17. *unequaled* 1. outstanding 2. different 3. praised 4. unique 5. strange
18. *adversity* 1. opponent 2. hardship 3. opening 4. public announcement 5. agency
19. *fastidious* 1. speedy 2. precise 3. squeamish 4. hungry 5. slow
20. *disconcert* 1. sing in harmony 2. pretend 3. cancel program 4. confuse 5. interrupt
21. *garrulous* 1. laconic 2. strangling 3. ecstatic 4. frozen 5. wordy
22. *mores* 1. morals 2. customs 3. taxes 4. fiscal year 5. swamp
23. *vestige* 1. clothing 2. trace 3. undergarment 4. hallway 5. hope
24. *perfunctory* 1. thorough 2. impossible 3. lively 4. listless 5. sly
25. *indigence* 1. nativity 2. tolerance 3. gossiping 4. poverty 5. eating
26. *virago* 1. bacillus 2. chastity 3. shrew 4. wanton 5. tirade
27. *persiflage* 1. banter 2. oppression 3. sarcasm 4. bigotry 5. simile
28. *loquacious* 1. situated 2. gregarious 3. taciturn 4. antisocial 5. garrulous
29. *phlegmatic* 1. stolid 2. respiratory 3. animated 4. pneumatic 5. aroused
30. *saturnine* 1. planetary 2. gloomy 3. astronomic 4. hopeful 5. temperate
31. *misanthropy* 1. badinage 2. generosity 3. vivacity 4. miserliness 5. hatred
32. *chicanery* 1. foulness 2. aroma 3. chastity 4. trickery 5. poultry
33. *penury* 1. custom 2. poverty 3. numismatics 4. affluence 5. criminology
34. *expiated* 1. vapid 2. assumed 3. disinclined 4. atoned 5. eroded
35. *vindictive* 1. revengeful 2. triumphant 3. strategic 4. demonstrative 5. bigoted
36. *frustration* 1. satiety 2. facility 3. thwarting 4. nostalgia 5. lethargy
37. *punctilious* 1. scrupulous 2. varied 3. ready 4. prompt 5. vicarious
38. *haggard* 1. gaunt 2. irascible 3. wise 4. sluggish 5. witty

39. *staid*   1. weary   2. remaining   3. sedate
    4. afraid   5. unkempt
40. *pedagogue*   1. demagogue   2. peddler   3. bicyclist   4. teacher   5. pupil
41. *decorous*   1. adorned   2. ugly   3. insane
    4. proper   5. childish
42. *onerous*   1. possessive   2. proud   3. droll
    4. burdensome   5. sly
43. *expedient*   1. precise   2. expert   3. expendable
    4. advisable   5. erratic
44. *succulent*   1. asking help   2. wicked   3. anxious   4. concise   5. juicy
45. *nepotism*   1. favoritism   2. pool   3. philosophy   4. rule of a despot   5. hedonism
46. *propensity*   1. inclination   2. intelligence
    3. probity   4. dishonesty   5. act
47. *tawdry*   1. refined   2. yellow-orange   3. ancient
    4. forward   5. gaudy
48. *inculcate*   1. corroborate   2. lack   3. teach
    4. destroy   5. avenge
49. *tortuous*   1. winding   2. sadistic   3. cruel
    4. like a turtle   5. carefree
50. *mollify*   1. sweeten   2. appease   3. applaud
    4. worry   5. discourage

Synonym Test B

Each of the questions below consists of a word printed in italics, followed by five words or phrases numbered 1 to 5. Choose the numbered word or phrase which is most nearly similar in meaning to the word in italics and write the number of your choice on your answer paper.

51. *regime*   1. military group   2. summary   3. rule
    4. estimate   5. manor
52. *tenacity*   1. persistence   2. game played on grass   3. large town   4. indifference   5. ecstasy
53. *professedly*   1. meekly   2. cruelly   3. bravely
    4. pedantically   5. ostensibly
54. *retrospect*   1. special kind of telescope   2. microscope   3. prism   4. review of the past
    5. forecast of future events
55. *impeccable*   1. poverty-stricken   2. faultless
    3. dirty   4. criminal   5. impervious
56. *abettor*   1. gambler   2. slaughter-house   3. encourager   4. factor   5. author
57. *debilitate*   1. argue   2. engage   3. remove hair
    4. soothe   5. enfeeble
58. *junto*   1. junction   2. jungle   3. small boat
    4. secret faction   5. embrace
59. *harass*   1. annoy   2. harness   3. involve
    4. injure   5. consider

60. *erudite*   1. rough   2. unpolished   3. scholarly
    4. magnificent   5. ornate
61. *abrade*   1. rub off   2. bleed   3. embellish
    4. erase   5. poison
62. *inane*   1. lifeless   2. senseless   3. hopeless
    4. faithless   5. crazy
63. *culpable*   1. free   2. guilty   3. vindicable
    4. wholesome   5. vindictive
64. *ingenuous*   1. sophisticated   2. clever   3. cunning   4. naive   5. artificial
65. *fealty*   1. sense of touch   2. loyalty   3. anger
    4. anxiety   5. personality
66. *cogent*   1. geared   2. formidable   3. strong
    4. weak   5. convincing
67. *expunge*   1. rationalize   2. purge   3. exhale
    4. eradicate   5. assign
68. *indigenous*   1. wealthy   2. having stomach trouble   3. native   4. scholarly   5. bald
69. *condiment*   1. vegetable   2. salad   3. meat dish
    4. relish   5. sugar
70. *fortuitous*   1. lucky   2. accidental   3. rich
    4. prearranged   5. concerted
71. *adipose*   1. liquid   2. weighty   3. major
    4. sharp   5. fatty
72. *duplicity*   1. two-pronged spear   2. mimeograph   3. hypocrisy   4. candor   5. two-story apartment
73. *cryptic*   1. obscure   2. written   3. copied
    4. dead   5. puzzling
74. *homily*   1. cereal   2. household   3. suburb
    4. sermon   5. pension
75. *dormant*   1. animated   2. hibernating
    3. active   4. vigorous   5. birdlike
76. *asperity*   1. roughness   2. dream   3. ambition   4. smoothness   5. sarcastic remark
77. *altercation*   1. adjustment   2. repair   3. quarrel   4. split personality   5. echo
78. *captious*   1. prominent   2. carping   3. critical
    4. caustic   5. epigrammatic
79. *accolade*   1. balcony   2. outer garment   3. drink
    4. honor   5. fruit
80. *deprecate*   1. plead earnestly against   2. denounce   3. belittle   4. devaluate   5. dishonor
81. *bombastic*   1. inflated   2. explosive   3. retaliatory
    4. meek   5. enraged
82. *inter*   1. carry   2. hint   3. bury   4. interfere
    5. act as go-between
83. *acumen*   1. keenness   2. brilliance   3. swiftness   4. greediness   5. ferocity.
84. *inundate*   1. overwhelm   2. surrender   3. flood
    4. destroy   5. conquer
85. *cantata*   1. symphony   2. concerto   3. opera
    4. choral work   5. military march
86. *sumptuous*   1. swampy   2. irritable   3. meagre
    4. fancy   5. lavish

87. *tractable*   1. practicable   2. amenable   3. indisposed   4. critical   5. artistic

88. *querulous*   1. questioning   2. critical   3. complaining   4. curious   5. ambiguous

89. *morose*   1. calm   2. gloomy   3. misty   4. damp   5. diseased

90. *surmise*   1. dawn   2. plan   3. unexpected event   4. tragedy   5. guess

91. *ubiquitous*   1. affluent   2. resigning   3. omnipresent   4. omnipotent   5. omniscient

92. *attrition*   1. addition   2. regret   3. attitude   4. abrasion   5. concentration

93. *reticence*   1. reserve   2. retention   3. regret   4. brazenness   5. hostility

94. *chagrin*   1. chin   2. mortification   3. elation   4. intuition   5. chamber

95. *plaudit*   1. concentration   2. commendation   3. complaint   4. comparison   5. scholar

96. *viva voce*   1. lively   2. in writing   3. belligerently   4. thematically   5. orally

97. *malfeasance*   1. seasickness   2. criticism   3. cure   4. misconduct   5. poor performance

98. *hamlet*   1. actor   2. benefactor   3. small rodent   4. village   5. introvert

99. *pneumatic*   1. pertaining to air   2. automatic   3. sick   4. elastic   5. plotted

100. *tepid*   1. enraged   2. equatorial   3. transported   4. lukewarm   5. embarrassed

Antonym Test A

Each of the questions below consists of a word printed in italics, followed by five words or phrases numbered 1 to 5. Choose the numbered word or phrase which is most nearly opposite in meaning to the word in italics and write the number of your choice on your answer paper.

EXAMPLE

win   1. *conquer*   2. *lose*   3. *forfeit*   4. *surrender*
Answer 2

1. *abominate*   1. love   2. loathe   3. abhor   4. despise   5. attach

2. *ravenous*   1. famished   2. nibbling   3. sated   4. starving   5. unsatisfied

3. *pithy*   1. central   2. federal   3. homogeneous   4. tautological   5. gregarious

4. *adamant*   1. yielding   2. primitive   3. elementary   4. primeval   5. inflexible

5. *ephemeral*   1. evergreen   2. deciduous   3. biennial   4. everlasting   5. tactile

6. *synthetic*   1. cosmetic   2. artificial   3. plastic   4. viscous   5. natural

7. *vivacious*   1. animated   2. dramatic   3. versatile   4. phlegmatic   5. vigilant

8. *audacity*   1. quivering   2. cowardice   3. conciseness   4. patricide   5. bravado

9. *irascible*   1. pictorial   2. piscatorial   3. bellicose   4. cranky   5. good-natured

10. *bucolic*   1. citified   2. rustic   3. intoxicated   4. sick   5. healthy

11. *infinitesimal*   1. everlasting   2. colossal   3. picayune   4. microscopic   5. telescopic

12. *gelid*   1. lurid   2. torpid   3. torrid   4. piebald   5. vapid

13. *circuitous*   1. entertaining   2. direct   3. roundabout   4. labyrinthine   5. radial

14. *provincial*   1. urbane   2. governmental   3. local   4. rural   5. native

15. *clandestine*   1. open   2. sunny   3. swampy   4. pugnacious   5. banal

16. *abhor*   1. detest   2. absolve   3. accuse   4. bedizen   5. adore

17. *flamboyant*   1. decorated   2. apparitional   3. plain   4. female   5. terse

18. *redundant*   1. tautological   2. repeated   3. curt   4. voluble   5. opulent

19. *impoverished*   1. impecunious   2. affluent   3. rococo   4. iniquitous   5. pendent

20. *obsequious*   1. fawning   2. servile   3. supercilious   4. improper   5. first

21. *discrete*   1. wise   2. foolish   3. unkempt   4. separate   5. continuous

22. *fatuous*   1. inane   2. thin   3. witty   4. planned   5. stout

23. *amenable*   1. responsive   2. intractable   3. indifferent   4. agreeable   5. correct

24. *fallacious*   1. erroneous   2. faulty   3. accurate   4. afraid   5. plucky

25. *altruism*   1. honesty   2. tolerance   3. bigotry   4. thievery   5. selfishness

26. *indifferent*   1. curious   2. varied   3. uniform   4. alike   5. uninquisitive

27. *cohesive*   1. attached   2. detached   3. associated   4. affiliated   5. sticky

28. *insipid*   1. tasty   2. silly   3. angry   4. active   5. emaciated

29. *discord*   1. noise   2. amity   3. irritation   4. scrap   5. use

30. *priority*   1. anxiety   2. irregularity   3. subsequence   4. piety   5. impishness

31. *crabbed*   1. crowded   2. saccharine   3. sour   4. condemned   5. salty

32. *corroboration*   1. proof   2. arrest   3. invalidation   4. alibi   5. alias

33. *decorum*   1. ribaldry   2. balladry   3. high collar   4. solo   5. freedom

34. *vivacious*   1. surgical   2. lively   3. girlish   4. inactive   5. boyish

35. *ingenuous*   1. clever   2. stupid   3. naive   4. young   5. sophisticated

36. *alleviate*   1. allow   2. aggravate   3. instigate   4. belittle   5. refuse
37. *obsolete*   1. mechanical   2. fancy   3. free   4. renovated   5. old
38. *blasé*   1. indifferent   2. awed   3. afraid   4. cultured   5. worldly
39. *sanguine*   1. bloody   2. gloomy   3. happy   4. thin   5. red-faced
40. *languid*   1. pusillanimous   2. indifferent   3. sad   4. vigorous   5. motley
41. *respite*   1. recess   2. intermission   3. exertion   4. dinner   5. anger
42. *obloquy*   1. shame   2. fame   3. name   4. colloquy   5. inquiry
43. *placate*   1. nettle   2. label   3. soothe   4. reply   5. retaliate
44. *complacent*   1. satisfied   2. agreeable   3. nasty   4. querulous   5. asking
45. *assent*   1. save   2. inquire   3. resent   4. introduce   5. disavow
46. *husbandry*   1. munificence   2. wife   3. frugality   4. matrimony   5. widower
47. *noisome*   1. quiet   2. fragrant   3. eager   4. foul   5. riotous
48. *permanent*   1. indifferent   2. tardy   3. mutable   4. improper   5. disheveled
49. *covetous*   1. unfinished   2. uncovered   3. undesirous   4. birdlike   5. plying
50. *corporeal*   1. earthy   2. privileged   3. solid   4. spiritual   5. ethical

Antonym Test B

Each of the questions below consists of a word printed in italics, followed by five words or phrases numbered 1 to 5. Choose the numbered word or phrase which is most nearly opposite in meaning to the word in italics and write the number of your choice on your answer paper.

51. *zealot*   1. heretic   2. hypocrite   3. person who is careless   4. person who is rich   5. person who is indifferent
52. *abstemious*   1. fastidious   2. punctilious   3. pusillanimous   4. dissipated   5. prodigal
53. *satiety*   1. starvation   2. dissatisfaction   3. pretense   4. lowest class   5. grandeur
54. *deciduous*   1. undecided   2. hesitant   3. evergreen   4. annual   5. perennial
55. *innocuous*   1. large   2. toxic   3. spotless   4. impeccable   5. sober
56. *germane*   1. Teutonic   2. healthful   3. irrelevant   4. massive   5. puny
57. *egregious*   1. notorious   2. splendid   3. abortive   4. maturing   5. birdlike
58. *nepotism*   1. midnight   2. partiality   3. impartiality   4. dawn   5. noon

59. *autonomous*   1. magnanimous   2. ambiguous   3. exiguous   4. dependent   5. operated by hand
60. *exculpate*   1. pardon   2. destroy   3. create   4. convict   5. admonish
61. *earthy*   1. pithy   2. salty   3. watery   4. refined   5. moldy
62. *contentious*   1. pacific   2. bellicose   3. satisfied   4. dissatisfied   5. hungry
63. *gainsay*   1. deny   2. lose money   3. audit   4. applaud   5. affirm
64. *ameliorate*   1. harden   2. coarsen   3. aggravate   4. improve   5. scrape
65. *ignominious*   1. disgraceful   2. erudite   3. scholarly   4. incognito   5. laudatory
66. *evanescent*   1. permanent   2. incandescent   3. ephemeral   4. putrid   5. perfunctory
67. *corpulent*   1. sallow   2. cooperative   3. emaciated   4. enterprising   5. red-blooded
68. *jocund*   1. round   2. flat   3. jocular   4. jugular   5. melancholy
69. *hibernal*   1. Irish   2. estival   3. English   4. festival   5. wintry
70. *ebullient*   1. intoxicated   2. placid   3. effervescent   4. gregarious   5. jovial
71. *assuage*   1. solve   2. abate   3. isolate   4. irritate   5. demonstrate
72. *indigenous*   1. alien   2. pleasing   3. comestible   4. disgusting   5. irate
73. *dearth*   1. birth   2. scantiness   3. abundance   4. brilliance   5. morning
74. *deleterious*   1. sane   2. intoxicated   3. sober   4. wholesome   5. adding
75. *fell*   1. downed   2. risen   3. propitious   4. cruel   5. official
76. *exemplary*   1. deplorable   2. imitative   3. outstanding   4. particular   5. additional
77. *choleric*   1. red   2. serene   3. severe   4. stern   5. irritable
78. *baroque*   1. common   2. boatlike   3. rococo   4. simple   5. stupid
79. *dilettante*   1. amateur   2. professional   3. postponement   4. party   5. frenzy
80. *amorphous*   1. diaphonic   2. translucent   3. organized   4. opaque   5. chaotic
81. *capricious*   1. whimsical   2. consistent   3. goatlike   4. honest   5. hypocritical
82. *salubrious*   1. healthy   2. plagued   3. rustic   4. fashioned   5. miasmic
83. *disparity*   1. equality   2. aspersion   3. allusion   4. equanimity   5. suture
84. *apothegm*   1. contradictory statement   2. pithy statement   3. prolix statement   4. terse statement   5. letter
85. *chary*   1. lavish   2. malevolent   3. insinuating   4. sparing   5. irritable

86. *candor*   1. hypocrisy   2. ingenuousness   3. sweetmeat   4. pleasure   5. velocity

87. *equivocate*   1. lie   2. whisper   3. balance   4. be truthful   5. be unequal

88. *estranged*   1. reconciled   2. separated   3. foreign   4. traded   5. embarrassed

89. *pretentious*   1. real   2. excusing   3. modest   4. unpardonable   5. typical

90. *sub rosa*   1. under the rose   2. clandestinely   3. fashionably   4. openly   5. simply

91. *subservient*   1. obsequious   2. omnipresent   3. fawning   4. haughty   5. miserly

92. *untenable*   1. rented   2. maintainable   3. occupied   4. permanent   5. picayune

93. *herbivorous*   1. ravenous   2. omnivorous   3. carnivorous   4. voracious   5. veracious

94. *opulence*   1. glamor   2. sobriety   3. badinage   4. penury   5. petulance

95. *threnody*   1. elegy   2. eulogy   3. ballade   4. paean   5. epic

96. *vaunted*   1. lauded   2. belittled   3. berated   4. worried   5. wicked

97. *cede*   1. yield   2. harvest   3. annex   4. examine   5. mimic

98. *obfuscate*   1. clarify   2. magnify   3. intensify   4. belittle   5. becloud

99. *concave*   1. hollow   2. solid   3. convex   4. complex   5. broken

100. *precipitate*   1. wary   2. steep   3. audacious   4. masterly   5. conquered

Vocabulary Test 1

In each line below you will find one italicized word followed by five words or phrases numbered 1 to 5. In each case choose the word or phrase that has most nearly the same meaning as the italicized word.

1. *filch*   1 hide   2 swindle   3 drop   4 steal   5 covet

2. *urbane*   1 well-dressed   2 polished   3 rural   4 friendly   5 prominent

3. *decant*   1 bisect   2 speak wildly   3 bequeath   4 pour off   5 abuse verbally

4. *antithesis*   1 contrast   2 conclusion   3 resemblance   4 examination   5 dislike

5. *heretical*   1 heathenish   2 impractical   3 quaint   4 rash   5 unorthodox

6. *coalesce*   1 associate   2 combine   3 contact   4 conspire   5 cover

7. *charlatan*   1 clown   2 philanthropist   3 jester   4 dressmaker   5 quack

8. *gauche*   1 clumsy   2 stupid   3 feeble-minded   4 impudent   5 foreign

9. *redundant*   1 necessary   2 plentiful   3 sufficient   4 diminishing   5 superfluous

10. *atrophy*   1 lose leaves   2 soften   3 waste away   4 grow   5 spread

11. *resilience*   1 submission   2 elasticity   3 vigor   4 determination   5 recovery

12. *analogy*   1 similarity   2 transposition   3 variety   4 distinction   5 appropriateness

13. *facetious*   1 obscene   2 shrewd   3 impolite   4 complimentary   5 witty

14. *diatribe*   1 debate   2 monologue   3 oration   4 tirade   5 conversation

15. *malediction*   1 curse   2 mispronunciation   3 grammatical error   4 tactless remark   5 epitaph

16. *aggregate*   1 result   2 difference   3 quotient   4 product   5 sum

17. *aplomb*   1 caution   2 timidity   3 self-assurance   4 shortsightedness   5 self-restraint

18. *therapeutic*   1 curative   2 restful   3 warm   4 stimulating   5 professional

19. *transmute*   1 remove   2 change   3 duplicate   4 carry   5 explain

20. *attrition*   1 annihilation   2 encirclement   3 counter attack   4 appeasement   5 wearing down

21. *truncate*   1 divide equally   2 end swiftly   3 cut off   4 act cruelly   5 cancel

22. *oscillate*   1 confuse   2 kiss   3 turn   4 vibrate   5 whirl

23. *inoculate*   1 make harmless   2 infect   3 cure   4 overcome   5 darken

24. *perusal*   1 approval   2 estimate   3 reading   4 translation   5 computation

25. *querulous*   1 peculiar   2 fretful   3 inquisitive   4 shivering   5 annoying

26. *autonomy*   1 tyranny   2 independence   3 plebiscite   4 minority   5 dictatorship

27. *machinations*   1 inventions   2 ideas   3 mysteries   4 plots   5 alliances

28. *schism*   1 government   2 religion   3 division   4 combination   5 coalition

29. *pusillanimous*   1 cowardly   2 extraordinary   3 ailing   4 evil-intentioned   5 excitable

30. *terminology*   1 technicality   2 finality   3 formality   4 explanation   5 nomenclature

31. *stipend*   1 increment   2 bonus   3 commission   4 gift   5 salary

32. *litigation*   1 publication   2 argument   3 endeavor   4 law suit   5 ceremony

33. *fiasco*   1 disappointment   2 turning point   3 loss   4 celebration   5 complete failure

34. *vagary*   1 caprice   2 confusion   3 extravagance   4 loss of memory   5 shiftlessness

35. *graphic*   1 serious   2 concise   3 short   4 detailed   5 vivid

36. *connotation*   1 implication   2 footnote   3 derivation   4 comment   5 definition

37. *tortuous*   1 crooked   2 difficult   3 painful   4 impassable   5 slow

38. *fulminating* 1 throbbing 2 pointed 3 wavelike
4 thundering 5 bubbling
39. *circumvent* 1 freshen 2 change 3 control
4 harass 5 frustrate
40. *cartel* 1 rationing plan 2 world government
3 industrial pool 4 skilled craft
5 instrument of credit

Vocabulary Test 2

In each line below you will find one italicized word
followed by five words or phrases numbered 1 to 5. In
each case choose the word or phrase that has most
nearly the same meaning as the italicized word.

1. *prolific* 1 meager 2 obedient 3 fertile
4 hardy 5 scanty
2. *assuage* 1 create 2 ease 3 enlarge 4 prohibit
5 rub out
3. *decorum* 1 wit 2 charm 3 adornment
4 seemliness 5 charity
4. *phlegmatic* 1 tolerant 2 careless 3 sensitive
4 stolid 5 sick
5. *intrepid* 1 quick-witted 2 brutal 3 fearless
4 torrid 5 hearty
6. *actuate* 1 frighten 2 direct 3 isolate
4 dismay 5 impel
7. *mountebank* 1 trickster 2 courier 3 scholar
4 cashier 5 pawnbroker
8. *laconic* 1 terse 2 informal 3 convincing
4 interesting 5 tedious
9. *boorish* 1 sporting 2 tiresome 3 argumentative
4 monotonous 5 rude
10. *erudite* 1 modest 2 egotistical 3 learned
4 needless 5 experienced
11. *acrimonious* 1 repulsive 2 enchanting
3 stinging 4 snobbish 5 disgusting
12. *embryonic* 1 hereditary 2 arrested
3 developed 4 functioning 5 rudimentary
13. *inexorable* 1 unfavorable 2 permanent
3 crude 4 relentless 5 incomplete
14. *protracted* 1 boring 2 condensed 3 prolonged
4 comprehensive 5 measured
15. *obsequious* 1 courteous 2 fawning
3 respectful 4 overbearing 5 inexperienced
16. *loquacious* 1 queer 2 logical 3 gracious
4 rural 5 voluble
17. *pugnacious* 1 bold 2 combative 3 brawny
4 pug-nosed 5 valiant
18. *astringent* 1 bossy 2 musty 3 flexible
4 corrosive 5 contracting
19. *escarpment* 1 threat 2 limbo 3 cliff
4 behemoth 5 blight
20. *amenities* 1 prayers 2 ceremonies
3 pageantries 4 pleasantries 5 social functions
21. *deplore* 1 condone 2 forget 3 forgive
4 deny 5 regret
22. *banal* 1 commonplace 2 flippant 3 pathetic
4 new 5 unexpected
23. *abacus* 1 casserole 2 blackboard 3 slide rule
4 adding device 5 long spear

24. *seismism* 1 inundation 2 tide 3 volcano
4 earthquake 5 tornado
25. *ameliorate* 1 favor 2 improve 3 interfere
4 learn 5 straddle
26. *chary* 1 burned 2 careful 3 comfortable
4 fascinating 5 gay
27. *corpulent* 1 dead 2 fat 3 full 4 organized
5 similar
28. *enigma* 1 foreigner 2 ambition 3 instrument
4 officer 5 riddle
29. *inept* 1 awkward 2 intelligent 3 ticklish
4 tawdry 5 uninteresting
30. *inveterate* 1 evil 2 habitual 3 inconsiderate
4 reformed 5 unintentional
31. *obeisance* 1 salary 2 justification 3 conduct
4 deference 5 afterthought
32. *pedantic* 1 stilted 2 odd 3 footworn
4 selfish 5 sincere
33. *petulant* 1 lazy 2 loving 3 patient 4 peevish
5 wary
34. *proclivity* 1 backwardness 2 edict 3 rainfall
4 slope 5 tendency
35. *trenchant* 1 keen 2 good 3 edible 4 light
5 subterranean
36. *vapid* 1 carefree 2 crazy 3 insipid 4 spotty
5 speedy
37. *prognosticate* 1 forecast 2 ravish 3 salute
4 scoff 5 succeed
38. *propriety* 1 advancement 2 atonement
3 fitness 4 sobriety 5 use
39. *pulchritude* 1 beauty 2 character 3 generosity
4 intelligence 5 wickedness
40. *scrupulous* 1 drunken 2 ill 3 masterful
4 exact 5 stony

Vocabulary Test 3

In each line below you will find one italicized word
followed by five words or phrases numbered 1 to 5. In
each case choose the word or phrase that has most
nearly the same meaning as the italicized word.

1. *invariable* 1 diverse 2 eternal 3 fleeting
4 inescapable 5 uniform
2. *voracious* 1 excitable 2 honest 3 greedy
4 inclusive 5 circular
3. *concentrate* 1 agitate 2 protest 3 debate
4 harden 5 consolidate
4. *plagiarize* 1 annoy 2 borrow 3 steal ideas
4 imitate poorly 5 impede
5. *cortege* 1 advisers 2 official papers 3 slaves
4 retinue 5 personal effects
6. *antipathy* 1 sympathy 2 detachment
3 aversion 4 amazement 5 opposition
7. *demur* 1 object 2 agree 3 murmur 4 discard
5 consider
8. *paragon* 1 dummy 2 lover 3 image 4 model
5 favorite
9. *finite* 1 impure 2 firm 3 minute 4 limited
5 unbounded
10. *autarchy* 1 laissez-faire 2 motor-mindedness
3 pacifism 4 lawless confusion 5 self-sufficiency

11. *discrimination* 1 acquittal 2 insight 3 caution
    4 indiscretion 5 distortion
12. *invective* 1 richness 2 goal 3 solemn oath
    4 praise 5 verbal abuse
13. *adroit* 1 hostile 2 serene 3 pompous
    4 skillful 5 allergic
14. *lesion* 1 injury 2 contortion 3 suffering
    4 convulsion 5 aggravation
15. *dilettante* 1 epicure 2 dabbler 3 procrastinator
    4 literary genius 5 playboy
16. *provisional* 1 military 2 tentative 3 absentee
    4 democratic 5 appointed
17. *condiment* 1 ledger 2 ore 3 telegraph device
    4 musical instrument 5 spice
18. *recalcitrant* 1 insincere 2 obstinate 3 crafty
    4 conservative 5 reconcilable
19. *bon mot* 1 witticism 2 pun 3 praise
    4 last word 5 exact meaning
20. *accoutrements*. 1 sealed orders 2 equipment
    3 cartons 4 correspondence 5 financial records
21. *hypothesis* 1 assumption 2 proof 3 estimate
    4 random guess 5 established truth
22. *alacrity* 1 slowness 2 indecision 3 caution
    4 promptness 5 fearlessness
23. *jettison* 1 throw overboard 2 dismantle
    3 scuttle 4 unload cargo 5 camouflage
24. *vacillate* 1 glitter 2 swerve 3 surrender
    4 soften 5 waver
25. *astute* 1 shrewd 2 futile 3 potent
    4 provocative 5 ruthless
26. *proviso* 1 final treaty 2 condition 3 demand
    4 official document 5 proclamation
27. *macabre* 1 gruesome 2 meager 3 sordid
    4 fantastic 5 cringing
28. *augment* 1 curtail 2 change 3 restore
    4 conceal 5 increase
29. *integral* 1 useful 2 powerful 3 essential
    4 mathematical 5 indestructible
30. *impunity* 1 shamelessness 2 power of action
    3 self-reliance 4 haughtiness 5 exemption from
    punishment
31. *latent* 1 inherent 2 lazy 3 dormant
    4 crushed 5 anticipated
32. *obdurate* 1 patient 2 stupid 3 rude
    4 stubborn 5 tolerant
33. *bizarre* 1 boastful 2 warlike 3 sluggish
    4 fantastic 5 oriental
34. *arroyo* 1 cliff 2 plain 3 ranch 4 gully
    5 cactus
35. *augur* 1 enrage 2 foretell 3 suggest
    4 evaluate 5 minimize
36. *contrite* 1 infectious 2 worried 3 penitent
    4 sympathetic 5 tolerant
37. *petulant* 1 silly 2 gay 3 sarcastic 4 officious
    5 quarrelsome
38. *paean* 1 prize 2 song of praise 3 decoration
    4 certificate 5 story of heroism
39. *exotic* 1 romantic 2 exciting 3 wealthy
    4 strange 5 tropical
40. *archipelago* 1 slender isthmus 2 long, narrow
    land mass 3 string of lakes 4 high, flat plain
    5 group of small islands

Vocabulary Test 4

In each line below you will find one italicized word
followed by five words or phrases numbered 1 to 5. In
each case choose the word or phrase that has most
nearly the same meaning as the italicized word.

1. *prevaricate* 1 hesitate 2 lie 3 protest
   4 ramble 5 remain silent
2. *incredulous* 1 argumentative 2 imaginative
   3 indifferent 4 irreligious 5 skeptical
3. *placate* 1 amuse 2 appease 3 embroil 4 pity
   5 reject
4. *cognizant* 1 afraid 2 aware 3 capable
   4 ignorant 5 optimistic
5. *dissonance* 1 disapproval 2 disaster 3 discord
   4 disparity 5 dissimilarity
6. *imminent* 1 declining 2 distinguished
   3 impending 4 terrifying 5 unlikely
7. *torsion* 1 bending 2 compressing 3 sliding
   4 stretching 5 twisting
8. *accrued* 1 added 2 incidental 3 miscellaneous
   4 special 5 unearned
9. *effrontery* 1 bad taste 2 conceit 3 dishonesty
   4 impudence 5 snobbishness
10. *acquiescence* 1 advice 2 advocacy
    3 compliance 4 friendliness 5 opposition
11. *reticent* 1 fidgety 2 repetitious 3 reserved
    4 restful 5 truthful
12. *stipulate* 1 bargain 2 instigate 3 prefer
    4 request 5 specify
13. *pseudo* 1 deep 2 obvious 3 pretended
    4 provoking 5 spiritual
14. *flotsam* 1 dark sand 2 fleet 3 life preserver
    4 shoreline 5 wreckage
15. *awry* 1 askew 2 deplorable 3 odd 4 simple
    5 striking
16. *nefarious* 1 clever 2 necessary 3 negligent
    4 short-sighted 5 wicked
17. *glib* 1 cheerful 2 delightful 3 dull 4 fluent
    5 gloomy
18. *paucity* 1 abundance 2 ease 3 hardship
    4 lack 5 stoppage
19. *lucrative* 1 debasing 2 fortunate 3 influential
    4 monetary 5 profitable
20. *indubitable* 1 doubtful 2 fraudulent
    3 honorable 4 safe 5 undeniable
21. *connivance* 1 approval 2 collusion 3 conflict
    4 permission 5 theft
22. *savant* 1 diplomat 2 inventor 3 learned man
    4 thrifty person 5 wiseacre
23. *incipient* 1 beginning 2 dangerous 3 hasty
    4 secret 5 widespread
24. *virile* 1 honest 2 loyal 3 manly
    4 pugnacious 5 virtuous
25. *assiduous* 1 courteous 2 diligent 3 discouraged
    4 frank 5 slow
26. *cataclysm* 1 blunder 2 superstition
    3 treachery 4 triumph 5 upheaval
27. *auspicious* 1 condemnatory 2 conspicuous
    3 favorable 4 questionable 5 spicy
28. *banter* 1 conversation 2 criticism 3 gossip
    4 irony 5 jesting

29. *vernacular* 1 common speech 2 correct usage 3 long words 4 oratory 5 poetic style
30. *emolument* 1 capital 2 compensation 3 liabilities 4 loss 5 output
31. *turgid* 1 dusty 2 muddy 3 rolling 4 swollen 5 tense
32. *expunge* 1 clarify 2 copy 3 delete 4 investigate 5 underline
33. *ethnology* 1 causation 2 morals 3 social psychology 4 study of races 5 word analysis
34. *deduce* 1 diminish 2 infer 3 outline 4 persuade 5 subtract
35. *panoramic* 1 brilliant 2 comprehensive 3 pretty 4 fluorescent 5 unique

36. *ignominy* 1 disgrace 2 isolation 3 misfortune 4 sorrow 5 stupidity
37. *relevant* 1 ingenious 2 inspiring 3 obvious 4 pertinent 5 tentative
38. *gamut* 1 game 2 range 3 risk 4 organization 5 plan
39. *apposite* 1 appropriate 2 contrary 3 different 4 spontaneous 5 tricky
40. *ambulatory* 1 able to walk 2 confined to bed 3 injured 4 quarantined 5 suffering from disease

Vocabulary Test 5

In each line below you will find one italicized word followed by five words or phrases numbered 1 to 5. In each case choose the word or phrase that has most nearly the same meaning as the italicized word.

1. *disparage* .... 1 belittle 2 degrade 3 erase 4 reform 5 scatter
2. *limpid* .... 1 calm 2 clear 3 crippled 4 delightful 5 opaque
3. *derisive* .... 1 dividing 2 furnishing 3 reflecting 4 expressing ridicule 5 suggesting
4. *debilitate* .... 1 encourage 2 insinuate 3 prepare 4 turn away 5 weaken
5. *opulent* .... 1 fearful 2 free 3 oversized 4 trustful 5 wealthy

6. *blandishment* ...... 1 dislike 2 flattery 3 ostentation 4 praise 5 rejection
7. *cryptic* .... 1 appealing 2 arched 3 deathly 4 hidden 5 intricate
8. *raucous* .... 1 harsh 2 loud 3 querulous 4 rational 5 violent
9. *avidity* .... 1 friendliness 2 greediness 3 resentment 4 speed 5 thirst
10. *epitome* .... 1 conclusion 2 effort 3 letter 4 summary 5 summit

11. *hiatus* .... 1 branch 2 disease 3 gaiety 4 insect 5 opening
12. *plenary* .... 1 easy 2 empty 3 full 4 rewarding 5 untrustworthy
13. *capricious* .... 1 active 2 fickle 3 opposed 4 sheeplike 5 slippery
14. *specious* .... 1 frank 2 particular 3 plausible 4 suspicious 5 vigorous
15. *extirpate* .... 1 besmirch 2 clean 3 eradicate 4 favor 5 subdivide

16. *equivocal* .... 1 doubtful 2 medium 3 monotonous 4 musical 5 well-balanced
17. *benison* .... 1 approval 2 blessing 3 gift 4 prayer 5 reward
18. *beatific* .... 1 giving bliss 2 eager 3 hesitant 4 lovely 5 sad
19. *sanguine* .... 1 limp 2 mechanical 3 muddy 4 red 5 stealthy
20. *surcease* .... 1 end 2 hope 3 resignation 4 sleep 5 sweetness

21. *sentient* .... 1 very emotional 2 capable of feeling 3 hostile 4 sympathetic 5 wise
22. *obviate* .... 1 grasp 2 reform 3 simplify 4 smooth 5 make unnecessary
23. *peruse* .... 1 endure 2 perpetuate 3 read 4 undertake 5 urge
24. *rancor* .... 1 dignity 2 fierceness 3 odor 4 spite 5 suspicion
25. *truncheon* .... 1 baton 2 canopy 3 dish 4 gun 5 rejected food

26. *sebaceous* .... 1 fatty 2 fluid 3 porous 4 transparent 5 watery
27. *dilatory* .... 1 hairy 2 happy-go-lucky 3 ruined 4 tardy 5 well-to-do
28. *ebullition* .... 1 bathing 2 boiling 3 refilling 4 retiring 5 returning
29. *relegate* .... 1 banish 2 deprive 3 designate 4 report 5 request
30. *recondite* .... 1 brittle 2 concealed 3 explored 4 exposed 5 uninformed

31. *redolent* .... 1 odorous 2 quick 3 refined 4 repulsive 5 supple
32. *dissimulate* .... 1 confound 2 pretend 3 question 4 separate 5 strain
33. *sublime* .... 1 below par 2 highly praised 3 extreme 4 noble 5 settled
34. *termagant* .... 1 fever 2 noisy woman 3 sea bird 4 sedative 5 squirrel
35. *sedulous* .... 1 deceptive 2 diligent 3 grassy 4 hateful 5 sweet

36. *vitiate* .... 1 contaminate 2 flavor 3 freshen 4 illuminate 5 refer
37. *curvet* .... 1 come around 2 follow 3 leap 4 restrain 5 warp

38. *adventitious*	......	1 accidental 2 courageous 3 favorable 4 risk taking 5 unexpected
39. *animus*	....	1 animosity 2 breath 3 faith 4 light 5 poison
40. *descried*	....	1 hailed 2 rebuffed 3 recalled 4 regretted 5 sighted

Vocabulary Test 6

In each line below you will find one italicized word followed by five words or phrases numbered 1 to 5. In each case choose the word or phrase that has most nearly the same meaning as the italicized word.

1. *adulation* .... 1 approach 2 echo 3 flattery 4 gift 5 imitation
2. *subsequently* ...... 1 continually 2 factually 3 farther 4 incidentally 5 later
3. *expurgate* .... 1 amplify 2 emphasize 3 offend 4 purify 5 renew
4. *liaison* .... 1 derivative 2 liability 3 link 4 malice 5 officer
5. *sedentary* .... 1 careful 2 inactive 3 notched 4 pleasant 5 uneventful

6. *lassitude* .... 1 childishness 2 energy 3 ignorance 4 languor 5 seriousness
7. *altruistically* ...... 1 egotistically 2 harmfully 3 harshly 4 highly 5 unselfishly
8. *perfidious* .... 1 ambiguous 2 flawless 3 perforated 4 treacherous 5 trusting
9. *consummate* ..... 1 achieve 2 devour 3 effuse 4 ignite 5 take
10. *munificently* ...... 1 acutely 2 awkwardly 3 cruelly 4 generously 5 militarily

11. *lugubrious* .... 1 calm 2 doleful 3 tepid 4 wan 5 warm
12. *apathetic* .... 1 desolate 2 emotional 3 incorrigible 4 passive 5 sad
13. *coterie* .... 1 clique 2 cure-all 3 expert judge 4 forerunner 5 society girl
14. *conduit* .... 1 doorway 2 electric generator 3 power 4 screen 5 tube
15. *shibboleth* ...... 1 friend in need 2 lonely home 3 personal complaint 4 reason for action
                        5 watchword

16. *evanescent* ...... 1 colorful 2 consecrated 3 converted 4 empty 5. vanishing
17. *parsimonious* ..... 1 cautious 2 ecclesiastical 3 luxurious 4 stingy 5 unique
18. *Machiavellian* .... 1 cunning 2 humble 3 kingly 4 machine-like 5 saintly
19. *compendium* ...... 1 amplification 2 appendix 3 expansion 4 paraphrase 5 summary
20. *megalomania* ...... 1 desire for beauty 2 mania for sympathy 3 miserliness 4 passion for grandness
                        5 pity for the poor

21. *torpor* .... 1 cyclone 2 frenzy 3 sluggishness 4 strain 5 twisting
22. *esoteric* .... 1 clear 2 external 3 popular 4 secret 5 uncertain
23. *superciliously* ...... 1 critically 2 disdainfully 3 hypersensitively 4 naïvely 5 softly
24. *abstemious* .... 1 blatant 2 exhilarating 3 greedy 4 temperate 5 wasteful
25. *ken* .... 1 acceptance 2 belief 3 dune 4 knowledge 5 woody glen

26. *germane* .... 1 diseased 2 foreign 3 infected 4 pertinent 5 polished
27. *vituperation* ...... 1 abuse 2 appendectomy 3 complication 4 rejuvenation 5 repeal
28. *chimerical* .... 1 clever 2 delusive 3 experimental 4 foreign 5 provisional
29. *dulcimer* .... 1 dolly 2 doublet 3 duenna 4 gadget 5 musical instrument
30. *sartorial* .... 1 disheveled 2 frozen 3 satirical 4 tailored 5 warm

31. *vertigo* .... 1 curiosity 2 dizziness 3 enlivenment 4 greenness 5 invigoration
32. *debacle* .... 1 ceremony 2 collapse 3 dance 4 deficit 5 dispute
33. *condign* .... 1 deserved 2 hidden 3 perplexed 4 pretended 5 unworthy
34. *ephemerally* .... 1 enduringly 2 lightly 3 openly 4 suspiciously 5 transiently
35. *histrionic* .... 1 authentic 2 hysterical 3 reportorial 4 sibilant 5 theatrical

36. *urbanity* .... 1 aggressiveness 2 mercenary 3 municipity 4 rustic 5 suavity
37. *truculent* .... 1 rambling 2 relenting 3 savage 4 tranquil 5 weary
38. *inveigh* .... 1 allure 2 entice 3 guide cautiously 4 originate 5 speak bitterly
39. *desultory* .... 1 delaying 2 disconnected 3 flagrant 4 insulting 5 irritating
40. *ingenuous* .... 1 clever 2 frank 3 ignorant 4 native 5 unkind

Vocabulary Test 7

In each line below you will find one italicized word followed by five words or phrases numbered 1 to 5. In each case choose the word or phrase that has most nearly the same meaning as the italicized word.

1. *cumulative* .... 1 additive 2 clumsy 3 cumbersome 4 incorrect 5 secretive
2. *epigram* .... 1 chemical term 2 exclamation 3 outer skin 4 pithy saying 5 tombstone
3. *gesticulate* .... 1 dance 2 digest easily 3 ridicule 4 travel 5 use gestures
4. *beguile* .... 1 benefit 2 bind 3 deceive 4 envy 5 petition
5. *avid* .... 1 eager 2 glowing 3 indifferent 4 lax 5 potent

6. *labyrinth* .... 1 laboratory 2 maze 3 path 4 portal 5 room
7. *regurgitate* .... 1 make new investments 2 obliterate 3 restore to solvency 4 slacken 5 surge back
8. *podium* .... 1 chemical element 2 dais 3 foot specialist 4 magistrate 4 Roman infantryman
9. *bereft* .... 1 annoyed 2 awarded 3 deprived 4 enraged 5 insane
10. *elucidate* .... 1 condense 2 escape 3 evade 4 explain 5 shine through

11. *emollient* .... 1 comical 2 despicable 3 enthusiastic 4 raucous 5 soothing
12. *nostalgic* .... 1 expressive 2 forgetful 3 homesick 4 inconstant 5 seasick
13. *expiate* .... 1 atone for 2 die 3 hasten 4 imitate 5 make holy
14. *paradox* .... 1 accepted opinion 2 axiom 3 contradiction 4 enigma 5 pattern
15. *archetype* .... 1 bowman 2 original model 3 public records 4 roguishness 5 star

16. *mundane* .... 1 deformed 2 free 3 rough-shelled 4 tearful 5 worldly
17. *palliative* .... 1 boring 2 callous 3 permanent 4 softening 5 unyielding
18. *foment* .... 1 curb 2 explode 3 rouse 4 turn into wine 5 undermine
19. *predacious* .... 1 beautiful 2 incongruous 3 peaceful 4 preying 5 valuable
20. *stark* .... 1 absent-minded 2 bristling 3 desolate 4 involuntary 5 shining

21. *blatant* .... 1 clamorous 2 conceited 3 prudish 4 reticent 5 unsuited
22. *adversity* .... 1 advertising 2 counsel 3 criticism 4 misfortune 5 proficiency
23. *cadaverous* .... 1 cheerful 2 contemptible 3 ghastly 4 hungry 5 ill-bred
24. *wraith* .... 1 anger 2 apparition 3 figurine 4 mannequin 5 model
25. *perspicacity* .... 1 clearness 2 dullness 3 keenness 4 vastness 5 wideness

26. *extraneous* .... 1 derived 2 foreign 3 unsuitable 4 visible 5 wasteful
27. *paroxysm* .... 1 catastrophe 2 convulsion 3 illusion 4 lack of harmony 5 loss of all bodily movement
28. *sapient* .... 1 discerning 2 foolish 3 mocking 4 soapy 5 youthful
29. *flaccid* .... 1 flabby 2 golden 3 hard 4 strong 5 wiry
30. *impecunious* .... 1 frugal 2 guiltless 3 miserly 4 monied 5 poor

31. *spurious* .... 1 concise 2 false 3 obstinate 4 sarcastic 5 severe
32. *subservient* .... 1 existing 2 obsequious 3 related 4 underlying 5 useful
33. *importune* .... 1 aggrandize 2 carry 3 exaggerate 4 prolong 5 urge
34. *indigenous* .... 1 confused 2 native 3 poor 4 unconcerned 5 wrathful

Items 35-40 are incomplete statements designed to test your understanding of words. Select the word that correctly completes the statement.

35. *Obstruct* is to *impede* as *impenetrable* is to
    1 forbearing   3 impervious   5 open
    2 hidden   4 merciful

36. *Felicity* is to *bliss* as *congenial* is to
    1 clever   3 fierce
    2 compatible   4 unfriendly   5 witty

37. *Cautious* is to *circumspect* as *precipitous* is to
    1 deep   3 high
    2 flat   4 prophetic   5 steep

38. *Inquisitive* is to *incurious* as *manifest* is to
    1 latent   3 obvious   5 unique
    2 many-sided   4 proclamation

39. *Fetish* is to *talisman* as *fealty* is to
    1 allegiance   3 payment   5 sensitivity
    2 faithlessness   4 real estate

40. *Perspicacious* is to *dull* as *pacific* is to
    1 arctic   3 giddy   5 restrained
    2 bellicose   4 quiet

ANSWERS

WORD TEST 1

1. 5	6. 5	11. 1	16. 2
2. 4	7. 3	12. 3	17. 3
3. 2	8. 1	13. 5	18. 4
4. 5	9. 3	14. 4	19. 1
5. 1	10. 2	15. 1	20. 1

WORD TEST 2

21. 2	26. 1	31. 4	36. 5
22. 2	27. 1	32. 4	37. 5
23. 4	28. 2	33. 3	38. 4
24. 5	29. 2	34. 4	39. 3
25. 5	30. 3	35. 4	40. 2

WORD TEST 3

41. 2	46. 3	51. 4	56. 4
42. 3	47. 3	52. 3	57. 2
43. 1	48. 4	53. 1	58. 3
44. 4	49. 4	54. 2	59. 3
45. 5	50. 5	55. 3	60. 4

WORD TEST 4

61. 4	66. 2	71. 4	76. 2
62. 5	67. 2	72. 4	77. 1
63. 2	68. 3	73. 2	78. 3
64. 1	69. 4	74. 1	79. 2
65. 3	70. 5	75. 2	80. 1

WORD TEST 5

81. 2	86. 2	91. 3	96. 2
82. 5	87. 4	92. 3	97. 3
83. 2	88. 3	93. 1	98. 1
84. 5	89. 5	94. 4	99. 5
85. 4	90. 3	95. 4	100. 1

WORD TEST 6

101. 2	106. 1	111. 1	116. 2
102. 1	107. 1	112. 5	117. 4
103. 1	108. 2	113. 5	118. 4
104. 4	109. 1	114. 4	119. 5
105. 5	110. 4	115. 3	120. 4

WORD TEST 7

121. 5	126. 1	131. 3	136. 2
122. 1	127. 1	132. 5	137. 3
123. 5	128. 4	133. 1	138. 4
124. 3	129. 3	134. 2	139. 4
125. 1	130. 2	135. 2	140. 4

WORD TEST 8

141. 4	146. 2	151. 4	156. 5
142. 1	147. 1	152. 4	157. 5
143. 3	148. 3	153. 1	158. 3
144. 2	149. 1	154. 2	159. 2
145. 2	150. 5	155. 1	160. 3

WORD TEST 9

161. 3	166. 3	171. 3	176. 1
162. 3	167. 4	172. 3	177. 3
163. 2	168. 3	173. 1	178. 2
164. 3	169. 2	174. 1	179. 4
165. 4	170. 2	175. 4	180. 2

WORD TEST 10

181. 3	186. 5	191. 1	196. 1
182. 3	187. 4	192. 4	197. 4
183. 3	188. 2	193. 5	198. 1
184. 3	189. 2	194. 1	199. 3
185. 4	190. 5	195. 5	200. 2

WORD TEST 11

201. 3	206. 1	211. 2	216. 5
202. 3	207. 5	212. 2	217. 1
203. 4	208. 1	213. 1	218. 2
204. 5	209. 3	214. 5	219. 3
205. 1	210. 4	215. 2	220. 1

WORD TEST 12

221. 1	226. 3	231. 3	236. 3
222. 4	227. 1	232. 4	237. 2
223. 3	228. 5	233. 1	238. 5
224. 2	229. 3	234. 4	239. 5
225. 1	230. 1	235. 1	240. 2

WORD TEST 13

241. 3	246. 4	251. 4	256. 2
242. 5	247. 3	252. 4	257. 1
243. 1	248. 1	253. 1	258. 3
244. 2	249. 3	254. 5	259. 2
245. 2	250. 2	255. 3	260. 2

WORD TEST 14

261. 4	266. 4	271. 1	276. 1
262. 2	267. 5	272. 1	277. 2
263. 1	268. 1	273. 3	278. 2
264. 1	269. 3	274. 5	279. 4
265. 3	270. 2	275. 2	280. 3

WORD TEST 15

281. 2	286. 3	291. 2	296. 1
282. 4	287. 3	292. 3	297. 4
283. 2	288. 1	293. 3	298. 3
284. 1	289. 4	294. 2	299. 2
285. 1	290. 1	295. 1	300. 2

WORD TEST 16

301. 2	306. 3	311. 2	316. 2
302. 5	307. 1	312. 1	317. 1
303. 2	308. 2	313. 3	318. 2
304. 2	309. 2	314. 3	319. 4
305. 5	310. 5	315. 1	320. 2

WORD TEST 17

321. 3	326. 5	331. 2	336. 4
322. 4	327. 2	332. 4	337. 5
323. 5	328. 2	333. 5	338. 5
324. 2	329. 5	334. 1	339. 2
325. 1	330. 1	335. 3	340. 3

WORD TEST 18

341. 3	346. 2	351. 1	356. 2
342. 3	347. 1	352. 1	357. 2
343. 1	348. 2	353. 2	358. 1
344. 2	349. 5	354. 4	359. 1
345. 4	350. 1	355. 5	360. 4

WORD TEST 19

361. 2	366. 2	371. 3	376. 1
362. 2	367. 5	372. 1	377. 4
363. 5	368. 5	373. 3	378. 3
364. 3	369. 2	374. 3	379. 1
365. 1	370. 3	375. 3	380. 2

WORD TEST 20

381. 1	386. 1	391. 2	396. 3
382. 3	387. 1	392. 4	397. 1
383. 1	388. 4	393. 2	398. 3
384. 5	389. 2	394. 2	399. 3
385. 4	390. 3	395. 3	400. 3

WORD TEST 21

401. 2	406. 3	411. 4	416. 4
402. 4	407. 2	412. 5	417. 3
403. 1	408. 3	413. 1	418. 2
404. 3	409. 4	414. 2	419. 5
405. 3	410. 5	415. 5	420. 2

WORD TEST 22

421. 2	426. 5	431. 1	436. 5
422. 3	427. 1	432. 2	437. 3
423. 3	428. 1	433. 5	438. 5
424. 4	429. 4	434. 1	439. 3
425. 5	430. 1	435. 1	440. 2

WORD TEST 23

441. 3	446. 3	451. 1	456. 1
442. 1	447. 2	452. 3	457. 5
443. 2	448. 4	453. 4	458. 1
444. 4	449. 5	454. 5	459. 1
445. 3	450. 2	455. 5	460. 3

WORD TEST 24

461. 2	466. 3	471. 1	476. 5
462. 3	467. 4	472. 4	477. 1
463. 2	468. 3	473. 2	478. 2
464. 5	469. 2	474. 5	479. 4
465. 4	470. 1	475. 2	480. 3

WORD TEST 25

481. 2	486. 1	491. 1	496. 2
482. 4	487. 4	492. 3	497. 3
483. 3	488. 2	493. 4	498. 1
484. 5	489. 2	494. 2	499. 1
485. 1	490. 4	495. 1	500. 1

WORD TEST 26

501. 3	506. 3	511. 1	516. 1
502. 1	507. 4	512. 4	517. 4
503. 4	508. 5	513. 2	518. 5
504. 5	509. 2	514. 2	519. 5
505. 3	510. 3	515. 2	520. 4

WORD TEST 27

521. 4	526. 5	531. 4	536. 1
522. 3	527. 1	532. 3	537. 3
523. 5	528. 1	533. 1	538. 3
524. 2	529. 3	534. 4	539. 5
525. 2	530. 1	535. 1	540. 3

WORD TEST 28

541. 3	546. 4	551. 3	556. 1
542. 2	547. 3	552. 4	557. 2
543. 4	548. 1	553. 4	558. 3
544. 1	549. 2	554. 4	559. 5
545. 1	550. 3	555. 2	560. 3

WORD TEST 29

561. 3	566. 1	571. 2	576. 2
562. 2	567. 4	572. 3	577. 1
563. 3	568. 1	573. 3	578. 2
564. 2	569. 1	574. 1	579. 2
565. 5	570. 4	575. 4	580. 5

WORD TEST 30

581. 3	586. 3	591. 3	596. 3
582. 1	587. 1	592. 4	597. 3
583. 3	588. 1	593. 4	598. 1
584. 2	589. 2	594. 2	599. 2
585. 1	590. 4	595. 3	600. 2

WORD TEST 31

601. 2	606. 3	611. 1	616. 3
602. 3	607. 1	612. 3	617. 5
603. 5	608. 2	613. 3	618. 5
604. 1	609. 2	614. 2	619. 3
605. 1	610. 4	615. 4	620. 3

WORD TEST 32

621. 2	626. 3	631. 4	636. 2
622. 3	627. 2	632. 5	637. 1
623. 1	628. 1	633. 4	638. 3
624. 4	629. 1	634. 5	639. 2
625. 5	630. 5	635. 1	640. 3

WORD TEST 33

641. 5	646. 4	651. 3	656. 1
642. 2	647. 5	652. 5	657. 3
643. 4	648. 3	653. 2	658. 5
644. 1	649. 1	654. 4	659. 4
645. 3	650. 2	655. 1	660. 2

WORD TEST 34

661. 5	666. 4	671. 4	676. 2
662. 4	667. 4	672. 1	677. 3
663. 3	668. 1	673. 1	678. 1
664. 3	669. 5	674. 5	679. 2
665. 1	670. 5	675. 4	680. 4

WORD TEST 35

681. 3	686. 5	691. 3	696. 3
682. 3	687. 2	692. 1	697. 1
683. 2	688. 1	693. 4	698. 2
684. 1	689. 5	694. 2	699. 5
685. 4	690. 4	695. 1	700. 4

WORD TEST 36

701. 1	706. 3	711. 4	716. 3
702. 2	707. 2	712. 1	717. 4
703. 2	708. 5	713. 2	718. 3
704. 3	709. 1	714. 2	719. 1
705. 3	710. 2	715. 5	720. 4

WORD TEST 37

721. 2	726. 4	731. 1	736. 4
722. 4	727. 5	732. 3	737. 1
723. 4	728. ?	733. 5	738. 5
724. 3	729. 1	734. 3	739. 4
725. 1	730. 1	735. 2	740. 3

WORD TEST 38

741. 5	746. 3	751. 1	756. 1
742. 3	747. 2	752. 2	757. 2
743. 5	748. 4	753. 5	758. 2
744. 1	749. 3	754. 5	759. 1
745. 1	750. 1	755. 3	760. 5

WORD TEST 39

761. 2	766. 2	771. 2	776. 4
762. 2	767. 2	772. 1	777. 3
763. 1	768. 1	773. 4	778. 3
764. 3	769. 1	774. 3	779. 2
765. 1	770. 5	775. 1	780. 4

WORD TEST 40

781. 2	786. 1	791. 3	796. 2
782. 5	787. 3	792. 1	797. 1
783. 3	788. 2	793. 2	798. 5
784. 3	789. 5	794. 4	799. 4
785. 3	790. 2	795. 2	800. 1

SYNONYM TEST A

1. 2	11. 2	21. 5	31. 5	41. 4
2. 4	12. 2	22. 2	32. 4	42. 4
3. 1	13. 4	23. 2	33. 2	43. 4
4. 1	14. 3	24. 4	34. 4	44. 5
5. 3	15. 5	25. 4	35. 1	45. 1
6. 4	16. 3	26. 3	36. 3	46. 1
7. 5	17. 4	27. 1	37. 1	47. 5
8. 3	18. 2	28. 5	38. 1	48. 3
9. 5	19. 3	29. 1	39. 3	49. 1
10. 1	20. 4	30. 2	40. 4	50. 2

SYNONYM TEST B

51. 3	61. 1	71. 5	81. 1	91. 3
52. 1	62. 2	72. 3	82. 3	92. 4
53. 5	63. 2	73. 1	83. 1	93. 1
54. 4	64. 4	74. 4	84. 3	94. 2
55. 2	65. 2	75. 2	85. 4	95. 2
56. 3	66. 5	76. 1	86. 5	96. 5
57. 5	67. 4	77. 3	87. 2	97. 4
58. 4	68. 3	78. 2	88. 3	98. 4
59. 1	69. 4	79. 4	89. 2	99. 1
60. 3	70. 2	80. 1	90. 5	100. 4

ANTONYM TEST A

1. 1	11. 2	21. 5	31. 2	41. 3
2. 3	12. 3	22. 3	32. 3	42. 2
3. 4	13. 2	23. 2	33. 1	43. 1
4. 1	14. 1	24. 3	34. 4	44. 4
5. 4	15. 1	25. 5	35. 5	45. 5
6. 5	16. 5	26. 1	36. 2	46. 1
7. 4	17. 3	27. 2	37. 4	47. 2
8. 2	18. 3	28. 1	38. 2	48. 3
9. 5	19. 2	29. 2	39. 2	49. 3
10. 1	20. 3	30. 3	40. 4	50. 4

ANTONYM TEST B

51. 5	61. 4	71. 4	81. 2	91. 4
52. 4	62. 1	72. 1	82. 5	92. 2
53. 1	63. 5	73. 3	83. 1	93. 3
54. 3	64. 3	74. 4	84. 3	94. 4
55. 2	65. 5	75. 3	85. 1	95. 4
56. 3	66. 1	76. 1	86. 1	96. 2
57. 2	67. 3	77. 2	87. 4	97. 3
58. 3	68. 5	78. 4	88. 1	98. 1
59. 4	69. 2	79. 2	89. 3	99. 3
60. 4	70. 2	80. 3	90. 4	100. 1

VOCABULARY TEST 1

1. 4	11. 2	21. 3	31. 5
2. 2	12. 1	22. 4	32. 4
3. 4	13. 5	23. 2	33. 5
4. 1	14. 4	24. 3	34. 1
5. 5	15. 1	25. 2	35. 5
6. 2	16. 5	26. 2	36. 1
7. 5	17. 3	27. 4	37. 1
8. 1	18. 1	28. 3	38. 4
9. 5	19. 2	29. 1	39. 5
10. 3	20. 5	30. 5	40. 3

VOCABULARY TEST 2

1. 3	11. 3	21. 5	31. 4
2. 2	12. 5	22. 1	32. 1
3. 4	13. 4	23. 4	33. 4
4. 4	14. 3	24. 4	34. 5
5. 3	15. 2	25. 2	35. 1
6. 5	16. 5	26. 2	36. 3
7. 1	17. 2	27. 2	37. 1
8. 1	18. 5	28. 5	38. 3
9. 5	19. 3	29. 1	39. 1
10. 3	20. 4	30. 2	40. 4

VOCABULARY TEST 3

1. 5	11. 2	21. 1	31. 3
2. 3	12. 5	22. 4	32. 4
3. 5	13. 4	23. 1	33. 4
4. 3	14. 1	24. 5	34. 4
5. 4	15. 2	25. 1	35. 2
6. 3	16. 2	26. 2	36. 3
7. 1	17. 5	27. 1	37. 5
8. 4	18. 2	28. 5	38. 2
9. 4	19. 1	29. 3	39. 4
10. 5	20. 2	30. 5	40. 5

VOCABULARY TEST 4

1. 2	11. 3	21. 2	31. 4
2. 5	12. 5	22. 3	32. 3
3. 2	13. 3	23. 1	33. 4
4. 2	14. 5	24. 3	34. 2
5. 3	15. 1	25. 2	35. 2
6. 3	16. 5	26. 5	36. 1
7. 5	17. 4	27. 3	37. 4
8. 1	18. 4	28. 5	38. 2
9. 4	19. 5	29. 1	39. 1
10. 3	20. 5	30. 2	40. 1

VOCABULARY TEST 5

1. 1	11. 5	21. 2	31. 1
2. 2	12. 3	22. 5	32. 2
3. 4	13. 2	23. 3	33. 4
4. 5	14. 3	24. 4	34. 2
5. 5	15. 3	25. 1	35. 2
6. 2	16. 1	26. 1	36. 1
7. 4	17. 2	27. 4	37. 3
8. 1	18. 1	28. 2	38. 1
9. 2	19. 4	29. 1	39. 1
10. 4	20. 1	30. 2	40. 5

VOCABULARY TEST 6

1. 3	11. 2	21. 3	31. 2
2. 5	12. 4	22. 4	32. 2
3. 4	13. 1	23. 2	33. 1
4. 3	14. 5	24. 4	34. 5
5. 2	15. 5	25. 4	35. 5
6. 4	16. 5	26. 4	36. 5
7. 5	17. 4	27. 1	37. 3
8. 4	18. 1	28. 2	38. 5
9. 1	19. 5	29. 5	39. 2
10. 4	20. 4	30. 4	40. 2

VOCABULARY TEST 7

1. 1	11. 5	21. 1	31. 2
2. 4	12. 3	22. 4	32. 2
3. 5	13. 1	23. 3	33. 5
4. 3	14. 3	24. 2	34. 2
5. 1	15. 2	25. 3	35. 3
6. 2	16. 5	26. 2	36. 2
7. 5	17. 4	27. 2	37. 5
8. 2	18. 3	28. 1	38. 1
9. 3	19. 4	29. 1	39. 1
10. 4	20. 3	30. 5	40. 2

The Sentence Completion Question

3

The type of question treated in this chapter tests your ability to use your vocabulary and recognize logical consistency among the elements in a sentence. Merely to know a synonym of a word does not assure success, for these questions put words to use. It is therefore unwise to memorize new words in rote fashion. Those who have prepared themselves in this manner will encounter difficulty with the exercises in this chapter. It is advisable to learn new words by studying their usage and then by using them correctly.

Sentence completion questions actually measure a phase of reading comprehension. If you can recognize the implications of a sentence you have no difficulty in choosing the answer that best fulfills the meaning of the sentence or provides a clear, logical statement of fact.

The subject matter of these questions may come from science, literature, music, art, social studies, or other fields. At times your knowledge of a particular fact may guide you in choosing the correct answer, but more often your success in answering a question will depend upon your ability to understand and use the English language.

In this type of question, which is extensively used on the SAT and other examinations, a sentence with one or two words omitted appears on the question paper. Five possible words or sets of words are provided. The candidate is asked to select the best of the five possible answers provided.

Illustration I

The simplest animals are those whose bodies are simplest in structure and which do the things done by all living animals, such as eating, breathing, moving, and feeling, in the most .... way.
1 haphazard **2** bizarre **3** primitive **4** advantageous **5** unique

This sentence calls for careful analysis on the part of the candidate. He or she should know from biology and reading that *primitive* life forms were simple in structure and that the more complex forms evolved later. To secure the most *advantageous* way of conducting the activities of life, the animal would have to become specialized and complex. Thus, Choice 3 (primitive) is best because it develops the concept of simplicity discussed in the sentence. There is no justification for the other choices.

Illustration II

Because the enemy had a reputation for engaging in sneak attacks, we were .... on the alert.
1 inevitably **2** frequently **3** constantly **4** evidently **5** occasionally

The best answer is 3 (constantly). We can eliminate Choices 2 and 5 because neither frequent nor occasional periods of alertness would provide for the necessary protection against sneak attacks at all times. Constant vigilance would have to be maintained. Choice 1 (inevitably) may be supported, but it is not as good as choice 3. The right word will relate closely to given parts of the sentence.

123

Illustration III

You may wonder how the expert on fossil remains is able to trace descent through teeth, which seem .... pegs upon which to hang whole ancestries.   **1** interesting   **2** reliable   **3** specious   **4** inadequate   **5** academic

If "you may wonder," it appears that it is inadvisable to rely on teeth for guidance in interpreting fossils. Choice 4 (inadequate) creates the element of doubt that the clause tries to develop. Choices 1 and 2 would not lead to the inquiry mentioned in the main clause. There is nothing to justify the idea that the reasoning is specious or false.

Illustration IV

.... has introduced the tremendous problem of the .... of the hundreds of workers replaced by machines.
1 Specialization—relocation   **2** Automation—retraining
3 Unemployment—education   **4** Disease—recovery
5 Machinery—training

The placement of workers deprived of their jobs by modern machinery calls for their retraining into more skilled activities. Thus, answers 2 and 5 are possibilities. The word "automation", however, is preferable to "machinery" because it connotes the replacement of men by machines. Number 2 is best.

Illustration V

To be .... is to be .... restrained.   **1** wanton—emotionally   **2** placid—morally   **3** continent—morally
4 despotic—fully   **5** succinct—thoroughly

This type of sentence completion question is actually a definition question. The best answer is number 3 because a continent person is temperate and restrained morally in his behavior. The other choices do not meet the meanings of the words supplied.

Illustration VI

After the .... of the city, he welcomed the .... of the state park where he camped for two weeks.
1 heat—excitement   **2** bustle—urbanity   **3** noise—turbulence   **4** monotony—routine   **5** commotion—tranquillity

This sentence calls for a contrast between city life and the life of a rural area. The best answer is number 5 because city life is usually associated with noise and commotion and this may be contrasted with the quiet-ness and tranquillity of the country. Choices 2, 3, and 4 do not provide a contrast, and Choice 1 does not make sense.

Illustration VII

Every .... person will .... the importance of an expressive, intelligently used vocabulary.
1 scholarly—impugn   **2** discriminating—accept
3 verbose—acknowledge   **4** literary—interrogate
5 illiterate—dispute

The best answer is number 2. A *discriminating* person is one with taste and sensitivity. He appreciates the accuracy and vividness of an exact vocabulary. Choices 1 and 4 contradict the meaning of the sentence; Choices 3 and 5 lack strong connectives between terms.

Illustration VIII

It was .... to everyone that the speaker told the truth.   **1** enigmatic   **2** veracious   **3** startling
4 officious   **5** patent

The best answer is number 5. *Patent* means obvious, clear. It is the only word that fits the thought of the sentence.

Illustration IX

Although he was theoretically an extremely .... individual, his testimony at the trial revealed that he had been very ....   **1** intrepid—valiant   **2** loyal—hypocritical   **3** loathsome—repulsive   **4** intelligent—erudite   **5** tidy—late

The words *although* and *theoretically* indicate an expectation that is the opposite of what is true. We are therefore looking for a strong contrast or for a pair of opposites among the answers. Choice 2 conveys this contrast.

Illustration X

While the disease is in a .... state it is almost impossible to determine its existence by ....
1 placid—placebo   **2** frenetic—observation   **3** critical—examination   **4** latent—application   **5** latent—observation

This question involves the meaning of the word *latent*. During a *latent* state, the disease would be hidden or undeveloped. Observation would not be able to discover such a state. Therefore, Choice 5 is best. *While* could mean *although*, but then none of the choices make sense.

Illustration XI

.... the heroic efforts of the firemen, the people who were on the roof of the burning building were ....   1 Because of—helpless   2 By means of—doomed   3 Despite—doomed   4 In addition to—helpless   5 In spite of—rescued

Note: Many sentence completions are based on a contrast between the ideas expressed in the first part of the sentence and the ideas expressed in the second half. Such a contrast is indicated by connecting words or phrases such as: *nevertheless, but, theoretically, despite, however, although, even though,* etc. In such a case, the answer is one which allows the first part of the sentence to be opposite in meaning to the second part.

In the sentence in this illustration, the phrases *because of, by means of,* and *in addition to* do not call for the contrast that is provided by the second word in the choice provided. *Despite* calls for the contrasting word *doomed*. Choice 3 is best.

Illustration XII

Were this tract of land .... and the access to the main road more direct, the builder would be more hopeful of........ .   1 more level—making a profit   2 larger—fewer houses   3 better forested—faster construction   4 cheaper—freedom from earthquakes   5 sold—landscaping

Reword the sentence into a plain statement, leaving the appropriate blanks:

If this tract of land were .... and the access to the main road (were) more direct, the builder would be more hopeful of ....

Choice 2: If the tract were larger, the builder might want to build more or the same number of houses, but probably not fewer. Choice 3: More trees slow down construction, since some probably would have to be removed. Choice 4: Freedom from earthquakes does not follow from low price. Choice 5: An argument can be made for this, but it requires an unusual situation—a builder who landscapes *after* he has sold, under a separate contract. Choice 1 is far more common. Level land normally requires less work from a builder and gives him a better chance of making a profit. Level land also makes a better pair with direct access to the main road.

Note: Often in the sentence completion questions, a choice may be complicated by an *unusual word order,* such as:
1. placing the subject after the verb:
    To the complaints window strode the angry customer.
2. placing the subject after an auxiliary of the verb:
    Only by unending search could some few Havana cigars be found.
3. inverting the subject and verb to give the sense of *if:*
    Were defeat to fall on his side, today's dear friends would be tomorrow's acquaintances, and next week's strangers.
4. placing a negative word or phrase first, which usually requires at least part of the verb to follow:
    Never have I seen such a fireworks display!
In all these instances, the candidate should rephrase the sentence to make a plain straightforward sentence. Then he or she may more easily see which of the choices fits the blanks.

For example:
The angry customer strode to the complaints window.
Some few Havana cigars could be found only by unending search.
If defeat were to fall on his side, today's dear friends would be tomorrow's acquaintances, and next week's strangers.
I have never seen such a fireworks display!

PRACTICE EXERCISES

The four exercises that follow will give you an indication of your ability to handle these sentence completion questions. The time for each exercise is fifteen minutes. Scoring for each of the exercises may be interpreted as follows:

21-25—SUPERIOR
16-20—ABOVE AVERAGE
11-15—AVERAGE
5-10—BELOW AVERAGE
0- 5—UNSATISFACTORY

Sentence Completion TEST A

1. The literary artist, concerned solely with the creation of a book or story as close to perfection as his powers will permit, is generally a quiet individual, contemplative, ...
   1. effuse   2. somnolent   3. retiring   4. poetic   5. gregarious
2. He was so .... at tying fishermen's flies that he was asked to demonstrate his technique at sports fairs and exhibitions.

1. applicable 2. adroit 3. fancy 4. gauche
5. impressed

3. No punishment is too severe for such an .... crime; it is almost impossible to understand its enormity.
   1. avaricious 2. apposite 3. exemplary
   4. arbitrary 5. egregious

4. He was so convinced that people were driven by .... motives that he could not believe that anyone could be unselfish.
   1. selfless 2. personal 3. altruistic
   4. ulterior 5. intrinsic

5. When the infant displayed signs of illness, the anxious parents called in a ....
   1. podiatrist 2. pediatrician 3. practitioner
   4. pedagogue 5. plagiarist

6. I can recommend him for this position because I have always found him .... and reliable.
   1. voracious 2. veracious 3. vindictive
   4. valorous 5. mendacious

7. No hero of ancient or modern times can surpass the Indian with his lofty contempt of death and the .... with which he sustained the cruelest affliction.
   1. assent 2. fortitude 3. guile 4. concern
   5. reverence

8. Sitting so close to the .... section of the orchestra, I found that the incessant beating of the drums gave me a headache.
   1. string 2. brass 3. wind 4. percussion
   5. front

9. I could not wish for a more .... occasion on which to announce my plans for enlarging our establishment.
   1. ominous 2. propitious 3. magnificent
   4. pronounced 5. portentous

10. We ask for .... from others, yet we are never merciful ourselves.
    1. clemency 2. culpability 3. sincerity
    4. selectivity 5. consideration

11. To prevent a repetition of this dreadful occurrence, we must discover the .... element in the food that was served.
    1. unknown 2. toxic 3. benign 4. tawdry
    5. heinous

12. The concept of .... grouping of people with similar interests and abilities was very popular among educators.
    1. segregated 2. integrated 3. heterogeneous
    4. homogeneous 5. congruent

13. His theories were so .... that few could see what he was trying to establish.
    1. logical 2. erudite 3. scholarly
    4. theoretical 5. nebulous

14. When I first began to study words in families, I was unaware that *protagonist* was the opposite of *antagonist*, that .... was the opposite of *zenith*.
    1. *apex* 2. *rood* 3. *solstice* 4. *nadir* 5. *hegira*

15. Your .... attitude will alienate any supporters you may have won to your cause.
    1. fascinating 2. humanitarian 3. logical
    4. truculent 5. tortuous

16. We do not mean to be disrespectful when we refuse to follow the advice of our .... leader.
    1. venerable 2. respectful 3. famous
    4. gracious 5. dynamic

17. I fail to understand why there is such a .... atmosphere; we have lost a battle, not a war.
    1. funereal 2. blatant 3. giddy 4. sanguine
    5. haughty

18. When he recited the passage by .... , he revealed that he was reproducing .... without understanding their meaning.
    1. sounds—meaning 2. sounds—pronunciation
    3. effects—cause 4. rote—sounds
    5. ideas—message

19. Something that is .... is not ....
    1. trite—boring 2. violent—vivid
    3. common—a cliché 4. elastic—resilient
    5. hackneyed—original

20. When he realized that he had been induced to sign the contract by .... , he threatened to institute legal proceedings to .... the agreement.
    1. force—nullify 2. innuendo—negate
    3. chicanery—cancel 4. flattery—liquidate
    5. hypnotism—validate

21. An individual who is .... is incapable of ....
    1. fettered—flight 2. modest—shame
    3. penurious—thought 4. militant—fear
    5. ambitious—failure

22. His .... was so marked that I teasingly suggested that he had seen a ....
    1. clumsiness—vision 2. pallor—spectre
    3. demeanor—physician 4. separation—lawyer
    5. visage—ghost

23. A .... statement is an .... comparison.
    1. sarcastic—unfair 2. blatant—overt
    3. sanguine—inherent 4. metaphorical—implied
    5. bellicose—ardent

24. The hostess attempted to .... a romantic atmosphere that would bring the two young people together in ....
    1. simulate—conflict 2. expand—fealty
    3. introduce—cacophony 4. contrive—matrimony 5. present—collusion

25. Old legends of extinct religions come down to us as .... and ....
    1. romance—chivalry 2. myths—fables
    3. dreams—visions 4. predictions—prophecies
    5. miracles—epiphanies

Sentence Completion TEST B

26. As I recall my plane trip around the world last July and August, I think my greatest difficulty was the adjustment to the different .... served with the food in the various cities we visited.
 1. ingredients 2. condiments 3. qualities
 4. grades 5. varieties

27. After several .... attempts to send the missile into space, the spacecraft was finally launched successfully.
 1. abortive 2. difficult 3. experimental
 4. preliminary 5. excellent

28. He worked .... at his task for weeks before he felt satisfied that the results would justify his long effort.
 1. occasionally 2. regularly 3. patiently
 4. assiduously 5. intermittently

29. His book was marred by the many .... remarks, which made us forget his main theme.
 1. inappropriate 2. humorous 3. digressive
 4. opinionated 5. slanted

30. Overindulgence .... character as well as physical stamina.
 1. strengthens 2. stimulates 3. debilitates
 4. maintains 5. provides

31. He was not .... and preferred to be alone most of the time.
 1. antisocial 2. gracious 3. gregarious
 4. cordial 5. handsome

32. The reasoning in this editorial is so .... that we cannot see how anyone can be deceived by it.
 1. coherent 2. special 3. cogent 4. specious
 5. chauvinistic

33. Since you have failed three of the last four tests, you cannot afford to be .... about passing for the term.
 1. courteous 2. relevant 3. sanguine
 4. passive 5. indolent

34. You are afraid to attack him directly; you, therefore, are resorting to ....
 1. guile 2. effrontery 3. criticism 4. innuendo
 5. condemnation

35. His .... remarks are often embarrassing because of their frankness.
 1. sarcastic 2. sadistic 3. frank 4. urbane
 5. ingenuous

36. The pioneers' greatest asset was not their material wealth but their ....
 1. fortitude 2. simplicity 3. largesse

 4. companions 5. possessions

37. Your .... tactics may compel me to cancel the contract because the job must be finished on time.
 1. dilatory 2. offensive 3. obstructive
 4. infamous 5. confiscatory

38. Some students are .... and want to take only the courses for which they see immediate value.
 1. theoretical 2. stupid 3. pragmatic
 4. foolish 5. opinionated

39. Because I find that hot summer weather .... me and leaves me very tired, I try to leave the city every August and go to Maine.
 1. irritates 2. bores 3. enervates 4. boils
 5. disturbs

40. Americans do not feel that .... obedience and implicit submission to the will of another is necessary in order to maintain good government.
 1. titular 2. blind 3. partial 4. verbal
 5. stark

41. Because his occupation required that he work at night and sleep during the day, he had an exceptionally .... complexion.
 1. ghastly 2. ruddy 3. livid 4. plain
 5. pallid

42. It is almost impossible at times to capture the .... of words when we translate them into a foreign language.
 1. implications 2. meanings 3. denotations
 4. connotations 5. essence

43. As .... head of the organization, he attended social functions and civic meetings but had no .... in the formulation of company policy.
 1. titular—voice 2. complete—vote
 3. titular—pride 4. real—competition
 5. actual—superior

44. Unlike the Shakespearean plays, the "closet dramas" of the nineteenth century were meant to be .... rather than ....
 1. seen—acted 2. read—acted 3. quiet—loud
 4. sophisticated—urbane 5. produced—acted

45. The collapse of the financial empire set up by the small group was more than a .... ; it affected millions of small ....
 1. threat—men 2 vision—speculators 3. debacle—investors 4. disaster—homeowners
 5. calamity—prospectors

46. Employers who retire people who are willing and able to continue working should realize that .... age is not an effective .... in determining whether an individual is capable of working.

1. physical—barrier   2. chronological—factor
3. intellectual—criterion   4. chronological—criterion   5. declining—standard

47. Her true feelings .... themselves in her sarcastic asides; only then was her .... revealed.
1. concealed—sweetness   2. manifested—bitterness   3. hid—sarcasm   4. developed—anxiety
5. grieved—charm

48. To .... is to try to .... an individual.
1. gainsay—corrupt   2. evacuate—dismiss
3. exhume—bury 4. proselytize—convert 5. inhibit—frighten

49. When I listened to his cogent arguments, all my .... were .... and I was forced to agree with his point of view.
1. senses—stimulated   2. doubts—confirmed
3. friends—present   4. questions—asked
5. doubts—dispelled

50. She was .... because her plans had gone ....
1. pleased—awry   2. imminent—efficiently
3. foiled—well   4. importunate—splendidly
5. distraught—awry

Sentence Completion TEST C

51. The ties that bind us together in common activity are so .... that they can disappear at any moment.
1. tentative 2. tenuous 3. restrictive
4. consistent 5. tenacious

52. I did not anticipate reading such an .... discussion of the international situation in the morning newspaper; normally, such a treatment could be found only in scholarly magazines.
1. erudite 2. arrogant 3. ingenious 4. overt
5. analytical

53. We need more men of culture and enlightenment; we have too many .... among us.
1. boors 2. students 3. philistines
4. pragmatists 5. philosophers

54. The Trojan War proved to the Greeks that cunning and .... were often more effective than military might.
1. treachery 2. artifice 3. strength 4. wisdom
5. beauty

55. His remarks were filled with .... which sounded lofty but presented nothing new to the audience.
1. aphorisms 2. platitudes 3. bombast
4. adages 5. symbols

56. Achilles had his .... , Hitler had his Elite Corps.
1. myrmidons 2. antagonists 3. arachnids
4. myriads 5. anchorites

57. In order to photograph .... animals, elaborate flashlight equipment is necessary.
1. predatory 2. wild 3. nocturnal 4. live
5. rare

58. He was deluded by the .... who claimed he could cure all diseases with his miracle machine.
1. salesman 2. inventor 3. charlatan
4. doctor 5. practitioner

59. The attorney protested that the testimony being offered was not .... to the case and asked that it be stricken from the record as irrelevant.
1. favorable 2. coherent 3. harmful
4. beneficial 5. germane

60. Automation threatens mankind with an increased number of .... hours.
1. meager 2. useless 3. active 4. complex
5. idle

61. I was so bored with the verbose and redundant style of that writer that I welcomed the change to the .... style of this author.
1. prolix 2. consistent 3. terse
4. logistical 5. tacit

62. Such doltish behavior was not expected from so .... an individual.
1. exasperating 2. astute 3. cowardly
4. enigmatic 5. democratic

63. Disturbed by the .... nature of the plays being presented, the Puritans closed the theaters in 1642.
1. mediocre 2. fantastic 3. moribund
4. salacious 5. witty

64. John left his position with the company because he felt that advancement was based on .... rather than on ability.
1. chance 2. seniority 3. nepotism
4. superciliousness 5. maturation

65. He became quite overbearing and domineering once he had become accustomed to the .... shown to soldiers by the natives; he enjoyed his new sense of power.
1. ability 2. domesticity 3. deference
4. culpability 5. insolence

66. Epicureans live for the .... of their senses.
1. mortification 2. removal 3. gratification
4. gravity 5. lassitude

67. I grew more and more aware of Iago's .... purpose as I watched him plant the seeds of suspicion in Othello's mind.
1. noble 2. meritorious 3. fell 4. insincere
5. hypocritical

68. Her reaction to his proposal was .... ; she rejected it ....
1. inevitable—vehemently   2. subtle—violently
3. clever—obtusely   4. sympathetic—angrily
5. garrulous—tersely

69. .... is the mark of the ....
1. Timorousness—hero   2. Thrift—impoverished

3. Avarice—philanthropist 4. Trepidation—coward 5. Vanity—obsequious

70. If you carry this .... attitude to the conference, you will .... any supporters you may have at this moment.
1. belligerent—delight 2. truculent—alienate
3. conciliatory—defer 4. supercilious—attract
5. ubiquitous—alienate

71. It hurt my pride to be forced to .... a person who always insulted me; nevertheless, I tried to .... him.
1. rebuke—condign 2. respect—avenge
3. propitiate—conciliate 4. repudiate—evaluate
5. intimidate—redeem

72. Because .... is such an unsightly disease, its victims have frequently been shunned.
1. leprosy 2. cancer
3. halitosis 4. poverty
5. tuberculosis

73. I am not attracted by the .... life of the .... , always wandering through the countryside, begging for charity.
1. proud—almsgiver 2. noble—philanthropic
3. urban—hobo 4. natural—philosopher
5. peripatetic—vagabond

74. The sugar dissolved in the water .... ; finally all that remained was an almost .... residue on the bottom of the glass.
1. quickly—lumpy 2. immediately—fragrant
3. gradually—imperceptible 4. subsequently—glassy 5. spectacularly—opaque

75. It is foolish to vent your spleen on an .... object; still, you make .... enemies that way.
1. inanimate—fewer 2. immobile—bitter
3. interesting—curious 4. insipid—fewer
5. humane—more

Sentence Completion TEST D

76. Architects travel to Greece and Italy to .... the marvels of classic design.
1. imitate 2. photograph 3. recall 4. embellish 5. study

77. The discoveries of science often are a mixed blessing; on the one hand they give us valuable pesticides that enable the farmer to grow more abundant crops and on the other hand they .... the benefits by destroying the balance of nature.
1. compromise 2. misplace 3. mollify
4. damage 5. counteract

78. If we .... these experienced people to positions of unimportance because of their political persuasions, we shall lose the services of valuably trained personnel.
1. define 2. propel 3. relegate 4. constrict
5. detract

79. His .... directions misled us; we did not know which of the two roads to take.
1. foolish 2. complicated 3. extenuating
4. ambiguous 5. arbitrary

80. I am afraid that you will have to alter your .... views in the light of the tragic news that has just arrived.
1. roseate 2. tragic 3. contrary 4. narrow
5. dour

81. You were frightened by a concept that you .... in your own mind.
1. accepted 2. idealized 3. sought
4. externalized 5. created

82. Although there are .... outbursts of gunfire, we can report that the major rebellion has been suppressed.
1. bitter 2. heinous 3. meager 4. nocturnal
5. sporadic

83. He was guided by .... rather than by ethical considerations.
1. expediency 2. precepts 3. morality
4. consequence 5. sophistry

84. We now know that what constitutes practically all matter is empty space; relatively enormous .... in which revolve with lightning velocity infinitesimal particles so small that they have never been seen or photographed.
1. seas 2. particles 3. areas 4. skies 5. voids

85. To be .... is to be without ....
1. credulous—gullibility 2. considerate—incredibility 3. belligerent—pugnacity
4. maudlin—tenacity 5. gullible—skepticism

86. His listeners enjoyed his .... wit but his victims often .... at its satire.
1. lugubrious—suffered 2. taut—smiled
3. bitter—smarted 4. lugubrious—smiled
5. trenchant—winced

87. An occasional .... remark spoiled the .... that made the paper memorable.
1. trite—clichés 2. colloquial—verisimilitude
3. hackneyed—originality 4. urbane—sophistication 5. jocund—gaiety

88. Unlike the carefully weighed and .... compositions of Dante, Goethe's writings have always the sense of .... and enthusiasm.
1. inspired—vigor 2. spontaneous—immediacy
3. contrived—languor 4. planned—immediacy
5. developed—construction

89. In Homer's work, Achilles is the .... of Greek warriors; Odysseus .... the shrewd man.
1. epitome—abhors 2. antithesis—exemplifies

3. paragon—exemplifies 4. prototype—eschews
5. adversary—abhors

90. .... enables us to know the past and to use it in preparing for the future.
    1. Beauty 2. Truth 3. Language
    4. Antiquity 5. Thought

91. Victims of glaucoma find that their .... vision is impaired and that they can no longer see objects not directly in front of them.
    1. peripatetic 2. peripheral 3. periphrastic
    4. ocular 5. perspicacious

92. The child's earliest words deal with concrete objects and actions, it is much later that he is able to grapple with ....
    1. decisions 2. abstractions 3. maxims
    4. opponents 5. mathematics

93. It is regrettable that the author saved many of his most brilliant lines for the ....; by that time, most of the audience had left.
    1. ingenue 2. epilogue 3. climax 4. curtain
    5. book

94. It would be difficult for one so .... to be led to believe that all men are equal and that we must disregard race, color, and creed.
    1. emotional 2. broadminded 3. tolerant
    4. intolerant 5. democratic

95. The .... of our civilization from an agricultural society to today's complex industrial world was accompanied by upheaval and, all too often, war.
    1. adjustment 2. migration 3. phasing
    4. metamorphosis 5. route

96. To be .... is to be ....
    1. petulant—agreeable 2. turbid—swollen
    3. torpid—sluggish 4. turgid—clear
    5. evergreen—deciduous

97. Man is essentially a .... animal and tends to .... others.
    1. selfish—resent 2. vicarious—work with
    3. maudlin—belittle 4. perverse—adopt
    5. gregarious—associate with

98. Singers have a definite advantage over musicians who play an instrument; they can appeal to us through .... as well as ....
    1. personality—charm 2. emotions—sounds
    3. thoughts—ideas 4. ideas—music
    5. sight—personality

99. Because the inspector gave the plant a .... examination, he .... many defects.
    1. semiannual—uncovered 2. significant—neglected 3. perfunctory—overlooked
    4. pertinent—unveiled 5. routine—discovered

100. The playwright was known not for his original ideas but for his .... of ideas that had been propounded by others.
    1. invention 2. reiteration 3. consideration
    4. enlightenment 5. rejection

ANSWERS   Chapter 3

SENTENCE COMPLETION TEST A

1. 3	6. 2	11. 2	16. 1	21. 1
2. 2	7. 2	12. 4	17. 1	22. 2
3. 5	8. 4	13. 5	18. 4	23. 4
4. 4	9. 2	14. 4	19. 5	24. 4
5. 2	10. 1	15. 4	20. 3	25. 2

SENTENCE COMPLETION TEST B

26. 2	31. 3	36. 1	41. 5	46. 4
27. 1	32. 4	37. 1	42. 4	47. 2
28. 4	33. 3	38. 3	43. 1	48. 4
29. 3	34. 4	39. 3	44. 2	49. 5
30. 3	35. 5	40. 2	45. 3	50. 5

SENTENCE COMPLETION TEST C

51. 2	56. 1	61. 3	66. 3	71. 3
52. 1	57. 3	62. 2	67. 3	72. 1
53. 3	58. 3	63. 4	68. 1	73. 5
54. 2	59. 5	64. 3	69. 4	74. 3
55. 2	60. 5	65. 3	70. 2	75. 1

SENTENCE COMPLETION TEST D

76. 5	81. 5	86. 5	91. 2	96. 3
77. 5	82. 5	87. 3	92. 2	97. 5
78. 3	83. 1	88. 4	93. 2	98. 4
79. 4	84. 5	89. 3	94. 4	99. 3
80. 1	85. 5	90. 3	95. 4	100. 2

The Analogy Question 4

The exercises in this chapter furnish drill in a type of question that challenges your ability to analyze relationships between words. In some questions you are asked to carry an analogy from a concrete relationship to a more abstract or less tangible situation. In others you may find questions involving synonyms, antonyms, cause and effect, etc. In this chapter you will find many different kinds of relationships listed so that you may be better able to examine the pair of words in each question.

Working with verbal relationships involves a kind of reasoning similar to mathematical thinking. Many students find it helpful to apply the ratio and proportion concept of mathematics to the verbal situations presented in the verbal analogy question.

Illustration I

In the word relationship question, the student is presented with a pair of words followed by five additional pairs of words. He or she must select the pair of words from among the five choices that best matches the relationship existing between the first two words.

tree : forest ::   **1** daisy : meadow   **2** grass : lawn   **3** wheat : field   **4** flower : garden   **5** frog : pond

In handling this type of question, it is necessary to determine the exact nature of the relationship existing between the two given words in the stem. In this case, the relationship is that a forest cannot exist without trees. The answer is 2 because a lawn cannot exist without grass. However, a meadow need not contain daisies. A field can be made of other grains than wheat. A garden may contain only vegetables and a pond need not contain frogs.

Illustration II

erosion : rocks ::   **1** flatless : landscape   **2** fatigue : task   **3** fasting : food   **4** dissipation : character   **5** forgery : signature

The idea of a wearing away of a substance (erosion : rocks) is continued in Choice 4. *Dissipation* implies a wasting away of energies that results in a loss of character.

Illustration III

campaign : objective ::   **1** motivation : energy   **2** misdeed : consequence   **3** victory : triumph   **4** talent : success   **5** voyage : destination

Just as a campaign should have a definite goal or objective, a voyage has a destination. Choice 5 is the best answer.

Illustration IV

possess : lose ::   **1** hesitate : advance   **2** cease : recur   **3** undertake : perform   **4** continue : desist   **5** produce : supply

This is more difficult. We can eliminate Choices 3 and 5 immediately, for they present synonyms and we are looking for opposites in meaning. Choice 1 does not provide a clear opposite; Choice 2 is good; Choice 4 is best. The objection to Choice 2 is found in the word *recur*, which carries the concept of repeated activity which is not found in the word *lose*.

Illustration V

chronometer : time :: **1** odometer : distance **2** thermometer : degrees **3** calendar : days **4** odometer : hatred **5** cardiograph : heart

A chronometer is an accurate timepiece and is used to measure time. An odometer is a device for measuring distance. (It is commonly confused with *speedometer.*) Number 1 is best.

Illustration VI

platitude : commonplace :: **1** cliché : pithy **2** proverb : moral **3** cliché : banal **4** parable : terse **5** paradox : loyal

Platitudes and clichés are trite, commonplace, banal statements. Therefore, number 3 best matches the relationship.

Illustration VII

chronometer : hourglass :: **1** watch : sand **2** rifle : bow **3** ticking : sand **4** metal : glass **5** spear : cannon

The hourglass was an instrument commonly used by people in ancient times to measure the passage of time. With the development of clocks and chronometers, the hourglass became obsolete. Likewise, with the development of gunpowder, the rifle replaced the bow (Choice 2).

Illustration VIII

apprentice : mechanic :: **1** doctor : intern **2** painter : artist **3** tyro : novice **4** amateur : expert **5** novice : nun

Choice 5 is best because the novice, like the apprentice, is a beginner or probationary student. After proper training, the apprentice will become a mechanic and the novice, a nun. (The amateur is not necessarily trying to become an expert.)

Illustration IX

abhorrence : distaste :: **1** shower : deluge **2** ecstasy : happiness **3** ache : pain **4** altruism : philanthropy **5** hatred : odium

In this analogy, we observe that *abhorrence* (repugnance, loathing) is much more extreme than *distaste.* The concept of extreme to mild is found in Choice 2 since *ecstasy* may be defined as extreme *happiness.*

Illustration X

doctor : lawyer :: **1** client : illness **2** client : ailment **3** patient : litigation **4** ailment : client **5** patient : client

Occasionally, too many possible relationships can be found when the first two words are examined. This is true when we begin to look for the relationship between *doctor and lawyer.*

> Note: When too many possible relationships can be found after the first two words in the stem are examined, seek a relationship between the first word of the original pair and the first word of the suggested answers. After finding a relationship between the first word in each case, examine whether the same relationship exists between the second word of the original pair and the second word of the suggested answers.

Using this method, Choice 5 becomes obvious because the person who utilizes the services of a *doctor* is called a *patient*, and the person who utilizes the services of a *lawyer* is called a *client*.

Illustration XI

blueberry : pea :: **1** sky : purity **2** potato : raspberry **3** sky : star **4** purity : world **5** sky : grass

In this illustration, we face a different problem. No apparent relationship can be found between *blueberry* and *pea*. However, if we examine the choices in the manner indicated in the previous illustration, we find that *blueberry* and *sky* have similar colors and that *pea* and *grass* have a color similarity. Thus, Choice 5 becomes the only acceptable answer.

> Note: When no apparent relationship can be found in the first two stem words, try to establish a relationship based on those commonly-used on this test. A list of possible relationships follows.

Kinds of Word Relationships

It is obvious that there are many possible relationships that may exist among words. Some of the more common ones are included in the following list.

1. **Worker and article created**
   carpenter : house
   writer : book
   composer : symphony
2. **Worker and tool used**
   carpenter : saw
   writer : typewriter
   surgeon : scalpel
3. **Tool and object worked on**
   pencil : paper
   saw : wood
4. **The act the tool does to the object it works on**
   saw : wood (cuts)
   knife : bread (cuts)
   brake : car (stops)
5. **Time sequence**
   early : late
   dawn : twilight
   sunrise : sunset
6. **Cause and effect**
   germ : disease
   carelessness : accident
   explosion : debris
7. **Degree of intensity**
   tepid : hot
   joy : ecstasy
   admiration : love
8. **Class—species**
   furniture : chair
   insect : grasshopper
   mammal : whale
   dog : poodle
9. **Type—characteristic**
   cow : herbivorous
   tiger : carnivorous
10. **Grammatical relationships**
   I : mine (first person nominative case : first person possessive case)
   wolf : vulpine (noun : adjective)
   have : had (present tense : past tense)
   alumnus : alumni (masculine singular noun : masculine plural noun)
11. **Synonyms**
   lie : prevaricate
   kind : benevolent
12. **Antonyms**
   never : always
   love : hate
   fancy : simple
   real : fictional
13. **Person and thing sought by person**
   alchemist : gold
   prospector : gold
14. **Person and thing avoided by person**
   child : fire
   pilot : reef
15. **Part to the whole**
   soldier : regiment
   star : constellation
16. **Sex**
   duck : drake
   bull : cow
17. **Symbol—what it stands for**
   flag : nation
   insignia : rank

PRACTICE EXERCISES

The four exercises that follow will give you an indication of your ability to handle verbal analogies. The time for each exercise is fifteen minutes. Scoring for each of the exercises may be interpreted as follows.

21-25—SUPERIOR
16-20—ABOVE AVERAGE
11-15—AVERAGE
6-10—BELOW AVERAGE
0- 5—UNSATISFACTORY

Word Analogy TEST A

1. quixotic : feasible :: 1. sudden : workable 2. theoretical : practical 3. fashionable : efficient 4. precise : practicable 5. sad : adept
2. debate : forensic :: 1. drama : histrionic 2. opera : spoken 3. concerto : harmonizing 4. argument : domestic 5. novel : original
3. anthology : poems :: 1. antipasto : hors d'oeuvres 2. volume : book 3. encyclopedia : words 4. thesaurus : synonyms 5. medley : arrangement
4. anhydrous : saturated :: 1. dry : wet 2. sweet : wet 3. cloying : full 4. stolid : liquid 5. physics : chemistry
5. wine : grapes :: 1. champagne : raisins 2. liquor : intoxicating 3. vineyard : winery 4. whiskey : hops 5. vodka : potatoes

6. notable : notorious ::   1. philanthropic : benevolent   2. philandering : pleasant   3. heinous : atrocious   4. nefarious : secret   5. philanthropic : miserly

7. entrepreneur : laborer ::   1. profits : wages   2. arbitrator : capitalist   3. mediator : conflict   4. moonlighting : worker   5. capitalism : communism

8. morphine : sedates ::   1. drug : addicts   2. liquor : intoxicates   3. medicine : soothes   4. oil : smears   5. bandage : heals

9. actor : soliloquy :: ::   1. playwright : tragedy   2. director : movie   3. musician : solo   4. drummer : march   5. singer : duet

10. continent : immoral ::   1. land : evil   2. dissolute : lascivious   3. restrained : wanton   4. shore : reef   5. conscience : sin

11. mendicant : impecunious ::   1. critic : quizzical   2. complainer : petulant   3. hat : askew   4. liar : poor   5. philanthropist : prodigal

12. apostate : religion ::   1. loyal : faith   2. traitor : country   3. renegade : Indian   4. vital : church   5. disloyal : colonies

13. dermatologist : skin ::   1. paleontologist : statues   2. genealogist : genes   3. cardiologist : heart   4. astrologist : future   5. psychologist : insanity

14. squint : eyes ::   1. grapple : iron   2. grope : hands   3. lisp : speech   4. limp : limbs   5. sneeze : nostrils

15. cynosure : brilliant ::   1. student : attentive   2. map : legible   3. rock : large   4. word : common   5. magnet : attractive

16. numerator : denominator ::   1. fraction : decimal   2. divisor : quotient   3. ratio : proportion   4. dividend : divisor   5. top : bottom

17. noisome : garbage ::   1. liquid : perfume   2. heavy : metal   3. loud : music   4. warmth : snow   5. fragrant : incense

18. sad : dolorous ::   1. rich : wealthy   2. smart : smattering   3. grief : healthy   4. giver : free   5. gratitude : frugal

19. school : tuition ::   1. game : loss   2. lawyer : client   3. hospital : insurance   4. church : tithe   5. library : fine

20. dissertation : ideas ::   1. propaganda : facts   2. novel : theme   3. poem : emotions   4. play : acting   5. essay : novel

21. naive : ingenuous ::   1. ordinary : ingenious   2. old : wise   3. simple : kind   4. eager : reserved   5. sophisticated : urbane

22. termagant : shrew ::   1. anteater : mouse   2. virago : harpy   3. supporter : nag   4. single : married   5. male : female

23. cloud : storm ::   1. container : contained   2. portent : disaster   3. cumulus : gale   4. thunder : lightning   5. rain : wind

24. conduit : water ::   1. pump : oil   2. behavior : liquid   3. artery : blood   4. wire : sound   5. electricity : television

25. bread : oven ::   1. ceramics : kiln   2. silo : corn   3. pottery : wheel   4. iron : furnace   5. cake : stove

Word Analogy TEST B

26. latitude : Equator ::   1. direction : declension   2. weight : length   3. warp : woof   4. longitude : Internationate Date Line   5. north pole : Arctic Circle

27. antimacassar : sofa ::   1. rug : floor   2. table : chair   3. door : window   4. picture : frame   5. pillow : bed

28. perimeter : addition ::   1. arithmetic : geometric   2. exponential : quadratic   3. linear : logarithmic   4. triangle : sphere   5. area : multiplication

29. actuary : insurance ::   1. librarian : school   2. historian : dates   3. veterinarian : animal husbandry   4. agronomist : agreement   5. vegetarian : meat

30. isolationist : aloof ::   1. altruist : selfish   2. pessimist : mournful   3. scholar : proud   4. bigot : tolerant   5. segregationist : gregarious

31. water : conduit ::   1. electricity : magnet   2. elevator : shaft   3. shell : rifle   4. noise : cannon   5. soda : bottle

32. plaintiff : defendant ::   1. court : law   2. injured : accused   3. judge : jury   4. district attorney : lawyer   5. nobleman : serf

33. explosive : volcano ::   1. cold : mountain   2. arid : desert   3. humid : valley   4. misty : morning   5. fertile : plain

34. bizarre : exotic ::   1. stage : dancer   2. commonplace : routine   3. wild : tame   4. ordinary : exceptional   5. lively : livid

35. doctor : disease ::   1. psychiatrist : maladjustment   2. teacher : pupils   3. scholar : knowledge   4. judge : crime   5. lawyer : law

36. shower : deluge ::   1. irritation : rage   2. April : May   3. passion : affection   4. surprise party : exceptional   5. flow : surge

37. drama : playwright ::   1. act : actor   2. words : author   3. poetics : poet   4. review : critic   5. opera : musician

38. always : never ::   1. often : rarely   2. frequently : occasionally   3. constantly : frequently   4. intermittently : casually   5. occasionally : constantly

39. President : Pope ::   1. elected : chosen   2. ballot : smoke   3. proclamation : bull   4. temporal : secular   5. leader : religion

40. permanent : evanescent ::   1. durable : fleeting

2. lasting : glittering   3. eternal : everlasting 4. hairdo : bleach   5. wave : scene
41. ornithologist : birds ::   1. aquarium : fish   2. anthropologist : insects   3. archeologist : artifacts 4. architect : buildings   5. botanist : animals
42. verbs : action ::   1. nouns : amplification   2. pronouns : demonstration   3. adjectives : modification 4. adverbs : connection   5. prepositions : definition
43. oafish : astute ::   1. net : gun   2. ocean : mountain 3. wise : smart   4. lake : thorough   5. simpleton : sage
44. suggest : demand ::   1. deny : request   2. affection : consolation   3. hint : blunder   4. give : receive   5. take : grab
45. vindicable : reprehensible ::   1. mild : serious 2. bitter : sad   3. mild : sad   4. solid : porous 5. vivid : dull
46. multiplication : division ::   1. increase : decrease 2. zero : infinity   3. calculate : estimate   4. digit : series   5. integers : numbers
47. sonnet : line ::   1. ballad : poetry   2. symphony : harmony   3. novel : chapter   4. game : score 5. epic : ode
48. triangle : quadrilateral ::   1. plane : solid   2. pentagon : hexagon   3. rectangle : octagon   4. cone : cube   5. regular : irregular
49. fine : imprisonment ::   1. sentence : judgment 2. bail : bond   3. jury : judge   4. magistrate : judge   5. misdemeanor : felony
50. satellite : orbit ::   1. ball : pitcher   2. missile : trajectory   3. moon : phase   4. rocket : projectile   5. auto : bridge

Word Analogy TEST C

51. liquefy : petrify ::   1. water : stone   2. soften : frighten   3. cash in : strenghten   4. solvent : rich 5. insolvent : bankrupt
52. belt : trousers ::   1. braces : garters   2. trunk : tree 3. pillar : society   4. cables : trolley   5. cables : bridge
53. gasoline : petrol ::   1. motor : car   2. engine : trunk   3. light : heavy   4. elevator : lift   5. refined : crude
54. rhythm : rhyme ::   1. poet : versifier   2. accent : sound   3. prose : poetry   4. versification : scansion 5. blank verse : free verse
55. scholar : entrepreneur ::   1. books : superstition 2. learning : studying   3. university : laboratory 4. knowledge : profits   5. knowledge : research
56. nectar : ambrosia :   1. frankincense : myrrh

2. vegetable : fruit   3. taste : smell   4. goddess : god   5. drink : food
57. muslin : brocade ::   1. ornate : decorated 2. simple : torn   3. gaudy : rich   4. plain : figured 5. multicolored : variegated
58. derivation : lexicographer ::   1. evolution : biologist   2. origin : typographer   3. politics : anarchist 4. laws : court   5. foundation : roofer
59. epaulet : shoulder ::   1. medal : chest   2. knapsack : back   3. sash : window   4. sword : scabbard 5. decoration : uniform
60. sheep : wool ::   1. fodder : animal   2. otter : fur 3. flax : cotton   4. animal : vegetable   5. stupid : good
61. nail : puncture ::   1. sword : scabbard   2. scalpel : incision   3. easel : picture   4. needle : sew   5. tire : flat
62. misdemeanor : felony ::   1. imprisonment : bail 2. joy : ecstasy   3. gale : breeze   4. judge : magistrate   5. coward : criminal
63. Secret service : F.B.I. ::   1. soldier : army 2. local : national   3. treasury : justice   4. policemen : detectives   5. open : undercover
64. fatuous : inane ::   1. clever : inchoate   2. querulous : picayune   3. fatal : mordant   4. portentous : significant   5. cloying : viscous
65. lungs : blood ::   1. heart : circulation   2. arteries : veins   3. carburetor : car   4. glands : secretions 5. carburetor : gasoline
66. scales : justice ::   1. weights : measures   2. markets : courts   3. torch : liberty   4. laurel : peace 5. balance : right
67. diaphanous : cacophonous ::   1. twofold : multiple 2. sheer : transparent   3. sheer : opaque   4. harmonious : discordant   5. transparent : noisy
68. bleeding : tourniquet ::   1. drowning : resuscitation 2. sunstroke : fatigue   3. traffic : red light 4. coughing : elixir   5. disease : microbe
69. detritus : glaciers ::   1. ice : icebergs   2. thaw : cold 3. silt : rivers   4. sediment : bottom   5. dregs : society
70. exculpate : incriminate ::   1. exonerate : involve 2. free : fine   3. blame : criticize   4. blame : pardon 5. excuse : free
71. trumpet : brass ::   1. drums : hide   2. bugle : bronze 3. cello : string   4. orchestra : band   5. horn : metal
72. sandpaper : abrasive ::   1. polish : floors   2. pumice : emulsion   3. gasoline : refined   4. oil : lubricant   5. gratuity : irritant
73. albeit : although ::   1. preposition : conjunction 2. conjunction : conjunction   3. conjunction : preposition   4. adjective : conjunction   5. conjunction : adverb
74. habits : instincts ::   1. work : play   2. training : heredity   3. acquired : cultivated   4. natural :

unusual   5. birds : animals

75. ambulatory : bedridden ::   1. wheelchair : bed
2. healthy : sick 3. strong : weak 4. broken arm :
broken limb 5. free : confined

Word Analogy TEST D

76. pariah : favorite ::   1. nephew : son   2. hypno-
tism : comatose   3. sycophant : obsequious
4. ostracism : nepotism   5. chosen : accepted

77. golf : holes ::   1. badminton : feather   2. football
: kick   3. baseball : innings   4. tennis : net
5. swimming : pool

78. infancy : senility ::   1. conclusion : climax
2. incipient : critical   3. dawn : dusk   4. day :
night   5. January : October

79. tirade : abusive :: 1. monologue : lengthy 2. aphorism : boring   3. prologue : precedent   4. encomium : laudatory 5. critique : insolent

80. goose : gander ::   1. lion : lioness 2. shark : shark-
skin   3. duck : drake   4. male : female 5. master :
slave

81. bushel : potatoes ::   1. container : fruit   2. ounce
: coal   3. wood : cord   4. point : diamond
5. bricks : mortar

82. paddle : canoe ::   1. engine : train 2. auto : motor
3. oar : row   4. walk : run   5. steer : rudder

83. thermometer : temperature ::   1. minute : time
2. gauge : pressure   3. calendar : year   4. stop-
watch : speed   5. barometer : air current

84. synthesis : construction ::   1. artificial : building
2. dissection : analysis   3. excuse : denial
4. inductive : logical   5. artificial : true

85. plebiscite : ukase ::   1. vote : musical instrument
2. lack : abundance   3. public : ruler   4. written :
oral   5. cancel : construct

86. poetry : rhythm :: 1. music : instrument 2. sculpture : clay 3. painting : form
4. architecture : builder   5. artist : model

87. partnership : corporation ::   1. two : many
2. local : national   3. agreement : conspiracy
4. conspiracy : plot 5. unlimited : limited

88. inkblot : eye chart ::   1. blurs : letters   2. blotter
: spectacles 3. physician : specialist 4. psychiatrist
: optometrist   5. oculist : opthalmologist

89. tulip : zinnia :: 1. flower : bud 2. garden : meadow 3. bulb : seed 4. annual : perennial
5. flower : grass

90. ligaments : bones ::   1. fat : muscles   2. inverte-
brates : vertebrates   3. tear : fracture   4. inverte-
brates : mammals   5. heart : arm

91. like : as ::   1. conjunction : conjunction   2. conjunction : preposition   3. me : I   4. me : me
5. comparison : contrast

92. debater : laryngitis :: 1. actor : aplause 2. doctor
: diagnosis 3. writer : paper 4. pedestrian : lame-
ness 5. swimmer : wet

93. daffodils : trees ::   1. spring : summer   2. fish :
frogs   3. lake : meadow   4. snakes : grass
5. garden : orchard

94. knight : shield ::   1. fencer : saber   2. soldier :
carbine 3. welder : goggles 4. mechanic : wrench
5. lord : escutcheon

95. furlong : mile ::   1. second : hour   2. degree :
thermometer   3. foot : yard   4. ounce : pound
5. pint : gallon

96. legislature : laws :: 1. judiciary : decisions 2. king : justice 3. election : candidates 4. democracy : freedom 5. army :
weapons

97. conviction : intellect ::   1. speech : propaganda
2. belief : religion 3. facts : statistics 4. court :
home   5. persuasion : emotion

98. bereaved : condolences :   1. guilty : accusations
2. faulty : eraser 3. robbed : insurance 4. victorious : wealth   5. destitute : charity

99. blow : retaliation :: 1. attack : violence 2. ac-
cusation : proof 3. criticism : sarcasm 4. insult :
retort 5. deception : unmasking

100. brush : paint ::   1. hammer : nail   2. polish :
floor 3. trowel : cement 4. match : fire 5. rake
: lawn

ANSWERS   **Chapter 4**

WORD ANALOGY TEST A

1. 2	*6.* 5	*11.* 2	*16.* 4	*21.* 5
2. 1	*7.* 1	*12.* 2	*17.* 5	*22.* 2
3. 4	*8.* 2	*13.* 3	*18.* 1	*23.* 2
4. 1	*9.* 3	*14.* 2	*19.* 4	*24.* 3
5. 5	*10.* 3	*15.* 5	*20.* 3	*25.* 1

WORD ANALOGY TEST C

51. 1	*56.* 5	*61.* 2	*66.* 3	*71.* 3
52. 5	*57.* 4	*62.* 2	*67.* 5	*72.* 4
53. 4	*58.* 1	*63.* 3	*68.* 3	*73.* 2
54. 2	*59.* 1	*64.* 4	*69.* 3	*74.* 2
55. 4	*60.* 2	*65.* 5	*70.* 1	*75.* 5

WORD ANALOGY TEST B

26. 4	*31.* 2	*36.* 1	*41.* 3	*46.* 1
27. 1	*32.* 2	*37.* 4	*42.* 3	*47.* 3
28. 5	*33.* 2	*38.* 1	*43.* 5	*48.* 2
29. 3	*34.* 2	*39.* 3	*44.* 5	*49.* 5
30. 2	*35.* 1	*40.* 1	*45.* 1	*50.* 2

WORD ANALOGY TEST D

76. 4	*81.* 4	*86.* 3	*91.* 3	*96.* 1
77. 3	*82.* 1	*87.* 5	*92.* 4	*97.* 5
78. 3	*83.* 2	*88.* 4	*93.* 5	*98.* 5
79. 4	*84.* 2	*89.* 3	*94.* 3	*99.* 4
80. 3	*85.* 3	*90.* 3	*95.* 5	*100.* 3

Typical Test A   Time: One Hour

DIRECTIONS: *Each item below consists of an italicized word followed by five alternatives. Decide which alternative means the same as or the opposite of the italicized word. Write the number of the word that you have chosen as your answer for each question.*

1. *bucolic* 1. sickly 2. meandering 3. pastoral 4. imaginative 5. hospitable
2. *ostentatious* 1. modest 2. factual 3. indifferent 4. sarcastic 5. magnanimous
3. *recondite* 1. miserly 2. recluse 3. conciliatory 4. bashful 5. abstruse
4. *vernal* 1. old 2. springlike 3. bubbling 4. tacit 5. uncouth
5. *diaphanous* 1. evanescent 2. ephemeral 3. topical 4. sheer 5. musical
6. *prolix* 1. terse 2. sheer 3. circular 4. curative 5. morbid
7. *spurious* 1. spacious 2. genuine 3. indicative 4. predictive 5. fundamental
8. *apostate* 1. fruit 2. cancel 3. loyal follower 4. teacher 5. pupil
9. *cognizant* 1. aware 2. follower 3. nonsense 4 tinkerer 5. author
10. *amelioration* 1. cancellation 2. worsening 3. forgetfulness 4. consideration 5. bribe
11. *malinger* 1. feign sickness 2. support 3. imbibe 4. become unconscious 5. slander
12. *loquacious* 1. juicy 2. voracious 3. laconic 4. basic 5. tutorial
13. *turbid* 1. limpid 2. activated 3. torpid 4. viscous 5. hungry
14. *aviary* 1. egg 2. bird cage 3. mountain peak 4. atoll 5. bee hive
15. *avid* 1. veracious 2. forgetful 3. insignificant 4. state 5. loath
16. *termagant* 1. virago 2. ant 3. hurricane 4. perennial 5. start
17. *omniscient* 1. powerful 2. scientific 3. wasteful 4. magnanimous 5. ignorant
18. *esoteric* 1. confidential 2. foreign 3. identical 4. summery 5. fashionable
19. *precious* 1. accurate 2. affected 3. absolute 4. cheap 5. reserved
20. *mollify* 1. grind 2. present 3. allay 4. quit 5. provoke
21. *retrogression* 1. imagination 2. deterioration 3. violation 4. articulation 5. amazement
22. *hamper* 1. food box 2. support 3. animal 4. treat lightly 5. caution
23. *banal* 1. fruit 2. dry 3. original 4. enthusiastic 5. noisy
24. *jocund* 1. small 2. frantic 3. amazing 4. gay 5. intelligent
25. *inveigle* 1. entice 2. encircle 3. intrude 4. inspect 5. envelop
26. *lucid* 1. fancy 2. rococo 3. embroiled 4. arrogant 5. obscure
27. *anathema* 1 national song 2. factual report 3. name 4. concept 5. benediction
28. *altruistic* 1. impartial 2. petulant 3. selfish 4. quizzical 5. luring
29. *devious* 1. ingenious 2. devilish 3. burdensome 4. erratic 5. sincere
30. *philandering* 1. trifling 2. loathing 3. inquisitive 4. masterful 5. borrowing

DIRECTIONS: *Questions 31-70 are incomplete statements, each followed by five alternatives. In each question, select the alternative that best completes the statement.*

31. *Scholar* is to *knowledge* as *entrepreneur* is to 1. love 2. profits 3. charity 4. books 5. privilege

32. *Rung* is to *ladder* as *story* is to 1. book 2. chapter 3. building 4. article 5. staircase
33. *Incite* is to *rebellion* as *ignite* is to 1. revolution 2. stockpile 3. insubordination 4. conflagration 5. revolt
34. *Insipid* is to *tasteless* as *innocuous* is to 1. innuendo 2. innocent 3. unambitious 4. tasteless 5. harmless
35. *Condoning* is to *forgive* as *loquacious* is to 1. punish 2. speak 3. frighten 4. lavish 5. mitigate
36. *Crime* is to *heinous* as *man* is to 1. nefarious 2. philanthropic 3. migratory 4. captive 5. woman
37. *Recondite* is to *ignorant* as *ecstatic* is to 1. frantic 2. scholarly 3. stupid 4. morose 5. mad
38. *Numismatist* is to *coins* as *lexicographer* is to 1. words 2. laws 3. books 4. stamps 5. maps
39. *Bellicose* is to *pacific* as *militant* is to 1. ocean 2. warlike 3. angry 4. panicky 5. peaceful
40. *Amulet* is to *evil* as *brake* is to 1. car 2. pedestrian 3. collision 4. stop 5. control
41. *Prologue* is to *play* as *overture* is to 1. concerto 2. symphony 3. sonata 4. tragedy 5. opera
42. *Chef* is to *culinary* as *barber* is to 1. tonsorial 2. hairy 3. hair 4. pole 5. barbarous
43. *X-axis* is to *y-axis* as *latitude* is to 1. tolerance 2. degrees 3. minutes 4. location 5. longitude
44. *Teacher* is to *ignorance* as *light* is to 1. darkness 2. bulb 3. electricity 4. current 5. stupidity
45. *Diamond* is to *baseball* as *court* is to 1. golf 2. tennis 3. lacrosse 4. football 5. hockey
46. *Paris* is to *Vatican City* as *the Louvre* is to 1. pyramids 2. Pope 3. Swiss Guards 4. Sistine Chapel 5. Italy
47. *Initial* is to *terminal* as *engine* is to 1. current 2. battery 3. motor 4. prong 5. caboose
48. *Potable* is to *edible* as *milk* is to 1. beer 2. cream 3. cheese 4. cow 5. fatty
49. *Numismatist* is to *coins* as *dermatologist* is to 1. stamps 2. insect 3. plants 4. skin 5. bones
50. *Salutatorian* is to *valedictorian* as *incipient* is to 1. clever 2. intelligent 3. final 4. habitual 5. stupid
51. *Easel* is to *palette* as *scalpel* is to 1. surgeon 2. blade 3. suture 4. hone 5. patient
52. *Hands* is to *tactile* as *nose* is to 1. aquiline 2. Roman 3. olfactory 4. tensile 5. broken
53. *Laws* is to *conduct* as *buoy* is to 1. float 2. pilot 3. captain 4. channel 5. lifeguard
54. *Lumber* is to *forest* as *stone* is to 1. mountain 2. sculptor 3. mason 4. quarry 5. valley
55. *Lexicographer* is to *dictionary* as *cartographer* is to 1. library 2. carriage 3. gazetteer 4. laundry 5. thief
56. *Islands* is to *archipelago* as *stars* is to 1. movies 2. planets 3. orbits 4. constellation 5. sun
57. *Ostracism* is to *censure* as *applause* is to 1. cheers 2. approval 3. boos 4. condemnation 5. prohibition

58. *Vault* is to *valuables* as *granary* is to 1. hospital 2. wheat 3. animals 4. bonds 5. stock market
59. *Quart* is to *liter* as *yard* is to 1. bed 2. garbage 3. meter 4. pint 5. inch
60. *Christmas* is to *poinsettia* as *Easter* is to 1. rabbit 2. Sunday 3. service 4. bonnet 5. lily
61. *Meager* is to *inordinate* as *scarcity* is to 1. irrational 2. plethora 3. paucity 4. magnitude 5. excessive
62. *Culinary* is to *kitchen* as *terpsichorean* is to 1. music hall 2. stage 3. pantry 4. dance studio 5. bedroom
63. *Hourglass* is to *arrow* as *clock* is to 1. bow 2. rifle 3. spear 4. direction 5. dart
64. *Individual* is to *group* as *island* is to 1. peninsula 2. isthmus 3. archipelago 4. galaxy 5. ocean
65. *Hercules* is to *Ulysses* as *brawn* is to 1. strength 2. agility 3. insincerity 4. travels 5. wiliness
66. *Dime* is to *decade* as *dollar* is to 1. year 2. century 3. hundredth 4. dealer 5. millenium
67. *Wealth* is to *indigent* as *food* is to 1. enervated 2. ascetic 3. parched 4. sated 5. emaciated
68. *Stocks* are to *bonds* as *owners* are to 1. buyers 2. sellers 3. brokers 4. lenders 5. bankers
69. *Cow* is to *crab* as *bovine* is to 1. crustacean 2. nipping 3. amphibian 4. edible 5. aquatic
70. *Tuberculosis* is to *infantile paralysis* as *bacillus* is to 1. child 2. crippling 3. eliminated 4. vaccine 5. virus

DIRECTIONS: *Items 71-100 contain sentences which have words omitted. Each sentence is followed by five alternatives. Indicate the number of the alternative which best completes the meaning of the sentence.*

71. He was guided by ———— rather than by ethical considerations.
    1. expediency 2. precepts 3. morality 4. consequences 5. sophistry
72. You were frightened by an ———— which you created in your mind.
    1. idea 2. image 3. hallucination 4. attitude 5. ideal
73. In times of war, we must take precautions against acts of ———— as well as of direct violence.
    1. heinousness 2. viciousness 3. subterfuge 4. sabotage 5. infiltration
74. They fired upon the enemy from behind trees, walls and any other ———— point they could find.
    1. conspicuous 2. obvious 3. vantage 4. safe 5. hidden
75. *Pilgrim's Progress* is an ———— of the temptations and victories of man's soul.
    1. anecdote 2. extension 3. opinion 4. idealization 5. allegory
76. His ———— directions misled us; we did not know which road to take.
    1. foolish 2. complicated 3. extenuating 4. ambiguous 5. arbitrary
77. The heavy meal and the overheated room made us all ———— and indifferent to the speaker.
    1. somnolent 2. belligerent 3. pacific 4. can-

did 5. noisy

78. He interpreted the departure of the birds as an _____ of evil.
    1. indication 2. action 3. outline 4. augury
    5. aspect

79. Overindulgence _____ character as well as physical stamina.
    1. strengthens 2. stimulates 3. debilitates
    4. maintains 5. provides

80. I am afraid you will have to alter your _____ views in the light of the tragic news that has just arrived.
    1. roseate 2. tragic 3. contrary 4. narrow
    5. dour

81. If you behave from now on, I will _____ this notation from your record card.
    1. extract 2. expunge 3. enter 4. absolve
    5. overlook

82. He was so convinced that people were driven by _____ motives that he could not believe that anyone could be unselfish.
    1. selfish 2. personal 3. altruistic 4. ulterior
    5. intrinsic

83. "The child is father to the man" is an example of _____.
    1. hyperbole 2. metaphor 3. iambic pentameter
    4. blank verse 5. paradox

84. Since Cyrano de Bergerac did not wish to be obligated to any man, he refused to be a _____ of Cardinal Richelieu.
    1. adherent 2. disciple 3. protege 4. follower
    5. recipient

85. The attorney protested that the testimony being offered was not _____ to the case.
    1. favorable 2. coherent 3. harmful 4. beneficial 5. germane

86. The detectives searched the area for the _____ who had set these costly fires.
    1. criminal 2. pyromanic 3. children
    4. sparks 5. megalomaniac

87. A pessimist has a _____ outlook on life.
    1. salubrious 2. contemputuous 3. intense
    4. placid 5. lugubrious

88. His blood _____ in his veins as he saw the dread monster rush toward him.
    1. curdled 3. burst 3. rushed 4. congealed
    5. coagulated

89. His remarks were filled with _____ which sounded

lofty but presented nothing new to the audience.
    1. aphorisms 2. platitudes 3. bombast
    4. adages 5. complaints

90. His is a _____ foe; you must respect and fear him at all times.
    1. redoubtable 2. invincible 3. courageous
    4. insignificant 5. craven

91. The _____ designs of the eighteenth century architecture seem grotesque to modern viewers.
    1. grotesque 2. rococo 3. Romanesque
    4. Gothic 5. Hellenic

92. Such homely virtues as _____, hard work, and simplicity seem old-fashioned in these days.
    1. parsimony 2. asceticism 3. prodigality
    4. thrift 5. wantonness

93. Your _____ attitude will alienate any supporters you may have won to your cause.
    1. fascinating 2. altruistic 3. logical 4. truculent 5. tortuous

94. Disturbed by the _____ nature of the plays being presented, the Puritans closed the theatres in 1642.
    1. mediocre 2. fantastic 3. moribund 4. salacious 5. witty

95. The _____ pittance the widow receives from the government cannot keep her from poverty.
    1. magnanimous 2. paltry 3. insignificant
    4. munificent 5. niggardly

96. He was not serious in his painting; he was rather a _____.
    1. hack 2. gamester 3. tyro 4. dilettante
    5. clown

97. I fail to understand why there is such a _____ atmosphere; we have lost a battle, not a war.
    1. funereal 2. blatant 3. giddy 4. sanguine
    5. murky

98. I can recommend him for this position because I have always found him _____ and reliable.
    1. voracious 2. veracious 3. vindictive
    4. valorous 5. mendacious

99. A musical piece for soloist with orchestral accompaniment is a _____.
    1. symphony 2. tone poem 3. concert piece
    4. concertina 5. concerto

100. When the infant displayed signs of illness, the anxious parents called in a _____.
    1. podiatrist 2. pediatrician 3. practitioner
    4. pedagogue 5. plagiarist

Typical Test B   Time: One Hour

DIRECTIONS: *Each item below consists of an italicized word followed by five alternatives. Decide which alternative means the* same as *or the* opposite of *the italicized word. Write the number of the word that you have chosen as the answer for each question.*

1. *impugn*   1. involve 2. insult 3. fight 4. admire
   5. accept

2. *grandiloquent*   1. gargoyle 2. bombastic 3. truculent 4. abashed 5. mediocre

3. *amenable*   1. intractable 2. likable 3. frantic
   4. magnificent 5. hectic

4. *sallow*   1. ruddy 2. deep 3. wise 4. conciliatory embarrassed

5. *remiss*   1. unduly 2. lose 3. consequential

4. negligent   5. sorry

6. *veracious*   1. hungry   2. avid   3. mendacious
4. tawdry   5. limited

7. *allay*   1. misplace   2. assuage   3. forget   4. honor
5. acquaint

8. *halcyon*   1. rough   2. meager   3. notable
4. varied   5. customary

9. *terse*   1. verse form   2. triad   3. vivid   4. mournful   5. curt

10. *complaisant*   1. agreeable   2. smug   3. intelligent
4. whining   5. unpleasant

11. *turgid*   1. logical   2. rhetorical   3. brilliant
4. bombastic   5. sluggish

12. *spurious*   1. goading   2. fantastic   3. melancholy
4. genuine   5. irritating

13. *tautological*   1. tense   2. vivid   3. syllogistic
4. repetitious   5. nonsensical

14. *vicarious*   1. deputed   2. deported   3. departed
4. disputed   5. discarded

15. *inimical*   1. imitated   2. hostile   3. alien   4. antiquated   5. morose

16. *ostensible*   1. showy   2. full   3. professed
4. followed   5. false

17. *urbane*   1. poison   2. rustic   3. scholarly   4. futile
5. naive

18. *pariah*   1. fruit   2. district   3. angel   4. outcast
5. devotee

19. *lugubrious*   1. stormy   2. heavy   3. portable
4. gay   5. famous

20. *mottled*   1. particolored   2. annoyed   3. mollified
4. questioned   5. alleviated

21. *soporific*   1. drink   2. toast   3. narcotic   4. wonderful   5. illegal

22. *intrepid*   1. courageous   2. contrary   3. pedestrian
4. philanthropic   5. stolid

23. *paltry*   1. admirable   2. faulty   3. palatable
4. fearful   5. food

24. *laconic*   1. cool   2. voluble   3. friendly   4. militant   5. fretful

25. *ubiquitous*   1. sycophantic   2. redundant   3. resolute   4. mordant   5. omnipresent

26. *panegyric*   1. remedy   2. malady   3. lament
4. customary   5. eulogy

27. *dais*   1. platform   2. meadow   3. flower   4. insect
5. orator

28. *redolent*   1. repetitious   2. alleged   3. disputed
4. recalled   5. fragrant

29. *tractable*   1. legible   2. logical   3. docile   4. valid
5. inscrutable

30. *condone*   1. overlook   2. derive   3. defy   4. deserve   5. abandon

DIRECTIONS: *Questions 31-70 are incomplete statements, each followed by five alternatives. In each question select the alternative that best completes the statement.*

31. *Alumnus* is to *alumnae* as *sheep* is to   1. ram
2. rams   3. ewe   4. ewes   5. sheep

32. *Benediction* is to *anathema* as *eulogy* is to   1. curse

2. vilification   3. paean   4. panegyric   5. blessing

33. *Coal* is to *coke* as *sand* is to   1. beach   2. mud
3. clay   4. glass   5. stone

34. *Brash* is to *reticence* as *bold* is to   1. brazenness
2. impudence   3. shyness   4. laziness
5. cowardice

35. *Regicide* is to *king* as *patricide* is to   1. father
2. queen   3. mother   4. patron   5. patroon

36. *Hen* is to *cluck* as *horse* is to   1. canter   2. gallop
3. whinny   4. check   5. snort

37. *Mountain* is to *peak* as *wave* is to   1. summit
2. valley   3. apex   4. pinnacle   5. crest

38. *Desert* is to *water* as *idiot* is to   1. wine   2. moron
3. strength   4. stupidity   5. intelligence

39. *Generous* is to *prodigal* as *frugal* is to   1. benevolent
2. philanthropic   3. lethargic   4. parsimonious
5. sanctimonious

40. *Director* is to *movie* as *choreographer* is to   1. ballet
2. opera   3. play   4. chorus   5. television show

41. *Leather* is to *felt* as *shoe* is to   1. tongue   2. lace
3. hat   4. cap   5. sole

42. *Business* is to *collapses* as *ship* is to   1. succumbs
2. fails   3. founders   4. settles   5. veers

43. *Conscience* is to *sin* as *pilot* is to   1. man   2. harbor
3. ship   4. captain   5. reef

44. *Joy* is to *ecstasy* as *shower* is to   1. tub   2. deluge
3. drizzle   4. drought   5. cloud

45. *Sheep* is to *mutton* as *deer* is to   1. forest   2. deer
3. doe   4. venison   5. antlers

46. *Horse* is to *bridle* as *ship* is to   1. propeller   2. bow
3. stern   4. engine   5. rudder

47. *Indigence* is to *affluence* as *beggar* is to   1. blind
2. Indian   3. thief   4. millionaire   5. lawyer

48. *Gold carat* is to *diamond carat* as *quality* is to
1. color   2. weight   3. size   4. price   5. quality

49. *Conservative* is to *garish* as *cautious* is to   1. rococo
2. fearful   3. daring   4. reactionary   5. liberal

50. *Jersey* is to *Holstein* as *Siamese* is to   1. Twins
2. Angora   3. Rhode Island   4. Vermont   5. cat

51. *Papal* is to *bull* as *presidential* is to   1. election
2. guards   3. proclamation   4. perquisites
5. goat

52. *Enigma* is to *riddle* as *labyrinth* is to   1. Jason
2. Minotaur   3. maze   4. fleece   5. Medea

53. *Philatelist* is to *stamps* as *entomologist* is to   1. insects   2. ancestors   3. words   4. bees   5. fish

54. *First* is to *last* as *alpha* is to   1. beta   2. zeta
3. omega   4. lambda   5. phi

55. *Whet* is to *knife* as *hone* is to   1. strop   2. stone
3. leather   4. barber   5. razor

56. *Doctor* is to *disease* as *phychiatrist* is to   1. imbecility   2. senility   3. maladjustment   4. poverty
5. idiocy

57. *Red* is to *green* as *rage* is to   1. frustration   2. envy
3. eagerness   4. fear   5. anger

58. *Hops* is to *beer* as *grapes* is to   1. vine   2. vineyard
3. vat   4. wine   5. raisin

59. *Bronze* is to *patina* as *iron* is to   1. steel   2. wrought
3. cast   4. galvanized   5. rust

60. *State* is to *nation* as *week* is to   1. month   2. day   3. country   4. hour   5. calendar

61. *Spartan* is to *laconic* as *pusillanimous* is to   1. courageous   2. curt   3. verbose   4. miserly   5. powerful

62. *Turgid* is to *turbid* as *thaw* is to   1. spring   2. muddy   3. drought   4. swollen   5. thud

63. *Impecunious* is to *hovel* as *affluent* is to   1. cringe   2. domicile   3. mansion   4. bank   5. indigent

64. *Isobars* are to *isotherms* as *pressure* is to   1. gauge   2. light   3. wind   4. heat   5. sound

65. *Laurel* is to *olive* as *victory* is to   1. justice   2. mercy   3. peace   4. tranquillity   5. greed

66. *Fire* is to *water* as *holocaust* is to   1. drought   2. sailor   3. arsonist   4. inundation   5. avalanche

67. *Crutches* are to *walking* as *mnemonic devices* are to   1. hearing   2. seeing   3. thinking   4. remembering   5. smelling

68. *Frugality* is to *parsimony* as *interest* is to   1. desire   2. apathy   3. usury   4. integrity   5. thrift

69. *Books* are to *jewels* as *errata* are to   1. gems   2. valuables   3. adornments   4. flaws   5. color

70. *Teacher* is to *pupil* as *master* is to   1. slave   2. child   3. bachelor   4. apprentice   5. minor

DIRECTIONS: *Items 71-100 contain sentences which have words omitted. Each sentence is followed by five alternatives. Indicate the number of the alternative which best completes the meaning of the sentence.*

71. He was not _____ and preferred to be alone most of the time.
    1. antisocial   2. gracious   3. gregarious   4. cordial   5. handsome

72. Although there are _____ outbursts of shooting, we may report that the major rebellion has been suppressed.
    1. sporadic   2. bitter   3. heinous   4. meager   5. nocturnal

73. His book was marred by his many _____ remarks which made us forget his main theme.
    1. inappropriate   2. humorous   3. digressive   4. opinionated   5. slanted

74. At such a serious moment in our history, your _____ is inappropriate and in bad taste.
    1. questioning   2. levity   3. attire   4. moodiness   5. maturation

75. John left his position with the company because he felt that advancement was based on _____ rather than ability.
    1. chance   2. seniority   3. nepotism   4. superciliousness   5. maturation

76. He worked _____ at his task for weeks before he felt satisfied that the results justified his effort.
    1. occasionally   2. regularly   3. patiently   4. assiduously   5. intermittently

77. Fear of enclosed places is called _____ .
    1. kleptomania   2. agoraphobia   3. hypochondria   4. insanity   5. claustrophobia

78. He discovered a small _____ in the wall, through which the insects had entered the room.
    1. niche   2. blemish   3. aperture   4. schism   5. crevasse

79. The robin has been called the _____ of spring.
    1. greeter   2. leviathan   3. spokesman   4. crimson herald   5. harbinger

80. Your _____ tactics may compel me to cancel the contract as the job must be finished on time.
    1. dilatory   2. offensive   3. obstructive   4. infamous   5. confiscatory

81. The members of the religious sect ostracized the _____ who had abandoned their faith.
    1. coward   2. suppliant   3. litigant   4. recreant   5. proselyte

82. We do not mean to be disrespectful when we refuse to follow the advice of our _____ leader.
    1. venerable   2. revered   3. famous   4. gracious   5. great

83. It is almost impossible at times to capture the _____ of words when we translate them into a foreign language.
    1. implications   2. meanings   3. denotations   4. connotations   5. essence

84. The Trojan War proved to the Greeks that cunning and _____ were often more effective than military might.
    1. treachery   2. artifice   3. strength   4. wisdom   5. beauty

85. If we _____ these experienced people to positions of unimportance because of their political persuasions, we shall lose the services of valuably trained personnel.
    1. assign   2. banish   3. relegate   4. restrict   5. condemn

86. This area has been preserved in all its _____ wildness to remind us the past.
    1. pristine   2. natural   3. rugged   4. untamed   5. virile

87. Before any agreement can be signed, the workers insist that no _____ against the strikers will be taken.
    1. reprisals   2. attacks   3. revenge   4. penalties   5. fines

88. No hero of ancient or modern times can surpass the Indian with his lofty contempt of death and the _____ with which he sustains the cruelest affliction.
    1. disdain   2. fortitude   3. guile   4. grace   5. reverence

89. He felt that the office routine was too _____ for a man of his dreams.
    1. enervating   2. exacting   3. rigorous   4. stimulating   5. prosaic

90. The Marines attacked the south beach at daybreak; _____ , as a diversionary maneuver, a company landed on the north side of the island.
    1. previously   2. later   3. simultaneously   4. at noon   5. subsequently

91. The seriousness of the drought could only be understood by those who had seen the _____ crops in the fields.
    1. copious 2. blighted 3. meager 4. verdant
    5. crippled

92. I intend to wait for a more _____ occasion before I announce my plans.
    1. propitious 2. prodigious 3. pronounced
    4. pathetic 5. positive

93. We were certain that disaster was _____ .
    1. impeccable 2. inherent 3. immutable
    4. invidious 5. imminent

94. The plot of this story is so _____ that I can predict its outcome.
    1. clever 2. inveterate 3. involved 4. trite
    5. insipid

95. "As idle as a painted ship" is an example of _____ .
    1. simile 2. metaphor 3. litotes 4. metonymy
    5. synecdoche

96. A _____ is a self-contradictory statement.
    1. paragon 2. paradox 3. maxim 4. aphorism
    5. motif

97. Because this liquid is highly _____ , it should be kept in a tightly stoppered bottle.
    1. voluble 2. voluptuous 3. expensive
    4. volatile 5. explosive

98. Because his occupation required that he work at night and sleep during the day, he had an exceptionally _____ complexion.
    1. ghastly 2. ruddy 3. livid 4. plain 5. pallid

99. We need more men of culture and enlightenment; we have too many _____ among us.
    1. boors 2. students 3. philistines 4. pragmatists 5. philosophers

100. The prodigal son _____ the family fortune.
    1. saved 2. coveted 3. inherited 4. squandered
    5. invested

Typical Test C   Time: One Hour

DIRECTIONS: _Each item below consists of an italicized word followed by five alternatives. Decide which alternative means the same as or the opposite of the italicized word. Write the number of the word that you have chosen as the answer for each question._

1. _emollient_ 1. lamentable 2. fantastic 3. picayune
    4. softening 5. cautious

2. _callow_ 1. experienced 2. crude 3. rustic
    4. migratory 5. exquisite

3. _chary_ 1. careful 2. frenetic 3. conciliatory
    4. migratory 5. militant

4. _renegade_ 1. Indian 2. warrior 3. prisoner
    4. liar 5. deserter

5. _meticulous_ 1. meretricious 2. remiss 3. ingenuous 4. carefree 5. complacent

6. _circuitous_ 1. encompassing 2. circumscribing
    3. direct 4. drastic 5. bombastic.

7. _propitious_ 1. magnanimous 2. maligning
    3. favorable 4. following 5. fallacious

8. _rococo_ 1. florid 2. quaint 3. futile 4. pastry
    5. earthworm

9. _decorum_ 1. ornateness 2. seemliness 3. politeness 4. fulfillment 5. mastery

10. _wax_ 1. grow larger 2. grow wilder 3. fight
    4. think 5. forget

11. _voluble_ 1. precious 2. precise 3. tactful
    4. taciturn 5. free

12. _plethora_ 1. despair 2. denial 3. average 4. glut
    5. constellation

13. _insipid_ 1. wise 2. flavorless 3. cowardly
    4. cautious 5. lax

14. _inhibit_ 1. restrain 2. restore 3. rescue
    4. refrain 5. feel •

15. _voracious_ 1. truthful 2. mendacious 3. reputable 4. ravening 5. lively

16. _extirpate_ 1. explain 2. add footnotes 3. amend
    4. question 5. destroy

17. _nebulous_ 1. hypothetical 2. querulous
    3. bickering 4. lamentable 5. distinct

18. _humility_ 1. comedy 2. queerness 3. meekness
    4. quality 5. loyalty

19. _dissuade_ 1. extort 2. exhort 3. extol
    4. assuage 5. intensify

20. _bland_ 1. pale 2. mild 3. angry 4. vital
    5. wipe out

21. _sanguine_ 1. hot 2. frantic 3. arctic 4. pessimistic 5. related

22. _resplendent_ 1. dull 2. dwelling 3. averring
    4. claiming 5. counseling

23. _cupidity_ 1. love 2. anguish 3. greed 4. fear
    5. despair

24. _recalcitrant_ 1. tractable 2. fearful 3. remembering 4. visitor 5. painter

25. _affluence_ 1. power 2. puerility 3. penury
    4. pensiveness 5. pomposity

26. _inequity_ 1. unequalness 2. justice 3. union
    4. sterility 5. monstrosity

27. _lampoon_ 1. satire 2. lantern 3. vessel
    4. parody 5. relief

28. _heterogeneous_ 1. blasphemy 2. piety 3. uniform
    4. villanous 5. palatable

29. _panacea_ 1. ocean 2. choir 3. herb 4. remedy
    5. hostility

30. _taciturn_ 1. revolving 2. maintaining 3. callous
    4. beautiful 5. garrulous

DIRECTIONS: _Questions 31-70 are incomplete statements, each followed by five alternatives. In each question, select the alternative that best completes the statement._

31. _Collie_ is to _dog_ as _whale_ is to 1. fish 2. water
    3. oil 4. mammal 5. Moby Dick

32. *Hero* is to *villain* as *protagonist* is to   1. heroine   2. *deus ex machina*   3. antagonist   4. guide   5. patron

33. *Fish* is to *bird* as *submarine* is to   1. tank   2. bird   3. airplane   4. hangar   5. ship

34. *Stethoscope* is to *physician* as *pestle* is to   1. pharmacist   2. sculptor   3. teacher   4. author   5. plagiarist

35. *Vixen* is to *fox* as *sow* is to   1. shrew   2. termagant   3. pig   4. Saxon   5. boar

36. *Taciturn* is to *verbose* as *epigrammatic* is to   1. laconic   2. pithy   3. dead   4. silent   5. redundant

37. *Shilling* is to *franc* as *Parliament* is to   1. France   2. Congress   3. pound   4. guinea   5. parlement

38. *Everlasting* is to *ephemeral* as *permanent* is to   1. evanescent   2. iridescent   3. obsolete   4. vivid   5. fundamental

39. *Libretto* is to *score* as *author* is to   1. game   2. team   3. opera   4. composer   5. critic

40. *Petulant* is to *affable* as *ignominious* is to   1. honorable   2. agreeable   3. affluent   4. indigenous   5. irritable

41. *Picture* is to *frame* as *diamond* is to   1. ring   2. brooch   3. setting   4. carat   5. ruby

42. *Virtuoso* is to *tyro* as *experienced* is to   1. taught   2. untried   3. talented   4. young   5. veteran

43. *Laurel* is to *victory* as *ashes* is to   1. fire   2. memory   3. remorse   4. defeat   5. dregs

44. *Sedulous* is to *indolent* as *static* is to   1. electricity   2. dynamic   3. noise   4. radio   5. inert

45. *Investor* is to *broker* as *litigant* is to   1. lawyer   2. doctor   3. realtor   4. accountant   5. chemist

46. *Awl* is to *auger* as *cobbler* is to   1. blacksmith   2. carpenter   3. prophet   4. mathematician   5. surveyor

47. *Carelessness* is to *accident* as *exertion* is to   1. casualty   2. care   3. exercise   4. fatigue   5. indifference

48. *Lift* is to *elevator* as *petrol* is to   1. bird   2. pennant   3. escalator   4. oil   5. gasoline

49. *Trumpet* is to *brass* as *drum* is to   1. kettle   2. bass   3. noisy   4. percussion   5. taut

50. *Cummerbund* is to *epaulets* as *waist* is to   1. neck   2. ankles   3. shoulders   4. sleeves   5. trousers

51. *Intrinsic* is to *extrinsic* as *inherent* is to   1. esoteric   2. real   3. concerned   4. extraordinary   5. extraneous

52. *Interest* is to *bond* as *royalty* is to   1. king   2. monarchy   3. book   4. sceptre   5. palace

53. *Square* is to *cube* as *triangle* is to   1. pyramid   2. cone   3. cylinder   4. sphere   5. prism

54. *Perennial* is to *annual* as *rose* is to   1. marigold   2. forsythia   3. spruce   4. tulip   5. shrub

55. *Dime* is to *cent* as *decade* is to   1. century   2. year   3. day   4. era   5. dollar

56. *Exuberant* is to *downcast* as *effusive* is to   1. verbose   2. reticent   3. gay   4. spirited   5. enthusiastic

57. *Poet* is to *eclogue* as *seamstress* is to   1. gown   2. stitch   3. pastoral   4. epic   5. sew

58. *Dog* is to *canine* as *cow* is to   1. herbivorous   2. bovine   3. milk   4. pasture   5. lethargic

59. *Scholarly* is to *erudite* as *ignorant* is to   1. educated   2. illiterate   3. wealthy   4. impoverished   5. emaciated

60. *Spruce* is to *pine* as *boxer* is to   1. pugilist   2. ring   3. gladiator   4. dog   5. collie

61. *Time* is to *scythe* as *liberty* is to   1. scales   2. flag   3 slogan   4. tocsin   5. torch

62. *Rococo* is to *simple* as *baroque* is to   1. exotic   2. esoteric   3. flamboyant   4. plain   5. futile

63. *Appease* is to *propitiate* as *agitate* is to   1. disturb   2. palliate   3. propagate   4. stagnate   5. hibernate

64. *Cylinder* is to *piston* as *shaft* is to   1. gun   2. elevator   3. round   4. sphere   5. pyramid

65. *Cornea* is to *corn* as *ophthalmologist* is to   1. famine   2. pediatrician   3. podiatrist   4. grazer   5. druggist

66. *Gauche* is to *deft* as *rough* is to   1. abrasive   2. lubricant   3. smooth   4. elegant   5. insipid

67. *Erudite* is to *scholar* as *mendacious* is to   1. beggar   2. traveler   3. victim   4. victor   5. liar

68. *Drum* is to *percussion* as *oboe* is to   1. tabor   2. string   3. brass   4. woodwind   5. horn

69. *Circuitous* is to *direct* as *tortuous* is to   1. painful   2. soporific   3. precise   4. straight   5. rectangular

70. *Soldier* is to *knight* as *carbine* is to   1. chivalry   2. gallantry   3. spear   4. armour   5. steed

DIRECTIONS: *Items 71–100 contain sentences which have words omitted. Each sentence is followed by five alternatives. Indicate the number of the alternative which best completes the meaning of the sentence.*

71. After we had waded through all the _____, we discovered that the writer had said very little.
   1. context   2. treatise   3. verbiage   3. volubility   5. vortex

72. Although her _____ tears were a sign of her remorse, they did not influence the judge when he imposed sentence.
   1. abundant   2. contrite   3. crocodile   4. copious   5. restrained

73. After his book had been published, he was invited to join the literary _____ that lunched daily at the hotel.
   1. coterie   2. clique   3. bunch   4. cohorts   5. crowd

74. In spite of the constant ridicule, he is always presenting one of his _____ schemes.
   1. grandiose   2. imaginative   3. fantastic   4. quixotic   5. quaint

75. Although we maintain that we shall never be the

first to attack, we are on the alert to _____.
1. reciprocate 2. mobilize 3. concentrate
4. defend 5. attack

76. In his usual _____ manner, he had insured himself against this type of loss.
1. indifferent 2. thoughtful 3. casual
4. intense 5. provident

77. He should be dismissed for his _____ remarks about the company's president.
1. impeccable 2. scurrilous 3. critical
4. subversive 5. laudatory

78. _____ pride did not prevent him from noticing his nephew's shortcomings.
1. Nepotistic 2. Paternal 3. False 4. Avuncular 5. Quixotic

79. In his researches on _____ diseases, he discovered many facts about the lungs of animals and human beings.
1. malignant 2. inherited 3. chronic
4. infectious 5. pulmonary

80. Because his _____ remarks were misinterpreted, he decided to write all his speeches in advance.
1. candid 2. extemporaneous 3. verbal
4. oral 5. studied

81. His interest in _____ activities took him to islands in the Bahamas and to icy mountain streams.
1. aquatic 2. physical 3. intellectual
4. piscatorial 5. community

82. Nylon can be woven into _____ or thick fabrics.
1. sturdy 2. gossamer 3. motley 4. variegated 5. gay

83. When he insisted on singing that _____ song, many of us were offended and left the room.
1. ribald 2. revolutionary 3. garish 4. lugubrious 5. maudlin

84. We felt that such a song was in _____ taste.
1. bitter 2. foul 3. execrable 4. extenuating
5. intrepid

85. I resent your _____ remarks because no one asked for them.
1. fantastic 2. insulting 3. scurrilous
4. gratuitous 5. gossiping

86. I am afraid to undertake this venture because of the _____ omens I have received.
1. auspicious 2. baneful 3. frightening
4. baleful 5. varied

87. He dropped his libel suit after the newspaper published a _____ of its statement.
1. summary 2. glossary 3. photograph
4. resume 5. retraction

88. I resent your _____ to belittle every contribution he makes to our organization.
1. intention 2. drive 3. propensity
4. predilection 5. failure

89. On June 21 of each year we have the summer _____.
1. equinox 2. nadir 3. zenith 4. solstice
5. apex

90. The _____ arguments used by the demagogue is certain to deceive many people.
1. plausible 2. involved 3. syllogistic
4. specious 5. splenetic

91. The physicians were worried about the possibility of finding a _____ growth in the patient.
1. benign 2. tumorous 3. malicious
4. malignant 5. benignant

92. Not only the _____ are fooled by propaganda; we can all be misled if we are not wary.
1. ignorant 2. gullible 3. people 4. masses
5. uneducated

93. Her critics maintained that you could tell she was an actress by her _____ manner of speaking.
1. affectionate 2. romantic 3. affected
4. dramatic 5. professional

94. I can think of nothing more _____ than arriving at the theatre and discovering that I had left the tickets at home.
1. aggravating 2. tantalizing 3. vexatious
4. vitiating 5. banal

95. Our only hope is to prove that the witness was _____ and guilty of perjury.
1. prejudiced 2. improper 3. mendacious
4. meretricious 5. meddlesome

96. Now that I realize the extent of your _____, I feel that it will be impossible for me to trust you implicitly in the future.
1. chicanery 2. lapse 3. ingenuousness
4. inconsistency 5. clemency

97. Such an _____ act of hostility can only lead to war.
1. overt 2. opportunistic 3. occasional
4. oscillating 5. unequaled

98. Gettysburg was the scene of as _____ a battle as any recorded in history.
1. sanguinary 2. meaningless 3. futile
4. historic 5. variable

99. After three years in Paris, he was filled with _____ and longed for the familiar scenes of New York City.
1. ennui 2. chagrin 3. nostalgia 4. lethargy
5. anxiety

100. "The road was a ribbon of moonlight" is an example of
1. simile 2. metaphor 3. personification
4. prosody 5. metonymy

ANSWERS TO TEST **A**

1. 3	*26.* 5	*51.* 3	*76.* 4
2. 1	*27.* 5	*52.* 3	*77.* 1
3. 5	*28.* 3	*53.* 4	*78.* 4
4. 2	*29.* 5	*54.* 4	*79.* 3
5. 4	*30.* 1	*55.* 3	*80.* 1
6. 1	*31.* 2	*56.* 4	*81.* 2
7. 2	*32.* 3	*57.* 2	*82.* 4
8. 3	*33.* 4	*58.* 2	*83.* 5
9. 1	*34.* 5	*59.* 3	*84.* 3
10. 2	*35.* 2	*60.* 5	*85.* 5
11. 1	*36.* 1	*61.* 2	*86.* 2
12. 3	*37.* 4	*62.* 4	*87.* 5
13. 1	*38.* 1	*63.* 2	*88.* 4
14. 2	*39.* 5	*64.* 3	*89.* 2
15. 5	*40.* 3	*65.* 5	*90.* 1
16. 1	*41.* 5	*66.* 2	*91.* 2
17. 5	*42.* 1	*67.* 5	*92.* 4
18. 1	*43.* 5	*68.* 4	*93.* 4
19. 2	*44.* 1	*69.* 1	*94.* 4
20. 5	*45.* 2	*70.* 5	*95.* 5
21. 2	*46.* 4	*71.* 1	*96.* 4
22. 2	*47.* 5	*72.* 3	*97.* 1
23. 3	*48.* 3	*73.* 4	*98.* 2
24. 4	*49.* 4	*74.* 3	*99.* 5
25. 1	*50.* 3	*75.* 4	*100.* 2

ANSWERS TO TEST **B**

1. 5	*26.* 5	*51.* 3	*76.* 4
2. 2	*27.* 1	*52.* 3	*77.* 5
3. 1	*28.* 5	*53.* 1	*78.* 3
4. 1	*29.* 3	*54.* 3	*79.* 5
5. 4	*30.* 1	*55.* 5	*80.* 1
6. 3	*31.* 4	*56.* 3	*81.* 4
7. 2	*32.* 2	*57.* 2	*82.* 1
8. 1	*33.* 4	*58.* 4	*83.* 4
9. 5	*34.* 5	*59.* 5	*84.* 2
10. 1	*35.* 1	*60.* 1	*85.* 3
11. 4	*36.* 3	*61.* 3	*86.* 1
12. 4	*37.* 5	*62.* 4	*87.* 1
13. 4	*38.* 5	*63.* 3	*88.* 2
14. 1	*39.* 4	*64.* 4	*89.* 5
15. 2	*40.* 1	*65.* 3	*90.* 3
16. 3	*41.* 3	*66.* 4	*91.* 2
17. 5	*42.* 3	*67.* 4	*92.* 1
18. 4	*43.* 5	*68.* 3	*93.* 5
19. 4	*44.* 2	*69.* 4	*94.* 4
20. 1	*45.* 4	*70.* 4	*95.* 1
21. 3	*46.* 5	*71.* 3	*96.* 2
22. 1	*47.* 4	*72.* 1	*97.* 4
23. 1	*48.* 2	*73.* 3	*98.* 4
24. 2	*49.* 1	*74.* 2	*99.* 3
25. 5	*50.* 2	*75.* 3	*100.* 4

ANSWERS TO TEST C

1. 4	26. 2	51. 5	76. 5
2. 1	27. 1	52. 3	77. 2
3. 1	28. 3	53. 5	78. 4
4. 5	29. 4	54. 1	79. 5
5. 2	30. 5	55. 2	80. 2
6. 3	31. 4	56. 2	81. 4
7. 3	32. 3	57. 1	82. 2
8. 1	33. 3	58. 2	83. 1
9. 2	34. 1	59. 2	84. 3
10. 1	35. 5	60. 5	85. 4
11. 4	36. 5	61. 5	86. 4
12. 4	37. 5	62. 4	87. 5
13. 2	38. 1	63. 1	88. 3
14. 1	39. 4	64. 2	89. 4
15. 4	40. 1	65. 3	90. 4
16. 5	41. 3	66. 3	91. 4
17. 5	42. 2	67. 5	92. 2
18. 3	43. 3	68. 4	93. 3
19. 2	44. 2	69. 4	94. 3
20. 2	45. 1	70. 3	95. 3
21. 4	46. 2	71. 3	96. 1
22. 1	47. 4	72. 2	97. 1
23. 3	48. 5	73. 1	98. 1
24. 1	49. 4	74. 4	99. 3
25. 3	50. 3	75. 1	100. 2

ANSWERS EXPLAINED—TYPICAL TEST A

1. 3. *Bucolic* and *pastoral* have the same meaning —pertaining to shepherds and rural life.

2. 1. *Ostentatious* (showy) and *modest* are opposites.

3. 5. *Recondite* (profound) and *abstruse* are synonyms.

4. 2. *Vernal* means *springlike.*

5. 4. *Diaphanous* means *sheer* and transparent.

6. 1. *Prolix* (verbose) and *terse* are opposites.

7. 2. *Spurious* (false, counterfeit) and *genuine* opposites.

8. 3. An *apostate* (person who forsakes his religion or cause) is not a *loyal follower.*

9. 1. *Cognizant* means *aware.*

10. 2. *Amelioration* (betterment) is the opposite of *worsening.*

11. 1. *Malinger* means to *feign sickness.*

12. 3. *Loquacious* (talkative) is the opposite of *laconic* (terse).

13. 1. *Turbid* (muddy, unclear) is the opposite of *limpid* (clear).

14. 2. An *aviary* is a large *bird cage.*

15. 5. *Avid* (eager) is the opposite of *loath* (unwilling).

16. 1. A *termagant* is a *virago* or shrew.

17. 5. *Omniscient* (having infinite knowledge) is the opposite of *ignorant.*

18. 1. *Esoteric* (private or secret) material is *confidential.*

19. 2. *Precious* means *affected* (feigned, assumed).

20. 5. *Mollify* (appease, placate) is the opposite of *provoke.*

21. 2. *Retrogression* (going backward, worsening) is the same as *deterioration.*

22. 2. *Hamper* (hinder, impede) is the opposite of *support.*

23. 3. *Banal* (trite) is the opposite of *original.*

24. 4. *Jocund* and *gay* are synonyms.

25. 1. *Inveigle* and *entice* are synonyms.

26. 5. *Lucid* (clear) is the opposite of *obscure.*

27. 5. *Anathema* (curse) is the opposite of *benediction* (blessing).

28. 3. *Altruistic* (unselfish) is the opposite of *selfish.*

29. 5. *Devious* (shifty, crooked) is the opposite of *sincere.*

30. 1. *Philandering* (making love without serious intentions) is a synonym for *trifling.*

31. 2. A *scholar* seeks *knowledge*; an *entrepreneur* seeks *profits.*

32. 3. A *ladder* has several *rungs*; a *building*, several *stories.*

33. 4. A person may *incite* (start) a *rebellion*; he may *ignite* (light) a *conflagration* (fire).

34. 5. *Insipid* and *tasteless* are synonyms; *innocuous* and *harmless* are synonyms.

35. 2. *Condoning* individuals *forgive*; *loquacious* individuals *speak.*

36. 1. A wicked *crime* is *heinous*; a wicked *man* is *nefarious.*

37. 4. *Recondite* (scholarly, learned) is the opposite of *ignorant*; *ecstatic* (extremely joyful) is the opposite of *morose.*

38. 1. A *numismatist* studies and collects *coins*; a *lexicographer* (editor of dictionaries) studies and collects *words.*

39. 5. *Bellicose* (belligerent) and *pacific* (peaceful) are opposites.

40. 3. An *amulet* (charm) is supposed to ward off *evil*; a *brake* is supposed to ward off the evil of *collision.*

41. 5. A *prologue* opens a *play* and an *overture* begins an *opera*.

42. 1. A *chef* practices *culinary* (pertaining to cooking) arts; a *barber* practices *tonsorial* (pertaining to a barber's work) arts.

43. 5. The *x-axis* and the *latitude* are horizontal lines; the *y-axis* and the *longitude* are vertical lines.

44. 1. A *teacher* tries to eliminate *ignorance* and *light* eliminates *darkness*.

45. 2. *Baseball* is played on a *diamond* and *tennis* is played on a *court*.

46. 4. *The Louvre* in *Paris* contains great works of art; the *Sistine Chapel* in *Vatican City* also contains great art works.

47. 5. *Initial* begins and *terminal* ends. The *engine* heads a train and the *caboose* is at the end of the freight trains.

48. 3. *Milk* is *potable* (drinkable); *cheese* is *edible* (fit to be eaten).

49. 4. A *numismatist* studies *coins*; a *dermatologist* studies the *skin*.

50. 3. A *salutatorian* usually gives an address at the beginning of a graduation and a *valedictorian* gives a speech at the end. *Incipient* means starting or beginning and *final* means the end.

51. 3. The *easel* (stand on which a painting rests) and the *palette* (board on which pigments are mixed) are used by a painter; the *scalpel* (knife used to make incisions) and the *suture* (material used to close a wound) are used by the surgeon.

52. 3. The *tactile* sense (sense of touch) is found in the *hands*; the *olfactory* sense (sense of smell) is found in the *nose*.

53. 4. *Laws* indicate the proper *conduct* for society to take; *buoys* indicate the proper *channel* for ships to take.

54. 4. *Lumber* is gotten in a *forest* and *stone* in a *quarry*.

55. 3. A *lexicographer* helps prepare a *dictionary*; a *cartographer* (map maker) helps prepare a *gazetteer* (geographical dictionary).

56. 4. An *archipelago* is made up of a group of *islands*; a *constellation* consists of a cluster of *stars*.

57. 2. *Ostracism* (exclusion from a group) is a form of *censure* (strong disapproval); *applause* is an indication of *approval*.

58. 2. *Valuables* are kept in a *vault*; *wheat* is stored in a *granary*.

59. 3. *Quart* and *yard* are units in liquid and linear measures used in England and America; their counterparts in the metric system are the *liter* and the *meter*.

60. 5. The *poinsettia* is a plant associated with *Christmas*; the *lily* is associated with *Easter*.

61. 2. *Meager* (scanty) is the opposite of *inordinate* (excessive); *scarcity* is the opposite of *plethora* (overabundance).

62. 4. *Culinary* (pertaining to cooking) arts are practiced in the *kitchen*; *terpsichorean* (pertaining to the dance) arts are practiced in the *dance studio*.

63. 2. Examining the relationship between *hourglass* and *clock*, we find that the *clock* is an improvement over the *hourglass* in the matter of time. Similarly, the *rifle* was an improvement over the *bow*.

64. 3. An *individual* is part of a *group*; an *island* is part of an *archipelago*.

65. 5. *Hercules* was renowned for his strength or *brawn*; *Ulysses* for his cunning or *wiliness*.

66. 2. A *dime* is a tenth of a *dollar*; a *decade*, a tenth of a *century*.

67. 5. A person who lacks *wealth* is *indigent* (poor); a person who lacks *food* is *emaciated* (made thin by lack of nutrition).

68. 4. People who buy *stocks* become *owners* of the company; people who buy *bonds* are *lenders* to the company.

69. 1. A *cow* is a *bovine*; a *crab* is a *crustacean*.

70. 5. *Tuberculosis* is caused by a *bacillus*; *infantile paralysis*, by a *virus*.

71. 1. *Expediency* is defined as consideration for what is advantageous rather than for what is just or right.

72. 3. A *hallucination* is a false idea or impression.

73. 4. A *vantage* point is a superior position for attack.

74. 3. *Sabotage* is underhand interference.

75. 4. An *allegory* is a symbolic narrative.

76. 4. *Ambiguous* directions leave people in doubt.

77. 1. *Somnolent* means very drowsy.

78. 4. An *augury* is an omen or prophesy.

79. 3. *Debilitates* means weakens.

80. 1. *Roseate* means optimistic.

81. 2. *Expunge* means delete.

82. 4. An *ulterior* motive is usually a selfish one.

83. 5. This line is an example of *paradox*, a figure of speech in which a seemingly self-contradictory statement contains an element of truth.

84. 3. A *protege* is a person who is assisted financially by an influential individual.

85. 5. *Germane* means pertinent.

86. 2. Fires are set by arsonists or *pyromaniacs*.

87. 5. *Lugubrious* means gloomy or mournful.

88. 4. *Congealed* means froze.

89. 2. A *platitude* is a trite remark.

90. 1. *Redoubtable* means to be feared.

91. 2. *Rococo* architecture involved elegant and ornate designs.

92. 4. *Thrift* is an old-fashioned virtue.

93. 4. *Truculent* means hostile.

94. 4. *Salacious* or lewd material would offend the Puritans.

95. 5. *Niggardly* means very stingy.

96. 4. A *dilettante* dabbles at his art.

97. 1. *Funereal* means gloomy.

98. 2. *Veracious* means truthful.

99. 5. A *concerto* fits the definition in the sentence.

100. 2. A *pediatrician* is a medical doctor who specializes in the care of children and their diseases.

TYPICAL TEST B

1. 5. *Impugn* (call in question, challenge) is the opposite of *accept*.

2. 2. *Grandiloquent* means *bombastic* (using pompous language).

3. 1. *Amenable* (willing to submit) is a synonym of *tractable*.

4. 1. *Sallow* (sickly in color) and *ruddy* (having a fresh reddish color) are antonyms.

5. 4. *Remiss* and *negligent* are synonyms.

6. 3. *Veracious* (truthful) and *mendacious* (lying) are opposites.

7. 2. *Allay* (ease) and *assuage* (lessen) are synonyms.

8. 1. *Halcyon* (calm) and *rough* are antonyms.

9. 5. *Terse* (concise, succinct) and *curt* are synonyms.

10. 1. *Complaisant* (inclined to please) and *agreeable* are synonyms.

11. 4. *Turgid* (inflated, as in writing) and *bombastic* (pompous, in language) are synonyms.

12. 4. *Spurious* (false) is the opposite of *genuine*.

13. 4. *Tautological* means needlessly *repetitious*.

14. 1. *Vicarious* (taking the place of another) and *deputed* (assigned as one's substitute) are synonyms.

15. 2. *Inimical* (unfriendly) and *hostile* are synonyms.

16. 3. *Ostensible* (apparent) and *professed* are synonyms.

17. 5. *Urbane* (sophisticated) and *naive* (unsophisticated) are opposites.

18. 4. A *pariah* is an *outcast*.

19. 4. *Lugubrious* (gloomy, morose) and *gay* are opposites.

20. 1. *Mottled* means *particolored* (having different colors).

21. 3. A *soporific* and a *narcotic* both induce sleep.

22. 1. *Intrepid* (fearless) and *courageous* are synonyms.

23. 1. *Paltry* (mean, contemptible) is the opposite of *admirable*.

24. 2. *Laconic* (brief, curt) is the opposite of *voluble* (speaking freely).

25. 5. *Ubiquitous* (being everywhere) and *omnipresent* are synonyms.

26. 5. A *panegyric* and a *eulogy* both are writings praising persons or things.

27. 1. A *dais* is a raised *platform*.

28. 5. *Redolent* (pleasantly odorous) and *fragrant* are synonyms.

29. 3. *Tractable* (easily controlled) and *docile* are synonyms.

30. 1. To *condone* an offense is to *overlook* it.

31. 4. *Alumnus* refers to a male graduate of a school (singular); *alumnae* to female graduates (plural). A *ram* is a male sheep; *ewes* are female sheep.

32. 2. *Benediction* (blessing) and *anathema* (curse) are opposites. *Eulogy* (praise) and *vilification* (use of abusive language) are opposites.

33. 4. *Coke* is derived from *coal*; *glass*, from *sand*.

34. 5. A person who is *brash* (rash, impudent) lacks *reticence* (reserve, shyness); a person who is *bold* lacks *cowardice*.

35. 1. *Regicide* is the killing of a *king*; *patricide* is the killing of a *father*.

36. 3. A *hen clucks* and a *horse whinnies*.

37. 5. A *peak* is the top of a *mountain* and a *crest* is the top of a *wave*.

38. 5. A *desert* lacks *water* and an *idiot* lacks *intelligence*.

39. 4. The relationship is one of degree. *Generous* carried to an extreme becomes *prodigal* (wastefully extravagant). *Frugal* (thrifty) carried to an extreme becomes *parsimonious* (extremely thrifty).

40. 1. A *director* stages a *movie* and a *choreographer* stages a *ballet*

41. 3. A *shoe* is made of *leather*; a *hat* is made of *felt*.

42. 3. A *business collapses* when it goes under; a *ship founders* when it sinks.

43. 5. *Conscience* helps man avoid *sin*; a *pilot* helps a ship avoid a *reef*.

44. 2. *Ecstasy* is extreme *joy*; a *deluge* is a very heavy *shower*.

45. 4. The meat of a *sheep* is called *mutton*; the meat of a *deer*, *venison*.

46. 5. The direction a *horse* takes is determined by the *bridle*; the direction of a *ship*, by its *rudder*.

47. 4. *Indigence* (poverty) and *affluence* (wealth) are opposites; *beggar* and *millionaire* are opposites.

48. 2. The *gold carat* marking indicates the degree of purity or *quality*; the *diamond carat* is an indication of *weight*.

49. 1. *Conservative* and *cautious* are synonyms; *garish* and *rococo* are synonyms.

50. 2. The *Jersey* and the *Holstein* are kinds of cows; the *Siamese* and the *Angora* are kinds of cats.

51. 3. Popes issue *papal bulls*; presidents issue *presidential proclamations*.

52. 3. An *enigma* is a *riddle*; a *labyrinth* is a *maze*.

53. 1. A *philatelist* collects and studies *stamps*; an *entomologist*, *insects*.

54. 3. *Alpha* is the *first* letter of the Greek alphabet; *omega*, the *last*.

55. 5. *Whet* means to sharpen a *knife*; *hone*, to sharpen a *razor*.

56. 3. A *doctor* combats *disease*; a *psychiatrist*, *maladjustments*.

57. 2. An individual may be *red* with *rage* and *green* with *envy*.

58. 4. *Hops* are used in the production of *beer* and *grapes* in the production of *wine*.

59. 5. The oxidation of *bronze* is called a *patina*; the oxidation of *iron*, *rust*.

60. 1. A *state* is part of a *nation*; a *week*, part of a *month*.

61. 3. *Spartan* (valorous) and *pusillanimous* (cowardly) are opposites; *laconic* (terse) and *verbose* (wordy) are opposites.

62. 4. Rivers and streams become *turgid* (swollen, agitated) when the spring *thaw* starts; they become *turbid* (muddy, cloudy) during the summer *drought*.

63. 3. *Impecunious* (poverty stricken) people live in *hovels* (wretched huts); *affluent* (wealthy) people, in *mansions*.

64. 4. *Isobars* are lines on weather maps connecting places with similar barometric *pressure*; *isotherms* connect places with similar temperature or *heat*.

65. 3. The *laurel* is the symbol of *victory* and the *olive* the symbol of *peace*.

66. 4. Destruction by *fire* is called a *holocaust*; destruction by *water*, an *inundation* (flood).

67. 4. *Crutches* assist the handicapped when *walking*; *mnemonic devices* assist in *remembering*.

68. 3. Excessive *frugality* (thrift) becomes *parsimony* (stinginess); excessive *interest* becomes *usury*.

69. 4. Mistakes in *books* are called *errata*; things that spoil the perfection of *jewels* are called *flaws*.

70. 4. A *teacher* works with his *pupil* and a *master* with his *apprentice*.

71. 3. A *gregarious* person likes the company of others.

72. 1. If the major battle has ended, we may assume that only *sporadic* or irregular and isolated shooting continues.

73. 3. *Digressive* remarks wander away from the main topic.

74. 2. *Levity* (gaiety) is inappropriate at a time of seriousness.

75. 3. *Nepotism* means favoritism shown on the basis of family relationships.

76. 4. A person who puts an effort in his work does so *assiduously* or *diligently*.

77. 5. *Claustrophobia* is the fear of enclosed places.

78. 3. An *aperture* is a small hole or slit.

79. 5. A *harbinger* heralds the arrival of someone or something.

80. 1. *Dilatory* (delaying) tactics will prevent finishing a job on time.

81. 4. A *recreant* is a traitor to a belief.

82. 1. *Venerable* means deserving respect.

83. 4. *Connotations* are the suggested meanings of words.

84. 2. *Artifice* (wiliness) best ties up with cunning.

85. 3. *Relegate* means to assign to a lower position or rank.

86. 1. *Pristine* means earliest.

87. 1. *Reprisals* (actions taken in retaliation) is best. It encompasses choices 4 and 5.

88. 2. *Fortitude* means patient courage.

89. 5. *Prosaic* means commonplace, humdrum.

90. 3. For best results, the diversionary maneuver should occur *simultaneously* (at the same time) as the real attack.

91. 2 Crops that are wilted and dying are *blighted*.

92. 1. *Propitious* means favorable.

93. 5. *Imminent* means likely to occur at any moment.

94. 4. A *trite* (made stale by repeated use) story is predictable.

95. 1. A *simile* is a comparison of two unlike things using the words "like" or "as."

96. 2. A *paradox* is a self-contradictory statement.

97. 4. A *volatile* liquid evaporates quickly.

98. 4. A person who is indoors would have a pale or *pallid* complexion.

99. 3. A *philistine* is a person lacking in culture and refinement.

100. 3. *Prodigal* means wastefully extravagant.

TYPICAL TEST C

1. 4. *Emollient* and *softening* are synonyms.

2. 1. *Callow* (inexperienced) and *experienced* are opposites.

3. 1. *Chary* and *careful* are synonyms.

4. 5. A *renegade* is a *deserter*.

5. 2. *Meticulous* (exact, precise) and *remiss* (negligent, careless) are opposites.

6. 3. *Circuitous* (roundabout) and *direct* are opposites.

7. 3. *Propitious* and *favorable* are synonyms.

8. 1. *Rococo* and *florid* (excessively ornate) are synonyms.

9. 2. *Decorum* (propriety) and *seemliness* (state of being in good taste) are synonyms.

10. 1. *Wax* means to *grow larger*.

11. 4. *Voluble* (fluent, glib) is the opposite of *taciturn* (laconic).

12. 4. *Plethora* (overabundance) and *glut* (excessive supply) are synonyms.

13. 2. *Insipid* (tasteless) and *flavorless* are synonyms.

14. 1. *Inhibit* (block, hold back) and *restrain* are synonyms.

15. 4. *Voracious* (eating large quantities of food) and *ravenous* (extremely hungry) are synonyms.

16. 5. *Extirpate* (uproot) and *destroy* are synonyms.

17. 5. *Nebulous* (hazy, cloudy) and *distinct* are opposites.

18. 3. *Humility* (quality of being humble) and *meekness* (humble patience) are synonyms.

19. 2. *Dissuade* (deter by persuasion) and *exhort* (urge) are antonyms.

20. 2. *Bland* (nonirritating, soothing) and *mild* are synonyms.

21. 4. *Sanguine* (cheerful, optimistic) and *pessimistic* (gloomy) are opposites.

22. 1. *Resplendent* (shining brightly) and *dull* are opposites.

23. 3. *Cupidity* means *greed* and *avarice*.

24. 1. *Recalcitrant* (hard to manage) and *tractable* (easily controlled) are opposites.

25. 3. *Affluence* (wealth, prosperity) and *penury* (poverty) are antonyms.

26. 2. *Inequity* (injustice) and *justice* are opposites.

27. 1. *Lampoon* means sharp *satire*.

28. 3. *Heterogeneous* (different in kind) and *uniform* (having the same quality) are opposites.

29. 4. A *panacea* is a cure-all or *remedy*.

30. 5. *Taciturn* (laconic) is the opposite of *garrulous* (excessively talking).

31. 4. A *collie* is a *dog*; a *whale* is a *mammal*.

32. 3. The *hero* is opposed by a *villain*; a *protagonist* (leading character), by the *antagonist*.

33. 3. *Fish* and *submarine* travel in the water; *bird* and *airplane*, in the air.

34. 1. A *stethoscope* is associated with a *physician*; a *pestle* (tool for grinding substances in a mortar), with a *pharmacist*.

35. 5. A *vixen* is a female *fox*; a *sow* is a female *boar* or swine. Note that "pig" is a young swine of either sex.

36. 5. *Taciturn* and *verbose* are opposites; *epigrammatic* (terse, pithy) and *redundant* (repetitious) are opposites.

37. 5. The *shilling* is an English coin; the *franc*, a French coin. *Parliament* is the English legislative body; *parlement*, the French legislative body.

38. 1. *Everlasting* and *ephemeral* (short-lived) are opposites; *permanent* and *evanescent* (vanishing) are opposites.

39. 4. The *libretto* (book) of an opera is written by an *author*; the *score* (music) by a *composer*.

40. 1. *Petulant* (showing irritation) is the opposite of *affable* (friendly); *ignominious* (disgraceful, dishonorable) and *honorable* are opposites.

41. 3. A *picture* is placed in a *frame*; a *diamond*, in a *setting*.

42. 2. A *virtuoso* (person with great skill) is the opposite of a *tyro* (beginner). *Experienced* is the opposite of *untried*.

43. 3. The *laurel* symbolizes *victory*; *ashes*, *grief* or *remorse*.

44. 2. *Sedulous* (diligent) and *indolent* (avoiding exertion) are opposites; *static* (not moving or changing) and *dynamic* (energetic) are opposites.

45. 1. An *investor* will use the services of a *broker*; a *litigant* (person engaged in a lawsuit) will use a *lawyer*.

46. 2. An *awl* (a pointed instrument for punching small holes is used by a *cobbler* (mender of shoes). An *auger* (a boring tool) is used by a *carpenter*.

47. 4. *Carelessness* may cause an *accident*; *exertion*, *fatigue*.

48. 5. In England, *elevators* are called *lifts* and gasoline is called *petrol*.

49. 4. In an orchestra, the *trumpet* is part of the *brass* section; the *drum*, of the *percussion* section.

50. 3. A *cummerbund* (sash) is worn about the *waist*; *epaulets* (ornamental shoulder pieces) are worn on the *shoulder*.

51. 5. *Intrinsic* (belonging to a thing) and *inherent* are synonyms; *extrinsic* (not essential or inherent) and *extraneous* are synonyms.

52. 3. The *bond* owner receives *interest*; the owner of the *book* copyright receives *royalties*.

53. 5. A *cube* is a three-dimensional figure with a *square* on top and bottom; a *prism* is a three-dimensional figure with a *triangle* on top and bottom.

54. 1. A *perennial* (living for more than two years) plant is a *rose*. An *annual* (living for only one year) plant is the *marigold*.

55. 2. A *dime* is ten times as much as a *cent*; a *decade* is ten times as much as a *year*.

56. 2. *Exuberant* and *downcast* are opposites; *effusive* (expressing feelings in an unrestrained manner) is the opposite of *reticent* (disinclined to speak).

57. 1. A *poet* can create an *eclogue* (pastoral poem); a *seamstress*, a *gown*.

58. 2. A *dog* belongs to the *canine* family and a *cow* to the *bovine* family.

59. 2. *Scholarly* and *erudite* are synonyms; *ignorant* and *illiterate* are synonyms.

60. 5. *Spruce* and *pine* trees are evergreens; a *boxer* and *collie* are dogs.

61. 5. Father *Time* carries a *scythe*; *liberty* carries a *torch*.

62. 4. *Rococo* (ornate) is the opposite of *simple*; *baroque* (elaborately ornamented) and *plain* are opposites.

63. 1. *Appease* and *propitiate* are synonyms; *agitate* and *disturb* are synonyms.

64. 2. A *piston* moves up and down in a *cylinder*; an *elevator*, in a *shaft*.

65. 3. An *ophthalmologist* (a doctor who treats diseases of the eye) will treat the *cornea*; a *podiatrist* (a doctor who treats foot ailments) will treat a *corn*.

66. 3. *Gauche* (clumsy) and *deft* (adroit) are opposites; *rough* and *smooth* are opposites.

67. 5. A *scholar* is *erudite* (learned); a *liar* is *mendacious* (lying).

68. 4. A *drum* is part of the *percussion* section of an orchestra; the *oboe* of the *woodwind* section.

69. 4. *Circuitous* and *tortuous* are synonyms; *direct* and *straight* are synonyms.

70. 3. A *soldier* uses a *carbine* (rifle); a *knight* used a *spear*.

71. 3. *Verbiage* means an abundance of useless words.

72. 2. *Contrite* means sincerely remorseful.

73. 1. *Coterie* means a group of people who have common interests.

74. 4. *Quixotic* means impractical, visionary.

75. 1. *Reciprocate* means to give in return.

76. 5. *Provident* means careful in providing for the future.

77. 2. *Scurrilous* remarks are abusive.

78. 4. *Avuncular* means pertaining to an uncle.

79. 5. Diseases that affect the lungs are *pulmonary* in nature.

80. 2. Remarks made on the spur of the moment are *extemporaneous*.

81. 4. *Piscatorial* means of fishing and fishermen.

82. 2. The use of "or" in the sentence indicates that a contrast to "thick" will best complete the thought of the sentence. *Gossamer* means sheer.

83. 1. A *ribald* (vulgar, lewd) song would be offensive to many.

84. 3. *Execrable* means detestable.

85. 4. Uncalled for remarks are *gratuitous*.

86. 4. *Baleful* means menacing.

87. 5. A *retraction* (withdrawal) of the statement might cause the dropping of a libel suit.

88. 3. *Propensity* means natural inclination.

89. 4. *Solstice* means the time when either the days or nights are longest. During the summer *solstice*, we have the longest day and the shortest night.

90. 4. *Specious* (seemingly reasonable but incorrect) remarks will fool many people.

91. 4. A *malignant* growth can cause death.

92. 2. *Gullible* means people who are easily deceived.

93. 3. *Affected* means falsely put on to impress people.

94. 3. *Vexatious* means irritating.

95. 3. A *mendacious* (lying) person would be guilty of perjury.

96. 1. *Chicanery* means trickery and deception.

97. 1. An *overt* act is open and discernible.

98. 1. *Sanguinary* means bloody.

99. 3. *Nostalgia* means a yearning for the past.

100. 4. A *metaphor* is an implied comparison of two dissimilar persons or things. The words "like" or "as" are not used.